Child and Adolescent Mental Health
in Social Work

Child and Adolescent Mental Health in Social Work

A Casebook

JACQUELINE CORCORAN

and

COURTNEY BENJAMIN WOLK

OXFORD
UNIVERSITY PRESS

OXFORD
UNIVERSITY PRESS

Oxford University Press is a department of the University of Oxford. It furthers the University's objective of excellence in research, scholarship, and education by publishing worldwide. Oxford is a registered trade mark of Oxford University Press in the UK and certain other countries.

Published in the United States of America by Oxford University Press
198 Madison Avenue, New York, NY 10016, United States of America.

Library of Congress Cataloging-in-Publication Data
Names: Corcoran, Jacqueline, editor. | Wolk, Courtney Benjamin, editor.
Title: Child and adolescent mental health in social work /
Jacqueline Corcoran and Courtney Benjamin Wolk.
Description: New York, NY : Oxford University Press, [2023] |
Includes bibliographical references and index.
Identifiers: LCCN 2023022881 (print) | LCCN 2023022882 (ebook) |
ISBN 9780197653562 (paperback) | ISBN 9780197653586 (epub) |
ISBN 9780197653593
Subjects: LCSH: Child mental health services—United States. | Social work
with children—United States. | Child psychopathology—United States. |
Psychiatric social work—United States.
Classification: LCC RJ501.A2 C46 2023 (print) | LCC RJ501.A2 (ebook) |
DDC 362.2083—dc23/eng/20230706
LC record available at https://lccn.loc.gov/2023022881
LC ebook record available at https://lccn.loc.gov/2023022882

DOI: 10.1093/oso/9780197653562.001.0001

Printed by Marquis Book Printing, Canada

CONTENTS

SECTION II. Neurodevelopmental Disorders

SECTION III. Externalizing Problems

1

Introduction and Overview

According to the 2016 National Survey of Children's Health (Whitney & Peterson, 2019), 7.7 million children in the United States have been diagnosed with at least one mental health disorder. This represents almost 17% of the child population. In high-income countries, the overall prevalence of childhood mental disorders was 13% (Barican et al., 2022). Anxiety (5.2%), attention-deficit/hyperactivity (3.7%), oppositional defiant (3.3%), substance use (2.3%), conduct (1.3%), and depressive (1.3%) disorders were the most common. Along with high prevalence, unmet treatment needs are apparent. Only 44% of youths in high-income countries received services (Barican et al., 2022).

This is especially true among children who live in poverty (Ghandour et al., 2018). Only 1% to 3% of youths with a serious emotional disturbance receive evidence-based treatments in the United States (Bruns et al., 2015). Despite calls for the use of evidence-based treatments in public community mental health centers to improve the efficiency and effectiveness of services (e.g., Garland et al., 2013), the uptake of such treatments has been low.

Social workers make up the majority of the mental health workforce (Tikkanen et al., 2020). Therefore, clinical social workers shoulder the work of providing effective mental health services to children, especially those who live in poverty and are marginalized and oppressed, consistent with the mission of social work. The purpose of *Child and Adolescent Mental Health in Social Work: A Casebook* is to provide a comprehensive text, including assessment, goal setting, and intervention, for the treatment of mental health problems in children and adolescents in contemporary social work practice settings. This book can be the primary text in a specialized course on working with children and adolescents and can also be used as a supplemental text for required courses on clinical assessment and clinical practice. We use several frameworks and teaching tools to meet the purpose of *Child and Adolescent Mental Health in Social Work: A Casebook*, that are described next.

1

Child and Adolescent Mental Health in Social Work. Jacqueline Corcoran and Courtney Benjamin Wolk, Oxford University Press.
© Oxford University Press 2023. DOI: 10.1093/oso/9780197653562.003.0001

THE AMERICAN PSYCHIATRIC ASSOCIATION'S *DIAGNOSTIC AND STATISTICAL MANUAL OF MENTAL DISORDERS*

The various disorders are catalogued and described in the *Diagnostic and Statistical Manual of Mental Disorders* (DSM), published by the American Psychiatric Association (APA, 2022). The DSM is the standard resource for clinical diagnosis in the United States. We discuss the use of the manual, both its advantages and disadvantages, and how it reconciles with social work's perspective and ethics in Chapter 3. The challenge is to teach social workers competence and critical thinking in the diagnostic process, while also considering diagnosis in a way that is consistent with social work values and principles. These values include a strengths-based orientation, concern for the worth and dignity of individuals, and appreciation for the environmental context of individual behavior.

RISK AND RESILIENCE FRAMEWORK

"Risk and resilience" considers the balance of risk and protective processes at the biological, psychological, and social levels that interact to determine an individual's propensity toward *resilience*, or the ability to function adaptively and achieve positive outcomes despite stressful life events (Werner, 2000). The "strengths" perspective underlies the concept of resilience, or the skills, abilities, knowledge, and insight that people accumulate over time as they struggle to surmount adversity and meet life challenges. It refers to the ability of clients to persist despite the difficulties they encounter (Saleeby, 2011).

Risk, on the other hand, can be understood as hazards or problems at the biological, psychological, or social levels that may lead to poor adaptation (Bogenschneider, 1996). *Protective factors* may counterbalance or buffer the individual against risk (Pollard et al., 1999; Werner, 2000), promoting successful adjustment in the face of risk (Dekovic, 1999). Risk and protective factors are sometimes the converse of each other. For instance, at the individual level, a difficult temperament is a risk factor, and an easy temperament is a protective factor. Indeed, researchers have found many pairs of risk and protective factors that are negatively correlated with each other (Jessor et al., 1997).

The biopsychosocial-cultural emphasis expands the focus beyond the individual to a recognition of systemic factors that can create and ameliorate problems. The nature of systems is that the factors within and between them have influence on each other. For instance, the presence of a certain risk or protective factor may increase the likelihood of other risk and protective factors. Wachs (2000) provides the example of how an aversive parenting style with poor monitoring increases children's risk for socializing with deviant peers. If parents are overwhelmed by many environmental stressors, such as unemployment, lack of transportation and medical care, and residence in an unsafe neighborhood, their ability to provide consistent warmth and nurturance may be compromised. This phenomenon also operates for protective factors. For example, adolescents whose parents provide emotional support and structure the environment with consistent rules and monitoring tend to associate with peers who share similar family backgrounds (Steinberg, 2001). Supportive parenting will, in turn, affect the characteristics of the child in that, through receiving it, the child learns to regulate emotional processes and develop cognitive and social competence (Wachs, 2000). Systemic influences also play themselves out from the perspective of a child's characteristics. A child who has resilient qualities, such as social skills, effective coping strategies, intelligence, and self-esteem, is more likely to attract high-quality caregiving, and attachment patterns formed in infancy tend to persist into other relationships across the life span.

Although precise mechanisms of action are not specified, data have begun to accumulate about the number of risk factors that are required to overwhelm a system and result in negative outcomes (e.g., Fraser et al., 1999; Kalil & Kunz, 1999). The cumulative results of different studies seem to indicate that four or more risk factors represent a threat to adaptation (Epps & Jackson, 2000; Frick, 2006; Runyan et al., 1998; Rutter et al.,1979). These findings align with results of the large-scale Adverse Childhood Experiences (ACEs) Kaiser-Permanente study (Centers for Disease Control and Prevention, 2019). The more ACEs experienced, the greater the risk conferred; four or more ACEs are associated with the most profound risk in terms of chronic health conditions, unsafe health behaviors, depression, and poor socioeconomic outcomes (Merrick et al., 2019).

Risk does not proceed in a linear fashion, however, and all risk factors are not equal (Greenberg et al., 2001). Some of the risk and protective factors play a role in multiple types of problems. From a prevention and intervention perspective, common risk factors occurring across multiple domains can be targeted for reduction or amelioration, and protective factors can be targeted for enhancement (Corcoran & Nichols-Casebolt, 2004).

For social work, in sum, there are several advantages to using the risk and resilience framework to consider mental disorder. First, it is a coherent way of considering mental disorder as having biopsychosocial influences rather than to overfocus on one aspect, such as on individual dysfunction. Relatedly and second, it keeps at the forefront the emphasis on the systems' influences on child functioning. Third, the risk and resilience framework offers a balanced appraisal of risk/adversity and strengths/protective factors. In Table 1.1, we summarize the risk and protective factors that have been identified as having an evidence base to support their relationship with children's adjustment. In each chapter, we cover the specific factors that have to do with that mental health condition.

EVIDENCE-BASED PRACTICE

Evidence-based practice (EBP) formally began in medicine in the early 1990s (Sackett et al., 1997) and was defined as the integration of the best available research knowledge informed by both clinical expertise and consumer values. In

Table 1.1 RISK AND RESILIENCE IN BIOPSYCHOSOCIAL-SPIRITUAL ASSESSMENT

Factor	Risk	Protective
Biological		
Genes and heritability • Not generally known because family environment interacts with genetic predispositions and a genetic vulnerability may be activated by adverse environmental events	Family with mental health and substance use disorders Physical and psychological adversity during prenatal or early childhood period when neural structures and connections develop may impair structure, connectivity, and functions in brain. Adversity may also result in toxic stress in which the cortisol response is impaired, and over time may become linked with inflammation that gives rise to health conditions.	No first-degree relatives with mental health disorders Lack of adversity in prenatal and early childhood period
Temperament • Provides the foundation for personality, involving qualities that are biologically driven, observed from infancy, and moderately stable across the life span • Involves activity level, intensity, attention span, quality of mood, adaptability, flexibility, and rhythmicity	Irritability Risk-taking (for conduct disorder)	Behavior inhibition (for conduct disorder, but is a risk factor for anxiety)
Physical health • Includes prenatal health	Medical problems Pregnancy and birth complications	Good physical health Regular prenatal care
Developmental stage	Adolescence for depression in females Young adulthood for onset of mental disorders	People with personality disorders may recover in middle age.
Psychological		
IQ	Low IQ Learning disorders	Average or high IQ Absence of learning disorders
Self-efficacy and self-esteem	Low self-esteem and efficacy	High self-esteem and efficacy
Self-regulation and emotion regulation	Dysregulation	Ability to regulate

Table 1.1 CONTINUED

Factor	Risk	Protective
Coping strategies	Avoidance, including substance use	Problem-solving
	Rumination	Ability to identify and express feelings
		Seek social support
Spiritual	Lack of meaning	Religious involvement
		Beliefs that provide meaning
		Mindfulness and other spiritual practices
Social		
Family	Poor attachment bonds	Secure attachment
	Lack of supervision and monitoring	Supervision and monitoring
	Harsh or inconsistent parenting	Warm, consistent, authoritative parenting
	Two-parent family	Single-parent household
	Isolation of nuclear family	Extended family involvement
Traumatic and stressful life events, loss	Frequent moving	Stability
	Abuse	Safety
	Loss	
	Stressful life events	
	Intimate partner violence	
Neighborhood	Unsafe	Safe
	Availability of alcohol outlets and drug dealing	Spacious
		Caring neighbors
	Segregated	Integrated
	Crowded	Presence of organized community activities
	Lack of organized community activities	
Ethnicity and culture	Ethnic minority risk for discrimination, segregation, health disparities, etc.	Culture can be a source of identity and support
Sexual identification and orientation	LGBTQ individuals are at risk for anxiety, depression, suicidality, bullying, and victimization.	Straight, cisgender
Welfare, tax policies, and legal sanctions	Current U.S. safety net inadequate	Safety nets can meet some basic needs
		Child support laws
		Earned income tax credits
Social class	Poverty	Mid to higher socioeconomic status

SOURCES OF COMPILATIONS: Corcoran & Nichols-Casebolt (2004).

other words, evidence-based treatment is a process of using research knowledge to make decisions about intervening with clients. In the current environment, however, the term *evidence based* has come to mean that there is an empirical basis to treatments and services (Zlotnik, 2007). The process of clinical decision-making according to EBP is therefore distinguished from the product, which involves compilations of the research evidence (Proctor, 2007).

What kind and number of accumulated studies meet criteria to be considered EBP? Numerous definitions, albeit vague in some cases, have been offered, such as that by Drake and colleagues (2001), who assert that EBPs "are interventions for which there is consistent scientific evidence showing that they improve client outcomes" (p. 180). The American Psychological Association Division 12 Task Force has developed a schema of "well-established," "probably efficacious," "promising," and "experimental" for many of the disorders discussed in this book. "Well-established" means that an intervention has been studied in at least two randomized controlled or quasi-experimental designs, with results on a salient outcome (e.g., "depression" for the problem of depression) reported as statistically significant. One of the experiments must have been conducted by an independent evaluator, meaning not the group of colleagues that originally conceptualized the treatment. In this text, we report on some of these evidence-based treatments and apply them to a case that is relevant for the types of populations and problems that social workers see. We rely heavily on systematic reviews and meta-analyses for the evidence basis of treatments as well as, when present, on assessments and risk factors. These concepts will be briefly defined here, although more information is available in Littel et al. (2008).

A *systematic review* aims to locate and synthesize the research that bears on a particular question using organized, transparent, and replicable procedures at each step in the process (Littel et al., 2008). *Meta-analysis* is a set of statistical methods for combining quantitative results from multiple studies to produce an overall summary of empirical knowledge on a given topic. Results of the original studies are converted to one or more common metrics, called *effect sizes*, which reveal the strength or magnitude of the relationships between variables. In meta-analysis, effect sizes are calculated for each study, weighted by sample size, and then averaged to produce an overall effect. The most commonly reported effect size in this book will be the *standardized mean difference* (SMD), also known as *Cohen's d* (Cohen, 1988), which is the mean difference divided by the pooled standard deviation (SD) of the two groups. For the SMD, a negligible effect ranges from 0.0 to 0.2; a small effect ranges between 0.2 and 0.5; a medium effect ranges from 0.5 to 0.8; and a large effect is greater than 0.8 (Cohen, 1988).

In this book, the criteria for including a disorder are that it is prevalent in mental health settings *and* has a solid research basis to determine which interventions might be effective as determined by systematic reviews. As a result, disorders such as reactive attachment disorder, bipolar disorder, and disruptive mood dysregulation disorder will not have their own chapters, although the latter two will appear as a discussion and critique of the DSM in Chapter 3.

Admittedly, the focus on what has been supported by research means that cognitive-behavioral therapy (CBT) is often used. Authors have commented in critiques of EBP that CBT has garnered the most research attention for a couple of reasons. First, CBT arose out of a research tradition, whereas other clinical paradigms have more of a practice basis. A second reason is that CBT is much more easily researched because it has a structured, step-by-step approach that can be manualized. However, that also means that students and beginning social workers can grasp the steps and use the resources that are available to guide their work with clients. The case study applications can help them understand how the theory can be used to treat clients and their families to promote adjustment and recovery. CBT also generally has a short-term, present-focused approach, which is compatible with the need of agencies and settings to serve many clients in efficient and effective ways and with the way families generally view problems and their treatment.

Another part of EBP involves using evidence to assess people for clinical levels of distress and symptoms and to determine that they are responding in the desired way to intervention. For this second component of EBP, standardized child self-report and parent/teacher measurement tools for specific disorders are presented in each chapter. The measurement tools presented have demonstrated reliability and validity and, when possible, are freely available. Social workers are encouraged to incorporate reliable, valid measurement tools such as these into their practice for both initial assessment and progress monitoring purposes. As a sample of their use, in the case example in Chapter 5 on attention-deficit/hyperactivity disorder, the clinician introduces the assessment process to the family and integrates information obtained from clinical interviews with the parent and child as well as from parent and teacher reports on standardized rating scales.

CASE STUDIES

Despite all this information about research, *Child and Adolescent Mental Health in Social Work: A Casebook* weaves the clinical work and research together to demonstrate to learners how they work in tandem. A brief case description opens each chapter, and this case is subsequently threaded through the rest of the chapter to illustrate the material. The cases were chosen to reflect the low-income and diverse populations to which social workers are committed. Our hope is that these case examples will bring to life the application of EBPs to real-world clients.

REFERENCES

American Psychiatric Association. (2022). *Diagnostic and statistical manual of mental disorders* (5th ed., Text Revision). Washington, DC: American Psychiatric Association.

Barican, J. L., Yung, D., Schwartz, C., Zheng, Y., Georgiades, K., & Waddell, C. (2022). Prevalence of childhood mental disorders in high-income countries: A systematic review and meta-analysis to inform policymaking. *Evidence-Based Mental Health*, *25*(1), 36–44. https://doi.org/10.1136/ebmental-2021-300277

Bogenschneider, K. (1996). An ecological risk/protective theory for building prevention programs, policies, and community capacity to support youth. *Family Relations: Journal of Applied Family & Child Studies*, *45*, 127–138.

Bruns, E., Kerns, S., Pullmann, M., Hensley, S., Lutterman, T., & Hoagwood, K. (2015). Research, data, and evidenced-based treatment use in state behavioral health systems, 2001–2012. *Psychiatric Services*, *67*(5), 496–503.

Centers for Disease Control and Prevention. (2019, November). Adverse childhood experiences (ACESs): Preventing early trauma to improve adult health. *Vital Signs*, https://www.cdc.gov/vitalsigns/aces/pdf/vs-1105-aces-H.pdf

Cohen, J. (1988). *Statistical power analysis for the behavioral sciences* (2nd ed.). Hillsdale, NJ: Erlbaum.

Corcoran, J., & Nichols-Casebolt, A. (2004). Risk and resilience ecological framework for assessment and goal formulation. *Child & Adolescent Social Work Journal*, *21*(3), 211–235.

Dekovic, M. (1999). Risk and protective factors in the development of problem behavior during adolescence. *Journal of Youth and Adolescence*, *28*(6), 667–685.

Epps, S., & Jackson, B. (2000). *Empowered families, successful children*. Washington, DC: American Psychiatric Publishing.

Fraser, M., Richman, J., & Galinsky, M. (1999). Risk, protection, and resilience: Toward a conceptual framework of social work practice. *Social Work Research*, *23*, 131–143.

Frick, P. J. (2006). Developmental pathways to conduct disorder. *Child and Adolescent Psychiatric Clinics of North America*, *15*, 311–331.

Garland, A., Haine-Schlagel, R., Brookman-Frazee, L., Baker-Ericzen, M., Trask, E., & Fawley-King, K. (2013). Improving community-based mental health care for children: Translating knowledge into action. *Administration and Policy in Mental Health*, *40*(1), 6–22.

Ghandour, R., Sherman, L., Vladutiu, C., Ali, M., Lynch, S., Bitsko, R., & Blumberg, S. (2018). Prevalence and treatment of depression, anxiety, and conduct problems in U.S. children. *Journal of Pediatrics*, *206*(1), 256–267.

Greenberg, M., Speltz, M., DeKlyen, M., & Jones, K. (2001). Correlates of clinic referral for early conduct problems: Variable- and person-oriented approaches. *Development & Psychopathology*, *13*, 255–276.

Jessor, R., Van Den Bos, J., Vanderryn, J., Costa, F. M., & Turbin, M. S. (1997). Protective factors in adolescent problem behavior: Moderator effects and developmental change. In G. A. Marlatt & G. R. Van Den Bos (Eds.), *Addictive behaviors: Readings on etiology, prevention, and treatment* (pp. 239–264). Washington, DC: American Psychological Association.

Kalil, A., & Kuntz, J. (1999). First births among unmarried adolescent girls: Risk and protective factors. *Social Work Research*, *23*, 197–208.

Littel, J., Corcoran, J., & Pillai, V. (2008). *Systematic reviews and meta-analysis*. New York: Oxford University Press.

Merrick, M., Ford, D., Ports, K., Guinn, A., Chen, J., Klevens, J., Metzler, M., Jones, C., Simon, T., Daniel, V., Ottley, P., & Mercy, J. (2019). Vital signs: Estimated proportion of adult health problems attributable to adverse childhood experiences and implications for prevention—25 states, 2015–2017. *Morbidity and Mortality Weekly Report*, 68(44), 222–1005.

Pollard, J. A., Hawkins, J. D., & Arthur, M. W. (1999). Risk and protection: Are both necessary to understand diverse behavioral outcomes in adolescence? *Social Work Research*, 23(3), 145–158.

Proctor, E. K. (2007). Implementing evidence-based practice in social work education: Principles, strategies, and partnerships. *Research on Social Work Practice*, 17(5), 583–591.

Runyan, D. K., Hunter, W. M., Scololar, R. R., Amaya-Jackson, L., English, D., Landsverk, J., Dubowitz, H., Browne, D. H., Bangdiwala, S. I., & Mathew, R. M. (1998). Children who prosper in unfavorable environments: The relationship to social capital. *Pediatrics*, 101(1), 12–19.

Rutter, M., Maughan, N., Mortimore, P., & Ouston, J. (1979). *Fifteen thousand hours.* Cambridge, MA: Harvard University Press.

Sackett, D. L., Richardson, W. S., Rosenberg, W., & Haynes, R. B. (1997). *Evidence-based medicine: How to practice and teach EBM.* New York: Churchill Livingstone.

Saleebey, D. (2012). *Strengths perspective in social work practice* (6th ed.). Pearson.

Steinberg, L. (2001). We know some things: Parent–adolescent relationships in retrospect and prospect. *Journal of Research on Adolescence*, 11, 1–19.

Tikkanen, R., Fields, K., Williams II, R., & Abrams, M. (2020). Mental health conditions and substance use: Comparing U.S. needs and treatment capacity with those in other high-income countries. The Commonwealth Fund. https://www.commonwealthfund.org/publications/issue-briefs/2020/may/mental-health-conditions-substance-use-comparing-us-other-countries

Wachs, T. (2000). *Necessary but not sufficient.* Washington, DC: American Psychiatric Association.

Werner, E. (2000). Protective factors and individual resilience. In J. Shonkoff & S. Meisels (Eds.), *Handbook of early childhood intervention* (2nd ed., pp. 115–132). New York: Cambridge University Press.

Whitney, D., & Peterson, M. (2018). US national and state-level prevalence of mental health disorders and disparities of mental health care use in children. *JAMA Pediatrics*, 173(4), 389–391.

Zlotnik, J. (2007). Evidence-based practice and social work education: A view from Washington. *Research on Social Work Practice*, 15(5), 625–629.

Professional Social Work Context

Where and How Do Social Workers Practice?

In this chapter, we discuss the context for the social work role and delivery of services in settings where child and adolescent mental health is treated. We explore first the variety of settings where youth mental health problems are addressed and then some of the key social work values and ethics involved in this type of practice. We offer case vignettes to illustrate these points and to involve the reader in reflection and discussion.

SETTINGS WHERE SOCIAL WORKERS PRACTICE

Clinical social workers practice in a variety of traditional mental health settings, including outpatient, inpatient, and residential treatment facilities, as well as in a range of settings where mental health care has not traditionally been provided, such as primary care, hospitals, schools, child welfare, and juvenile justice. In some instances, the majority of mental health care is provided in these nonspecialty mental health settings (Freed, 2020; Proctor et al., 1999; Regier et al., 1978). Most youths with mental health care needs do not present to treatment with a mental health specialist (American Academy of Child and Adolescent Psychiatry Committee on Health Care Access and Economics Task Force on Mental Health, 2009; U.S. Department of Health and Human Services, 1999). Research indicates that children are more likely to receive their mental health services in school than in any other public system (Green et al., 2013; President's New Freedom Commission on Mental Health, 2003). Adults with depression predominantly receive treatment in primary care and not in outpatient mental health clinics (Kroenke & Unutzer, 2017). Most children attend primary care visits annually, though evidence-based mental health screening is not often routine in pediatric primary care (American Academy of Child and Adolescent Psychiatry Committee on Health Care Access and Economics Task Force on Mental Health, 2009). It has also been well documented that people living with mental health conditions are overrepresented in criminal justice settings (Borschmann et al.,

Child and Adolescent Mental Health in Social Work. Jacqueline Corcoran and Courtney Benjamin Wolk, Oxford University Press.
© Oxford University Press 2023. DOI: 10.1093/oso/9780197653562.003.0002

2020; Prins, 2014) and in juvenile justice in particular (Collins et al., 2010), where conduct disorder and substance use disorders are common. Finally, mental health needs are high among youths in the child welfare system, where nearly half of youths have mental health conditions but only about one-fourth receive specialty treatment (Bronsard, 2016; Burns et al., 2004).

Specialty Mental Health Settings

OUTPATIENT

Services in community mental health settings include individual or group psychotherapy and range in intensity. Outpatient therapy is often offered on a weekly or biweekly basis. There are also intensive outpatient models and day treatment programs, where youths are seen more frequently but still live at home. Most of the case examples in this book illustrate clinical work in an outpatient context.

RESIDENTIAL

In residential treatment facilities, youths who cannot safely remain in the home live in a supervised facility and receive therapeutic and educational services on site. Often these youths have not improved sufficiently in lower levels of care (e.g., outpatient) before stepping up to more intensive residential services, have child welfare system involvement, and may have had or are at risk for juvenile justice placements (Huefner et al., 2010). Social workers are often an integral part of residential care teams, which also typically include psychiatrists, psychologists, teachers, and professionals from a range of other disciplines, including occupational therapy, physical therapy, and nutrition. Chapter 12 includes a residential treatment case example. The appropriateness of residential care has been much debated, and the evidence for what constitutes effective, evidence-based residential care is lacking (Butler & McPherson, 2007). However, four evidence-based treatment models have been identified (James, 2012): the Positive Peer Culture (Vorrath & Brendtro, 1985), Teaching-Family (Phillips et al., 1974), Sanctuary (Bloom, 1997), and Stop-Gap (McCurdy & McIntyre, 2004) Models. Boot camps and wilderness-programs have less empirical support. Almost all existing designs for wilderness programs are pretest, posttest designs and are therefore limited, the meta-analyses of studies involving both adjudicated and private pay youth show medium effects on most outcomes (Beck & Wong, 2022; Bettmann et al., 2016); research has demonstrated that boot camps in particular can be harmful to youths (Coventry & Swanson, 2011).

INPATIENT

More than 150,000 youths are hospitalized for a psychiatric reason annually; hospitalizations among youths with a primary mental health diagnosis account for nearly 10% of pediatric hospitalizations in the United States (Bardach et al., 2014). Social workers are often critical members of inpatient psychiatric care teams. Inpatient treatment teams often include an attending psychiatrist, nurses, and a case manager. Psychologists, occupational therapists, physical therapists, and nutritionists also often are involved in inpatient treatment programs. Inpatient psychiatric facilities range from units within larger general or children's hospitals to freestanding psychiatric treatment facilities.

Children and adolescents are admitted for inpatient treatment for a variety of reasons, most commonly following suicidal behavior or because of acute suicide risk or concerns of harm to self or others. Additionally, youths exhibiting manic or psychotic symptoms are sometimes admitted for inpatient treatment because they require stabilization.

The social worker's role includes providing individual and family therapy as well as coordinating with the rest of the treatment team around treatment decisions and discharge planning. Social workers on interdisciplinary teams also have key roles around advocating for client psychosocial needs; providing resources to meet basic family needs, such as housing, transportation, food, and utilities; and reminding the team of the person–environment context rather than having an exclusive focus on individual pathology. Typically, the core members of the care team round each morning, meeting as a team to discuss each patient on the unit and meeting with each patient. These rounds provide opportunities to clarify diagnoses and key areas of concern, to plan and adjust treatment during the in-patient stay, and to develop an appropriate follow-up plan for the patient after discharge. The rest of the social worker's day is spent meeting individually with patients to understand their needs and priorities, providing brief interventions such as safety planning and motivational interviewing to support engagement in follow-up services planned for after discharge, and conducting family meetings. Family meetings are opportunities to understand family strengths and challenges, provide psychoeducation to caregivers, and support families in developing and using healthy communication and in navigating any interpersonal challenges. Social workers in inpatient settings also often engage with existing outpatient therapists (when patients already have those in place).

Throughout their work with patients and their families, the social worker is in close communication with the rest of the care team. This takes many forms, including sharing pertinent information gleaned from individual and family meetings with the rest of the team, providing recommendations for treatment, and ensuring appropriate connections to outpatient or follow-up treatments that are arranged as part of discharge planning. In this role, the social worker helps the team understand the patient's psychosocial risk and protective factors and engages the patient and family in the treatment and in planning for after discharge

CASE APPLICATIONS

Michael is a social worker on a child and adolescent inpatient mental health unit within a large urban children's hospital. The unit has 20 beds divided into two 10-bed wings: one for children aged 12 and younger and one for adolescents aged 13 to 18. The unit serves youths experiencing psychiatric emergencies; most youths who are admitted are transferred from the hospital's emergency department (ED) or transported from another area hospital or crisis response center. Next, we present case examples from Michael's work to illustrate common roles and responsibilities for clinical social workers in inpatient psychiatric settings.

Mood Dysregulation

Leroy is an 8-year-old Black male who had been adopted by Deborah Randles at 2 years of age after serving as his foster parent. Leroy was admitted overnight from the ED because of concerns about extreme mood dysregulation and possible emergent bipolar disorder. The police, accompanied by Ms. Randles, had brought him to the ED after Leroy had taken Ms. Randles's car keys, gotten into the car, and driven it down the block and into a ditch. This had all occurred without Ms. Randle's knowledge while she was socializing in the backyard with a neighbor and under the impression that Leroy was in bed sleeping. The police had found Leroy in the car, unharmed, and escorted him to the ED after consulting with Ms. Randles, who reported that Leroy's behavior had been increasingly impulsive and concerning as of late. Ms. Randles had accompanied Leroy to the inpatient unit, had given information about Leroy's current symptoms and relevant history to the nurse, and then had gone home to sleep.

During morning rounds, the team nurse presented the reasons for Leroy's hospitalization and his relevant history as reported by Ms. Randles on admission. In addition to the scenario with the car that had prompted admission, Ms. Randles said Leroy is frequently angry, easily loses his temper, and can be "unpredictable." She also noted that he seems to be sleeping less than usual. Ms. Randles described impulsive behavior, such as running into the street without looking first and taking things from others without asking (e.g., grabbing a ball from another child on the playground). She described these behaviors not as discrete episodes but rather as symptoms that wax and wane but are always present.

When the team met with Leroy, they noted that he did not appear sleepy even though he had been up most of the night, and that he spoke quickly and often switched topics unexpectedly, consistent with pressured speech and racing thoughts. Leroy said he didn't know why he had taken his mother's car, stating, "I don't know, I just did it." Ms. Randles had little information about his family history other than that Leroy's birth mother had "some sort of mental illness and was in and out of the hospital and jail." Leroy reportedly struggled to make friends and performed below average academically in school.

Throughout Leroy's inpatient stay, the psychiatrist, with input from the rest of the care team, worked to clarify Leroy's diagnosis and determine the most appropriate course of treatment. Ultimately, Leroy was assigned a diagnosis of unspecified bipolar and related disorder; the unspecified type is often used in youths when manic symptoms are assessed that cause impairment but episodes cannot be clearly defined as is necessary for bipolar I disorder (American Psychiatric Association [APA], 2022). Given the level of impairment and risk involved with some of Leroy's behaviors, the psychiatrist prescribed risperidone (a second-generation antipsychotic medication) during his hospital stay, which Leroy tolerated well. Before beginning the medication, the psychiatrist and social worker met with Ms. Randles to discuss potential medication side effects, such as the potential for weight gain, and to weigh the pros and cons of medication in the context of Leroy's significant impairment. (See Chapter 3 for discussion of the diagnosis of bipolar disorder in children and concerns about antipsychotic medication.)

Leroy spent a total of 5 days on the inpatient unit. During that time, the team met with Leroy daily during morning rounds, and Michael met with Leroy individually each day, spoke with his mother by phone each day, and conducted two family meetings jointly with Leroy and his mother. Michael's work with Ms. Randles largely focused on psychoeducation. This included psychoeducation about mood disorders and medications, what to expect in terms of future mental health treatment needs and how to navigate the mental health system, problem-solving around how to keep Leroy safe and how to respond when he is angry or irritable, the importance of having good sleep routines and nutrition, and effective family communication. They also discussed signs and symptoms that would indicate an exacerbation of symptoms and would warrant immediate evaluation in the future.

Michael explained the vulnerability-stress model of pediatric bipolar spectrum disorders, stating, "There is not one factor that leads to bipolar illness; rather, there are a range of genetic, biological, environmental, and psychological factors that may predispose one to bipolar disorder, and these factors often interact with one another. The good news is that, with support from a therapist, families can often understand what the unique factors are for each child and how to manage the ones that you may have some control over so that you can set Leroy up for success as best as you can. I know that Leroy was adopted and that you don't have a lot of information about his biological family, just that his mother had mental health concerns and legal involvement. We know from research that about 50% of pediatric bipolar disorder can be accounted for genetically, and it is possible based on what you described that his mother had it too. Having a caring family and good communication at home, along with early identification of the illness, has been shown to be related to better prognosis. Based on my observations of your relationship with Leroy, I'm encouraged to see that you seem to have a great foundation to build on in terms of your relationship."

The social worker explained to Ms. Randles that youths with bipolar illnesses may experience "a range of emotions, from extreme irritability or mania to severe depression and everything in between." Michael described the various ways that hypomania and mania can present, including "extreme elation, feeling that you are on top of the world or that no harm can come to you, overactivity or hypersexuality, not sleeping much, or intense irritability" and that "it can look different in kids than adults. In adults, we may see very clear manic and depressive episodes. In kids those episodes may not be well defined—they may shift or cycle more quickly from one to another, or there can be a mix of symptoms present, and the core feature is really the presence of those extreme elevated or irritable moods." He also explained that "it is fairly common for kids with bipolar illness to also experience other mental health conditions, including attention-deficit/hyperactivity disorder (ADHD), anxiety, and disruptive behavioral challenges. We want to make sure that you'll have a good team in place for treatment and monitoring going forward to support Leroy as well as your family. This team can help you navigate how to keep him safe and how to respond to challenging behaviors, for example."

The social worker explained that evidence-based treatment for pediatric bipolar disorder typically includes medication prescribed by a child psychiatrist, therapy, and school supports. "We have some providers in our outpatient division who have a lot of experience in this area and will help you understand the illness, ensure you have a good treatment plan in place, and support you in this process. There are good evidence-based treatments available, and most kids can do quite well with on-going treatment and support." Michael also suggested, "While you are getting started with therapy, it will be important for Leroy to be closely monitored. Let's problem-solve some ways we can ensure he stays safe." Michael and Ms. Randles discussed strategies such as alarms on the doors that would alert her if Leroy left his room at night or attempted to leave the house again, locking up items such as car keys when not in use, and identifying other adults who could help provide supervision to Leroy when Ms. Randles, a single parent, needs a break. They also discussed setting up a consistent daily schedule for Leroy, including ensuring he was getting enough sleep and regular nutritious meals. Michael stated, "I know this is a lot, but you'll have a team in place to help you."

The family was connected to an outpatient psychiatrist and therapist, and appointments were made to meet with those individuals within 1 week of discharge. Ms. Randles was also given relevant community resources such as information about the local National Alliance on Mental Illness (NAMI) affiliate (www.NAMI.org) and how to obtain respite services through the county. On day 5, Leroy was discharged home to his mother.

Self-Harm and Suicidal Ideation

Sienna is a 16-year-old white female who was referred to a local ED by her outpa-tient therapist after she presented to her therapy appointment with a large, visible cut on her wrist that appeared in need of medical attention. Sienna had been attending weekly outpatient therapy for more than a year because of frequent interpersonal struggles, depression, and self-injury in the form of cutting that, until the day of ad-mission, had involved frequent, but always superficial, cutting of her arms and legs with a razor blade. Sienna had a history of stating "I'd be better off dead," she had not previously attempted suicide or disclosed a plan or intent to engage in suicidal behavior. She had been making little progress in weekly supportive talk therapy. The notes from the referring ED clinician indicate that Sienna had told them she was "unsure" if she was trying to die when she cut her wrist that day. After her wrist was treated (she required stiches), she was transferred to the inpatient unit.

Michael met with Sienna and her parents soon after her admission. She was quiet and tearful about being hospitalized, stating, "I just want to go home." She and her parents described a long history of emotional dysregulation, including often feeling sad or angry and having difficulty managing these intense emotions. They noted that Sienna has often turned to cutting herself when she experiences intense emotions because, according to Sienna, "it sort of grounds me." Sienna's parents reported that she is popular at school but that "there is always some sort of drama with her friends or with some boy." They said that Sienna has been in therapy for a while now where "we talk about my feelings and why I shouldn't cut" but that this has not been *particularly helpful. Sienna is prescribed a low dose of an antidepressant by an out-patient psychiatrist whom she sees monthly.*

During her time at the inpatient unit, Sienna met with Michael daily for individual meetings, which focused largely on safety planning. She also attended daily groups with the other teens on the unit. During group and leisure time, staff noted that Sienna was flirtatious with male patients and staff and that clear boundaries needed to be established. She also got into several arguments with female patients while simultaneously developing fast friendships with others. Her parents reported this was consistent with her relationships outside of the hospital. Sienna's antidepressant medication was adjusted during her stay, and she was able to develop a safety plan with Michael. Sienna's parents were included in safety planning, and Michael counseled them as to how to minimize Sienna's access to lethal means and cutting instruments. Michael and Sienna's parents discussed Sienna's treatment needs and agreed that her progress in therapy to date had not been optimal. Michael recommended a local adolescent dialectical behavior therapy (DBT) program in which Sienna would receive both individual therapy and group skills training on an outpatient basis while also having access to a clinician 24/7 for crises. Sienna would learn skills for distress tolerance, emotion regulation, mindfulness, and interpersonal functioning. The family agreed that this type of program sounded like a good fit for Sienna, and the unit case manager was able to arrange for her to have an intake with the DBT program following discharge from the hospital. After 4 days on the unit, Sienna was discharged home. Chapter 11 includes a case involving a DBT program.

Nonspecialty Mental Health Settings

Social workers, in addition to traditional mental health, also work in "host settings" (Sweifach, 2015), such as primary care, hospitals, schools, child welfare, and juvenile criminal justice, where social work is not the principal profession and mental health is not the primary mission or purpose (e.g., Atkins et al., 2010). There are some disadvantages to working in host settings, such as role confusion (Sweifach, 2015). Staff at the setting may not understand the role of the social worker, and sometimes in low-resource settings, social workers are asked to perform tasks unrelated to their training or role. Social workers also sometimes feel they lack authority when they are not in the most senior leadership role of a care team. Additionally, resources such as space (e.g., to meet individually with clients), office supplies, and access to technology (e.g., computers with Internet access) may be preferentially allocated to individuals in the setting whose work more closely aligns with the site's primary mission (Wolk et al., 2018). For example, physicians have prioritized access to private rooms for exams when space is limited in a primary care clinic.

Social workers may find themselves working in settings where multiple organizations are involved. For example, schools often contract with community mental health agencies for mental health service provision on site. Results of a comprehensive national survey demonstrated that about half of U.S. school districts contracted with community providers for mental health services (Foster et al., 2005). When this happens, the social worker is employed by the community mental health agency where they report to a clinical director, but they spend most their time working in a school where a principal is the lead authority. When these situations arise, social workers must know the reporting and supervisory structures and expectations, whom to consult if they receive competing or confusing messages, and the limits to privacy and confidentiality across roles and organizations. Despite these potential challenges, because mental health access issues persist in the United States (Henderson et al., 2013; Walker et al., 2015), the demand for more integrated mental health care models is only likely to continue to grow.

Schools and primary care are the most common nonspecialty mental health settings where children and adults, respectively, receive their mental health care. Next, we illustrate common roles for social workers in these settings.

School Mental Health

Public schools have become a primary provider of mental health services to children and may improve access to care for low-income youths (Hoover & Bostic, 2020). There are numerous models of school mental health services. Underresourced schools often utilize mental health teams composed of both school district and community mental health agency employees (Markle et al., 2014), or they may rely exclusively on contracted mental health agency employees to provide co-located services in schools (Taras & American Academy of Pediatrics Committee on School Health, 2004). Community agency employees typically bill Medicaid or private insurance for delivered services. (See the case illustration in Chapter 10 for an example of a co-located school provider.)

Social workers may be independent clinicians working in schools, may work on a team led by a school or clinical psychologist, or may be leaders of the school mental health team where they oversee other clinicians and paraprofessional support staff; the role varies considerably by region and school district. Support staff and other personnel on the mental health team may not be trained mental health providers but may nonetheless be responsible for implementing some mental health supports with students (Benjamin et al., 2014).

There are many effective prevention programs and interventions for the mental health problems youths most commonly present with for treatment in schools (Kutash et al., 2006), many of which are discussed in this book. Children are commonly referred for school-based mental health services because of behavioral challenges that are disruptive in the classroom (Little & McLennan, 2010). However, internalizing disorders such as anxiety, depression, and trauma are also common among school-aged youths (Merikangas et al., 2010). One challenge is that there are few treatments that have been specifically developed for use in schools or validated in school settings (Eiraldi et al., 2015). This can make it challenging for social workers because they will often need to adapt interventions to fit within the context of the school day (e.g., 40-minute class periods) while also ensuring they maintain fidelity to core intervention components.

In addition to providing direct mental health services to students in school, which may include individual or group therapy and encompass intervention and prevention services, social workers in schools have critical interprofessional functions. The social worker's role in the school regularly includes collaborating with parents and consulting with teachers. Social workers also may be involved with broader wellness or social emotional education for students and staff. They may collaborate with school administrators and school psychologists around the identification of students in need of additional supports, and they may aid in connecting students with behavioral and emotional concerns to appropriate services and accommodations. They often participate in interdisciplinary meetings, such as those for students with Individualized Education Programs (IEPs) and 504 Plans. Many schools employ both academic counselors, who support students with activities such as vocational or college planning, and clinical social workers. In these cases, social workers and school counselors can benefit greatly from working together to identify and support students' academic and emotional needs. Additionally, social workers in schools can play an important role in promoting school culture and climate (Kelly et al., 2016).

PRIMARY CARE

Primary care clinics may employ social workers in case management roles and as licensed mental health clinicians to provide direct mental health interventions. Integrated mental health services in primary care are increasingly common; the collaborative care model is a commonly employed evidence-based team approach for mental health treatment in the primary care setting. Collaborative care has been shown to increase access to mental health services and to lead to better outcomes for primary care patients (Archer et al., 2012; Miller et al., 2013; Woltmann et al., 2012). While much of the research on collaborative care to date has been with adult populations, it has demonstrated that this model is also effective in pediatric settings (Kolko et al., 2014; Richardson et al., 2014).

The core collaborative care team consists of the primary care provider (PCP), a mental health provider or care manager, and a consulting psychiatrist. Licensed clinical social workers often are employed in the mental health provider/care manager role. In the collaborative care model, the PCP is generally the billing provider of record. The PCP continues to manage the patient's overall health and prescribes psychotropic medications when indicated. The mental health provider typically coordinates care for patients and liaises with other relevant clinicians. The mental health provider also often provides brief psychotherapy as an embedded member of the primary care practice and typically takes the lead on following the patient over time to monitor the patient's mental health symptoms, medication adherence, and side effects. The mental health provider keeps the PCP apprised of the patient's progress and engages collaboratively with the PCP and consulting psychiatrist regarding the need to adjust treatment as necessary. The collaborative care model includes a consulting psychiatrist who provides guidance to the mental health provider and PCP regarding the patient's psychotropic medications. The consulting psychiatrist does not typically interact with the patient directly but instead collaborates closely with the mental health provider, who then shares the psychiatrist's recommendations with the PCP.

In collaborative care, the social worker functions as an integral member of the primary care team. Integration in the practice and effective collaboration are key components of the role. This can come in different forms, including attending team meetings, sharing documentation in the electronic health record, providing consultation and receiving warm handoffs (i.e., a direct handoff from the primary care provider to the mental health specialist during a visit) for patients in crisis, and treating patients with mild to moderate mental health needs (e.g., depression, anxiety) with brief evidence-based psychotherapy approaches. Common empirically supported psychotherapy approaches used by social workers in primary care include problem-solving therapy (Malouff et al., 2007), motivational interviewing (Lundahl et al., 2013), and brief cognitive behavioral therapy (Kolko et al., 2014).

Central to collaborative care is shared decision-making among the care team and between patients and providers. Another critical component of the model is the use of measurement-based care. Measurement-based care is the practice of adjusting care and treatment based on the results of data collected during ongoing treatment. Collaborative care programs use patient registries to track their patients and progress. At each encounter, the social worker assesses current symptoms using brief, validated measures, and these results guide treatment decisions. The specific measures selected will vary based on the patient and clinic; common choices in primary care include the nine-item Patient Health Questionnaire (PHQ; Johnson et al., 2002; Kroenke et al., 2001) for depressive symptoms and the Generalized Anxiety Disorder seven-item scale (GAD-7; Mossman et al., 2017; Spitzer et al., 2006) for anxiety symptoms. Sessions between the social worker and patient and family are conducted in person, by telephone, or through telehealth platforms; research supports that collaborative care can be effectively delivered remotely (e.g., Fortney et al., 2013).

Home-Based Services

Social work has a long history of home visiting, and in many settings, services are routinely provided in the home. Most recently, home visiting has been used when the child is at risk for being placed outside the home or moved to another setting. Often, services are presented intensively, meaning more than once a week and for more than an hour at a time. See Chapter 7 for descriptions of models that have this family preservation component.

Home-based services have many advantages (Corcoran, 2012). Logistically speaking, the limitations of clients who don't have reliable transportation or accessible public transportation are reduced, and disabilities, as well as childcare problems, can be eliminated by going to the client's home. The social worker can view clients in their natural environment, which gives a more accurate picture of conditions and functioning. It also helps the social worker identify challenges that must be overcome in terms of basic needs or safety. The social worker also might meet other people who are living with the client, assessing their level of support and engaging them as needed in services to assist the client. When social workers introduce clients to new behaviors, they can practice with the client in the setting where the new behaviors will be used, thereby improving generalizability.

For all the positives, however, there are also potential problems with home visiting. Foremost is the lack of structure and boundaries that exist in an office setting. Overcrowded living conditions are common, and the client may not have a private space in which to see the clinician. There must be creativity and flexibility in these cases. Porches, backyards, nearby parks, and fast-food restaurants may be options.

Clients may view the relationship to the clinician as more social than professional when clinicians come to their homes. A time limit and a clear purpose help to maintain structure in the visit. In some settings, home-based services are provided for a required number of hours per week. One problem with this arrangement is that it ignores the need to base goals and progress on the way services are structured rather than on time. This could encourage the client and the social worker to just "hang out," filling in the required time. For those motivated to change, it does not reward positive movement toward goals because the social worker will continue to be there regardless of whether the client is working on goals.

Numerous people may be in the home at the time of a visit for a variety of reasons, including a multigenerational family system, overcrowded living conditions, a chaotic family life, diffuse boundaries, and so forth. That is why it is important that social workers introduce themselves to those in the home and explain their role and purpose. Sometimes clients elect to involve people who appear from the outside to be tangential to the issue at hand (e.g., a son's girlfriend of 3 months, or a family friend who is sticking around for a ride later). In these cases, emphasizing the private nature of the work and the need for confidentiality is a way to limit the number of people being seen in the home.

Other issues that arise in making home visits include sanitary conditions and safety of the home. Although social workers must take care to remain nonjudgmental in the face of what may be the result of poverty, basic needs must be addressed first if they are being neglected. This may involve helping caregivers figure out how they will tackle such issues and connecting them to available supports in the community. This work may also involve providing necessary advocacy, such as empowering the client or contacting an apartment manager, for example, about spraying for pests or fixing unsafe appliances or electrical wiring. Social workers involved in the home should also take care of their own safety. Following commonsense precautions is important: informing the agency about destinations and expected time frames, keeping a door visible and accessible, and always carrying a fully charged mobile telephone.

Another issue with home visiting and its social nature is that clients may offer food and drinks. It is a generally accepted practice that social workers do not eat with clients, but in some cultures, turning down an offer of food or drink is interpreted as an insult. Distractions, such as the television playing, can also get in the way of work. One way to handle televisions and other loud, ongoing noise is to make an assertive statement, taking ownership over your own level of concentration (e.g., "Do you mind if we turn that off? I get easily distracted, and I want to be able to focus on you"). If the television is allowed to stay on, the message is that these are not professional services on which clients should be focused and that the work is not important. Distractions and the other issues briefly addressed here are some typical examples of home-based work, although there are others that unexpectedly arise.

TELEHEALTH

Teletherapy may present similar challenges and opportunities to home-based services, given that the client and family are receiving services in the home setting. Teletherapy may be more convenient for families and allows the clinician a glimpse into home life. However, it can also be important and helpful to establish boundaries and structure for teletherapy visits in advance. For example, it can be useful to discuss with families the importance of identifying a private and quiet space for sessions to occur in the home. They are best conducted seated at a table or desk with a computer, for instance, as opposed to logging in for a session from a cell phone while lying down or moving around. Teletherapy sessions may work best for older youths and teens participating in individual therapy or for parent consultation sessions. However, younger children may engage best with the therapist in person when feasible. Nelson, Cain, and Sharp (2017) provide practice guidelines and ethical consideration for teletherapy with children and adolescents from the American Telemedicine Association (Myers et al., 2017). Their review of the studies involving mental health concerns demonstrates the acceptability and feasibility of using these platforms. They also found that teletherapy services were at least as effective as in-person psychotherapy with youth. Finally, they noted that most of the treatments delivered involved cognitive-behavioral therapy and that such skills-based, structured approaches may lend themselves particularly to teletherapy services.

ETHICS AND VALUES IN SOCIAL WORK IN MENTAL HEALTH WITH CHILDREN

The National Association of Social Workers (NASW; 2017) code of ethics guides social workers' professional conduct. At times, social work clinicians may practice alongside other professionals who do not share their values, even when united to help youths in need. Following are some of the key social work values and their corresponding ethical standards that are invoked in this work.

Value: Service and Social Justice

The value of service is that social workers' primary goals are to help people in need and to address social problems. Front and center is the social work commitment to helping those who are disenfranchised to receive quality services. This mission is part of our rationale for teaching students, through this book, how to offer treatments that have received evidence support, which we believe is an important standard for selecting quality services. As well as providing treatment, we address disparities by connecting clients with the resources they need to meet their basic needs and improve their well-being. We may also advocate for our clients to receive the resources and services to which they are entitled.

The person-in-environment orientation of social work means that if we treating a child who is reacting to stress in the environment, such as family violence or conflict, we have a duty to address the environmental stress. In other words, we should not "psychologize" problems in a child who is dealing with an environment that we can work toward changing.

Understandably, in mental health settings, the medical model often pervades the work. However, social workers should instead of overfocusing on individual pathology, acknowledge, and, at times, articulate to colleagues the force of social oppression on constraining individuals' opportunities for advancement. Social workers are committed to improving conditions related to poverty, discrimination, and other forms of social injustice and operating with understanding and sensitivity to oppression and cultural and ethnic diversity (NASW, 2021).

Value: Importance of Human Relationships

Critical for working with children is the understanding that we must also engage with parents as well as the family unit. Consider the NASW (2017) value of the importance of relationships, which demands our engagement with parents as partners in the helping process, recognizing that the relationship between parent and child is an important vehicle for change and child well-being. This also holds true for adolescents, who are by definition gaining more independence and personal responsibility; therefore, the therapy sessions are typically a large part of the work, depending on the presenting problem. However, parents are still important, and their involvement is necessary. At the very least, they typically schedule and bring their child to appointments and arrange for payment. The adolescent still resides within the family system, and that environment continues to shape development in critical ways. Many of the evidence-supported interventions presented and illustrated in this book involve parents to a great extent, so this orientation aligns with research evidence as well.

Ethical Standard: Informed Consent

Under the central values of the profession are social work's ethical standards for working with clients. The ethical standard of informed consent entails informing parents and children that we will use an intervention that has evidence backing it. See the example in Chapter 9 where children with impairing anxiety problems that also affected their families received prior services that were not effective before receiving the evidence-supported intervention. There is also a stipulation in the code of ethics (section 5.02) for social workers to "critically examine and keep current with emerging knowledge relevant to social work and fully use evaluation and research evidence in their professional practice." This standard means that we should know how to deliver research-supported treatments (see also Chapter 1).

Ethical Standard: Cultural Competency

Individualizing the client and cultural humility are other values of the social work profession. Research-supported interventions have sometimes been criticized as being rote and mechanistic, without regard for the individual (Norcross et al., 2006). However, adapting the intervention to clients' unique circumstances, including cultural considerations, and making treatment relevant are important for collaborative work. Recently, a useful heuristic, the Cultural Treatment Adaptation Framework, was derived from an analysis of 45 studies (Chu & Leino, 2017). The framework involves (1) components of treatment; (2) participation and engagement; and (3) treatment delivery. In these authors' analysis, few of the adaptations involved changes to the core components; instead, case management to address housing, health care, and transportation needs was often the add-on. All the studies made changes to address engagement/participation and delivery, including the following:

- Incorporation of cultural themes/examples
- Changes to materials and semantics to avoid language that was stigmatizing or an orientation that was too focused on the individual instead of collectivism and interdependence
- Session structure, allowing for time to talk about racism and acculturative stress
- Changing the style of the provider–client relationship, whether the need was for hierarchical relationships or casual and personal relationships
- Using medical, tribal, or spiritual providers rather than mental health providers or locations

The Cultural Treatment Adaptation Framework is a useful way to consider treatment adaptations, when necessary, using the empirically derived categories that Chu and Leino (2017) found. They argue that since core components are not typically changed, fidelity to the treatment remains. In Chapter 7, the clinician considers and applies cultural adaptations in the case example.

The last NASW (2017) code of ethics standards we discuss here are privacy and confidentiality, which can sometimes be a source of confusion for practitioners, especially when working with adolescents. Informed consent covers the limits of confidentiality, such as imminent harm to self or others and abuse to older adults or children. But the situation sometimes becomes more complicated when adolescents reveal risky behavior, such as self-harm, sexual behavior that may result in a sexually transmitted infection or pregnancy, illegal drug use, and criminal activity. Rather than invoking these as abstractions, we present a series of vignettes that speak to some of the ethical dilemmas that arise when working with youths. We offer multiple-choice questions to aid in reflection and for discussion in class.

CASE APPLICATIONS
Case #1: Charlene

Charlene, a 10-year-old white female, was adopted at birth by her middle-class parents, who also have a son in high school. Charlene's parents reported out-of-control behaviors, such as hitting her mother, screaming at high volume when angry, trashing her room, and physically fighting a classmate at a birthday party. Both parents ran an organized household, and limit-setting was clear, but Charlene pushed at most boundaries, trying to get her way. Her parents didn't give in to her demands, but her behavior was difficult to manage on an almost daily basis.

One day, her father was assigned to take Charlene to her weekly therapy session. Charlene was playing with a much younger neighbor child (she tended to hang around younger children) and refused to go with her father. A power struggle ensued because he was aware that he would be charged for the session if they did not appear. Charlene ran to their house, lodged herself in the doorway, and adamantly refused to come. Her father pulled her out of the doorway forcibly and pushed her into the car.

In the session for which they arrived late, Charlene's father was seen first because he reported that Charlene was sulking in the bathroom. He relayed what had happened before the appointment. When they were finished talking, the clinician found Charlene in the women's bathroom, spraying air fresheners. She willingly followed the clinician back to the therapy room. There, Charlene was as friendly as ever, lying on the couch and chatting. She was angry at her father, however, for "making her" come to the session when she was having fun. She then pulled up her sleeve to reveal a bruise on her wrist where he had grabbed her to pull her toward the car.

Out of time in the session and with another client in the waiting room, the clinician did not have the chance to bring the father back in to talk. After hours, the clinician consulted with a colleague, and they discussed the necessity of making a report to Child Protective Services (CPS), which the clinician then did, being clear about the context of the injury. The CPS intake worker said that an investigator would contact the family but that since the family was receiving therapy, they would likely only be warned and nothing further would be done.

After a social worker contacted them, Charlene's parents were angry about the clinician's report, and the father said, "I'm not a child abuser." The clinician said that she did not consider him this way, validated his frustration both with her and his daughter's behavior, and explained the limits of confidentiality and the duty to report any signs of injury caused by a parent. The parents abruptly terminated treatment and said they would find someone else.

What could the clinical social worker have done to avoid the parents terminating treatment?

A. *Call the parents back in for a session alone in which the clinician explained that she had a duty to report and encourage them to call themselves from her office.*

B. *Call the parents and have a phone conversation before making the CPS report.*

C. *Cancel the next appointment and keep the father there to talk to him about the necessity of a report.*

D. *Refer the child for a higher level of care given that the father had to resort to physical means to get his child to obey his command.*

E. *Nothing else could have been done to prevent the parents from terminating treatment.*

Case #2: Emily

Emily, a 15-year-old white female, was seen in outpatient treatment for self-harm and suicidal ideation (with a vague plan involving a razor, her typical means of "cutting"). The clinician developed a safety plan with Emily and included Emily's mother so that she could restrict her daughter's access to sharp objects. The mother also started sleeping in Emily's room because she was afraid her daughter would harm herself in the middle of the night (Emily had threatened to do so).

During a beginning session when they were discussing cues and coping strategies, Emily revealed to the clinician that she'd had a bad week. She said she wanted to show the clinician what she'd done to her arms, but only if the clinician promised not to tell her mother, who was in the waiting room. The ensuing discussion processed Emily's reasons for not wanting to tell her mother: that she didn't want to be hospitalized (she had not been before) and that her mother "didn't need to know" because the actions weren't life-threatening. The clinician conveyed her concern for Emily's safety, reviewed some of the limits of confidentiality, and explored some other treatment options available short of hospitalization, such as partial hospitalization. They finally agreed, after a great deal of exploration and discussion, that Emily would show her injuries to the clinician and, if safety was deemed a concern, that her mother would be informed.

With some degree of pride, Emily revealed her forearms, both of which had multiple cut marks. Nearing the end of the time for the appointment, the clinician reacted by saying that the marks were of sufficient severity to talk to Emily's mother about safety concerns. Emily grew angry and said the clinician had violated her confidentiality, that the cuts weren't "that bad," and that she'd "done worse" without any threat to her safety. She fumed and refused to say good-bye to the clinician as they left.

When she returned 4 weeks later from a partial hospitalization program, Emily dismissed the helpfulness of the program and complained that the clinician had "put her in there." She said she didn't want the clinician talking to her mother again. The clinician advised that she would have to involve her mother because she was the primary person involved in Emily's care (her father, though caring, said he did not feel equipped to deal with the severity of Emily's behavior). Emily refused to see the clinician after this and switched therapists.

How could this situation have been improved?

A. Seeing the teenager alone and having the mother come in at another time for a separate session to avoid confrontation between the two
B. There was nothing different that should have been done.
C. Keeping confidentiality when the teen revealed the severity of her cuts; after all, she hadn't died from them
D. Bringing the mother into the session sooner and not engaging in the long, process-based discussion with the teen because this was entertaining her manipulation
E. Talking to the mother about the fact that giving in to her teen's desire to switch therapists inadvertently gave her power to make decisions in the home

A clinical social worker was the therapist for a juvenile justice program that contracted with the court to provide community monitoring. One of her clients was Eli, a 14-year-old Latino boy who had ended up in the program after being an accessory to a burglary. Eli's parents were frustrated with his lack of effort at school and that he had allowed himself to be talked into partaking in the burglary. They said that he tended to want to appear tougher than he was, and this made him vulnerable to being "used" and "talked into trouble." They were pleased, however, that he would receive therapeutic services in the home. After a couple of meetings, Eli revealed to the clinical social worker that he was selling the stimulants he was supposed to be taking for an ADHD diagnosis. The clinician led him through a discussion of the pros and cons, including if someone suffered a medical emergency from taking unprescribed medicine, but Eli remained adamant that he would keep doing it, mainly because it boosted his status. The social worker then told his case manager. The parents were furious and complained to the program director that the clinician had broken their son's confidentiality.

What is your reasoning for the optimal course of action in this scenario?

A. Because selling stimulants didn't involve an imminent risk of harm, the clinician should not have revealed this criminal activity to the case manager.
B. Because Eli was in the program for criminal activity, all criminal activity should have been revealed to the case manager.
C. Because Eli was adamant that he was going to keep selling his medication with full knowledge of potential risks, the clinician should have reported this to the case manager.
D. The program director should have learned from this incident that the informed consent for admission into the program needed to specify that any illegal activity uncovered as a part of services, even therapeutic services, would be reportable.

These scenarios provide examples of some of the ethical dilemmas that arise in work with children and adolescents and their families. Careful reading of the NASW code, discussions in class, and consultations with field supervisors and other administrative personnel will help in negotiating some of these boundaries.

SUMMARY

This chapter sets up the context for working with youths and families. The different settings where social workers work alongside colleagues from other mental health/counseling disciplines include traditional mental health settings such as outpatient, inpatient, and residential treatment settings. A case vignette involving a bipolar disorder diagnosis in inpatient care is illustrated here because this is a rare disorder in children and most of the book deals with more common disorders that social workers will typically see in outpatient services. Social workers also practice in settings where mental health treatment is delivered to youths outside the traditional mental health system, especially the school context, but also primary care and home-based services. We illustrate these with brief vignettes. Values of social work, namely service and the importance of working with family relationships, are discussed, along with the place of evidence-based treatment within these values. When working with children, ethical issues and dilemmas sometimes arise, and many of these have to do with confidentiality. For this reason, we explore with vignettes and reader reflection some common dilemmas surrounding confidentiality. In Chapter 3, we discuss the APA *Diagnostic and Statistical Manual of Mental Disorders* (DSM) and the organizing framework for this book.

REFERENCES

American Academy of Child and Adolescent Psychiatry Committee on Health Care Access and Economics Task Force on Mental Health. (2009). Improving mental health services in primary care: Reducing administrative and financial barriers to access and collaboration. *Pediatrics, 123*(4), 1248–1251. doi:10.1542/peds.2009-0048

American Psychiatric Association. (2022). *Diagnostic and statistical manual of mental disorders* (5th ed., Text Revision). Washington, DC: American Psychiatric Association.

Archer, J., Bower, P., Gilbody, S., Lovell, K., Richards, D., Gask, L., ... Coventry, P. (2012). Collaborative care for depression and anxiety problems. *Cochrane Database of Systematic Reviews, 10*, Cd006525. doi:10.1002/14651858.CD006525.pub2

Atkins, M. S., Hoagwood, K. E., Kutash, K., & Seidman, E. (2010). Toward the integration of education and mental health in schools. *Administration and Policy in Mental Health and Mental Health Services Research, 37*(1–2), 40–47.

Bardach, N. S., Coker, T. R., Zima, B. T., Murphy, J. M., Knapp, P., Richardson, L. P., Edwall, G., & Mangione-Smith, R. (2014). Common and costly hospitalizations for pediatric mental health disorders. *Pediatrics, 133*(4), 602–609. https://doi.org/10.1542/peds.2013-3165

Beck, N., & Wong, J. S. (2022). A meta-analysis of the effects of wilderness therapy on delinquent behaviors among youth. *Criminal Justice and Behavior, 49*(5), 700–729. https://doi.org/10.1177/00938548221078002

Benjamin, C. L., Taylor, K. P., Goodin, S., & Creed, T. A. (2014). Dissemination and implementation of cognitive therapy for depression in schools. In R. Beidas & P. C. Kendall (Eds.), *Dissemination and implementation of evidence-based practices in child and adolescent mental health* (pp. 277–293). New York: Oxford University Press.

Bettmann, J. E., Gillis, H. L., Speelman, E. A., Parry, K. J., & Case, J. M. (2016). Meta-analysis of Wilderness Therapy Outcomes for Private Pay Clients. *Journal of Child Family Studies, 25*, 2659–2673. https://doi-org.proxy.library.upenn.edu/10.1007/s10826-016-0439-0

Bloom, S. L. (1997). *Creating sanctuary: Toward the evolution of sane societies.* New York: Routledge.

Borschmann, R., Janca, E., Carter, A., Willoughby, M., Hughes, N., Snow, K., Stockings, E., Hill, N., Hocking, J., Love, A., Patton, G. C., Sawyer, S. M., Fazel, S., Puljević, C., Robinson, J., & Kinner, S. A. (2020). The health of adolescents in detention: A global scoping review. *Lancet Public Health, 5*(2), e114–e126. https://doi.org/10.1016/S2468-2667(19)30217-8

Bronsard, G., Alessandrini, M., Fond, G., Loundou, A., Auquier, P., Tordjman, S., & Boyer, L. (2016). The prevalence of mental disorders among children and adolescents in the child welfare system: A systematic review and meta-analysis. *Medicine, 95*(7), e2622. https://doi.org/10.1097/MD.0000000000002622

Burns, B. J., Phillips, S. D., Wagner, H. R., Barth, R. P., Kolko, D. J., Campbell, Y., & Landsverk, J. (2004). Mental health need and access to mental health services by youths involved with child welfare: A national survey. *Journal of the American Academy of Child & Adolescent Psychiatry, 43*(8), 960–970.

Chu, J., & Leino, A. (2017). Advancement in the maturing science of cultural adaptations of evidence-based interventions. *Journal of Consulting and Clinical Psychology, 85*(1), 45–57. http://dx.doi.org/10.1037/ccp0000145

Colins, O., Vermeiren, R., Vreugdenhil, C., van den Brink, W., Doreleijers, T., & Broekaert, E. (2010). Psychiatric disorders in detained male adolescents: A systematic literature review. *Canadian Journal of Psychiatry, 55*(4), 255–263. https://doi.org/10.1177/070674371005500409

Corcoran, J. (2012). *Helping skills in direct practice for social work.* New York: Oxford.

Coventry, G., & Swanson, L. G. (2011). Alternative treatments for conduct problems: Brats, boot camps, and bungee jumps. In R. C. Murrihy, A. D. Kidman, & T. H. Ollendick (Eds.), *Clinical handbook of assessing and treating conduct problems in youth* (pp. 365–381). New York: Springer.

Cummings, J. R., Ponce, N. A., & Mays, V. M. (2010). Comparing racial/ethnic differences in mental health service use among high-need subpopulations across clinical and school-based settings. *Journal of Adolescent Health, 46*(6), 603–606.

Eiraldi, R., Wolk, C. B., Locke, J., & Beidas, R. (2015). Clearing hurdles: The challenges of implementation of mental health evidence-based practices in under-resourced schools. *Advances in School Mental Health Promotion, 8*(3), 124–145. https://doi.org/10.1080/1754730X.2015.1037848

Fortney, J. C., Pyne, J. M., Mouden, S. B., Mittal, D., Hudson, T. J., Schroeder, G. W., Williams, D. K., Bynum, C. A., Mattox, R., & Rost, K. M. (2013). Practice-based versus telemedicine-based collaborative care for depression in rural federally qualified health centers: A pragmatic randomized comparative effectiveness trial. *American Journal of Psychiatry, 170*(4), 414–425. https://doi.org/10.1176/appi. ajp.2012.12050696

Foster, S., Rollefson, M., Doksum, T., Noonan, D., Robinson, G., & Teich, J. (2005). *School mental health services in the United States 2002–2003.* Washington, DC: U.S. Department of Health and Human Services.

Freed, M. C. (2020). Remember the denominator: Improving population impact of translational behavioral research. *Translational Behavioral Medicine, 10*(3), 667–673. https://doi.org/10.1093/tbm/ibz184

Green, J. G., McLaughlin, K. A., Alegría, M., Costello, E. J., Gruber, M. J., Hoagwood, K., Leaf, P. J., Olin, S., Sampson, N. A., & Kessler, R. C. (2013). School mental health resources and adolescent mental health service use. *Journal of the American Academy of Child and Adolescent Psychiatry, 52*(5), 501–510. https://doi.org/10.1016/j.jaac.2013.03.002

Henderson, C., Evans-Lacko, S., & Thornicroft, G. (2013). Mental illness stigma, help seeking, and public health programs. *American Journal of Public Health, 103*(5), 777–780. doi:10.2105/AJPH.2012.301056

Hoover, S., & Bostic, J. (2020). Schools as a vital component of the child and adolescent mental health system. *Psychiatric Services, 72*(1), 37–48. https://doi.org/10.1176/appi.ps.201900575

Huefner, J. C., James, S., Ringle, J., Thompson, R. W., & Daly, D. L. (2010). Patterns of movement for youth within an integrated continuum of residential services. *Children and Youth Services Review, 32*(6), 10. https://doi.org/10.1016/j.childyouth.2010.02.005

James S. (2011). What works in group care? A structured review of treatment models for group homes and residential care. *Children and Youth Services Review, 33*(2), 308–321. https://doi.org/10.1016/j.childyouth.2010.09.014

Johnson, J. G., Harris, E. S., Spitzer, R. L., & Williams, J. B. (2002). The patient health questionnaire for adolescents: Validation of an instrument for the assessment of mental disorders among adolescent primary care patients. *Journal of Adolescent Health, 30*(3), 196–204. https://doi.org/10.1016/s1054-139x(01)00333-0

Kelly, M. S., Frey, A., Thompson, A., Klemp, H., Alvarez, M., & Berzin, S. C. (2016). Assessing the National School Social Work Practice Model: Findings from the Second National School Social Work Survey. *Social Work, 61*(1), 17–28. https://doi.org/10.1093/sw/swv044

Kolko, D. J., Campo, J., Kilbourne, A. M., Hart, J., Sakolsky, D., & Wisniewski, S. (2014). Collaborative care outcomes for pediatric behavioral health problems: A cluster randomized trial. *Pediatrics, 133*(4), e981–e992. https://doi.org/10.1542/peds.2013-2516

Kroenke, K., Spitzer, R. L., & Williams, J. B. (2001). The PHQ-9: Validity of a brief depression severity measure. *Journal of General Internal Medicine, 16*(9), 606–613. https://doi.org/10.1046/j.1525-1497.2001.016009606.x

Kroenke, K., & Unutzer, J. (2017). Closing the false divide: Sustainable approaches to integrating mental health services into primary care. *Journal of General Internal Medicine, 32*, 404–410. https://doi.org/10.1007/s11606-016-3967-9

Kutash, K., Duchnowski, A. J., & Lynn, N. (2006). *School-based mental health: An empirical guide for decision-makers.* Tampa, FL: University of South Florida, The Louis de la Parte Florida Mental Health Institute, Department of Child & Family Studies., Research and Training Center for Children's Mental Health.

Little, M., & McLennan, J. D. (2010). Teacher perceived mental and learning problems of children referred to a school mental health service. *Journal of the Canadian Academy of Child and Adolescent Psychiatry,* 19(2), 94–99.

Lundahl, B., Moleni, T., Burke, B. L., Butters, R., Tollefson, D., Butler, C., & Rollnick, S. (2013). Motivational interviewing in medical care settings: A systematic review and meta-analysis of randomized controlled trials. *Patient Education and Counseling,* 93(2), 157–168. https://doi.org/10.1016/j.pec.2013.07.012

Malouff, J. M., Thorsteinsson, E. B., & Schutte, N. S. (2007). The efficacy of problem solving therapy in reducing mental and physical health problems: A meta-analysis. *Clinical Psychology Review,* 27(1), 46–57. https://doi.org/10.1016/j.cpr.2005.12.005

Markle, R. S., Splett, J. W., Maras, M. A., & Weston, K. J. (2014). Effective school teams: Benefits, barriers, and best practices. In M. D. Weist, N. A. Lever, C. P. Bradshaw, & J. S. Owens (Eds.), *Handbook of school mental health: Research, training, practice, and policy* (2nd ed., pp. 59–73). New York: Springer.

McCurdy, B. L., & McIntyre, E. K. (2004). And what about residential. . . ? Reconceptualizing residential treatment as a stop-gap service for youth with emotional and behavioral disorders. *Behavioral Interventions, 19,* 137–158.

Merikangas, K. R., He, J. P., Burstein, M., Swanson, S. A., Avenevoli, S., Cui, L., Benjet, C., Georgiades, K., & Swendsen, J. (2010). Lifetime prevalence of mental disorders in U.S. adolescents: Results from the National Comorbidity Survey Replication—Adolescent Supplement (NCS-A). *Journal of the American Academy of Child and Adolescent Psychiatry,* 49(10), 980–989. https://doi.org/10.1016/j.jaac.2010.05.017

Miller, C. J., Grogan-Kaylor, A., Perron, B. E., Kilbourne, A. M., Woltmann, E., & Bauer, M. S. (2013). Collaborative chronic care models for mental health conditions: Cumulative meta-analysis and metaregression to guide future research and implementation. *Medical Care, 51*(10), 922–930. https://doi.org/10.1097/MLR.0b013e3182a3e4c4

Mossman, S. A., Luft, M. J., Schroeder, H. K., Varney, S. T., Fleck, D. E., Barzman, D. H., Gilman, R., DelBello, M. P., & Strawn, J. R. (2017). The Generalized Anxiety Disorder 7-item scale in adolescents with generalized anxiety disorder: Signal detection and validation. *Annals of Clinical Psychiatry,* 29(4), 227–234A.

Myers, K., Nelson, E., Rabinowitz, T., Hilty, D., Baker, D., Barnwell, S. S., Boyce, G., Bufka, L. F., Cain, S., Chui, L., Comer, J. S., Cradock, C., Goldstein, F., Johnston, B., Krupinski, E., Lo, K., Luxton, D. D., McSwain, S. D., McWilliams, J., . . . Bernard, J. (2017). American telemedicine association practice guidelines for telemental health with children and adolescents. *Telemedicine Journal and e-Health,* 23(10), 779–804. https://doi.org/10.1089/tmj.2017.0177

National Association of Social Workers. (2021). *Code of ethics.* Retrieved from https://www.socialworkers.org/About/Ethics/Code-of-Ethics/Code-of-Ethics-English

Nelson, E. L., Cain, S., & Sharp, S. (2017). Considerations for conducting telemental health with children and adolescents. *Child and Adolescent Psychiatric Clinics,* 26(1), 77–91.

Norcross, J., Beutler, L., & Levant, R. (2005). *Evidence-based practices in mental health: Debate and dialogue on the fundamental questions.* Washington, DC: APA.

Phillips, E. L., Phillips, E. A., Fixsen, D. L., & Wolk, M. M. (1974). *The teaching-family handbook* (2nd ed.). Lawrence, KS: University Press of Kansas.

President's New Freedom Commission on Mental Health. (2003). *Achieving the promise: Transforming mental health care in America. Final report.* (DHHS Pub. No. SMA-03-3832). Rockville, MD.

Prins, S. J. (2014). Prevalence of mental illnesses in US State prisons: A systematic review. *Psychiatric Services, 65*(7), 862–872. doi:10.1176/appi.ps.201300166

Proctor, E. K., Morrow-Howell, N., Rubin, E., & Ringenberg, M. (1999). Service use by elderly patients after psychiatric hospitalization. *Psychiatric Services, 50*(4), 553–555.

Regier, D. A., Goldberg, I. D., & Taube, C. A. (1978). The de facto US mental health services system: A public health perspective. *Archives of General Psychiatry, 35*(6), 685–693.

Richardson, L. P., Ludman, E., & McCauley, E. (2014). Collaborative care for adolescents with depression in primary care: A randomized clinical trial. *JAMA, 312*(8):809–816. doi:10.1001/jama.2014.9259

Spitzer, R. L., Kroenke, K., Williams, J. B., & Löwe, B. (2006). A brief measure for assessing generalized anxiety disorder: The GAD-7. *Archives of Internal Medicine, 166*(10), 1092–1097. https://doi.org/10.1001/archinte.166.10.1092

Sweifach, J. S. (2015). Social workers and interprofessional practice: Perceptions from within. *Journal of Interprofessional Education & Practice, 1*(1), 21–27. https://doi.org/10.1016/j.xjep.2015.03.004

Taras, H. L., & American Academy of Pediatrics Committee on School Health. (2004). School-based mental health services. *Pediatrics, 113*(6), 1839–1845. https://doi.org/10.1542/peds.113.6.1839

U.S. Department of Health and Human Services. (1999). *Mental health: A report of the surgeon general—executive summary.* Rockville, MD: U.S. Department of Health and Human Services, Substance Abuse and Mental Health Services Administration, Center for Mental Health Services, National Institutes of Health, National Institute of Mental Health.

Vorrath, H., & Brendtro, L. (1985). *Positive peer culture* (2nd ed.). New York: Aldine.

Walker, E. R., Cummings, J. R., Hockenberry, J. M., & Druss, B. G. (2015). Insurance status, use of mental health services, and unmet need for mental health care in the United States. *Psychiatric Services, 66*(6), 578–584. https://doi.org/10.1176/appi.ps.201400248

Wolk, C. B., Stewart, R. E., Eiraldi, R., Cronholm, P., Salas, E., & Mandell, D. S. (2019). The implementation of a team training intervention for school mental health: Lessons learned. *Psychotherapy, 56*(1), 83–90. https://doi.org/10.1037/pst0000179

Woltmann, E., Grogan-Kaylor, A., Perron, B., Georges, H., Kilbourne, A. M., & Bauer, M. S. (2012). Comparative effectiveness of collaborative chronic care models for mental health conditions across primary, specialty, and behavioral health care settings: Systematic review and meta-analysis. *American Journal of Psychiatry, 169*(8), 790–804. https://doi.org/10.1176/appi.ajp.2012.11111616

3

The *Diagnostic and Statistical Manual of Mental Disorders* and the Medical Model

In the introductory chapter, we presented the *Diagnostic and Statistical Manual of Mental Disorders* (DSM) as one of the frameworks for the book. In this chapter, we detail further guidelines for the use of the manual and some principles for diagnosis, and we critique the medical model more generally as it relates to a social work perspective. We illustrate this critique using the diagnoses of bipolar disorder (BP) and disruptive mood dysregulation disorder (DMDD) and the use of medication to treat these disorders in children.

DSM DEFINITION OF MENTAL DISORDER

The definition of *mental disorder* in DSM-5 (American Psychiatric Association [APA], 2022) is a "syndrome characterized by clinically significant disturbance in an individual's cognition, emotion regulation, or behavior that reflects a dysfunction in the psychological, biological, or developmental processes underlying mental functioning" (p. 20). Such a disorder usually represents significant distress in the person's social or occupational functioning. The DSM represents a *medical* perspective, only one of many possible perspectives on human behavior. The medical definition focuses on underlying disturbances *within* the person and is sometimes referred to as the *disease model* of abnormality. This model implies that the abnormal person must experience changes within the self (rather than enact environmental change) to be considered "normal" again.

In its desire to promote the "objectivity" of its manual, the APA does not recognize the notion of mental illness as a *social construction*. A social construction is any belief system in a culture that is accepted as factual or objective by many of its members, when in fact the belief system is constructed by influential members of that society (Perone, 2014). The medical profession holds great

Child and Adolescent Mental Health in Social Work. Jacqueline Corcoran and Courtney Benjamin Wolk, Oxford University Press.
© Oxford University Press 2023. DOI: 10.1093/oso/9780197653562.003.0003

influence in Western society, so when mental health diagnoses are presented as scientifically based disorders, many people accept them as such. Social constructionism asserts that many "accepted" facts in a society are, in actuality, ideas that reflect the values of the times in which they emerge. Until 1974, for example, "homosexuality" was included as a mental disorder in DSM-II. Another example is the concept of gender incongruence, which has evolved over the past 65 years from being considered a mental disorder to one that is not. During that time, it has been considered a sexual deviation (APA, 1952), a sexual orientation disturbance (APA, 1968), an identity disturbance (APA, 1980), and now a source of dysphoria. The changing classifications of gender dysphoria in the DSM provide an example of how social and cultural norms may drive decisions about mental illness (Knudson et al., 2010).

RATIONALE FOR USE BY SOCIAL WORKERS

The DSM classification system does not fully represent the knowledge base or values of the social work profession, which emphasizes a transactional, person-in-situation perspective on human functioning. Still, the DSM is extensively used by social workers, for many positive reasons. Worldwide, the medical profession is preeminent in setting standards for mental health practice, and social workers are extensively employed in mental health settings, where clinical diagnosis is considered necessary for selecting appropriate interventions and insurance reimbursement. In fact, social workers account for more than half of the mental health workforce in the United States (Heisler & Bagelman, 2015). Competent use of the DSM is beneficial to social workers (and clients) for the following reasons:

- Social workers are employed in a variety of settings, not just mental health facilities, where they meet people who are vulnerable to mental health disorders because of poverty, minority status, and other social factors. No matter what their setting, social workers must be able to recognize the symptoms of possible disorders in their clients and appropriately refer them for treatment services.
- The diagnostic system provides a *partial* basis of a comprehensive biopsychosocial assessment.
- An accurate diagnosis helps to facilitate the development of an appropriate intervention plan (although many interventions are available for persons with the same diagnosis).
- The diagnostic categories enable social workers to help clients, and possibly also their families, learn about the nature of the clients' problems. Although stigma is often attached to the assignment of a diagnostic label, many people take comfort in learning that their painful experiences can be encapsulated in a diagnosis that is shared by others. It validates and legitimizes the experience and offers a path to recovery (Probst, 2012).

- Use of the DSM allows practitioners from various disciplines to converse in a common language about clients.
- The DSM perspective is incorporated into professional training programs offered by a variety of human service professions and portions of state social worker licensing examinations.
- Insurance companies usually require a formal DSM diagnosis for reimbursement.

Child and Adolescent Mental Health in Social Work might be used as a supplement in a course on clinical assessment or in a clinical treatment course. For that reason, we assume that readers will have received guidance on the use of the DSM and will only summarize it briefly here.

GUIDELINES FOR DSM DIAGNOSIS

Clinical disorders include all those discussed in the manual, as well as adjustment disorders. Most major diagnoses contain subtypes or specifiers (e.g., "mild," "moderate," and "severe") for added diagnostic clarity. When uncertain if a diagnosis is correct, social workers should use the "provisional" qualifier, which means a need for additional time or information to be confident about the choice. More than one diagnosis may apply to a client (called comorbid disorders), and medical diagnoses should also be listed. Social workers cannot make medical diagnoses, of course, but they can be included if they are noted in a client's history, or the client reports their existence. It is good practice to indicate the source for medical diagnosis (e.g., per doctor or self-report). Social and environmental problems can be captured from a chapter in the DSM titled "Other Conditions That May Be a Focus of Clinical Attention," which includes a list of conditions (popularly known as *Z-codes*) that are not considered formal diagnoses but can be used for that descriptive purpose.

The following is a list of hierarchical principles that can help the social worker decide which diagnoses to use in situations where several might be considered:

- "Disorders due to a general medical condition" and "substance-induced disorders," which include not only substances people consume but also medications they are prescribed and preempt a diagnosis of any other disorder that could produce the same symptoms.
- The fewer diagnoses that account for the symptoms, the better, which is the rule of "parsimony." Social workers need to understand the power of the diagnostic label in its negative as well as positive aspects and use such labels judiciously. For example, post-traumatic stress disorder (PTSD) and reactive attachment disorder are sometimes diagnosed together. Although they share some symptoms, when they are used together, the diagnostic picture becomes imprecise and does not lead to a coherent treatment plan.

- When a more pervasive disorder has essential or associated symptoms that are the defining symptoms of a less pervasive disorder, the more pervasive disorder is diagnosed if its criteria are met. For example, if symptoms of both "autism spectrum disorder" and "specific communication disorder" are present, the social worker should use the former diagnosis because its range of criteria subsumes the criteria for the latter one.
- Use the least restrictive diagnosis; in other words, use a diagnosis that is less stigmatizing, unless specified in the DSM that one diagnosis supersedes another. One diagnosis to always consider if the symptoms seem to be related to a recent stressful life event that has occurred in the past 3 months is "adjustment disorder." The adjustment disorder can be in reaction to an acute situation (one time) or a chronic situation that persists over time, such as parental divorce (APA, 2022). There are adjustment disorders that feature symptoms of anxiety, depression, and both together (mixed), as well as those that are conduct related or a mixed presentation of acting-out behavior and mood symptoms. In this book, we will mention adjustment disorders in the chapters that discuss that symptom profile (see, e.g., Chapter 10).

These principles are, of course, applied only after a comprehensive client assessment is carried out.

CRITIQUE OF THE MEDICAL MODEL

Now that we have described the DSM and briefly outlined guidance for diagnosis, we turn to a critique. Any classification of mental, emotional, and behavioral disorders is likely to be flawed because it is difficult for any system to capture the complexity of human life. As noted earlier, the DSM classification system is based on a medical model of diagnosis, while the profession of social work is characterized by the consideration of systems and the reciprocal impact of persons and their environments on human behavior. That is, for social workers, the quality of a person's social functioning should be assessed regarding the interplay of biological, psychological, and social factors. Three types of person-in-environment situations likely to produce problems in social functioning include life transitions, relationship difficulties, and environmental unresponsiveness (Carter & McGoldrick, 2005). Social work interventions, therefore, may focus on the person, the environment, or, more commonly, both.

Various specific criticisms of the DSM formulation of mental disorders have been postulated. First, as noted previously, it tends to view clients in isolation and decontextualizes the disorder from the person and the life circumstances that have given rise to it. Generally speaking, the DSM does not highlight the roles played by systems in the emergence of problems, except for the "adjustment disorders," in which people are seen as having difficulty adjusting to environmental stressors.

However, some practitioners might feel pressure to assign a more serious diagnosis for clients to receive certain services (Probst, 2012). Social workers can make references to the personal and social aspects of life in the diagnosis using Z-codes, but these are not generally reimbursable. Having to make a diagnosis for reimbursement means that social workers and other mental health professionals may reinforce the notion of the "identified patient" or the "sick one" when problems may have arisen as part of a family system (Probst, 2012) or a larger social system, such as structural inequality.

A related criticism is that, arising as it does from the psychiatric profession, the DSM may overstate the case for biological influences on some mental disorders (Paris, 2015). For instance, heritability for major depressive disorder, anxiety, and substance use disorder is about 30% to 40%. Although other biological factors may play a role in the development of mental disorders aside from genetics (e.g., complications at birth, exposure to lead), environmental factors exert a large influence.

Next, because not all symptoms need to be met for any diagnosis to be made, two people with the same diagnosis can have very different symptom profiles. There is also an acknowledged abundance of "subthreshold cases"—those that do not quite meet the minimum number of symptom criteria. However, subthreshold cases may produce as much impairment as those that meet full diagnostic criteria (Shah, 2015). The DSM has dealt with this problem, in part, by the addition over time of new subtypes of disorders and by the introduction of severity qualifiers (mild, medium, severe). In contrast to the International Classification of Diseases (ICD), which is used outside the DSM for the diagnosis of mental disorders as well as physical diseases, the DSM relies on symptom counting. The ICD approach is more about pattern recognition, generally avoiding arbitrary cutoffs and precise symptom counts, reflecting the approach clinicians usually take toward diagnosing (Reed et al., 2019). In the DSM, the current practice of basing diagnoses on symptom checklists seems problematic (Duffy et al., 2020).

Because of this limitation, many people have argued that mental disorders should be assessed through a *dimensional* approach, on a continuum of health and disorder. A dimensional approach allows more flexibility; a clinician can take severity into account instead of categorizing symptoms as either "normal" or "disordered." Many measurement instruments assess symptoms in a dimensional context rather than through a categorical system like the DSM, in which a person either meets certain criteria or does not. Several systems of this type are described in Part III of the DSM-5 (e.g., regarding personality disorders), but they have not yet been adopted for "official" use.

The problem of comorbidity, in which a person may qualify for more than one diagnosis, is also a point of confusion among practitioners. As will be evident throughout this book, comorbidity rates among populations social workers treat are often substantial. The DSM encourages the recording of more than one diagnosis when the assessment justifies doing so. Many disorders, however (e.g., anxiety disorders and depression), correlate strongly with one another (Balon, 2016). It may be that an anxious depression differs from either a "pure" major depressive disorder or anxiety disorder in critical ways. In addition, research on treatment generally confines itself to people without comorbid disorders, so that results are often not generalizable to the treatment population at large. For instance, we discuss BP in youths in the next section. The symptom profiles that supposedly are indicative of BP in youths—"manic-like" irritability, mood lability, and emotional reactivity—may show up in other conditions, including disruptive behavior disorders, PTSD, and pervasive developmental disorders (Carlson & Glovinsky, 2009). Further, youths diagnosed with BP show high rates of comorbid disorders, including attention-deficit/hyperactivity disorder (ADHD), disruptive behavior disorders, PTSD, anxiety disorders, and developmental disorders. The lack of a gold standard for confirming diagnosis remains elusive.

Moreover, the DSM lacks provisions for recording client strengths. Strengths-oriented practice implies that social workers should assess all clients in light of their capacities, talents, competencies, possibilities, visions, values, and hopes (Tan & Yuen, 2013; Saleeby, 2008). This perspective emphasizes human *resilience*—the skills, abilities, knowledge, and insight that people accumulate over time as they struggle to surmount adversity and meet life challenges.

Another concern about the DSM is that the reliability of diagnosis (agreement among practitioners about the same clients) is not high for some disorders, and generally has not risen significantly since DSM-II (Vanheule et al., 2014). There is no gold standard for confirming most diagnoses, and instead a great deal of subjectivity is present as to what might comprise a particular symptom within the sometimes broad and vague language of the DSM (McClellan et al., 2007; Morgan et al., 2013). The application of diagnostic criteria to a client case is dependent on the clinician's views as to what constitutes a symptom (McClellan & Werry, 2000).

Along with this subjectivity, cultural bias can occur. As described by Garb (2021), the way that symptoms are expressed affects diagnoses assigned. For example, Black individuals are more likely to report their symptoms of depression as irritability or agitation, as opposed to stating they often feel depressed. For many years, there has been a phenomenon, for instance, in which Black people are more likely to be diagnosed with the more serious mental illness, schizophrenia, rather than an affective illness (e.g., Adebimpe, 1981; Trierweiler et al., 2000). For youths, Chapter 7 explores the propensity of clinicians to diagnose Black children with oppositional defiant disorder (ODD) or conduct disorder rather than ADHD, which is seen as comprising less volitional behavior and has a better treatment profile (Atkins-Loria et al., 2015; Ballentein, 2019). Therefore, social work clinicians must ensure they are using the power they have to define clients' suffering through the DSM in careful and considered ways (Atkins-Loria et al. 2015).

Relatedly, a feminist critique is that the DSM is gender biased, conferring a much higher prevalence of many disorders to females than males (notably depression, anxiety, PTSD, and borderline personality disorder; Ussher, 2013). It has been argued that the DSM diagnoses may inadvertently blame girls and young women for their responses to oppressive social conditions. For example, sexual abuse is much more commonly experienced by females (Smith et al., 2018). Another concern is that many diagnoses reinforce societal gender biases (Wheeler et al., 2016).

Gender bias has been observed most notably in diagnoses of autism spectrum disorder, ADHD, conduct disorder, and some personality disorders (Garb, 2021).

Finally, the DSM classification system and the trend toward adding new diagnoses with each edition have been critiqued as potentially furthering the interests of the pharmaceutical companies (Moynihan et al., 2013). The pharmaceutical industry plays a significant role in medical prescribing practices. The more disorders there are, the more companies can market a particular medication for a certain disorder. Concerns have been raised about companies funding medication studies because they may be biased toward not publishing or disseminating null findings. Additional concerns include potential influence over individual doctors by offering consultancy fees, free meals, outings, or other perks and by sponsoring continuing education events. There have been some reforms around these practices. For example, doctors must disclose their relationship with pharmaceutical companies when they publish so that readers can examine the extent of influence that may have occurred.

BIPOLAR DISORDER

Now that we have detailed the DSM and its shortcomings from a social work perspective, we'll discuss the specific case of the bipolar and disruptive mood dysregulation disorders in children as illustrative of some of these critiques.

BP diagnosis increased dramatically in the United States among youths from 1996 when the rate was 1.3 per 10,000 to 7.3 per 10,000 children in 2004. Similarly, BP-related disorders increased fourfold among teens (Blader & Carlson, 2007).

The DSM describes the symptoms of BP as comprising a cyclical pattern, characterized by distinct episodes of mania and depression. Although age-specific criteria are not provided (McClellan et al., 2007), doctors began to give the diagnosis to youths in community settings who showed chronic difficulty regulating moods, emotion, and behavior (Geller et al., 2004; Wozniak et al., 1995). The broadening of the criteria was a controversial practice (Le et al., 2020). In an investigation of the controversy, Parry and Bastiampillai (2019) found 787 articles commenting on *pediatric bipolar disorder*. Among the 624 articles with U.S. authorship, the majority (83%) supported the concept of pediatric biology, whereas in the 163 articles by authors outside the United States, most (60%) endorsed the "traditional view" that such disorders are rare before mid-adolescence.

Pharmacologic intervention, specifically mood stabilizers, is considered primary for the treatment of BP. Mood stabilizers include lithium and the anticonvulsants. In 2000, the definition was expanded to include antipsychotics (see López-Muñoz et al., 2018, for a history). Because of some ill effects of lithium and the anticonvulsants, atypical antipsychotics were viewed as being safe, easy to use, and well tolerated. Antipsychotics in the past were reserved for the spectrum of schizophrenia disorders and psychosis that occurred during manic episodes; following this shift in perspective, in 2000 four antipsychotic medications were approved by the U.S. Food and Drug Administration (FDA) for "pediatric bipolar mania" (Correll et al., 2011, as cited in Toteja et al., 2014).

Most antipsychotic prescriptions written for youths in the United States are given for the diagnosis of BP (Burcu et al., 2016). Further, a study of prescriptions in one U.S. state indicated that of 10,000 children 6 years and younger enrolled in Medicaid, 4% received an antipsychotic prescription, and 75% of those prescriptions were for a diagnosis of BP (Lohr et al., 2015). However, the validity of the diagnosis in children has not been well established, much less for preschoolers (McClellan et al., 2007). Unfortunately, publicly insured youths are twice as likely to be prescribed antipsychotic medications as the privately insured (Burcu et al., 2016). Within the Medicaid population, children in foster care were even more likely to be given antipsychotics (Burcu et al., 2014).

Additionally, the practice of polypharmacy, meaning prescribing more than two medications, is increasingly common. Antipsychotic polypharmacy nearly doubled from 8% in the 1990s to 15% in the 2000s (Toteja et al., 2014). Systematic reviews have found that antipsychotic medications can be associated with serious side effects, including sudden weight gain and associated metabolic disturbances, with a heightened risk of type 2 diabetes (DeHert et al., 2011; Pringsheim et al., 2011).

At this point, it is established that BP in youths is very rare (Parry et al., 2021). The APA attempted to tackle the dramatic increase in bipolar diagnoses in youths by introducing the diagnosis of DMDD. Explosive behavior was subsumed under the umbrella of chronic irritability and studied originally as *severe mood dysregulation* (Leibenluft et al., 2003; Leibenluft, 2011), the forerunner to DMDD (Vidal-Ribas et al., 2016). Therefore, scientific support for DMDD is based primarily on studies of severe mood dysregulation (Mayes et al., 2016). Although severe mood dysregulation includes the main criteria of DMDD, it also requires symptoms of hyperarousal similar to those of ADHD (Leibenluft et al., 2003).

Researchers and clinicians have argued about the challenge of differentiating DMDD from ODD. Most youths with DMDD will meet criteria for ODD, although the opposite is not always the case (Stringaris et al., 2018). Further, the interrater reliability of DMDD was low in the DSM-5 field trials ($k = 0.25$), as was temporal stability, in that only a small fraction of children with DMDD met full criteria across time (Vidal-Ribas et al., 2016). Despite its flaws, the diagnosis of DMDD has now been on the rise to replace what is seen as the more serious disorder of BP, which has now shown a modest decrease in its diagnosis (Faheem et al., 2017). Psychiatrists and general doctors may prescribe medication, and sometimes multiple medications, despite potentially serious long-term health consequences, for youths with DMDD.

SUMMARY

This chapter provides an overview of the DSM diagnostic system, the reasons for its use among social workers, and its many drawbacks, particularly as it comes to the guiding principles and ethics of social work. We illustrate these concerns with the case of the BP diagnosis. However, we recognize that the DSM system will likely remain, so social workers need to be conversant with the manual and its use. We have used the DSM as an organizing framework for this book to present a survey of the mental health disorders that are commonly seen in community settings. We encourage critical thinking and a balanced appraisal of the use of the DSM. We urge the use of the evidence-based treatments, such as those described and applied in these chapters; in many cases (but not all, as described in this book), evidence-based psychotherapy can help youths adjust and recover without the need for medications. We now turn to the engagement of youths and their families in treatment, followed by a survey of the common mental health disorders that social workers may see, the research support for various interventions, and their clinical applications.

REFERENCES

Adebimpe, V. R. (1981). Overview: White norms and psychiatric diagnosis of Black patients. *American Journal of Psychiatry, 138*, 279–285.

American Psychiatric Association. (1980). *Diagnostic and statistical manual of mental disorders* (3rd ed.). American Psychiatric Association.

American Psychiatric Association (APA). (2022). *Diagnostic and statistical manual of mental* disorders (5th ed., Text Revision). Washington, DC: APA.

Atkins-Loria, S., Macdonald, H., & Mitterling, C. (2015). Young African American men and the diagnosis of conduct disorder: The neo-colonization of suffering. *Clinical Social Work Journal, 43*, 431–441. https://doi-org.proxy.library.upenn.edu/10.1007/s10615-015-0531-8

Ballentein, K. (2019). Understanding racial differences in diagnosing ODD versus ADHD using critical race theory. *Families in Society: The Journal of Contemporary Social Services, 100*(3), 282–292.

Balon, R. (2016). The confusion of psychiatric comorbidity. *Annals of Clinical Psychiatry, 28*(3), 153–154.

Blader, J., & Carlson, G. (2007). Increased rates of bipolar disorder diagnoses among U.S child, adolescent and adult inpatients, 1996–2004. *Biological Psychiatry, 62*(2), 107–114.

Burcu, M., Safer, D., & Zito, J. (2016). Antipsychotic prescribing for behavioral disorders in US youth: Physician specialty, insurance coverage, and complex regiments. *Pharmacoepidemiology and Drug Safety, 25*(1), 26–34.

Burcu, M., Zito, J., Ibe, A., & Safer, D. (2014). Atypical antipsychotic use among Medicaid-insured children and adolescents: Duration, safety, and monitoring implications. *Journal of Child and Adolescent Psychopharmacology, 24*, 112–119.

Carlson, G., & Glovinsky, I. (2009). The concept of bipolar disorder in children: A history of the bipolar controversy. *Child and Adolescent Psychiatric Clinics of North America, 18*(2), 257–271.

Carter, E., & McGoldrick, M. (2005). *The expanded life cycle.* Boston: Allyn & Bacon.

De Hert, M., Dobbelaere, M., Sheridan, E., Cohen, D., Sheridan, E., & Correll, C. (2011). Metabolic and endocrine adverse effects of second-generation antipsychotics in children and adolescents: A systematic review of randomized, placebo controlled trials and guidelines for clinical practice. *European Psychiatry, 26*(3), 144–158.

Duffy, A., Carlson, G., Dubicka, B., & Hillegers, M. H. J. (2020). Pre-pubertal bipolar disorder: origins and current status of the controversy. *International Journal of Bipolar Disorders, 8*(1), NA.

Faheem, S., Petti, V., & Mellos, G. (2017). Disruptive mood dysregulation disorder and its effect on bipolar disorder. *Annals of Clinical Psychiatry: Official Journal of the American Academy of Clinical Psychiatrists, 29*(1), 84–91.

Garb, H. N. (2021). Race bias and gender bias in the diagnosis of psychological disorders. *Clinical Psychology Review, 90*, 102087. https://doi.org/10.1016/j.cpr.2021.102087

Geller, B., Tillman, R., Craney, J., & Bolhofner, K. (2004). Four-year prospective outcome and natural history of mania in children with a prepubertal and early adolescent bipolar disorder phenotype. *Archives of General Psychiatry, 61*(5), 459–467. doi:10.1001/archpsyc.61.5.459

Heisler, E., & Bagelman, E. (2015). The mental health workforce: A primer. Congressional Research Service. Retrieved from https://ecommons.cornell.edu/bitstream/handle/1813/79418/CRS_The_Mental_Health_Workforce.pdf?sequence=1&isAllowed=y

Le, J., Feygin, Y., Creel, L., Lohr, W., Jones, F., Williams, G., & Myers, J. (2020). Trends in diagnosis of bipolar and disruptive mood dysregulation disorders in children and youth. *Journal of Affective Disorders, 264*, 242–248.

Leibenluft, E. (2011). Severe mood dysregulation, irritability, and the diagnostic boundaries of bipolar disorder in youths. *American Journal of Psychiatry, 168*(2), 129–142.

Leibenluft, E., Charney, D., Towbin, K., Bhangoo, R., & Pine, D. (2003). Defining clinical phenotypes of juvenile mania. *American Journal of Psychiatry, 160*(3), 430–437. https://doi.org/10.1176/appi.ajp.160.3.430Lohr, W., Chowning, R., Stevenson, M., & Williams, P. (2015). Trends in atypical antipsychoics prescribed to children six years of age or less on Medicaid in Kentucky. *Journal of Child and Adolescent Psychopharmacology, 25*(5), 440–443.

López-Muñoz, F., Shen, W. W., D'Ocon, P., Romero, A., & Álamo, C. (2018). A history of the pharmacological treatment of bipolar disorder. *International Journal of Molecular Sciences, 19*(7), 2143. https://doi.org/10.3390/ijms19072143

Mayes, S., Baweja, R., Hameed, U., & Waxmonsky, J. (2016). Disruptive mood dysregulation disorder: Current insights. *Neuropsychiatric Disease and Treatment, 12*, 2115–2124. https://doi.org/10.2147/NDT.S100312

McClellan, J., Kowatch, R., & Findling, R. (2007). Practice parameter for the assessment and treatment of children and adolescents with bipolar disorder. *Journal of the American Academy of Child & Adolescent Psychiatry, 46*(1), 107–125.

McClellan, J., & Werry, J. (2000). Introduction—research psychiatric diagnostic interviews for children and adolescents. *Journal of the American Academy for Children and Adolescent Psychiatry, 39*(1), 19–27.

Morgan, P., Staff, J., Hillemeier, M., Farkas, G., & Maczuga, S. (2013). Racial and ethnic disparities in ADHD diagnosis from kindergarten to eighth grade. *Pediatrics, 132*(1), 85–93.

Moynihan, R. N., Cooke, G. P. E., Doust, J. A., Bero, L., Hill, S., & Glasziou, P. P. (2013). Expanding disease definitions in guidelines and expert panel ties to industry: A cross-sectional study of common conditions in the United States. *PLoS Medicine, 10*(8).

Paris, J. (2015). *Overdiagnosis in psychiatry.* New York: Oxford University Press.

Parry, P., Allison, S., & Bastiampillai, T. (2019). The geography of a controversial diagnosis: A bibliographic analysis of published academic perspectives on "paediatric bipolar disorder." *Clinical Child Psychology and Psychiatry, 24*(3), 529–545. https://doi.org/10.1177/1359104519836700

Parry, P., Allison, S., & Bastiampillai, T. (2021). "Pediatric Bipolar Disorder" rates are still lower than claimed: A re-examination of eight epidemiological surveys used by an updated meta-analysis. *International Journal of Bipolar Disorders, 9*(1), 21. https://doi.org/10.1186/s40345-021-00225-5

Perone, A. (2014). The social construction of mental illness for lesbian, gay, bisexual, and transgender persons in the United States. *Qualitative Social Work, 13*(6), 766–771.

Pringsheim, T., Lam, D., Ching, H., & Patton, S. (2011). Metabolic and neurological complications of second-generation antipsychotic use in children. *Drug-Safety, 34,* 651–668. https://doi.org/10.2165/11592020-000000000-00000

Probst, B. (2012). "Walking the tightrope:" Clinical social workers' use of diagnostic and environmental perspectives. *Clinical Social Work Journal, 41,* 184–191.

Reed, G. M., First, M. B., Kogan, C. S., Hyman, S. E., Gureje, O., Gaebel, W., . . . Saxena, S. (2019). Innovations and changes in the ICD-11 classification of mental, behavioural and neurodevelopmental disorders. *World Psychiatry, 18,* 3–19. doi:10.1002/wps.20611

Saleebey, D. (2008). *The strengths perspective in social work practice.* London: Rugby.

Shah, J. L. (2015). Sub-threshold mental illness in adolescents: Within and beyond DSM's boundaries. *Social Psychiatry and Psychiatric Epidemiology, 50*(5), 675–677. doi:10.1007/s00127-015-1015-4

Smith, S. G., Zhang, X., Basile, K. C., Merrick, M. T., Wang, J., Kresnow, M., & Chen, J. (2018). *The National Intimate Partner and Sexual Violence Survey: 2015 Data brief— updated release.* Centers for Disease Control and Prevention.

Stringaris, A., Vidal-Ribas, P., Brotman, M. A., & Leibenluft, E. (2018). Practitioner review: Definition, recognition, and treatment challenges of irritability in young people. *Journal of Child Psychology and Psychiatry, 59,* 721–739. doi:10.1111/jcpp.12823

Tan, N., & Yuen, F. (2013). Social work, strengths perspective, and disaster management: Roles of social workers and models for intervention. *Journal of Social Work in Disability & Rehabilitation, 12,* 1–7

Toteja, N., Gallego, J., Saito, E., Gerhard, T., Winterstein, A., Olfson, M., & Correll, C. (2014). Prevalence and correlates of antipsychotic polypharmacy in children and adolescents receiving antipsychotic treatment. *International Journal of Neuropsychopharmacology, 17,* 1095–1105.

Trierweiler, S. J., Neighbors, H. W., Munday, C., Thompson, E. E., Binion, V. J., & Gomez, J. P. (2000). Clinician attributions associated with the diagnosis of schizophrenia in African American and non-African American patients. *Journal of Consulting and Clinical Psychology, 68*(1), 171–175. https://doi.org/10.1037/0022-006X.68.1.171

Ussher, J. M. (2013). Diagnosing difficult women and pathologising femininity: Gender bias in psychiatric nosology. *Feminism & Psychology, 23*(1), 63–69.

Vanheule, S., Desmet, M., Meganck, R., Inlegers, R., Willemsen, J., DeSchryver, M., & Devisch, I. (2014). Reliability in psychiatric diagnosis with the DSM: Old wine in new barrels. *Psychotherapy and Psychosomatics, 83*, 313–314.

Vidal-Ribas, P., Brotman, M. A., Valdivieso, I., Leibenluft, E., & Stringaris, A. (2016). The status of irritability in psychiatry: A Conceptual and Quantitative Review. *Journal of the American Academy of Child and Adolescent Psychiatry, 55*(7), 556–570. https://doi.org/10.1016/j.jaac.2016.04.014

Wheeler, E. E., Kosterina, E., & Cosgrove, L. (2016). *Diagnostic and Statistical Manual of Mental Disorders* (DSM), Feminist critiques of. *The Wiley Blackwell Encyclopedia of Gender and Sexuality Studies*, 1–3.

Wozniak, J., Biederman, J., Kiely, K., Stuart Ablon, J., Faraone, S., Mundy, E., & Mennin, D. (1995). Mania-like symptoms suggestive of childhood-onset bipolar disorder in clinically referred children. *Journal of the American Academy of Child and Adolescent Psychiatry, 34*(7), 867–876.

4

Engagement

We devote a chapter to engagement for several reasons. Families must invest time, energy, effort, and money in the child's treatment. Dropout rates are substantial— ranging from 34% to 46% (de Haan et al., 2013). Many youths do not come to the treatment process voluntarily; the school, the courts, and parents may require that the child attends. Engagement techniques must address the nonvoluntary nature of children's role in the process. Additionally, many parents initially believe their child's treatment will only involve the child. However, many of the evidence-based practices (EBPs) discussed in this book involve parents in the treatment process. Fortunately, some of the techniques that engage youths are also helpful for encouraging parental involvement.

In this chapter, we review the practice models of solution-focused therapy (SFT) and motivational interviewing (MI) for their ability to engage and motivate clients in treatment. We also review the empirical literature on evidence-based engagement strategies in child mental health treatment and describe promising approaches.

SOLUTION-FOCUSED THERAPY

Developed by deShazer, Berg, and colleagues (Berg, 1994; Berg & Miller, 1992; Cade & O'Hanlon, 1993; de Shazer et al., 1986; O'Hanlon & Weiner-Davis, 1989), SFT emphasizes the strengths people bring to therapy and how these can be applied to the change process. Clients are assumed to have the capability to solve their own problems using resources that are illuminated through elicitation and exploration of times when the problem does not exert its negative influence or when the client has coped successfully. Rather than focusing on the past and the history of the problem, SFT orients attention on a future without the problem as a way to build vision, hope, and motivation for the client. The assumption in SFT is that change occurs in a systemic way. A small change is all that is necessary to create a "spiral effect": the client takes a step in the right direction; others in the context respond differently; the client feels more empowered and is encouraged

Child and Adolescent Mental Health in Social Work. Jacqueline Corcoran and Courtney Benjamin Wolk, Oxford University Press.
© Oxford University Press 2023. DOI: 10.1093/oso/9780197653562.003.0004

toward further change. Behaving differently *and* thinking differently are part of the processes of change (deShazer, 1994).

Although SFT has not yet attained the status of an evidence-based treatment in terms of the systematic reviews that have been published and the categorical systems that rank treatments, SFT has excellent techniques for promoting initial engagement and a unique emphasis on assessing the client's relationship to the change process, recognizing that youths and parents have a different orientation.

Solution-Focused Therapy for Youths

Overall, engagement in SFT involves building a collaborative relationship, recognizing and eliciting strengths in the client, and orienting the client toward goals and change. One surefire way to start off with young clients, especially those who are reluctant or resistant, is to *orient the client toward meeting the requirements of the mandate*: "Whose idea was it that you come here? "What does ____ need to see happen to say that you don't have to come here anymore?" Along with the directive toward formulating goals implicit in these questions is a *relationship question*, defined in SFT as a way to help clients to view themselves from the perspective of another (de Jong & Berg, 2012). When people are in the midst of a problem, they often have difficulty seeing alternatives. By viewing the problem from another person's point of view (e.g., "What would your mom say needs to happen in our work together to know that our time has been successful?"), they can sometimes see other possibilities. Relationship questions also are useful when people respond with "I don't know" to questions, a common response from youths. They help relieve people of having to come up with the answers when they may feel pressured or stuck. A related engagement technique in SFT is *siding with the client against an external entity* so that the social worker and the child are on the same side rather than being polarized: "What will we need to do to convince your probation officer that you no longer need to come here?" If we hold one perspective and the client is in a completely different position, we risk becoming polarized, and the client is likely to become defensive and even more entrenched in a position against change (Berg, 1994). This question, although collaborative in nature, places the responsibility for change on clients so that you do not have to talk them into change or otherwise convince them of its necessity.

Solution-Focused Therapy for Parents

Parents, when they accompany their children to treatment, are often more motivated for their children to change than are the youths themselves. Parents are also not generally motivated to change their own parenting behaviors. One way to help a parent who continually focuses on a child's challenging behavior is to assist the parent in identifying positive replacement behaviors (i.e., "What would you like to see him doing instead?"). Generally, people have a difficult time answering this question because they have been so focused on problem behavior. To probe for behavioral indicators, follow-up questions are suggested: "If I were videotaping her, what would I see her doing when she is acting the way you want?" This type of question places responsibility on parents to be clear and concrete about what they want from their children. Therapy can then proceed to working toward achieving those goals. Another solution-focused technique is to *emphasize the circular nature of interaction patterns*: "What will you be doing when your child is behaving?" An additional technique for parents who have struggled with their child's emotions and behaviors is to ask what are called *coping questions*. These questions not only validate the extent to which people have been challenged but also ask clients to reflect on the resources they have used to manage their struggles. Types of coping questions include the following (Bertolino & O'Hanlon, 2002):

- "How have you coped with the problem?"
- "How do you manage? How do you have the strength to go on?"
- "This has been a very difficult problem for you. How have you managed to keep things from getting even worse?"
- "What percentage of the time are you dealing with this? How do you cope during this time? What makes it a little better the other percentage of the time?"

For both parents and children, complimenting is a technique to reduce the sense of defensiveness clients may feel initially and to reinforce strengths and resources. De Jong and Berg (2012) suggest a form of complimenting called "indirect complimenting" in which positive traits and behaviors are implied. Examples of indirect complimenting include:

- "How were you able to do that?"
- "How did you figure that out?"

These questions push the client to become aware of the resources they used to achieve success and to articulate their own strengths.

MOTIVATIONAL INTERVIEWING

MI is a person-centered, collaborative method for exploring ambivalence and enhancing motivation to change (Miller & Rollnick, 2012). MI involves both a philosophy and a method. The spirit of MI involves several elements that are very much in line with the values and ethics of social work: partnership, acceptance, compassion, and evocation. The emphasis in MI is on partnership and collaboration rather than confrontation and labeling, which aligns with the fundamental social work value of human dignity. Part of an appreciation for human dignity is that intervention addresses the whole person, including strengths as well as challenges. MI is strengths-based by nature (Manthey et al., 2011), building on the client's motivation and activating the client's expertise (Miller & Rollnick, 2012). The emphasis is on the collaborative relationship as a vehicle for change. Rather than being seen as a fixed state or a stable characteristic within the client, motivation is seen as a product of the interaction between client and social worker. Therefore, it avoids the labeling of "client resistance," which sometimes turns into client blame.

MI is discussed in Chapter 8, noting that it was originally designed for substance use disorders. A couple of studies have also recently used MI in an initial session or infused throughout behavioral approaches for disruptive behavior disorders. As an example, Sibley et al. (2016) combined MI with behavioral treatment for culturally diverse teens with attention-deficit/hyperactivity disorder (ADHD). Positive results were reported on ADHD symptoms and on teen organizational and planning ability, even at the 6-month follow-up.

The point in MI is to steer the conversation in a way so that people talk themselves into change, rather than trying to persuade, argue, or scare them into it. This task is accomplished by reinforcing statements about change and handling comments about not changing (called *sustain talk*) by using a variety of reflecting statements to evoke the side of the client that is desirous of change. Discussion of client goals and values is important in this model because it helps the client understand to what extent the problem behavior aligns with these. A variety of questions have been designed to elicit statements about wanting to change: problem recognition (e.g., "What things make you think that this is a problem?"); concern (e.g., "What is there about the problem that you or other people might see as reasons for concern?"); and querying extremes (e.g., "What concerns you the most about this in the long run?"). However, questions do not predominate in this model; in fact, Miller and Rollnick (2012) offer a general guideline of asking one question to two to three statements.

The decisional balance technique in which a client addresses the pros and cons of a problem behavior can provide a framework for discussion of client ambivalence (Westra, 2012), and both children and adolescents can engage in this discussion. Asking about the "good things" associated with problems, such as aggression, serves several important functions. First, it disarms the defensiveness people often feel when they are threatened with loss of autonomy. People expect to be judged for their behaviors and are pleasantly surprised when they are encouraged to speak about the payoffs to the behavior. Second, people are given credit for the fact that the problem behavior, though seemingly irrational and perhaps even destructive from an outside perspective, must serve some key purposes for the individual for the problem to remain in place. The intent can be reframed. "Your main goal is to stick up for yourself like your parents taught you. The way you have figured out how to do that is by fighting." Therefore, in addition to helping clients feel more understood, "asking about the advantages" can help both the client and the social worker learn about the function that the problem behavior serves.

Some clinicians may worry that asking about the "good things" of a behavior condones it. It does not. Asking about what people get out of a behavior facilitates your and the client's understanding of the problem. As part of the exploration, you can ask at the end of this conversation if they'd be interested in trying to meet these needs in alternative ways, even if they are uninterested in the moment in reducing or ameliorating the behavior. For instance, carrying on with the problem of aggression, the practitioner can ask, "Are you interested in figuring out how you can stick up for yourself without getting into trouble?"

In the process of talking about what clients like about their problem behavior, they will sometimes spontaneously initiate exploration of its downsides. If not, you can say, "Now that we've talked about what you get out of fighting, let's talk about the not so good things."

Discussion of the disadvantages of the problem can be very effective for work with children and adolescents for several reasons. First, it distinguishes the role of the social worker from other people in the child's life, namely parents and teachers, who lecture and scold the child about what he or she must do. Instead, the social worker's role is to guide a process where the child takes more ownership of the problem through a nonjudgmental approach of talking about what needs it meets for the child, developing ways to articulate internal processes and motivations. Additionally, and, according to MI, the process of hearing themselves have an internal debate about the positive and negative consequences of the problem may help them gain more clarity about the necessity of changing. For more information about the use of MI for youths, see Naar-King and Suarez (2010), and for MI in social work, see Corcoran (2016) and Hohman (2015).

EVIDENCE-BASED ENGAGEMENT

Another way to build engagement is to draw on approaches that have been studied and found effective for child and family intervention. In the literature, engagement is defined as attendance, adherence, and readiness/understanding (Lindsay et al., 2014). In a comprehensive review involving 40 years of child treatment studies, 89 engagement strategies in 50 randomized controlled trials were distilled (Becker et al., 2018). Successful strategies involved the following:

1. *Accessibility promotion*—providing services that allow people to attend sessions, such as childcare and transportation. In the meta-analysis on dropout, consistent family predictors involved social disadvantage (de Haan et al., 2013), so increasing accessibility is key to engagement.
2. *Assessment.* A skilled therapist can use the process of gathering information to connect with the client and build rapport.
3. *Psychoeducation about services*—explaining how treatment would help with the presenting problem and the details of the treatment. In the meta-analysis on dropout, families that perceived a lack of cohesion in treatment had higher dropout (de Haan et al., 2013). It is recommended that the practitioner convey a clear treatment plan or protocol to families, including the approximate number of sessions to expect, that is,

communicating that treatment has a rationale and a clear purpose and plan. See Chapter 2 for a case example that includes psychoeducation.

A skilled provider delivers *psychoeducation* in a conversational, not pedantic, style, soliciting parents' and children's knowledge about what they already know, checking in with their understanding about information shared, and correcting any misperceptions (Becker et al., 2018). Like the assessment process, a provider can use *psychoeducation* to build rapport by attending to client perspectives, instilling hope about treatment success, encouraging attendance, and facilitating participation in sessions.

Other researchers have studied engagement, seeing its critical importance in children receiving an effective course of therapy. A social work academic, McKay (2004) has built on Szapocznik's Brief Strategic Family Therapy engagement strategies (Szapocznik et al., 1988), using two structural family therapy techniques (Minuchin, 1974) for Latino families with a child with substance use disorders. The first was joining and the second was restructuring interactions in the family that block members from participating in treatment. McKay's engagement intervention, now described in a manual called *Training Intervention for the Engagement of Families* (http://www.tiesengagement.com/), has been both tested as a 30-minute intake call and infused in the initial therapy session. Testing of this intervention against "treatment as usual" has shown that both first-session and continuing attendance are improved through the engagement intervention (McKay et al., 1996).

SUMMARY

Engagement is a critically important phase of the helping process; children and families cannot receive an effective dose of treatment without it. A variety of considerations and techniques are explored in this chapter to improve families' attendance. SFT and MI offer useful ways to engage youths who may be attending treatment involuntarily. Finally, an evidence basis has accumulated on engagement strategies that may aid youths and families in need of treatment for child mental health problems.

REFERENCES

Becker, K., Boustani, M., Gellatly, R., & Chorpita, B. (2018). Forty years of engagement research in children's mental health services: Multidimensional measurement and practice elements. *Journal of Clinical Child & Adolescent Psychology, 47*(1), 1–23. doi:10.1080/15374416.2017.1326121

Berg, I. L. (1994). *Family-based services: A solution-focused approach.* New York: Norton.

Berg, I. K., & Miller, S. D. (1992). *Working with the problem drinker: A solution-focused approach.* New York: Norton.

Bertolino, B., & O'Hanlon, B. (2002). *Collaborative, competency-based counseling and therapy*. Boston: Allyn & Bacon.

Cade, B., & O'Hanlon, W. H. (1993). *A brief guide to brief therapy*. New York: Norton.

Corcoran, J. (2016). *Motivational interviewing: A workbook for social work*. New York: Oxford University Press.

de Haan, A. M., Boon, A. E., de Jong, J. T. V. M., Hoeve, M., & Vermeiren, R. R. J. M. (2013). A meta-analytic review on treatment dropout in child and adolescent outpatient mental health care. *Clinical Psychology Review, 33*(5), 698–711.

de Jong, P., & Berg, I. K. (2012). *Interviewing for solutions* (4th ed.). Pacific Grove, CA: Brooks/Cole.

de Shazer, S. (1994). *Words were originally magic*. New York: Norton.

de Shazer, S., Berg, I. K., Lipchick, E., Nunnally, E., Molnar, A., Gingerich, W., & Weiner-Davis, M. (1986). Brief therapy: Focused solution development. *Family Process, 25*, 207–221.

Hohman, M. (2015). *Motivational interviewing in social work practice*. New York: Guilford.

Lindsey, M., Brandt, N., Becker, K., Lee, B., Barth, R., Daleiden, E., & Chorpita, B. (2014). Identifying the common elements of treatment engagement interventions in children's mental health services. *Clinical Child and Family Psychology Review, 17*, 283–298.

Manthey, T. J., Knowles, B., Asher, D., & Wahab, S. (2011). Strengths-based practice and motivational interviewing. *Advances in Social Work, 12*(2), 126–151.

McKay, M. M., Hibbert, R., Hoagwood, K., Rodriguez, J., Murray, L., Legerski, J., & Fernandez, D. (2004). Integrating evidence-based engagement interventions into "real world" child mental health settings. *Brief Treatment and Crisis Intervention, 4*(2), 177–186. https://doi.org/10.1093/brief-treatment/mhh014

McKay, M. M., McCadam, K., & Gonzales, J. J. (1996). Addressing the barriers to mental health services for inner city children and their caretakers. *Community Mental Health Journal, 32*, 353–361. https://doi.org/10.1007/BF02249453

Miller, W., & Rollnick, S. (2012). *Motivational interviewing* (3rd ed.). New York: Guilford.

Minuchin, S. (1974). *Families & family therapy*. Cambridge, MA: Harvard University Press.

Naar-King, S., & Suarez, M. (2010). *Motivational interviewing with adolescents and young adults*. New York: Guilford.

O'Hanlon, W. H., & Weiner-Davis, M. (1989). *In search of solutions: A new direction in psychotherapy*. New York: Norton.

Szapocznik, A., Perez-Vidal, A., Brickman, A., Foot, F., Santisteban, D., Hervis, O., & Kurtines, W. (1988). Engaging adolescent drug abusers and their families in treatment: A strategic structural systems approach. *Journal of Consulting and Clinical Psychology, 56*, 552–557.

Sibley, M., Graziano, P., Kuriyan, A., Coxe, S., Pelham, W., Rodriguez, L., Sanchez, F., Derefinko, K., Helseth, S., & Ward, A. (2016). Parent–teen behavior therapy + motivational interviewing for adolescents with ADHD. *Journal of Consulting and Clinical Psychology, 84*(8), 699–712. https://doi.org/10.1037/ccp0000106

Westra, H. A. (2012). *Applications of motivational interviewing. Motivational interviewing in the treatment of anxiety*. New York: Guilford.

Neurodevelopmental Disorders

5

Attention-Deficit/ Hyperactivity Disorder

Jayden Carter is a 5-year-old African American male who presented with his 26-year-old mother, Ms. Najah Carter, to a child behavior consultation clinic at the recommendation of Jayden's school. Since Jayden began kindergarten 4 months earlier, his teachers have frequently relayed to Ms. Carter their concerns about Jayden's behavior, including calling out in class, getting up from his seat, and having trouble following directions. Ms. Carter also expressed concerns that Jayden is "all over the place, just bouncing off the walls" at home, and "he just doesn't do what he's told." When asked to provide examples of Jayden's challenging behaviors at home, Ms. Carter shared: "If I tell him to go upstairs and get dressed and brush his teeth, he might go up and do one of those things, or nothing—I might just find him playing in his room. Or, I go in there after him, and the drawers are all open, the lights are on, but he's already off doing the next thing. He knows the rules. I don't know why he can't just do what he's supposed to." Jayden had been asked to leave two childcare centers previously because of hyperactive behavior, and since starting kindergarten, Ms. Carter described being called into the school several times for meetings. "I can't have him kicked out of another school, or I'm going to lose my job." She shared that she supports herself and Jayden, who is an only child, with little financial help from his father, who doesn't see Jayden often. Ms. Carter has limited psychosocial support or respite from caregiving responsibilities, contributing to her stress and frustration. Ms. Carter also shared concerns about Jayden's peer relationships: "The other kids seem to get annoyed that he talks so much." She reported that Jayden's teacher has said that his peers at times seem frustrated by his frequent interruptions and difficulty waiting his turn.

OVERVIEW

Attention-deficit hyperactivity disorder (ADHD) in childhood and adolescence costs the United States per year $19.4 billion for children and $13.8 billion for adolescents (Schein et al., 2022). ADHD is characterized by a chronic pattern of

Child and Adolescent Mental Health in Social Work. Jacqueline Corcoran and Courtney Benjamin Wolk, Oxford University Press.
© Oxford University Press 2023. DOI: 10.1093/oso/9780197653562.003.0005

Table 5.1 DSM CRITERIA FOR ATTENTION-DEFICIT/HYPERACTIVITY
DISORDER(APA, 2022)

Pattern of inattention or hyperactivity-impulsivity that interferes with functioning or development. Characterized by:
1. Inattention: six or more symptoms for at least 6 months
   a. Often fails to give close attention to details or makes careless mistakes
   b. Often has difficulty sustaining attention in tasks
   c. Often does not seem to listen when spoken to directly
   d. Often does not follow through on instructions and fails to finish tasks
   e. Often has difficulty organizing tasks and activities
   f. Often avoids, dislikes, or is reluctant to engage in tasks that require mental effort
   g. Often loses things necessary for tasks or activities
   h. Is often easily distracted by extraneous stimuli
   i. Is often forgetful in daily activities
2. Hyperactivity-impulsivity: six or more symptoms for at least 6 months
   a. Often fidgets with or taps hands/feet
   b. Often leaves seat in situations when remaining seated is expected
   c. Often runs about or climbs in inappropriate situations
   d. Often is unable to play or engage in leisure activities quietly
   e. Is often "on the go," acting as if "driven by a motor"
   f. Often talks excessively
   g. Often blurts out an answer before a question has been completed
   h. Often has difficulty waiting his or her turn
   i. Often interrupts or intrudes on others
Symptoms present before 12 years, in two or more settings, impair functioning.

inattention or *hyperactive/impulsive behavior* (or both) that is more severe than what is typically observed in peers (American Psychiatric Association [APA], 2022). See Table 5.1. The *Diagnostic and Statistical Manual of Mental Disorders* (DSM) requires making a determination about subtype: inattentive, hyperactive/impulsive, or combined type in which both features are present. The ADHD diagnosis was once largely restricted to children and adolescents, but the condition can persist into adulthood (36% in the United States; Breslau et al., 2011).

Prevalence

In 2016, 6.1 million children in the United States 4 to 17 years of age had a diagnosis of ADHD. These numbers include the following age groups: 388,000 preschool children, 4 million elementary school–aged children; and 3 million children aged 12 to 17 years (Danielson et al., 2018). The rate of diagnosis is 9.4% in youths. These rates are higher than in previous years (Centers for Disease Control and Prevention, 2019); hypothesized reasons for the increase in diagnosis since 2003 include the shifting of diagnostic criteria throughout the years, the worldwide variability of diagnostic criteria, the changing social mores about childhood behavior, and the marketing efforts of pharmaceutical companies (Hinshaw & Scheffler, 2014).

Worldwide rates of ADHD are lower than in the United States. European countries rely on the International Classification of Diseases (ICD) criteria, which use the term *hyperkinetic disorder* rather than *ADHD*. Hyperkinetic disorder requires a more severe and extreme threshold of behavior. Therefore, fewer children are diagnosed in European countries, although rates have been increasing.

Even within the United States, however, the number of children diagnosed with ADHD varies widely (Danielson et al., 2018). For example, diagnostic rates are higher in the southern states than the western states. In terms of rates for ethnic minority groups in the United States, both Black and Latino children are diagnosed at lower rates than are whites (Centers for Disease Control and Prevention, 2019; Dong et al., 2020). In a more recent longitudinal study of more than 4,000 children, rates of diagnosis for ADHD were consistently higher among white children, with 19% of white youths diagnosed by the 10th grade compared with 10% of Black and 4% of Latino youths (Coker et al., 2016). Heartening news is that the disparity gap in diagnosis my be starting to close (Glasofer et al. 2022).

Prevalence rates for Latino children are estimated at 3.3% compared with 6.5% for white children. The condition may go unrecognized in Latino children because of language barriers, underreporting by caregivers who lack knowledge of symptoms and perhaps have differing developmental expectations, physician bias against taking concerns of parents seriously, and a lack of access to treatment resources (Bloom & Dey, 2006; Rothe, 2005).

RISK AND PROTECTIVE FACTORS

Biological

ADHD is assumed to be an inherited genetic disorder, with a risk of about 40% in children of parents with ADHD (Uchida et al., 2021). However, the precise genetic mechanisms that contribute to the onset of ADHD are not known (Neale et al., 2010). Dopamine transmitter and receptor genes, as well as several serotonin transporter and receptor genes, have been linked to the disorder (Faraone & Khan, 2006; Gizer et al., 2009; Levy et al., 2006).

The pattern of cognitive or neuropsychological impairment that is manifested in ADHD involves executive functioning (Barkley, 2006; Johnson et al., 2009). Executive functioning refers to goal-directed regulation of thought and action and key functions, including the following:

1. Working memory—the capacity to hold information actively in the mind and mentally work with it to guide behavior
2. Inhibition—the ability to override a habitual but incorrect response

3. Mental set-shifting—the ability to flexibly switch between tasks or mental sets

Stephen Hinshaw (2018), a longtime researcher in the ADHD field, has conceptualized ADHD "as a deficit in the regulation of attention to varying environmental demands" (p. 297). A meta-analysis of functional magnetic resonance imaging studies (using magnetic resonance imaging technology to measure brain activity) of people with ADHD confirmed that attention and impulsivity deficits are associated with several areas of the brain that involve impairments in cognitive function (Hart et al., 2013). At the same time, we must recognize that deducing brain activity from blood flow to the brain in a controlled laboratory environment may be a reductionist view and cannot determine the exact causality of ADHD (Johnson et al., 2009). Additionally, ADHD is defined by its behavioral symptoms rather than by any biological marker (Visser & Jehan, 2009).

Aside from genetics, other biological reasons may influence the development of ADHD. Children who are born prematurely are at twice the risk for ADHD as full-term children (Bhutta et al., 2002; Tung et al., 2016). Maternal smoking and drinking during pregnancy may independently act as predisposing influences (Kahn et al., 2003). Moreover, maternal prepregnancy obesity and overweight, preeclampsia, hypertension, acetaminophen exposure (Kim et al., 2020), pregnancy complications, and fetal exposure to high testosterone (Bitsko et al., 2022) are strongly related to ADHD. Fortunately, the systematic review by Bitsko and colleagues did not find any risk factors present during birth, such as labor complications.

Lead exposure in childhood is another route to the development of ADHD and is more common in low socioeconomic housing (Choi et al., 2016). Other environmental toxins, including organophosphate pesticides at levels common among U.S. children, may contribute to a diagnosis of ADHD (Bouchard et al., 2010).

One biological manifestation of ADHD is the gender disparity between boys and girls, with ADHD more common in boys (Gershon & Gershon, 2002), which is similar to the neurodevelopmental disorder of autism spectrum disorder. The gender disparity might involve true differences between genders, but girls also may be underdiagnosed (Arnold, 1996; Ohan & Johnston, 2005).

Compared with boys, who tend to have higher energy levels, girls with ADHD do not seem as active. Additionally, girls are more likely to have the inattentive type of ADHD. They may daydream and be distracted but are not disruptive and therefore are not as apt to garner the attention of school authorities (Arnold, 1996; Ohan & Johnston, 2005). However, it is important for providers to identify ADHD in girls. The Berkeley Girls With ADHD Longitudinal Study found that females with ADHD had significant impairments, with few showing positive adjustment over time into early adulthood (summarized in Hinshaw, 2022). Serious outcomes included self-harm, suicidal attempts, interpersonal violence, and early pregnancy.

For adjustment, physical exercise seems to be important for those with ADHD. Sun, Yu, and Zhou (2022) conducted a systematic review of 15 intervention studies and found that exercise was associated with improved attention and executive functioning. Another systematic review on this topic specified that a 20-minute session of sports, exercise, or other physical activity improved executive functioning (Montalva-Valenzuela et al., 2022). However, hyperactivity, depression, social problems, and aggression were not affected at a statistically significant level (Sun et al., 2022).

Psychological

Having higher baseline symptoms of ADHD and a disorder that is more severe, as well as being diagnosed with a co-occurring oppositional defiant disorder/conduct disorder (see Chapter 7), puts a child at risk for poor outcomes, but only when untreated (Groenman et al., 2022). Therefore, behavioral treatment (discussed later) plays a key protective role.

Mindfulness practices, such as meditation, guided visualization, and progressive muscle relaxation, can be developed as a coping strategy. Although children and parents didn't report benefit from these practices in terms of improved ADHD symptoms, teachers did see improvement, according to findings of a systematic review (Vekety et al., 2021). Therefore, mindfulness practices could be used in the school setting to set children with ADHD up for success in the classroom.

Social

Although many experts vigorously assert that ADHD is a neuropsychological disorder, others suggest that family and social risk influences play a causal role (Counts et al., 2005) and certainly influence outcome. In ADHD, adversity likely affects children with a genetic vulnerability to develop ADHD (Laucht et al., 2007). An interesting line of evidence involves how attachment difficulties may give rise to attention problems that are severe enough to meet diagnostic criteria for ADHD (Storebe et al., 2016). Severe early deprivation, as often occurs in institutional rearing, may be one way this occurs. Institutional rearing was associated with elevated inattention and overactivity into early adolescence, even when a child had been adopted at an earlier stage (Stevens et al., 2008). Cavichhioli, Stefanazzi, Tobia, and Ogliari (2022) argue that insecure attachment and ADHD have symptom overlap and that the attachment system plays a role in the development of self-regulation.

More broadly, the parent–child relationship, as well as family functioning and composition, may have a role in the development of ADHD and the adjustment of the child. Daily negative interactions and behavioral management difficulties demand considerable parental resources (Coghill et al., 2008). Additionally, if parents meet diagnostic criteria for ADHD, it may be even more difficult for parents to follow through with behavior management strategies and to cope with child irritability and tantrums without escalating situations. These demands often result in failure, fatigue, demoralization, isolation, strained marital relationships, and compromised health and occupational functioning (Corcoran et al., 2016a,b). A systematic review of correlational studies indicated that parental stress associated with having a child diagnosed with ADHD is considerable and is worse with male children and when hyperactivity is present (Theule et al., 2013).

Other systematic reviews provide evidence that child ADHD and maternal mental health, namely anxiety and depression, are associated (Cheung et al., 2018; Clavarino et al., 2010; Tucker & Hobson, 2022; Wüstner et al., 2019). Causality is undetermined; mothers predisposed to depression may pass along inherited deficits that manifest as child ADHD. Children's inherited anxiety potential could influence their responsiveness to the environment through an alteration in the hormonal and autonomic nervous system, or to the responsiveness of anxious mothers to their children's needs and behaviors. In utero influences may also be present, or having a child with an early difficult temperament could influence maternal mental health (Tucker & Hobson, 2022). Coping strategies for parents with children diagnosed with ADHD seem to be sparse (Corcoran et al., 2016a,b) and typically depend on avoidance, which means denying, minimizing, or escape; parents of youths with ADHD are often in need of more social support (Craig et al., 2020). Implications are that providers may need to demonstrate support, link parents to other informal and formal supports, and, if possible, work with the family to activate more support within the network.

A parent's ADHD diagnosis may increase the child's risk of receiving lax or harsh parenting because of organizational and emotion regulation demands. Recent systematic reviews found that maltreatment particularly (González et al., 2019) and, more broadly, parent–child interaction quality involving sensitivity/warmth, intrusiveness/reactivity, and negativity/harsh discipline, parental incarceration, and child media exposure were associated with ADHD outcomes (Claussen et al., 2022).

Single-parent status is also associated with ADHD (Claussen et al., 2022; Groenman et al., 2022). Having a child with ADHD puts a strain on marriages and is associated with a higher likelihood of divorce (Wymbs et al., 2008). A two-parent home may serve as a protective influence; two adults can more likely manage the stress related to a child's ADHD.

SES also appears to have a relationship to the diagnosis. A systematic review of 42 studies found that children from lower SES backgrounds were more likely to have an ADHD diagnosis than their counterparts from higher SES homes (Russell et al., 2016). In a more recent review of national and statewide data indicated positive associations between ADHD diagnosis and unsafe schools and neighborhood, as well as economic hardship (Bozinovic et al., 2021). The relationship in Russell et al. (2016) was partly explained by factors associated with low SES, including parental mental health and smoking during pregnancy. Unfortunately, children in poverty tend to be less successful than their nonpoor counterparts in terms of ADHD improvement when undergoing treatment (Jensen et al., 2007). Families living in poverty often lack access to quality health care and help in managing the stressors of poverty, and child ADHD symptoms are often assigned a lower priority in these families. Even into adulthood, a person's lower family income growing up and lower parental education contribute to poor adult outcome for those diagnosed with ADHD as children (Roy et al., 2017).

One social factor that involves a common source of *misdiagnosis* of ADHD involves the age of children relative to their classmates. Children who are the youngest in their classes are identified by their teachers as having more ADHD symptoms (Elder, 2010; Layton et al., 2018). The youngest kindergartners were 60% more likely to be diagnosed with ADHD than the oldest children in the same grade. Similarly, when that group of classmates reached the fifth and eighth grades, the youngest were more than twice as likely to be prescribed stimulants (Elder, 2010). Overall, this misdiagnosis likely accounts for about 20%—or 900,000—of the 4.5 million children currently identified as having ADHD.

Although childhood onset is required for appropriate diagnosis, many cases persist into adolescence, which can become a time of increased risk taking in terms of impulsive and distracted driving, criminal activity, substance use, and sexual impulsivity. While adults diagnosed with ADHD as children were more likely to have a substance use disorder than those who did not have a diagnosis in childhood (Levy et al., 2014), substance use seems to be curtailed by the appropriate use of medication targeted at the ADHD symptoms in youths (Quinn et al., 2017). A national longitudinal study done in Denmark by Østergaard et al. (2017) found that, compared with individuals without ADHD, those with ADHD were significantly more likely to become parents at 12 to 16 years of age, particularly the girls. Because adolescents with ADHD are at increased risk for pregnancy, attention to risky sexual behavior with appropriate education and medical services, as well as parental monitoring, is important.

ASSESSMENT

Who makes the diagnosis of ADHD? In a synthesis of qualitative studies, parents of youths with ADHD indicated no standardized route by which their children were diagnosed (Corcoran et al., 2016). The school system often first identified a child in need of further assessment; in other cases, parents sought out primary care providers. Given that primary care providers play a large role in diagnosis and treatment, attempts to educate them on appropriate practices have led to improvement in diagnostic accuracy (Wolraich et al., 2010). Most physicians report using the DSM criteria (81%) and teacher rating scales (67%) to arrive at a diagnosis. However, because of time constraints and lack of training, primary care providers are sometimes ill equipped to assess and manage a mental health disorder, and much variation exists. As a result, ADHD is both overdiagnosed (given to those who meet few symptoms of the criteria) and underdiagnosed (not given to those who meet full criteria; Danielson et al., 2018).

When are children diagnosed? Most cases emerge with the demands of elementary school. A comprehensive assessment should first involve a physical examination and medical history to rule out any physical basis for symptoms (American

Academy of Pediatrics, 2011; Barkley, 2006). Interviews with the child and the parent are critical, although children tend to underreport symptoms (Pelham et al., 2005). Freely available rating scales are listed in Table 5.2. Teacher input is valid for the diagnosis (Mannuzza et al., 2002), and the social worker may play a certain role in conducting the clinical interviews, assessing the interactions between parent and child, administering rating scales, and making referrals to psychologists for a full battery of testing to assess for intellectual functioning, cognitive processing, working memory, and any potential learning disorders. Part of the diagnosis of ADHD is assigning a severity code (mild, moderate, or severe). More severe ADHD is more persistent (Biederman et al., 2008; Kessler et al., 2005) and is associated with worse outcomes (Barkley, 2006), even into adulthood (Roy et al., 2017).

In assessment, making a differential diagnosis between ADHD and other disorders is critical, although comorbid disorders are common (Jensen et al., 2007). Comorbidities are associated with persistence of ADHD symptoms (Riglin et al., 2016) and poor outcomes (Roy et al., 2017). The most common concurrent disorders are oppositional defiant disorder (ODD) and conduct disorder (CD) (e.g., Connor et al., 2010). Children with ODD behave in a way that purposely provokes, annoys, and antagonizes others, whereas ADHD symptoms are not willful. White youths are more likely to have a diagnosis of ADHD without ODD/CD than are minority youths (Visser et al., 2016).

As part of gathering information, the practitioner must explore the possibility of trauma history. Some of the symptoms of post-traumatic stress disorder (PTSD), such as chronic hyperarousal and physiologic reactivity to trauma cues and intrusive thinking, may mimic those of hyperactivity, impulsivity, inattention, and inability to focus (Perrin et al., 2000).

It is critically important to ensure that Black and Latino youths are assessed carefully for the presence of ADHD symptoms because studies have indicated cultural biases. For example, providers may overdiagnose disruptive behavior disorders among these youths, attributing their behavioral challenges to criminality (Cameron & Guterman, 2007; Morgan et al., 2013). Additionally, ADHD often requires some parental advocacy to procure the diagnosis. Black parents and those from other minority cultural groups may not recognize ADHD as a biological disorder in need of treatment and rather attribute it to poor parenting or a normal developmental stage that will be outgrown (Dong et al., 2020; Glasofer et al., 2020).

The diagnostic process is similar for adolescents, with a few considerations. Although teacher report is advised, obtaining such reports is difficult given that adolescents typically have many teachers throughout the day. Despite these challenges, the American Academy of Pediatrics advises that at least two adults who know the child in some formal capacity should provide ratings. There are also problems with parent report. Parents do not observe their adolescent children as closely as when they were younger. Adolescents are also not as overtly hyperactive as when they were younger, so some behaviors may be less noticeable. Generally, adolescents underreport and minimize their symptoms. Adolescents

Table 5.2 MEASURES FOR ATTENTION-DEFICIT/HYPERACTIVITY DISORDER

Psychometric Support	Measure Name	No. of Items	Completed by[a]	Ages[b]	Link to Measure
Excellent	Strengths and Weaknesses of ADHD Symptoms and Normal-Behavior Scale (SWAN; Swanson et al., 2012)	18	P, T	Children and adolescents[c]	https://www.phenxtoolkit.org/protocols/view/121502
Excellent	Swanson, Nolan, and Pelham Rating Scale (SNAP-IV; Swanson, 2013)	18 or 26 versions	P, T	5–17	http://www.shared-care.ca/toolkits-adhd
Excellent	Vanderbilt ADHD Diagnostic Teacher Rating Scale (VADTRS; Wolraich et al., 2003)	43	T	4–12	https://www.nichq.org/resource/nichq-vanderbilt-assessment-scales
Good	Children's Scale of Hostility and Aggression: Reactive/Proactive (C-SHARP; Farmer & Aman, 2010, 2010)*	48	P	3–21	https://psychmed.osu.edu/index.php/instrument-resources/c-sharp/

[a] Completed by: Y = youth, P = parent/caregiver, C = clinician, T = teacher.
[b] Exact age range for specific forms (e.g., self-report, parent report) may vary.
[c] Exact age range not specified.
* Available in multiple languages.

NOTE: Table adapted from Becker-Haimes, E. M., Tabachnick, A. R., Last, B. S., Stewart, R. E., Hasan-Granier, A., & Beidas, R. S. (2020). Evidence base update for brief, free, and accessible youth mental health measures. *Journal of Clinical Child & Adolescent Psychology*, 49(1), 1–17, reprinted by permission of the publisher (Taylor & Francis Ltd, http://www.tandfonline.com).

(continued)

Table 5.2 CONTINUED

References for measures in Table 5.2:

Farmer, C. A., & Aman, M. G. (2010). Psychometric properties of the children's scale of hostility and aggression: Reactive/proactive (C-SHARP). *Research in Developmental Disabilities, 31*(1), 270–280.

Swanson, J. M., Kraemer, H. C., Hinshaw, S. P., Arnold, L. E., Conners, C. K., Abikoff, H. B., . . . Hechtman, L. (2001). Clinical relevance of the primary findings of the MTA: Success rates based on severity of ADHD and ODD symptoms at the end of treatment. *Journal of the American Academy of Child & Adolescent Psychiatry, 40*(2), 168–179.

Swanson, J. M., Schuck, S., Porter, M. M., Carlson, C., Hartman, C. A., Sergeant, J. A., . . . Wigal, T. (2012). Categorical and dimensional definitions and evaluations of symptoms of ADHD: History of the SNAP and the SWAN Rating Scales. *International Journal of Educational and Psychological Assessment, 10*(1), 51–70.

Wolraich, M. L., Lambert, W., Doffing, M. A., Bickman, L., Simmons, T., & Worley, K. (2003). Psychometric properties of the Vanderbilt ADHD diagnostic parent rating scale in a referred population. *Journal of Pediatric Psychology, 28*(8), 559–568.

with ADHD also need to be assessed for mood and anxiety disorders, risky sexual behaviors, substance use, and self-harm and suicidal behaviors. Like their younger counterparts, they should be screened for comorbid conditions, including emotional or behavioral, developmental, and physical conditions (e.g., tics, sleep apnea; Wolraich et al., 2019).

The clinician explained the assessment process to Ms. Carter.

Clinician: *I'll be asking you several questions today to better understand what behaviors are occurring at home, at school, and with other children. I'll also talk with Jayden so that I can learn about him, his strengths, and any challenges from his perspective. I also have some forms for you and Jayden's teacher to complete. These forms will help us understand how Jayden's behaviors compare with what is developmentally typical of other boys his age from both of your perspectives. When I have received those forms back, I'll combine that information with what I learn from you and Jayden today, and then we can meet to discuss my overall impressions and recommendations. Do you have any questions before we begin?*

Mother: *That sounds fine, but what if his teacher and I disagree? I think she sees things a little differently than I do. And Jayden probably won't have a lot to say (laughs).*

Clinician: *It's very common for each person to have a somewhat different perspective. In fact, that's part of the reason it's so important for me to hear from each of you—it will help me understand what Jayden's behavior looks like in different contexts and how he and important adults in his life perceive it. Part of my job is to integrate these different perspectives and information.*

Mother: *Okay.*

Clinician: *It's also really helpful for me to know that you think the teacher sees things a bit differently than you do, and I'll ask you to tell me more about that in a bit. Are you ready to get started?*

Mother: *Yes, I am.*

Clinician: *Great. I'll start by asking some questions about Jayden's developmental and medical histories and your family history, and then I have some specific questions I'll ask about symptoms he may or may not be experiencing. It is likely that some things I ask about may sound a lot like Jayden, and others won't. The reason is that I want to be thorough and make sure I don't miss anything.*

The clinician then proceeded to conduct a clinical interview with Ms. Carter and then with Jayden. She also sent Ms. Carter home with standardized rating scales for her to complete as well as a separate set of measures for Jayden's teacher. Ms. Carter was instructed to return the forms at their next appointment.

Based on a clinical interview with Jayden's mother, interview with and observation of Jayden, and parent and teacher ratings on the National Institute for Children's Health Quality Vanderbilt assessment scales (2002), Jayden met DSM-5 criteria for

ADHD-combined presentation, of moderate severity. Inattentive symptoms included failure to give close attention to details, difficulty sustaining attention, seeming not to listen when spoken to, often not following through on instructions or tasks, difficulty organizing tasks (e.g., trouble managing sequential tasks), distractibility, and forgetfulness. Symptoms of hyperactivity and impulsivity included fidgeting, difficulty remaining seated, often being "on the go," talking excessively, blurting out, and frequently interrupting and intruding. The symptoms were evident both at home and school, and they also were affecting peer relationships.

Jayden's mother and teacher initially conceptualized his difficulties as behavioral.

Mother: *His teacher says he is always acting up, and I believe it. He's always just not doing what he's supposed to. Can you teach him to act right?*

Clinician: *I understand that the behaviors Jayden has been exhibiting have been very frustrating for you and his teacher. Because you know that he understands the rules, you rightly wonder, "Why can't he just do what he is supposed to do?" My impression of Jayden is that he does understand the rules and tries to do his best but has trouble doing what he is supposed to do because of his difficulties paying attention and impulsivity. Children with ADHD often present this way.*

Mother: *But I don't want him to think he can just have an excuse, like, "Oh, I have ADHD?" I don't think he should have a label that just gets him out of stuff.*

Clinician: *You're right, ADHD is not an excuse to get out of schoolwork or chores, for example. But it does make it harder for Jayden to do things that require focus and organization. We can work together to help him learn strategies to do his best, and we can also make sure we are working to set up his environment in a way that will give him the best chance of being successful.*

Mother: *You know, Jayden's dad had a lot of trouble in school. Never made it through high school in fact. And he was always getting into trouble with the law, drugs, you name it. Maybe he had ADHD too.*

Clinician: *Maybe.*

Mother: *I'm just exhausted. It's overwhelming dealing with this, and everyone thinks I'm a bad mom. Like I just let him act up and get away with it. But I've tried everything I can think of. I'm just too tired sometimes to deal. So, if he forgets to do his chores, I'll either just do them myself or end up yelling.*

Given that Jayden presented as a 5-year-old kindergarten student, the clinician took care to evaluate Jayden's symptoms with an eye toward the developmental appropriateness of his presentation. Jayden had a March birthday, so he was not especially young for his grade.

Additionally, given the long-standing nature of his symptoms (i.e., he had been dismissed from two childcare settings before kindergarten) and the impairment noted at both home and school, the clinician determined that the diagnosis of ADHD was appropriate in this case.

As part of the clinical intake, the clinician inquired as to when the last time was that Jayden had been seen by his primary care doctor. Ms. Carter reported that she had discussed her concerns about Jayden's behavior and school performance with his pediatrician, Dr. Barker, last month, who had examined him and suggested they meet with a therapist. The clinician obtained a release of information to share the results of her assessment with the pediatrician. She also suggested Ms. Carter set a follow-up appointment with Dr. Barker to discuss Jayden's ADHD diagnosis.

> **Clinician:** *I'd also like you to talk with Dr. Barker about whether medication may be helpful. The research for young kids, like Jayden, suggests that it is often best to try behavioral treatments first but that sometimes medication can also be needed. It would be good to hear Dr. Barker's thoughts on the matter.*
>
> **Mother:** *Oh, I don't know about that—medication. He's so young.*
>
> **Clinician:** *I completely understand your hesitation. I'm not suggesting that we go down that path yet, but kids with ADHD often require medication at some point to be as successful as they can be. So, it never hurts to start learning more about that and discussing with his doctor how he approaches decision-making about meds.*
>
> **Mother:** *That makes sense then I guess. I'll ask him what he thinks.*

Both Jayden's mother and teacher reported clinically significant symptoms of inattention and hyperactivity/impulsivity on the Vanderbilt assessment scale. In addition to having Jayden's teacher complete the Vanderbilt, with Ms. Carter's permission, the clinician also conducted a brief phone call with the teacher to gather her impressions and understand the resources available at Jayden's school. The clinician was also able to provide psychoeducation to the teacher about ADHD and discuss ways they could work together to implement behavioral strategies to support Jayden in school and to ensure consistency with home. This is discussed further later.

As previously noted, Jayden's symptoms were consistent with moderate severity. He was not exhibiting many symptoms beyond those required by the diagnosis, and although he had previously been dismissed from childcare because of his behavior, the clinician determined that those centers had made little effort to use appropriate strategies to help Jayden succeed (such as implementing positive reinforcement strategies).

The clinician conducted a careful differential diagnostic assessment and determined that Jayden's symptoms were not better explained by trauma, anxiety, or a mood disorder. Given the academic challenges experienced, the clinician recommended further educational assessment to rule out a learning disability and to determine whether academic accommodations would be warranted. Finally, it was important to assess carefully for ODD and CD given their common co-occurrence with ADHD and Ms. Carter's description of Jayden's presentation ("He just doesn't do what he's supposed to") and his previous dismissals from childcare. There was no evidence that Jayden was resisting conforming or acting defiantly, which is characteristic of ODD and CD; rather, his perceived noncompliance appeared to be best explained by impulsivity and forgetting instructions.

INTERVENTION

ADHD is a chronic developmental condition that requires ongoing management and monitoring. That is, intervention will not "cure" ADHD, but it will help the person manage and improve functioning. Intervention should focus on helping clients learn to cope with, compensate for, and accommodate to symptoms, as well as on reducing additional problems that may arise because of these symptoms (Barkley, 2006).

Receiving intervention in childhood appears to affect long-term functioning. A systematic review of 351 studies compared adults with ADHD who were treated as children, those who were not treated, and those who were not diagnosed (Shaw et al., 2012). When studies were pooled, the findings indicated that lack of treatment was associated with worse long-term results in all areas compared with the receipt of treatment. Participants who were treated improved in 72% of all outcome categories over those who were not treated, although they still did not tend to function within "normal" levels. The outcomes most responsive to treatment were obesity and driving; the least responsive were drug use/addictive behavior, antisocial behavior, services use, and occupation. Therefore, it appears that treatment in childhood is important for improving the long-term course of ADHD, but it still may not help people attain a "normal" level of functioning in all areas. An associated factor related to better adjustment is treatment response (Molina et al., 2009). Those who had responded well to treatment and had maintained gains for at least 2 years tended to be functioning the best at 8-year follow-up.

We will discuss both psychosocial intervention and medication. Generally, almost two-thirds (62.0%) of youths take medication, and slightly less than half (46.7%) receive therapy (Danielson et al., 2018). Almost one-fourth receive neither. In general, African American and Latino parents prefer psychosocial treatment to medication for ADHD (Pham et al., 2010).

Psychosocial

Goals of psychosocial treatment usually include improved school functioning, peer relationships, and family relationships (Pelham et al., 2005). Psychosocial interventions may be targeted toward parents, children, and the school system and typically include behavioral and cognitive-behavioral strategies. Generally, behavioral management with parents is more effective than individual interventions with children.

PSYCHOEDUCATION

In Canada and the United Kingdom, psychoeducation is recommended as the first-line treatment (Canadian Attention Deficit Hyperactivity Disorder Resource Alliance, 2020; National Institute for Health and Care Excellence, 2018).

Psychoeducation involves offering information about ADHD, its contributing factors, parenting and coping strategies, support, and available treatments. The goal is not to blame families but to empower them to determine the best course of treatment. A systematic review indicated that psychoeducation holds promise on its own and as part of other treatment approaches, such as behavioral treatment (Dahl et al., 2020). However, Dekker et al. (2021) found that in parent training, other techniques, namely working with antecedents and reinforcements, are more important than offering psychoeducation. Their recommendation is that psychoeducation, while important, should be minimal in relation to the other techniques.

BEHAVIORAL TREATMENT

The empirical literature on psychosocial intervention for ADHD mainly involves parent training, which is a brief treatment model with a behavioral theoretical orientation. Psychoeducation is usually part of behavioral treatment models for ADHD. During the psychoeducation phase of treatment, providers define and describe ADHD, provide information about contributing factors, and discuss options for intervention. Parents are taught to manage antecedent conditions to set up behavior success for their children, and this seems an important component of parent training for enhancing parenting competence and mental health (Dekkers et al., 2021). Through positive reinforcements, children learn prosocial behavior such as following directions, completing homework, doing household chores, and getting along with siblings. Teaching parents how to provide reinforcements helps to reduce negative parenting behavior (Dekkers et al., 2021). Parents are taught to respond to children's challenging behaviors by ignoring (i.e., to avoid reinforcing these behaviors with attention) or by implementing consequences. Parents are taught these principles through didactic instruction, behavior rehearsal, modeling, and role playing. Because children with ADHD have problems with schoolwork, other interventions for parents include structuring the home environment so that the child has a place to work relatively free of distractions, getting regular teacher verification of satisfactory homework completion, and establishing a home-based reinforcement system featuring regular school–home communication.

At least 12 meta-analyses and systematic reviews have looked at psychosocial treatments for children with ADHD (and most involved training parents in behavioral management strategies). Critical appraisal of these reviews (Fabiano et al., 2015; Watson et al., 2015) determined that the studies included were different ones in each and were of varying quality, which has contributed to some difficulty aggregating results across studies. Overall, however, behavioral parent training approaches are considered a well-established treatment (Evans et al., 2014) that is effective for ADHD in youths (Dekkers et al., 2022; Fabiano et al., 2015), according to both parent and observational report, and gains are maintained over follow-up intervals.

In the United States, parent management training is the treatment of choice for young children, aged 6 to 8, and is suggested for elementary school-aged and adolescent youths (Wolraich et al., 2019). Younger children benefit more from parent training than do older youths (Dekkers et al., 2022). Despite this recommendation, insurance claims data over a 7-year period found that among 827,396 youths with ADHD, less than half received behavioral therapy (Waxmonsky et al., 2019).

SCHOOL-BASED SERVICES

Several federal laws are relevant regarding school-based services for children with ADHD. The Americans With Disabilities Act ensures that reasonable accommodations must be made for individuals who have a substantial limitation of a major life activity, such as learning. Section 504 of the 1973 Rehabilitation Act prohibits schools from discriminating against people with handicaps. The Individuals With Disabilities Education Act (IDEA) of 1990 (the reauthorization of the Education for All Handicapped Children Act, PL 94-142) also has several relevant provisions for persons with ADHD. ADHD may qualify children for special education services and accommodations under the classification of "other health impairment" when symptoms affect school performance. These policy changes may have led to an increase in ADHD diagnoses (Hinshaw, 2018). The IDEA further provides free and appropriate public education for children with ADHD and a multidisciplinary evaluation process toward the development of an Individualized Educational Program (IEP); however, IEPs are not typically granted for children who have ADHD without other learning impairments (504 plans are more commonly used for youths with ADHD in need of school accommodations; Hinshaw, 2018). Fabiano et al. (2022) compared children with ADHD who had an IEP with those who did not have one. There were no differences on any factors between groups, including learning disorders or behavioral profiles, except for lower academic performance among those with an IEP.

School-based accommodations for ADHD involve altering the delivery of academics, such as by adjusting scheduling, setting, presentation style, or response format, while retaining the content (Lovett & Nelson, 2020). Many in-school accommodations afforded youths with ADHD have a limited evidence base. The exception is reading-aloud test responses. Surveys of youths with ADHD, teachers, administrators, and parents indicate ambivalence and dissatisfaction with the process of establishing accommodations as well as with the accommodations themselves. Lovett and Nelson (2020) suggest that accommodations should be implemented on a time-limited basis and assessed regularly to determine whether they improve students' school performance. They caution against long-term use of blanket accommodations so as not to create unintended dependence on them.

Like the recommendation for behavioral management training for parents, contingency management strategies in the classroom are supported by meta-analyses, systematic reviews, and practice guidelines. Emerging evidence indicates that training children in organizational skills and offering homework supports also help school performance (Fabiano & Pyle, 2019).

Medication

Although the social work role does not involve prescribing, social workers can play a vital role in providing psychoeducation, allowing parents to process any advantages and disadvantages, and connecting families with physicians and psychiatrists for a medication consultation when indicated. Medication is the most effective treatment option in the short term for addressing core symptoms of ADHD (Wolraich et al., 2019). The primary psychostimulant drugs are methylphenidate (e.g., Ritalin) and amphetamines (e.g., Adderall), the latter of which has recently taken over as the most prescribed class of stimulants (Safer, 2016). Stimulants are classified as Schedule II drugs by the Drug Enforcement Agency because of their abuse potential. Schedule II is the most restrictive classification for medications, prohibiting both their prescription by telephone and the writing of refills.

For preschoolers, medication is not a first-line recommendation, but when behavioral interventions fail to produce significant improvement and functioning is moderately or severely disturbed, then methylphenidate is recommended (Wolraich et al., 2019). Methylphendiate has been the only agent studied with this age group. A recent large-scale meta-analysis of 133 randomized controlled trials on medication for ADHD supports methylphenidate in children and adolescents as the preferred first-choice medication for the short-term treatment of ADHD (Cortese et al., 2018). A meta-analysis of functional magnetic resonance imaging studies of ADHD suggests that stimulant use (for 6 months to 3 years) is associated with more normal basal ganglia function in youths, supporting medication's effectiveness at least in the short term (Hart et al., 2013). Children often take medication for an extended time, perhaps years, owing to the chronic nature of the disorder (Greenhill et al., 2020).

Although the stimulants have traditionally been the drug of first choice in treating ADHD, alternatives are sometimes necessary owing to lack of positive impact and side effects, which include insomnia and appetite suppression (Punja et al., 2016; Storebø et al., 2015). Common stimulant alternatives for the treatment of ADHD in children include atomoxetine (Strattera), a selective norepinephrine reuptake inhibitor (Newcorn et al., 2009), and guanfacine (Tenex or Intuniv) and clonidine (Catapres or Kapvay), both originally designed to lower blood pressure.

For adolescents, clinical practice guidelines are derived either from studies with school-aged and preschool-aged children or from data that aggregates adolescents with children. In a review of treatments, Chan, Fogler, and Hammerness (2016) recommend stimulant class medications as first-line agents for adolescents, followed by atomoxetine and extended-release guanfacine. In their study, less than half (45%) of 12- to 17-year-olds with ADHD reported receiving medication during the past week (Chan et al., 2016), and this phenomenon was even more pronounced among Black and Latino teens (Visser et al., 2016).

Another consideration about medication has to do with the way it is provided. In the Multimodal Treatment of ADHD (MTA) study, medication was only a superior condition when dosages were monitored frequently and titrated upward to an optimal dose (Swanson et al., 2008). A study using a large claims database from U.S.-managed health care organizations showed that the titration of dosage in usual practice is less than at recommended levels, suggesting that at least some children are not receiving optimal treatment (Olfson et al., 2009). Additionally, nonadherence among youths for ADHD medicine is higher than medicine prescribed for other disorders (Edgcomb & Zima, 2018).

Valid concerns about long-term medication exist. In a 16-year follow-up of the MTA study, height and weight of adults who had been medicated as children were examined (Greenhill et al., 2020). Overall, children who were consistently medicated over the 16-year follow-up were about 1½ inches shorter and had higher weight and body mass index than those who had been negligibly medicated and community control adults. The authors advise that families should be informed about these long-term effects so that they can decide whether these are outweighed by the risks of not treating ADHD symptoms with medication.

Jayden's treatment had several components, including psychoeducation, behavioral parent training, and a school–home note. The clinician provided psychoeducation to Ms. Carter about ADHD and its treatment. She also worked with Ms. Carter to help her learn more effective strategies for behavior management and to help her better scaffold the environment to give Jayden the best chance for success. As part of Jayden's treatment, the clinician also worked with Ms. Carter to help her identify individuals in her life who could provide support and respite. She identified a supportive cousin out of state whom she could call to talk to, as well as a friend with a similar-aged child who was willing to have Jayden over for playdates from time to time to allow Ms. Carter a break.

The clinician also worked with the teacher by telephone to help her implement strategies for managing behavior in the classroom and instituted a school–home note. As previously noted, Jayden's mother was encouraged to discuss the possibility of medication with Jayden's pediatrician. Finally, the clinician helped Jayden's mother request an educational evaluation through the school.

For Ms. Carter and Jayden, behavioral treatment started with psychoeducation about ADHD and its core symptoms. It was important for the clinician to align with Ms. Carter by empathizing with the stress and frustration she has experienced raising a child with ADHD with little support, while also helping her to better understand the etiology of Jayden's behavior:

> **Clinician:** *You have been doing this mostly on your own for quite some time. It must be exhausting to do all you do at work and to keep your household running while also dealing with the extra calls and conferences with school.*
> **Mother:** *You've got that right.*
> **Clinician:** *Jayden's ADHD means that his brain works differently than yours in terms of how he organizes, plans, and focuses. This has made schoolwork particularly challenging for him and contributes to some of the challenges you've told me about at home, such as difficulty completing tasks or chores.*
> **Mother:** *I've never really thought about it that way.*

Clinician: *There are some things we can do to help set him up to be more successful while gradually helping him take more responsibility as he is able. We call this scaffolding the environment.*

Mother: *Scaffolding?*

Clinician: *Right. We want to set things up at home and school so that he has the support he needs to succeed, like by helping him organize his backpack and school assignments, and then we gradually work to pull back these supports as he shows us that he can do it more independently.*

Mother: *That makes sense, but what do I do when he just isn't listening at home or doesn't get stuff done?*

Clinician: *I'm glad you asked. There are some things we can do to make sure we are giving Jayden instructions clearly, for example, by getting down physically to his eye level, stating in the simplest terms what we want him to do, and giving instructions one at a time.*

Mother: *How does that work exactly?*

Clinician: *Can you give me an example of a time recently when you asked Jayden to do something, and it didn't get done?*

Mother: *Yeah, just this morning we were running late, and I said finish your breakfast, brush your teeth, and get your backpack and shoes so we can go! He got as far as breakfast and then he got distracted by a toy.*

Clinician: *That's a great example, there are lots of things we can try here. When providing directions to children with ADHD, it helps to say them one at a time as opposed to giving multistep commands. So first, while making eye contact at his level, you'll say, "Jayden please finish your breakfast now." Then, when he has completed the task, ask him to brush his teeth.*

Mother: *I think I understand. So, break it up more so that he doesn't miss steps. This sounds like it could take a while though, to get through all the steps he needs to do to get out the door.*

Clinician: *We can use a timer if needed to help move him along since I know you don't have unlimited time in the morning. To help motivate him to do things, let's also put together a morning routine chart in which he can earn points for each activity he completes before the timer goes off, and determine a reward he can earn for those points.*

Mother: *Isn't that just bribing him to do stuff?*

Clinician: *It can be hard for children with ADHD to complete certain tasks, and a reward can be highly motivating. By using rewards, we can motivate Jayden to change his behavior until the activities become easier and more routine. The rewards can be temporary, just until Jayden had demonstrated success in doing the desired behaviors regularly.*

Mother: *I guess that makes sense.*

Clinician: *The rewards Jayden may earn don't need to be tangible items like toys. Screen time's a highly motivating reward to many children Jayden's age. Also, things like playing a board game with you, picking what's for dinner, or staying up 15 minutes late on the weekend can be great rewards.*

Let's spend some time with Jayden coming up with a menu of rewards he can earn that you feel comfortable with and that he would enjoy.

Mother: That's a good idea.

Clinician: Another way we can reinforce the behavior we want to see more of is to catch Jayden being good and to praise him for his behavior in a very specific way. For example, since you mentioned that he usually leaves his dirty clothes on the floor, when he does put them away, let's try saying something like, "I really like that you put your clothes in the hamper without my asking!"

Mother: I do praise him a lot already.

Clinician: That's great to hear. Children with ADHD often receive lots of negative feedback. They hear lots of no's, reminders to pay attention, and things like "stay in your seat." It's important for shaping the behavior we want to see and for his self-esteem to make sure he gets lots of positive feedback too.

Mother: I guess he does hear a lot of those negative comments too.

Clinician: And if we can be very specific in our praise, like saying, "I like how you are sitting in your seat at the dinner table" instead of a more generic "good job," it helps kids learn the exact behaviors that will get them more of the positive attention that they often find very rewarding.

Mother: I think I can try that.

To illustrate these concepts, the clinician asked Ms. Carter to role-play Jayden on a typical school morning while the clinician role-played Ms. Carter giving Jayden clear, specific instructions one at a time and using praise to reinforce desired behavior. They developed a concrete plan for Ms. Carter to try at home, and then at the next session they reviewed and made adjustments to maximize success. As the clinician and Ms. Carter worked together, they identified strategies that worked well for Jayden. For example, they found that he was highly motivated by rewards. Because treatment also involved engaging Jayden's kindergarten teacher, the clinician was able to translate what worked well at home to the school setting and to ensure consistency.

The clinician spoke to the teacher to provide psychoeducation about ADHD and provided Ms. Carter with handouts to give to Jayden's teacher. They collaboratively developed a school–home note (sometimes also referred to as a daily report card). The school–home note consisted of several target behaviors that Ms. Carter and the teacher agreed were important for Jayden to make progress on at school (e.g., stays in seat, waits to be called on to speak). For each behavior, Jayden's teacher would indicate each day if he had been successful to the agreed-on degree (e.g., stayed in seat most class periods) and would put the note in Jayden's backpack at the end of the day, and then Ms. Carter would reward success each night at home. Throughout treatment, Ms. Carter and the teacher periodically rated Jayden's behavior on the Vanderbilt assessment scale (Wolraich et al., 2003; see also Table 5.2) to monitor progress.

Ms. Carter was initially reluctant to try medications because she wanted Jayden to learn skills and "not think a pill is the answer." The clinician provided *psychoeducation about medication. This included (1) basic information about the efficacy of stimulants: "These medications have been around for a long time and work quite well for many kids, helping them to focus and learn"; (2) common side effects: "They are generally mild and can be addressed. For example, if Jayden has a decreased appetite when taking this medication, it can be helpful to make sure he has a large breakfast before taking it and a larger dinner in the evening to make up for eating less at lunch"; and (3) risks associated with not medicating children with ADHD who continue to struggle despite behavioral interventions, including the impact on peer relationships, academic performance, and risk for engagement in risky behavior, such as substance misuse and risky sexual behavior, as he gets older and continues to exhibit ADHD symptoms without adequate treatment. The clinician also helped her to understand that a medication consultation "doesn't mean you have to give him medication; it's just a conversation so that you can learn more and see if the doctor thinks it would be helpful."*

Ms. Carter initially agreed to discuss medication as an option for Jayden with his primary care provider Dr. Barker. Dr. Barker was reluctant to introduce a stimulant given Jayden's young age, preferring to try behavioral therapy first. Jayden's therapist, mother, and teacher monitored progress, and despite improvements in behaviors like remaining in his seat and calling out, Jayden continued to struggle academically with sustaining attention. Dr. Barker suggested that a referral to a child psychiatrist would be helpful. That referral was initiated, and Jayden was prescribed methylphenidate. He tolerated the medication well with minimal side effects, and improvements in attention and behavior were noted quickly at home and school. The therapist collected ongoing rating scales from Ms. Carter and Jayden's teacher and relayed this information to the psychiatrist, who used it to inform the methylphenidate titration.

SUMMARY

This chapter focuses on ADHD in children, which in the United States has become a highly prevalent diagnosis. Controversies with the diagnosis are also covered. The current formulation of ADHD as a neurodevelopmental disorder means that biological contributors are emphasized. However, social factors may play a role in development because low SES households are overrepresented among children diagnosed with ADHD, whereas ethnic minority children might be underdiagnosed. ADHD is often comorbid with other diagnoses, especially ODD and CD, which makes treatment more challenging. School intervention and behavior therapy, the most researched psychosocial intervention, are reviewed, as are medications, the most commonly prescribed of which are stimulants. Assessment and intervention strategies are applied to a case example. Recovery from ADHD may happen over time but often continues in adolescence and into early adulthood; therefore, interventions should focus on helping clients learn to cope with, compensate for, and accommodate to symptoms (Barkley, 2004).

REFERENCES

American Psychiatric Association. (2022). *Diagnostic and statistical manual of mental disorders* (5th ed., Text Revision). Washington, DC: American Psychiatric Assocation.

Barkley, R. A. (2006). Attention-deficit/hyperactivity disorder. In D. A. Wolfe & E. J. Mash (Eds.), *Behavioral and emotional disorders in adolescents: Nature, assessment, and treatment* (pp. 91–152). New York: Guilford Press.

Bhutta, A. T., Cleves, M. A., Casey, P. H., Cradock, M. M., & Anand, K. J. S. (2002). Cognitive and behavioral outcomes of school-aged children who were born preterm: A meta-analysis. *Journal of American Medical Association, 288*(6), 728–737. doi:10.1001/jama.288.6.728

Biederman, J., Petty, C. R., Dolan, C., Hughes, S., Mick, M., Monuteaux, M. C., & Faraone, S. V. (2008). The long-term longitudinal course of oppositional defiant disorder and conduct disorder in ADHD boys: Findings from a controlled 10-year prospective longitudinal follow-up study. *Psychological Medicine, 38*, 1027–1036. doi:10.1017/ S0033291707002668

Bitsko, R. H., Holbrook, J. R., O'Masta, B., Maher, B., Cerles, A., Saadeh, K., Mahmooth, Z., MacMillan, L. M., Rush, M., & Kaminski, J. W. (2022). A systematic review and meta-analysis of prenatal, birth, and postnatal factors associated with attention-deficit/hyperactivity disorder in children. *Prevention Science.* doi:10.1007/s11121-022-01359-3. Epub ahead of print. PMID: 35303250.

Bloom, B., & Dey, A. N. (2006). Summary health statistics for U.S. children: National Health Interview Survey, 2004. *Vital and Health Statistics, 10*, 1–85.

Bouchard, M. F., Bellinger, D. C., Wright, R. O., & Weisskopf, M. G. (2010). Attention-deficit/hyperactivity disorder and urinary metabolites of organophosphate pesticides. *Pediatrics, 125*(6), 1270–1277. doi:10.1542/peds.2009-3058

Bozinovic, K., McLamb, F., O'Connell, K., Olander, N., Feng, Z., Haagensen, S., & Bozinovic, G. (2021). U.S. national, regional, and state-specific socioeconomic factors correlate with child and adolescent ADHD diagnoses pre-COVID-19 pandemic. *Scientific Reports, 11*(1), 22008–22008. https://doi.org/10.1038/s41 598-021-01233-2

Breslau, J., Miller, E., Chung, J., & Schweitzer, J. B. (2011). Childhood and adolescent onset psychiatric disorders, substance use, and failure to graduate high school on time. *Journal of Psychiatric Research, 45*(3), 295–301.

Cameron, M., & Guterman, N. B. (2007). Diagnosing conduct problems of children and adolescents in residential treatment. *Child & Youth Care Forum, 36*(1), 1–10. https://doi.org/10.1007/s10566-006-9027-6

Canadian Attention Deficit Hyperactivity Disorder Resource Alliance. (2020). Retrieved from https://www.caddra.ca/wp-content/uploads/CADDRA-ADHD-Practice-Gui delines-4.1-English.pdf

Cavicchioli, M., Stefanazzi, C., Tobia, V., & Ogliari, A. (2022). The role of attachment styles in attention-deficit hyperactivity disorder: A meta-analytic review from the perspective of a transactional development model. *European Journal of Developmental Psychology*, 1–29. https://doi.org/10.1080/17405629.2022.2069095

Centers for Disease Control and Prevention. (2019). Health conditions among children under age 18, by selected characteristics: United States, average annual, selected years 1997–1999 through 2016–2018. Table 12. Retrieved from https://www.cdc.gov/nchs/data/hus/2019/012-508.pdf

Chan, E., Fogler, J., & Hammerness, P. (2016). Treatment of attention-deficit/hyperactivity disorder in adolescents: A systematic review. *Journal of American Medical Association*, *315*(8), 1997–1008.

Cheung, K., Aberdeen, K., Ward, M. A., & Theule, J. (2018). Maternal depression in families of children with ADHD: A meta-analysis. *Journal of Child and Family Studies*, *27*(4), 1015–1028. https://doi.org/10.1007/s10826-018-1017-4

Choi, W., Kwon, H., Lim, M., Lim, J., & Ha, M. (2016). Blood lead, parental marital status and the risk of attention-deficit/hyperactivity disorder in elementary school children: A longitudinal study. *Psychiatry Research, 236*, 42–46. doi:10.1016/j.psychres.2016.01.002

Clavarino, A. M., Mamun, A. A., O'Callaghan, M., Aird, R., Bor, W., O'Callaghan, F., Williams, G. M., Marrington, S., Najman, J. M., & Alati, R. (2010). Maternal anxiety and attention problems in children at 5 and 14 years. *Journal of Attention Disorders, 13*(6), 658–667. doi:10.1177/108 7054709347203

Claussen, A. H., Holbrook, J. R., Hutchins, H. J., Robinson, L. R., Bloomfield, J., Meng, L., Bitsko, R. H., O'Masta, B., Cerles, A., Maher, B., Rush, M., & Kaminski, J. W. (2022). All in the family? A systematic review and meta-analysis of parenting and family environment as risk factors for attention-deficit/hyperactivity disorder (ADHD) in children. *Prevention Science: The Official Journal of the Society for Prevention Research.* Advance online publication. https://doi.org/10.1007/s11121-022-01358-4

Coghill, D., Soutullo, C., D'Aubuisson, C., Preuss, U., Lindback, T., Silverberg, M., & Buitelaar, J. (2008). Impact of attention-deficit/hyperactivity disorder on the patient and family: Results from a European survey. *Child and Adolescent Psychiatry and Mental Health, 2*(1), 31. https://doi.org/10.1186/1753-2000-2-31

Coker, T. R., Elliott, M. N., Toomey, S. L., Schwebel, D. C., Cuccaro, P., Emery, S. T., . . . Schuster, M. A. (2016). Racial and ethnic disparities in ADHD diagnosis and treatment. *Pediatrics, 138*(3), e20160407. https://doi.org/10.1542/peds.2016-0407

Connor, D., Steeber, J., & McBurnett, K. (2010). A review of attention-deficit/hyperactivity disorder complicated by symptoms of oppositional defiant disorder or conduct disorder. *Journal of Developmental and Behavioral Pediatric, 31*, 427–440.

Corcoran, J., & Dattalo, P. (2006). Parent involvement in treatment for ADHD: A meta-analysis of the published studies. *Research on Social Work Practice*, *16*(6), 561–570.

Corcoran, J, Schildt, B., Hochbrueckner, R., & Abell, J. (2017a). Parents of children with attention deficit/hyperactivity disorder: A meta-synthesis, part i. *Child and Adolescent Social Work Journal*, *34*(1), 281–335. doi:10.1007/s10560-016-0465-1

Corcoran, J, Schildt, B., Hochbrueckner, R., & Abell, J. (2017b). Parents of children with attention deficit/hyperactivity disorder: A meta-synthesis, part II. *Child and Adolescent Social Work Journal*, *34*(1), 337–348. doi:10.1007/s10560-017-0497-1

Cortese, S., Adamo, N., Del Giovane, C., Mohr-Jensen, C., Hayes, A., Carucci, S., Atkinson, L., Tessari, L., Banaschewski, T., Coghill, D., Hollis, C., Simonoff, E., Zuddas, A., Barbui, C., Purgato, M., Steinhausen, H., Shokraneh, F., Xia, J., & Cipriani, A. (2018). Comparative efficacy and tolerability of medications for attention-deficit hyperactivity disorder in children, adolescents, and adults: a systematic review and network meta-analysis. *Lancet, 5*(9), 727–738. https://doi.org/10.1016/S2215-0366(18)30269-4

Counts, C. A., Nigg, J. T., Stawicki, J. A., Rappley, M., & Eye, A. V. (2005). Family adversity in DSM-IV ADHD combined and inattentive subtypes and associated disruptive behavior problems. *Journal of the American Academy of Child and Adolescent Psychiatry, 44*(7), 690–698.

Craig, F., Savino, R., Fanizza, I., Lucarelli, E., Russo, L., & Trabacca, A. (2020). A systematic review of coping strategies in parents of children with attention deficit hyperactivity disorder (ADHD). *Research in Developmental Disabilities, 98*, 103571. https://doi.org/10.1016/j.ridd.2020.103571

Dahl, V., Ramakrishnan, A., Spears, A. P., Jorge, A., Lu, J. Bigio, N. A. & Chacko, A. (2020). Psychoeducation interventions for parents and teachers of children and adolescents with ADHD: A systematic review of the literature. *Journal of Development and Physical Disabilities, 32*, 257–292. https://doi-org.proxy.library.upenn.edu/10.1007/s10882-019-09691-3

Danielson, M. L., Bitsko, R. H., Ghandour, R. M., Holbrook, J. R., Kogan, M. D., & Blumberg, S. J. (2018). Prevalence of parent-reported ADHD diagnosis and associated treatment among U.S. children and adolescents, 2016. *Journal of Clinical Child and Adolescent Psychology, 47*(2), 199–212. https://doi.org/10.1080/15374 416.2017.1417860

Dekkers, T. J., Hornstra, R., van der Oord, S., Luman, M., Hoekstra, P. J., Groenman, A. P., & van den Hoofdakker, B. J. (2022). Meta-analysis: Which components of parent training work for children with attention-deficit/hyperactivity disorder? *Journal of the American Academy of Child & Adolescent Psychiatry, 61*(4), 478–494. https://doi.org/10.1016/j.jaac.2021.06.015

Dong, Q., Garcia, B., Pham, A. V., & Cumming, M. (2020). Culturally responsive approaches for addressing ADHD within multi-tiered systems of support. *Current Psychiatry Reports, 22*(6), 27–27. https://doi.org/10.1007/s11920-020-01154-3

Edgcomb, J. B., & Zima, B. (2018). Medication adherence among children and adolescents with severe mental illness: A systematic review and meta-analysis. *Journal of Child and Adolescent Psychopharmacology, 28*(8), 508–520.

Elder, T. (2010). The importance of relative standards in ADHD diagnoses: Evidence based on exact birth dates. *Journal of Health Economics, 29*(5), 641–656.

Evans, S., Owens, J., & Bunford, N. (2014). Evidence-based psychosocial treatments for children and adolescents with attention-deficit/hyperactivity disorder. *Journal of Clinical Child and Adolescent Psychology, 43*(4), 527–551. https://doi.org/10.1080/15374416.2013.850700

Fabiano, G. A., Naylor, J., Pelham, W. E., Gnagy, E. M., Burrows-MacLean, L., Coles, E., Chacko, A., Wymbs, B. T., Walker, K. S., Wymbs, F., Garefino, A., Mazzant, J. R., Sastry, A. L., Tresco, K. E., Waschbusch, D. A., Massetti, G. M., & Waxmonsky, J. (2022). Special education for children with ADHD: Services received and a comparison to children with ADHD in general education. *School Mental Health. 14*, 818–830. https://doi.org/10.1007/s12310-022-09514-5

Fabiano, G., & Pyle, K. (2019). Best practices in school mental health for attention deficit/hyperactivity disorder: A framework for intervention. *School Mental Health, 11*(1), 72–91. https://doi.org/10.1007/s12310-018-9267-2

Fabiano, G. A., Schatz, N. K., Aloe, A. M., Chacko, A., & Chronis-Tuscano, A. (2015). A systematic review of meta-analyses of psychosocial treatment for attention-deficit/

hyperactivity disorder. *Clinical Child and Family Psychology Review, 18*(1), 77–97. https://doi.org/10.1007/s10567-015-0178-6

Faraone, S. V., Biederman, J., Spencer, T., Mick, E., Murray, K., Petty, C., Adamson, J. J., & Monuteaux, M. C. (2006). Diagnosing adult attention deficit hyperactivity disorder: Are late onset and subthreshold diagnoses valid? *American Journal of Psychiatry, 163*(10), 1720–1729.

Gershon, J., & Gershon, J. (2002). A meta-analytic review of gender differences in ADHD. *Journal of Attention Disorders, 5*(3), 143–154. https://doi.org/10.1177/108 705470200500302

Gizer, I. R., Ficks, C., & Waldman, I. D. (2009). Candidate gene studies of ADHD: A meta-analytic review. *Human Genetics, 126,* 51–90. doi:10.1007/s00439-009-0694x

Glasofer, A., & Dingley, C. (2022). Diagnostic and medication treatment disparities in African American children with ADHD: A literature review. *Journal of Racial and Ethnic Health Disparities, 9*(5), 2027–2048. https://doi.org/10.1007/s40 615-021-01142-0

Glasofer, A., Dingley, C., & Reyes, A. (2020). Medication decision making among African American caregivers of children with ADHD: A review of the literature. *Journal of Attention Disorders.* https://doi.org/10.1177/1087054720930783

González, R., Vélez-Pastrana, M., McCrory, E., Kallis, C., Aguila, J., Canino, G., & Bird, H. (2019). Evidence of concurrent and prospective associations between early maltreatment and ADHD through childhood and adolescence. *Social Psychiatry and Psychiatric Epidemiology, 54*(6), 671–682. https://doi.org/10.1007/s00 127-019-01659-0

Greenhill, L., Swanson, J., Hechtman, L., Waxmonsky, J., Arnold, L., Molina, B., Hinshaw, S., Jensen, P., Abikoff, H., Wigal, T., Stehli, A., Howard, A., Hermanussen, M., & Hanć, T. (2020). Trajectories of growth associated with long-term stimulant medication in the multimodal treatment study of attention-deficit/hyperactivity disorder. *Journal of the American Academy of Child & Adolescent Psychiatry, 59*(8), 978–989. https://doi.org/10.1016/j.jaac.2019.06.019

Groenman, A. P., Hornstra, R., Hoekstra, P. J., Steenhuis, L., Aghebati, A., Boyer, B. E., . . . van den Hoofdakker, B. J. (2022). An individual participant data meta-analysis: Behavioral treatments for children and adolescents with attention-deficit/hyperactivity disorder. *Journal of the American Academy of Child & Adolescent Psychiatry, 61*(2), 144–158. https://doi.org/10.1016/j.jaac.2021.02.024

Hart, H., Radua, J., Mataix-Cols, D., & Rubia, K. (2013). Meta-analysis of functional magnetic resonance imaging studies of inhibition and attention in attention-deficit/hyperactivity disorder: Exploring task-specific, stimulant medication, and age effects. *Journal of American Medical Association Psychiatry, 70*(2), 185–198.

Hinshaw, S. (2018). Attention Deficit Hyperactivity Disorder (ADHD): Controversy, developmental mechanisms, and multiple levels of analysis. *Annual Review of Clinical Psychology, 214*(1), 291–316.

Hinshaw, S. P., & Scheffler, R. M. (2014). *The ADHD explosion: Myths, medications, money, and today's push for performance.* New York: Oxford University Press.

Hinshaw, Nguyen, P. T., O'Grady, S. M., & Rosenthal, E. A. (2022). Annual Research Review: Attention-deficit/hyperactivity disorder in girls and women: Under-representation, longitudinal processes, and key directions. *Journal of Child Psychology and Psychiatry and Allied Disciplines*, 63(4), 484–496. https://doi.org/10.1111/jcpp.13480

Jensen, P. S., Arnold, L. E., Swanson, J. M., Vitiello, B., Abikoff, H. B., Greenhill, L. L., . . . Hur, K. (2007). 3-year follow-up of the NIMH MTA Study. *Journal of the American Academy of Child & Adolescent Psychiatry*, 46(8), 989–1002. doi:10.1097/CHI.0b013e3180686d48

Johnson, K. A., Wiersema, J. R., & Kuntsi, J. (2009). What would Karl Popper say? Are current psychological theories of ADHD falsifiable? *Behavioral and Brain Functions*, 5(15), 1–11.

Kahn, R. S., Khoury, J., Nichols, W. C., & Lanphear, B. P. (2003). Role of dopamine transporter genotype and maternal prenatal smoking in childhood hyperactive-impulsive, inattentive, and oppositional behaviors. *Journal of Pediatrics*, 143(1), 104–110.

Kessler, R. C., Adler, L., Ames, M., Demler, O., Faraone, S., Hiripi, E., Howes, M. J., Jin, R., Secnik, K., Spencer, T., Ustu, B., . . . Walters, E. E. (2005). The world health organization adult ADHD self-report scale (ASRS): A short screening scale for use in the general population. *Psychological Medicine*, 35(2), 245–256.

Kim, J., Kim, J., Lee, J., Jeong, G., Lee, E., Lee, S., Lee, K., Kronbichler, A., Stubbs, B., Solmi, M., Koyanagi, A., Hong, S., Dragioti, E., Jacob, L., Brunoni, A., Carvalho, A., Radua, J., Thompson, T., Smith, L., & Oh, H. (2020). Environmental risk factors, protective factors, and peripheral biomarkers for ADHD: an umbrella review. *Lancet*, 7(11), 955–970. https://doi.org/10.1016/S2215-0366(20)30312-6

Laucht, M., Skowronek, M. H., Becker, K., Schmidt, M. H., Esser, G., Schulze, T. G., & Rietschel, M. (2007). Interacting effects of the dopamine transporter gene and psychosocial adversity on attention-deficit/hyperactivity disorder symptoms among 15-year-olds from a high-risk community sample. *Archives of General Psychiatry*, 64, 585–590.

Layton, T. J., Barnett, M. L., Hicks, T. R., & Jena, A. B. (2018). Attention deficit–hyperactivity disorder and month of school enrollment. *New England Journal of Medicine*, 379(22), 2122–2130.

Levy, F., Hay, D. A., & Bennett, K. S. (2006). Genetics of attention-deficit/hyperactivity disorder: A current review and future prospects. *International Journal of Disability, Development and Education*, 53(1), 5–20.

Levy, S., Katusic, S. K., Colligan, R. C., Weaver, A. L., Killian, J. M., Voight, R. G., & Barbaresi, W. J. (2014). Childhood ADHD and risk for substance dependence in adulthood: A longitudinal, population-based study. *PLOS One*, 9(8), e105640.

Lovett, B. J., & Nelson, J. M. (2020). Systematic review: Educational accommodations for children and adolescents with attention-deficit/hyperactivity disorder. *Journal of the American Academy of Child and Adolescent Psychiatry*, S0890-8567(20), 31333-2. Advance online publication. https://doi.org/10.1016/j.jaac.2020.07.891

Mannuzza, S., Klein, R., & Moulton, J. (2002). Young adult outcome of children with "situational" hyperactivity: A prospective, controlled, follow-up study. *Journal of Abnormal Child Psychology*, 30, 191–198.

Miller, T. W., Nigg, J. T., & Miller, R. L. (2008). Attention deficit hyperactivity disorder in African American children: What can be concluded from the past ten years? *Clinical Psychology Review*. Advance online publication. doi:10.1016/j.cpr.2008.10.001

Molina, B. S. G., Hinshaw, S., Swanson, J., Arnold, L. E., Vitiello, B., Jensen, P. S., Epstein, J. N., Hoza, B., Hechtman, L., Abikoff, H. B., Elliott, G. R., Greenhill, L. L., Newcorn, J. H., Wells, K. C., Wigal, T., Gibbons, R. D., Hur, K., Houck, P. R.; & MTA Cooperative Group. (2009). The MTA at 8 years: Prospective follow-up of children treated for combined-type ADHD in a multisite study. *Journal of the American Academy of Child and Adolescent Psychiatry, 48*(5), 484–500. doi:10.1097/CHI.0b013e31819c23d0

Montalva-Valenzuela, F., Andrades-Ramírez, O., & Castillo-Paredes, A. (2022). Effects of physical activity, exercise and sport on executive function in young people with attention deficit hyperactivity disorder: A systematic review. *European Journal of Investigation in Health, Psychology and Education, 12*(1), 61–76. https://doi.org/10.3390/ejihpe12010006

Morgan, P. L., Staff, J., Hillemeier, M. M., Farkas, G., & Maczuga, S. (2013). Racial and ethnic disparities in ADHD diagnosis from kindergarten to eighth grade. *Pediatrics, 132*(1), 85–93.

National Institute for Health and Care Excellence. (2018, March). *Attention deficit hyperactivity disorder: Diagnosis and management.* Retrieved from https://www.nice.org.uk/guidance/ng87/chapter/Recommendations.

Neale, B. M., Medland, S. E., Ripke, S., Asherson, P., Franke, B., Lesch, K. P., Faraone, S. V., Nguyan, T. T., Schafer, H., Holmans, P., Daly, M., Steinhausen, H-C., Frietag, C., Reif, A., Renner, T. J., Romanos, M., Romanos, J., Walitza, S., Warnke, A., . . . Psychiatric GWAS Consortium: ADHD Subgroup. (2010). Meta-analysis of genome-wide association studies of attention-deficit/hyperactivity disorder [Abstract]. *Journal of the American Academy of Child and Adolescent Psychiatry, 49*(9), 884–897.

Newcorn, J. H., Sutton, Y. K., Weiss, M. D., & Sumner, C. R. (2009). Clinical responses to atomoxetine in attention-deficit/hyperactivity disorder: The integrated data exploratory analysis (IDEA) study. *Journal of the American Academy of Child & Adolescent Psychiatry, 48*(5), 511–518.

Olfson, M., Marcus, S., & Wan, G. (2009). Stimulant dosing for children with ADHS: A medical claims analysis. *Journal of the American Academy of Child & Adolescent Psychiatry, 48*(1), 51–59.

Ostergaard, S. D., Dalsgaard, S., Faraone, S. V., Munk-Olsen, T., & Laursen, T. M. (2017). Teenage parenthood and birth rates for individuals with and without attention-deficit/hyperactivity disorder: A nationwide cohort study. *Journal of American Academy of Child and Adolescent Psychiatry, 56*(7), 578–584.

Park, J. L., Hudec, K. L., & Johnston, C. (2017). Parental ADHD symptoms and parenting behaviors: A meta-analytic review. *Clinical Psychology Review, 56*, 25–39. https://doi.org/10.1016/j.cpr.2017.05.003

Pelham, W. E., Fabiano, G. A., & Massetti, G. M. (2005). Evidence-based assessment of attention deficit hyperactivity disorder in children and adolescents. *Journal of Clinical Child and Adolescent Psychology, 34*(3), 449–476.

Perrin, S., Smith, P., & Yule, W. (2000). Practitioner review: The assessment and treatment of post-traumatic stress disorder in children and adolescents. *Journal of Child Psychology and Psychiatry and Allied Disciplines, 41*(3), 277–289.

Pham, A. V., Carlson, J. S., & Kosciulek, J. F. (2010). Ethnic differences in parental beliefs of attention-deficit/hyperactivity disorder and treatment. *Journal of Attention Disorders, 13*(6), 584–591.

Punja, S., Shamseer, L., Hartling, L., Urichuk, L., Vandermeer, B., Nikles, J., & Vohra, S. (2016). Amphetamines for attention deficit hyperactivity disorder (ADHD) in children and adolescents. *Cochrane Library, 2*. doi:10.1002/14651858.CD009996.pub2

Quinn, P., Chang, Z., Hur, K., Gibbons, R., Lahey, B., Rickert, M. E., Sjölander, A., Lictenstein, P., Larsson, H., & D'Onofrio, B. M. (2017). ADHD medication and substance-related problems. *American Journal of Psychiatry, 174*, 877–885.

Riglin, L., Collishaw, S., Thapar, A. K., Dalsgaard, S., Langley, K., Smith, G. D, Stergiakouli, E., Maughan, B., O'Donovan, M. C., & Thapar, A. (2016). Association of genetic risk variants with attention-deficit/hyperactivity disorder trajectories in the general population. *Journal of the American Medical Association Psychiatry, 73*(12), 1285–1292. doi:10.1001/jamapsychiatry.2016.2817

Rothe, E. (2005). Considering cultural diversity in the management of ADHD in Hispanic patients. *Journal of the National Medicine Association, 97*, S17.

Roy, A., Hechtman, L., Arnold, L., Swanson, J., Molina, B., Sibley, M., & Howard, (2017). Childhood predictors of adult functional outcomes in the multimodal treatment study of attention-deficit/hyperactivity disorder (MTA). *Journal of the American Academy of Child & Adolescent Psychiatry, 56*(8), 687–695.e7. doi:10.1016/j.jaac.2017.05.020

Russell, A. E., Ford, T., Williams, R., & Russell, G. (2016). The association between socioeconomic disadvantage and attention deficit/hyperactivity disorder (ADHD): A systematic review. *Child Psychiatry and Human Development, 47*(3), 440–458. https://doi.org/10.1007/s10578-015-0578-3

Safer, J. D. (2016). Recent trends in stimulant usage. *Journal of Attention Disorders, 20*(6), 471–477.

Shaw, M., Hodgkins, P., Caci, H., Young, S., Kahle, J., Woods, A. G., & Arnold, L. E. (2012). A systematic review and analysis of long-term outcomes in attention deficit hyperactivity disorder: Effects of treatment and non-treatment. *BMC Medicine, 10*, 99. http://doi.org/10.1186/1741-7015-10-99

Stevens, S. E., Sonuga-Barke, E. J. S., Kreppner, J. M., Beckett, C., Castle, J., Colvert, E., Groothues, C., Hawkins, A., & Rutter, M. (2008). Inattention/overactivity following early severe institutional deprivation: Presentation and associations in early adolescence. *Journal of Abnormal Child Psychology, 36*, 385–398.

Storebø, O., Ramstad, E., Krogh, H., Nilausen, T., Skoog, M., Holmskov, M., . . . Gluud, C. (2015). Methylphenidate for children and adolescents with attention deficit hyperactivity disorder (ADHD). *Cochrane Database of Systematic Reviews, 11*, CD009885. doi:10.1002/14651858.CD009885.pub2

Storebø, O. J., Rasmussen, P. D., & Simonsen, E. (2016). Association between insecure attachment and ADHD: Environmental mediating factors. *Journal of Attention Disorders, 20*(2), 187–196.

Sun, W., Yu, M., & Zhou, X. (2022). Effects of physical exercise on attention deficit and other major symptoms in children with ADHD: A meta-analysis. *Psychiatry Research, 311*, 114509. https://doi.org/10.1016/j.psychres.2022.114509

Swanson, J. (2013). Swanson, Nolan, & Pelham Teacher and Parent Rating Scale (SNAP-IV). Retrieved from: https://www.mcpap.com/pdf/SNAPIV.pdf

Swanson, J., Arnold, L., Kraemer, H., Hechtman, L., Molina, B., Hinshaw, S., . . .Wial, T. (2008). Evidence, interpretation, and qualification from multiple reports of long-term outcomes in the multimodal treatment study of children with ADHD (MTA). Part I: Executive summary. *Journal of Attention Disorders, 12*(1), 4–14.

Swanson, J. M., Schuck, S., Porter, M. M., Carlson, C., Hartman, C. A., Sergeant, J. A., Clevenger, W., Wasdell, M., McCleary, R., Lakes, K., & Wigal, T. (2012). Categorical and dimensional definitions and evaluations of symptoms of ADHD: History of the SNAP and the SWAN rating scales. *International Journal of Educational and Psychological Assessment, 10*(1), 51–70.

Theule, J., Wiener, J., Tannock, R., & Jenkins, J. M. (2013). Parenting stress in families of children with ADHD: A meta-analysis. *Journal of Emotional and Behavioral Disorders, 21*(1), 3–17.

Tucker, J. R., & Hobson, C. W. (2022). A systematic review of longitudinal studies investigating the association between early life maternal depression and offspring ADHD. *Journal of Attention Disorders, 26*(9), 1167–1186. https://doi.org/10.1177/10870547211063642

Tung, I., Li, J. J., Meza, J. I., Jezior, K. L., Kianmahd, J. S., Hentschel, P. G., . . . Lee, S. S. (2016). Patterns of comorbidity among girls with ADHD: A meta-analysis. *Pediatrics, 138*(4).

Uchida, M., Driscoll, H., DiSalvo, M., Rajalakshmim, A., Maiello, M., Spera, V., & Biederman, J. (2021). Assessing the magnitude of risk for ADHD in offspring of parents with ADHD: A systematic literature review and meta-analysis. *Journal of Attention Disorders, 25*(13), 1943–1948. https://doi.org/10.1177/1087054720950815

Uchida, M., Driscoll, H., DiSalvo, M., Rajalakshmim, A., Maiello, M., Spera, V., & Biederman, J. (2021). Assessing the magnitude of risk for ADHD in offspring of parents with ADHD: A Systematic Literature Review and Meta-Analysis. *Journal of Attention Disorders, 25*(13), 1943–1948. https://doi.org/10.1177/1087054720950815

Visser, J., & Jehan, Z. (2009). ADHD: A scientific fact or a factual opinion? A critique of the veracity of attention deficit hyperactivity disorder. *Emotional & Behavioral Difficulties, 14*(2), 127–140. doi:10.1080/13632750902921930Visser, S. N., Deubler, E. L., Bitsko, R. H., Holbrook, J. R., & Danielson, M. L. (2016). Demographic differences among a national sample of US youth with behavioral disorders. *Clinical Pediatrics, 55*(14), 1358–1362. https://doi.org/10.1177/0009922815623229

Waxmonsky, J. G., Baweja, R., Liu, G., Waschbusch, D. A., Fogel, B., Leslie, D., & Pelham Jr., W. E. (2019). A commercial insurance claims analysis of correlates of behavioral therapy use among children with ADHD. *Psychiatric Services, 70*(12), 1116–1122. doi:10.1176/appi.ps.201800473

Wolraich, M. L., Bard, D. E., Stein, M. T., Rushton, J. L., & O'Connor, K. G. (2010). Pediatricians' attitudes and practices on ADHD before and after the development of ADHD pediatric practice guidelines. *Journal of Attention Disorders, 13*(6), 563–572. doi:10.1177/1087054709644194

Wolraich, M. L., Hagan, J. F., Allan, C., Chan, E., Davison, D., Earls, M., . . . Holbrook, J. R. (2019). Clinical practice guideline for the diagnosis, evaluation, and treatment of attention-deficit/hyperactivity disorder in children and adolescents. *Pediatrics, 144*(4), e20192528.

Wolraich, M. L., Lambert, W., Doffing, M. A., Bickman, L., Simmons, T., & Worley, K. (2003). Psychometric properties of the Vanderbilt ADHD diagnostic parent rating scale in a referred population. *Journal of Pediatric Psychology, 28*(8), 559–568.

Wüstner, A., Otto, C., Schlack, R., Hölling, H., Klasen, F., et al. (2019). Risk and
    protective factors for the development of ADHD symptoms in children and
    adolescents: Results of the longitudinal BELLA study. *PLOS ONE, 14*(3), e0214412.
    https://doi.org/10.1371/journal.pone.0214412

Wymbs, B. T., Pelham Jr., W. E., Molina, B. S. G., Gnagy, E. M., Wilson, T. K., &
    Greenhouse, J. B. (2008). Rate and predictors of divorce among parents of youths
    with ADHD. *Journal of Consulting and Clinical Psychology, 76*(5), 735–744. http://
    dx.doi.org/10.1037/a0012719

6

Autism Spectrum Disorder

JACQUELINE CORCORAN, JULIE WORLEY, AND
COURTNEY BENJAMIN WOLK ■

Timothy is a 15-year-old male who was referred for treatment by his current psychologist, Dr. Warren, because of concern that he may be exhibiting symptoms of obsessive-compulsive disorder (OCD). Dr. Warren had been providing educational consultation and supportive counseling services to Timothy and his family for autism spectrum disorder (ASD) for approximately 1 year. Recently, Timothy had begun to exhibit great concern about cleanliness and was repeatedly showering and washing his hands. Dr. Warren identified these challenges as new and discrete from repetitive behaviors that were more characteristic of Timothy's ASD, prompting referral to a clinician with expertise in treating OCD.

Timothy lives with his mother and father, Mr. and Mrs. Beckett, and 10-year-old sister in a low- to middle-income suburb. His mother works part-time as a teacher's aide in a public school, and his father is a manager at a landscaping company. Mr. and Mrs. Beckett reported that several extended family members have a history of anxiety and depression.

Timothy is currently homeschooled by his mother, having left the public school system 3 years earlier because he was being bullied. Timothy does not often socialize with peers. He was diagnosed with Asperger's syndrome at age 8 (in the DSM IV) and has a history of difficulty engaging socially. He gets along well with his parents, who are very supportive. His parents stated that they planned to transition him back into a traditional school for the next academic year and have been working with Dr. Warren to identify a school that could meet his needs and prepare for the transition. Timothy's parents described his primary interests as outer space and watching online videos and cooking shows.

Timothy had a trial of a selective serotonin receptor inhibitor (SSRI) lasting 3 to 4 months several years earlier, but his parents report that it was not effective in reducing his anxiety and thus was discontinued. They have been participating in supportive therapy with Dr. Warren, which has focused on social skills and preparing Timothy to transition back into a traditional school setting. Dr. Warren encouraged

Child and Adolescent Mental Health in Social Work. Jacqueline Corcoran and Courtney Benjamin Wolk, Oxford University Press.
© Oxford University Press 2023. DOI: 10.1093/oso/9780197653562.003.0006

Mr. and Mrs. Beckett to receive consultation from an expert in OCD because she was concerned that Timothy was exhibiting symptoms of the disorder that were distinct from the symptoms of his ASD.

Timothy presented to the intake appointment with his mother and father. He was initially quiet, but he began to warm up as the interview progressed. His attention was within normal limits for his age, and he demonstrated fair insight. He frequently fidgeted with his hands during the intake and spoke with a monotone. Timothy appeared to be answering questions in an open and honest manner. Overall, Timothy presented as a pleasant and likable young man. His parents presented as supportive, and they and Timothy communicated openly about Timothy's OCD symptoms.

OVERVIEW

As defined by the American Psychiatric Association (APA) in the *Diagnostic and Statistical Manual of Mental Disorders* (DSM; APA, 2022), ASD is a pervasive developmental disorder with symptoms typically emerging during the early developmental period. Children with ASD demonstrate impairments in social interaction and social communication, as well as restricted and repetitive behaviors (APA, 2022). More specifically, symptoms within the social-communication domain include (1) deficits in social-emotional reciprocity (e.g., responding to or initiating social interactions, conversations); (2) deficits in nonverbal communicative behavior (e.g., impaired eye contact and facial expressiveness, difficulty integrating verbal and nonverbal behaviors); and (3) deficits in developing, maintaining, and understanding relationships (e.g., decreased interest in peers; lack of age-appropriate friendships). Symptoms within the restricted, repetitive patterns of behavior or interests domain include (1) stereotyped or repetitive motor movements, use of objects, or speech (e.g., hand flapping, nonfunctional play with objects, echolalia, or scripting); (2) insistence on sameness, inflexible adherence to routines, and ritualized patterns of behavior (e.g., difficulty with changes and transitions); (3) restricted, fixated interests that are abnormal in intensity (i.e., a strong interest in a specific topic); and (4) hyposensitivity or hypersensitivity to sensory input (e.g., aversions to loud noises or textures, sensory-seeking behaviors).

The DSM-5 classification allows professionals to identify levels of disability based on observations of symptoms in each domain (i.e., impairments in social-communication and social interaction and restricted, repetitive patterns of behavior). The severity levels are *requiring support, requiring substantial support*, and *requiring very substantial support*. Individuals "requiring very substantial support" typically present with significant impairments in their communication skills, limited responding and initiating of social interactions, significant distress with changes to their usual routine, and intense preoccupation with specific interests, and it is often difficult to redirect them away from their interests. In its mildest form (i.e., individuals "requiring support," the deficits in social-communication skills are less impairing. Individuals may be socially interested, but without support, they do not successfully navigate social relationships or social conversations. They will also present with some restricted, repetitive behaviors (e.g., difficulty navigating changes to their schedule or using stereotyped language).

It should be mentioned that a new DSM disorder, social pragmatic communication disorder, characterizes children and adolescents who have persistent difficulty with verbal and nonverbal communication that cannot be explained by low cognitive ability. Some individuals previously diagnosed with ASD may now meet the criteria for this disorder.

Prevalence

The prevalence of ASD is difficult to gauge because of differences in assessment techniques both worldwide and in the United States (Ramsey et al., 2016). Diagnostic variability is believed to be an indicator of differences in the training of professionals, the availability of pediatricians and psychologists trained to assess symptoms of ASD, and the accessibility of health care resources. A review of prevalence studies indicates that the worldwide rate for ASD is about 11 per 10,000 (Baxter et al., 2015). The Centers for Disease Control and Prevention (2016) found that the prevalence of ASD in the United States is 1 in 54 and that ASD occurs more often in males than in females, with a ratio of approximately 4:1 (Maenner et al., 2021).

RISK AND PROTECTIVE FACTORS

Biological

ASD is a neurodevelopmental disorder, although its specific causes have not yet been identified. A scoping review of environmental factors associated with ASD identified support for the following risk factors in the literature: chemical factors (e.g., air pollution); physiologic factors, including pregnancy complications, low birth weight or preterm birth, advanced maternal age, hyperbilirubinemia; and the mother identifying as having immigrant status (Ng et al., 2017). There is no association of ASD with any psychological or social influences in the absence of biological mechanisms and no evidence of an association with vaccines (Ng et al., 2017). Although ASD has many potential causes, in this section we will further explore risks related to heredity and brain abnormalities.

HEREDITY
Evidence that ASD is a neurodevelopmental disorder is indicated by its high rates of heredity transmission (Tick et al., 2016). The concordance rate for ASD in identical twins ranges between 64% and 91%, depending on the diagnostic criteria used. A large-scale family study found that 10.1% of siblings also develop ASD, with the risk being highest for siblings born within 18 months of

each other (Risch et al., 2014). The chances of half-siblings developing ASD were 3% to 6.5%.

The research suggests that many genes, perhaps as many as 100, contribute to the development of ASD (Ji et al., 2016). Knowledge is developing rapidly in this area. Chromosomal damage appears to occur in genes that control growth and development in early life; influence speech and language development; cause behavioral symptoms associated with ASD; contribute to tuberous sclerosis (a multisystem disorder characterized by seizures and intellectual disability); are associated with metabolic and serotonin deficiencies; and prompt the development of fragile X, a type of intellectual disability. There is strong evidence that advanced parental age (>40 years) in either mothers or fathers creates an increased risk of having a child with ASD (Vierck & Silverman, 2015). Possible biological mechanisms at work here include mutations associated with advancing age or alterations in genetic imprinting. Environmental toxicants, at least for a subset of children, may have an equal contribution to the development of ASD as that of genetics (Rossignol et al., 2014). Genetics and toxicants may interact in synergistic ways.

Brain Abnormalities

Approximately 70% of people with ASD experience distinct neurologic abnormalities and some degree of intellectual disability (Rivard et al., 2015). Several relevant brain abnormalities have been identified. Brain imaging studies indicate that ASD is associated with enlarged overall brain size (as much as 10% larger than other toddlers) and decreased size and activity in specific areas of the brain (Hutsler & Zhang, 2010). These areas possibly include the midsagittal area of the cerebellum, thought to be involved in the sequencing of motor activities; the lower hippocampus (in the midbrain), associated with complex learning processes; the amygdala (located in the temporal lobe), which is believed to contribute to the recognition of faces and emotional expression; and a portion of the brain stem associated with attention. Children with ASD may have an overgrowth of neurons, coupled with an underdeveloped organization of neurons in specialized systems in some areas of the brain, although related findings have not been consistently replicated.

It has long been suspected that problems leading to ASD symptoms may be present in neurotransmitter systems (the chemicals in neurons that send messages to each other) that include serotonin, dopamine, norepinephrine, acetylcholine, oxytocin, endogenous opioids, cortisol, glutamate, and gamma-aminobutyric acid, but no clear evidence has yet emerged in this regard (Dickinson et al., 2016). Promising new areas of study include possible dysfunction of the cholinergic system, oxytocin, and amino acid neurotransmitters.

With regard to its deficits in brain functioning, ASD has been conceptualized in various ways—among them as a disorder of *central coherence*, in which the person is unable to process information holistically and instead develops a bias toward part-oriented processing; a disorder of *executive function*, in which the person is unable to process bits of information or regulate behavior and is thus inclined toward rigid, repetitive behaviors and impoverished interactions; and a deficit in *social cognition*, in which the person fails to understand the internal mental states of other people and has difficulty making attributions of mental states to others and themselves (Van Schalkwyk & Volkmar, 2015).

Other than the timing of assessment and intervention (discussed in the next section), protective influences for the course of ASD include an absence of pregnancy and birth complications (Ng et al., 2017); milder level of impairment; absence of intellectual disability; early acquisition of nonverbal communication, functional play skills, and speech capacity (Baghdadli et al., 2012); and better adaptive functioning (Farley et al., 2009).

There is no evidence that the avoidance of certain vaccines serves as a protective factor. Males have higher rates of autism, although there seem to be a gender bias in diagnosing (Loomes et al., 2017).

Psychological

Children and adolescents with ASD experience a range of comorbid medical and psychiatric disorders. Co-occurring mental health conditions are more prevalent in the autism population than in the general population at overall pooled prevalence estimates of 28% for attention-deficit/hyperactivity disorder (ADHD); 20% for anxiety disorders; 13% for sleep–wake disorders; 12% for disruptive disorders; 11% for depressive disorders; and 9% for OCD (Lai et al., 2019). The likelihood of comorbid psychiatric disorders is largely due to the broadly debilitating features of ASD, their associated medical disorders, and the problematic life experiences related to having the disorder (Richards et al., 2017). Individuals with ASD also commonly engage in problem behaviors such as physical aggression, self-injurious behaviors (head banging, hand biting), and elopement. Biological factors (such as seizures), cognitive and emotional impairments (leading to impulsivity and low frustration tolerance), an inability to verbally communicate needs and wants, difficulty managing change, and learned behaviors to avoid certain tasks or situations contribute to individuals engaging in problem behaviors.

Social

Social factors are involved, not in the development of the disorder itself, but in when the diagnosis is made. Low socioeconomic status (SES) is one of the factors associated with a later diagnosis of autism (Hildago et al., 2015). Higher SES parents are better able to navigate the medical system and have more access to resources to obtain an assessment for ASD for their child.

Although family environment does not influence the development of ASD, learning of a child's diagnosis and raising the child are typically disruptive to the entire family system, as demonstrated in two qualitative reviews. In a systematic review and meta-synthesis of 14 studies, six major themes related to family challenges were identified, including everyday emotional stress and strain, on-going problems with adaptation, an overall negative impact on the family, needing to make decisions about professional services, managing the sense of stigmatization, and learning to better appreciate the little things (Corcoran et al., 2015). In another metasynthesis of 31 articles, six themes were noted as well, several of them similar to those in the first study, including family confusion during the prediagnosis stage, accepting the diagnosis, challenges to family life adjustment, learning to navigate the services system, developing a sense of parental empowerment, and moving forward (DePape & Lindsay, 2015). A literature review on resilience factors for caregivers included the availability of social support, spousal support, changing cognitive appraisals of life situations (reframing), acceptance, optimism, self-efficacy, and a belief that one's actions can have an impact (Bekhet et al., 2012). Parents tended to develop resilience as the child got older and more time passed since the diagnosis. There are certain aspects of the family that lead to better outcomes for a child with ASD, including high-quality parent–child interactions.

School-aged youths, perhaps partly because of their lack of social skills and difficulties with interaction, experience bullying at a high rate. A systematic literature search indicated that half of all children/adolescents with ASD experienced victimization (Maiano et al., 2015).

ASSESSMENT

The goals of assessment are to determine first whether a child meets diagnostic criteria for ASD and then to offer appropriate interventions and educational environments to maximize the child's potential for change. Professionals must set the stage for a long-term collaborative relationship with parents and help them become better-informed advocates for their child.

A major thrust in health care is the early diagnosis of ASD so that intervention can begin as soon as possible (Rosenberg et al., 2011). Early diagnosis is associated with urban residence, middle SES, pediatric referral to a specialist, having a child with severe language deficits, having an IQ of 70 or lower, and symptoms such as hand flapping and toe walking. Later diagnosis is associated with rural residence, low SES, oversensitivity to pain, hearing impairment, female gender, and having seen at least four primary care providers. Parental concern is a more important factor than pediatric testing in identifying a child with ASD because 90% of parents of such children recognize developmental delays in their child by the age of 24 months (Matheis et al., 2017).

The symptoms of ASD can be observed when a child is as young as 6 to 12 months. During the first year of life, the child typically displays unusual social development, being less likely to imitate the movements and vocal sounds of others, and exhibits problems with attention and responding to external stimulation (Daniels & Mandell, 2014). Between 1 and 3 years of age, when parents are most likely to seek an evaluation, differences from peers are more apparent, and the child's idiosyncratic, self-focused behaviors and communication problems are notable. Parents report a regression in their child's skills in approximately 30% of cases (Barger et al., 2013). Often, neurologists, psychologists, and developmental pediatricians are responsible for diagnosing ASD, with primary pediatricians doing so only 12% of the time (Emerson et al., 2016). Many children with ASD are initially evaluated at a mean age of 48 months but are not diagnosed until 61 months (with no differences by gender or SES; Deconinck et al., 2013), and 20% to 25% of children are not diagnosed until after entering school. More severely impaired children tend to be diagnosed earlier.

Assessment is a challenging process because no biochemical tests are available to assess ASD, nor does a single behavior or set of behaviors unequivocally characterize it. While an ideal assessment is multidisciplinary in nature, including evaluations by a clinical or school psychologist, medical doctor, and speech and language pathologist as well as a social worker, that is not always feasible or necessary. At a minimum, an assessment should include a developmental interview and direct observation of the child's skills. A core assessment for ASD comprises the following elements (Hathorn et al., 2014):

- *Developmental interview with caregivers.* This includes information about the mother's pregnancy, labor, and delivery; the child's early neonatal course; the parents' earliest concerns about their child; family history of developmental disorders; inquiry about current and past social-communication skills; presence of restricted, repetitive behaviors; observations of problem behaviors (e.g., aggression, self-injury); the child's prior response to any educational programs or behavioral interventions; and results of any previous evaluations.
- *Direct observation of skills.* This includes directly assessing the individual's social and communication abilities. The gold standard assessment tool for this purpose is the Autism Diagnostic Observation Schedule, Second Edition (ADOS-2; Lord et al., 2012). While the ADOS-2 can be used for individuals 12 months of age through adulthood, many practitioners are not trained to administer or interpret the ADOS-2. Another commonly used tool is the Childhood Autism Rating Scales, Second Edition (CARS-2; Schopler et al., 2010).
- *Medical evaluation.* This includes information about possible seizures, visual and hearing examinations for possible sensory problems, and testing for lead levels if the child has had exposure.
- *Developmental or cognitive assessment.* This establishes the level of developmental functioning or intellectual functioning.
- *Assessment of adaptive functioning*
- *Speech and language assessment*

An evaluation was conducted to assess Timothy's appropriateness for receiving exposure and response prevention (ERP) treatment for OCD. Timothy and his parents were interviewed separately using the Children's Yale-Brown Obsessive Compulsive Scale

(CY-BOCS; Goodman et al, 1991; see also page 182). A clinical interview and history were also conducted to evaluate for the presence of anxiety, mood, and externalizing symptoms. Timothy and his parents individually completed self-report and parent-report measures of anxiety and OCD. Based on Timothy and his parents' reports, Timothy was determined to be experiencing symptoms consistent with a diagnosis of OCD with fair insight. Timothy had reportedly been experiencing OCD symptoms for a couple of years, with an exacerbation of symptoms occurring in the past few months.

Timothy and his parents reported that he experienced the following obsessions/ intrusive thoughts: concern or disgust with bodily waste/secretions, namely saliva and urine, and contamination concerns that have no consequences, except that things reportedly do not feel right. Additionally, Timothy's parents report a history (not current) of avoiding even numbers. Regarding compulsions, Timothy and his parents described Timothy as needing to frequently wash his hands and clean his body/clothes to remove possible traces of saliva, urine, or feces. For example, after using the bathroom Timothy would wash his hands and then splash water repeatedly on his pants to remove possible contamination. This frequently resulted in significant amounts of water on the bathroom floor and his hands becoming chapped/cracked and bleeding because of excessive washing. He would reportedly utilize approximately 15 hand towels per day, saturating them with water and would go through a bottle of hand soap approximately every few days. Timothy also reportedly had concerns that furniture (e.g., the coffee table) had become contaminated with saliva and required it to be cleaned before he would have contact with it or, for example, eat a snack at the table. He refused to wear clothes that had been previously worn even when they were not soiled and reportedly needed to shower before bed to ensure his bed did not become contaminated.

Timothy reported experiencing nearly constant intrusion of obsessive thoughts and engagement in compulsive behaviors approximately 2 hours per day. He and his parents described considerable distress associated with both obsessions and compulsions, and impairment was evidenced primarily in the home environment. He did not typically try to resist the obsessive thoughts and compulsions. Timothy demonstrated fair insight into his OCD. Overall, Timothy was experiencing moderate OCD and functioning with effort at the time of intake. His symptoms were not consistent with fixated or repetitive behaviors common in ASD and were determined to warrant an additional diagnosis of OCD.

Timothy was also experiencing symptoms indicating high-functioning ASD, consistent with his previously documented diagnosis of Asperger's syndrome. No other significant anxiety, mood, or externalizing symptoms were reported by Timothy or his parents at the time of intake.

INTERVENTION

Comprehensive interventions for children with ASD include strategies that address its core deficits of communication, social interaction, and flexibility in thinking and behavior. They are often delivered for many hours per week over periods of time ranging from months to years (Bishop-Fitzpatrick et al., 2013), and this is especially true for young children before starting elementary school.

After conducting a thorough literature review and evaluating treatment effectiveness, the National Clearinghouse on Autism Evidence and Practice (Steinbrenner et al., 2020) and the National Standards Project (National Autism Center, 2015) list interventions that have evidence supporting their use when treating individuals diagnosed with ASD. While many of the interventions listed are strategies used when applying the principles of behavior analysis, some other interventions include social skills training, social narratives, and cognitive-behavioral instructional strategies.

Depending on the child's needs, the range of interventions can include behavior treatment, special education services, family support, and social skills training. Some parents find complementary and alternative interventions appealing as a means of controlling behavioral symptoms, but considerable caution should be exercised when using these interventions because of the lack of research on them. Additionally, evidence-based treatments for other disorders, such as cognitive-behavioral therapy (CBT) for anxiety, can be successfully modified and utilized for children with ASD experiencing comorbidities (such as in the case example from this chapter; Sukhodolsky et al., 2013).

Behavior Management

Behavioral interventions rely on the principles of applied behavior analysis (ABA) to treat impairments related to the core features of ASD, improve skills of independence (i.e., adaptive skills), and treat problem behaviors. Treatment intensity (i.e., hours per week) and duration (i.e., months, years) have significant effects on outcomes (Linstead et al., 2017). Treatment intensity is highest (i.e., 20 to 40 hours per week) for younger children, typically before they begin school.

Evidence-based practice research suggests there are two intervention models to be recommended for children, which are ABA and developmental social pragmatic (DSP) strategies (Smith & Iadarola, 2015). In ABA, practitioners and parents utilize learning principles to teach socially significant behaviors to the child. Preacademic skills such as imitation, matching, numbers concepts, communication, self-management, and social and academic skills are broken down into small, discrete steps and taught to the child systematically, using reinforcers. In contrast, DSP interventions are based on observations that show a strong association between caregiver responsiveness to young children and the children's subsequent acquisition of skills for communicating and interacting with others. DSP intervention aims to promote these two sets of skills by being responsive to the child in ways such as imitating, expanding on, and joining into play activities initiated by the child. ABA is often associated with specific intervention strategies (e.g., discrete trial training [DTT]), and there are criticisms of the highly structured ABA interventions strategies utilized as part of ABA treatment packages. There is a movement toward using more naturalistic interventions, especially for toddlers and young children with ASD. Naturalistic developmental behavioral interventions (NDBIs) are informed by the merging of developmental sciences and principles of ABA. They are highly effective for young children with ASD and are implemented in the child's natural environment, rely on the use of natural reinforcement and contingencies, give the child shared control, capitalize on the child's motivation and interests, and allow the child to be an active participant in treatment (Schreibman et al., 2015).

For adolescents, intervention emphasis is often placed on adaptive and vocational skills. Sexual development in adolescence may bring some additional behavioral issues. Parents of adolescents with ASD are more likely than parents of non-ASD youths to report inappropriate sexual behavior and to have problems with privacy norms (Hancock et al., 2017). Adolescents with ASD also receive less formal and informal sex education.

Meta-analyses and systematic reviews support the efficacy of behavioral interventions, although with generally small to moderate effects. In a review of five meta-analyses published in 2009 and 2010, Reichow (2012) noted that four of the studies concluded that behavioral interventions were effective for many children, although outcomes varied among studies. One limitation of empirically validated programs is the challenge to families of maintaining the intensity recommended (the number of hours of involvement and consistent use of specific exercises).

Cognitive-Behavioral Therapy

Anxiety is a common comorbid problem in children and adolescents with ASD, and two meta-analyses investigated the efficacy of cognitive-behavioral interventions targeted at this condition (Kreslins et al., 2015). In one, 10 randomized control trials including 470 participants and using clinical and parent-reported outcome measures showed that such interventions were effective and that individual treatment was superior to group intervention. Another review of 14 studies and 511 youths with high-functioning ASD also found strong evidence of positive outcomes (Ung et al., 2015). While CBT is listed as an established treatment for ASD (National Autism Center, 2015), adaptations are often needed when utilizing this treatment approach for individuals with ASD (e.g., using visuals, incorporating the child's intense interests; Moree & Davis, 2010).

Family Support

Parents and caregivers can benefit greatly from educational and supportive interventions. They should be encouraged to participate in programs for their children with ASD to enhance consistency in intervention at home and at school and to facilitate the child's generalization of skills across settings. Family members can also be invited to join parent and family groups for information and support.

Many programs are parent-mediated, meaning that the parental caregiver takes on a primary intervention role. In a meta-analysis of 17 studies conducted since 2002 that included 916 children, it was found that such parent-mediated interventions can be helpful, especially in enhancing the relationship between parent and child, although these programs do not affect the child's core symptoms (Oono et al., 2013).

Social Skills Training

Interventions emphasizing social skills development have emerged as a major theme in the treatment literature in recent years, with a special focus on older children and adolescents. These interventions can be carried out through integrated peer groups, class-wide interventions, adult social groups, and videotapes to help clients observe themselves as they try to gain new interactional skills. Three meta-analyses have found that these interventions produce modest positive effects. One analysis of five randomized controlled studies involving clients 6 to 21 years old found that group interventions improved overall social competence and friendship quality but had no effect on the capacity for emotional regulation (Reichow et al., 2013). Another analysis of 19 group interventions found that overall positive effects for task-based measures of impact were modest (Gates et al., 2017). A review of 115 single-case studies of 343 participants also concluded that there were modest benefits to social skills intervention (Wang et al., 2013).

Medication

The core features of ASD unfortunately do not respond to medication. Drug intervention may, however, improve symptoms of aggression, severe irritability, interfering repetitive behaviors, ADHD, anxiety, depression, sleep dysregulation, and self-injury (Earle, 2016). The range of medications used for these purposes include risperidone, aripiprazole, and haloperidol (traditionally classified as antipsychotic medications); methylphenidate, atomoxetine, and alpha-agonists (ADHD medications); SSRI antidepressants; and mood stabilizers, including the anticonvulsants. All these medications, except risperidone and aripiprazole when used for severe irritability, are considered off-label because they have not been approved by the U.S. Food and Drug Administration (FDA) for treating ASD. A review by Earle (2016) suggests that risperidone and aripiprazole are effective for reducing severe irritability, but that antidepressants and stimulants should be used with caution because of their lower levels of effectiveness and high rates of adverse side effects. Children appear to be particularly sensitive to the adverse effects of the SSRI medications (including agitation).

Medications are used extensively in children with ASD. In a study of 7,901 children in five U.S. health systems, it was found that almost half (48.5%) received drugs during the year observed (Madden et al., 2017). The most frequently used medications were stimulants, alpha-antagonists, or atomoxetine (30.2%); antipsychotics (20.5%); and antidepressants (17.8%). Use of medication by children with ASD was 7.7% more prevalent than use by children with other DSM diagnoses, although evidence for the effectiveness of any medication was weak. In another study of a Medicaid program covering 41 states, it was found that 65% of children and adolescents with ASD received at least one psychotropic medication, most often from the antipsychotic class (Schubart et al., 2014). Rates of polypharmacy are also significant, a finding that supported in an insurance company study of 33,000 children with ASD (Jain et al., 2013). In that study, 64% of the children had filled at least one prescription, 35% had been prescribed two drugs, and 15% were prescribed drugs from three classes. The median length of polypharmacy was 346 days. Older children and those with comorbid diagnoses (e.g., seizures, ADHD, anxiety, depression, bipolar depression) received more medications.

There is little compelling support for claims of effectiveness for most medications for children with ASD. Hiorta, Veenstra-VanderWheele, Hollander, and Kishi (2014) conducted a systematic review and meta-analysis of seven randomized, placebo-controlled studies with 171 participants and concluded that there were no significant differences between those with ASD and control groups in regard to irritability and global impairment. Dove and colleagues (2012) conducted a systematic review of adolescents and young adults, including eight studies of 13- to 30-year-olds, and found that the strength of evidence for effectiveness was poor except regarding the use of risperidone for aggression.

Complementary and Alternative Treatments

Complementary and alternative therapies (CATs) for ASD include any that are believed by some professionals and family members to be helpful but have not been widely researched or endorsed by medical professionals. The National Center for Complementary and Alternative Medicine organizes these therapies into four domains: mind–body medicine, biologically based practices, manipulative and body-based practices, and energy medicine (Levy & Hyman, 2015). They tend to be used more often by parents with higher educational levels and lower functioning children.

One large-scale study involving 18 European countries examined the prevalence of CAT use among a sample of children with ASD who were younger than 7 years (Salomone et al., 2015). Of the 1,680 parent participants, 47% reported having tried any CAT approach in the past 6 months, with the most common approaches being diets and supplements (25%) and mind–body practices (24%). Other unconventional approaches were used by 25% of the families. Children with lower verbal ability and those using prescribed medications were more likely to be receiving diets or supplements. Concurrent use of high levels of conventional psychosocial intervention was significantly associated with use of mind–body practices. Higher parental educational level also increased the likelihood of use of diets, supplements, and mind–body practices. In another study 80.9% of parents (N = 194) from a local ASD organization and clinical practice in southeastern Virginia reported that they had tried some form of CAT for their child with autism (Hopf et al., 2016). The most frequently used therapies in this sample were multivitamins (58.6%), the gluten-free casein-free diet (54.8%), and methyl B-12 injections (54.1%). While research on CAT is varied and lacking for some approaches, a review of CATs for ASD found the most empirical support for melatonin, an RDA/RDI multivitamin/mineral supplement (when limited diet or poor appetite are concerns), and massage therapy (Lofthouse et al., 2012).

Based on the results of the intake assessment, Timothy was determined to be an appropriate candidate for ERP. ERP involves exposing oneself to the thoughts or situations that cause anxiety/obsessions and then not engaging in the compulsive behavior that is subsequently triggered. This is done gradually and collaboratively with an experienced ERP therapist, with the ultimate goal of learning how to manage the OCD more independently over time. The clinician discussed ERP treatment with Timothy, his parents, and Dr. Warren, and all parties agreed to a trial of ERP. It was agreed that Timothy would pause treatment with Dr. Warren for the time while ERP was initiated, and then resume with her as needed for support related to school and ASD. The clinician and Dr. Warren, with the family's agreement, established monthly consultations throughout the course of treatment; Dr. Warren provided consultation to the clinician in ASD, and the ERP clinician ensured that Dr. Warren was aware of the skills and strategies being utilized so that Dr. Warren could support and reinforce them as Timothy transitioned back to her care following ERP.

Timothy participated in a total of eight 45-minute ERP sessions over the course of 2.5 months. Throughout treatment, he was engaged, motivated, and actively participated in his treatment. His parents were also highly motivated, supportive, and consistently followed through with recommendations. In their first session together, the clinician provided Timothy and his parents with psychoeducation about OCD, explained ERP, and established an initial exposure hierarchy. Timothy and the clinician also discussed externalizing, or "bossing back" his OCD (March & Benton, 2007), which Timothy immediately took to. In subsequent sessions they engaged in in-session exposure and response prevention, and regular out-of-session exposure tasks were assigned each week. They also worked together to establish clear rules and expectations around handwashing and cleaning, which Timothy responded well to. The clinician, Timothy, and his parents identified rewards Timothy could earn, leveraging his special interests. For example, for successfully completing weekly exposure homework, Timothy was able to earn pieces for the model space station he and his father had been working on together. After completing in-session exposures, Timothy and the clinician would celebrate with 5 minutes for Timothy to share a favorite video clip with the clinician. They also agreed that when he reached the top of his hierarchy, Timothy would earn a trip to the nearest city's aerospace museum, a favorite destination of his. Finally, the family monitored Timothy's anxiety and compulsive behavior in an effort to identify triggers that exacerbated Timothy's symptoms and, with support from the clinician, identified ways to reduce triggers for Timothy or proactively offer additional support to him.

Exposures completed in treatment included engaging in the following without washing or cleaning afterward: contaminating a table with saliva and touching it (first touching with his leg, then the back of his hands, then his palms and fingers for longer and longer periods of time), licking his fingers, spitting into his hands, going to bed without showering first, wearing clothes that were folded on a table that may have been "contaminated" with saliva, going to the grocery store and not washing his hands afterward, and touching and using his "dirty" backpack (i.e., a backpack that had not been washed recently despite having been taken on public transit). Throughout, Timothy found that exposures were easier to engage in than he had initially suspected, and he and his parents reported a rapid reduction of symptoms. After successfully completing all items on his hierarchy, Timothy and the clinician discussed relapse prevention and worked to generalize the gains he had made to help him see how his new skills could apply in other situations (such as transitioning back to school). Treatment was mutually terminated given that Timothy had reached his goals and his parents were satisfied with the considerable reduction in OCD symptoms. Additionally, with the start of the school year approaching, it was important for Timothy to resume work with Dr. Warren to prepare for the transition. The family transitioned back to Dr. Warren's care and was invited to contact the ERP clinician if needed in the future.

The clinician provided Timothy's parents and Dr. Warren with the following suggestions. First, they were encouraged to provide Timothy with positive feedback and praise for efforts to cope with anxiety-provoking situations and efforts to resist engagement in compulsions. They were also cautioned to try not to accommodate anxiety or rituals. The clinician stated, "Sometimes it might seem easier to assist Timothy in rituals when he asks. However, doing so communicates that anxiety is dangerous or harmful and that the rituals are reasonable and should be completed. Accommodation also reinforces Timothy's beliefs that the feared situation is indeed dangerous or too difficult, that he is incapable of coping, and that he will not succeed in the situation. In fact, accommodating anxiety makes it more likely that he will be anxious the next time he faces a similar situation." The clinician also conveyed that it will be important that Timothy knows his parents understand that he is anxious or experiencing compulsive urges and that they are allies to help solve the problem. His parents were encouraged to coach Timothy to use proactive coping strategies to face feared situations rather than avoiding them, to help him to problem-solve strategies to manage his anxiety, and to encourage him to adopt an "exposure mindset" in which Timothy and his family are always on the lookout for opportunities to practice exposure and response prevention when obsessions or compulsions emerge.

Dr. Warren was also given tips and tools for supporting the family as part of their ongoing ASD work and in how to utilize principles of exposure, when appropriate, to support challenges that were more closely related to ASD. Given that Timothy had done so well with exposure, this proved a helpful tool for Dr. Warren. For example, when Timothy returned to school, he reported some distress related to students and teachers calling him "Tim" because he strongly preferred "Timothy" and had difficulty being flexible in this regard. In addition to problem-solving and role-playing how to advocate for use of his preferred name, Dr. Warren was able to help Timothy become more desensitized to occasionally being called Tim (in conjunction with anger management and social support work). Initially when called Tim, Timothy would become very upset and yell. With repeated, graduated exposure that started with seeing the name Tim in writing, then writing it himself, then saying it aloud, then hearing it spoken by the clinician, Timothy was able to respond more calmly, and instead of yelling would inform the speaker that he preferred to be called Timothy.

SUMMARY

ASD is a neurodevelopmental disorder, although its specific causes have not yet been identified. Rates of diagnosis have increased over time, although low-SES and ethnic minority children are at risk for not receiving a diagnosis in a timely manner. Early identification is important for intervention. Assessment is a complex process ideally conducted by multidisciplinary teams. Comorbidity is high for ASD, especially comorbid ADHD and anxiety. Behavioral interventions have the most research support for their effectiveness. A case involving a child comorbid for ASD and OCD illustrates the application of assessment and intervention strategies.

REFERENCES

American Psychiatric Association. (2022). *Diagnostic and statistical manual of mental disorders* (5th ed., Text Revision). Washington, DC: American Psychiatric Association.

Baghdadli, A., Assouline, B., Sonié, S., Pernon, E., Darrou, C., Michelon, C., Picot, M-C., Aussilloux, C., & Pry, R. (2012). Developmental trajectories of adaptive behaviors from early childhood to adolescence in a cohort of 152 children with autism spectrum disorders. *Journal of Autism and Developmental Disorders, 42*, 1314–1325. https://doi.org/10.1007/s10803-011-1357-z

Barger, B. D., Campbell, J. M., & McDonough, J. D. (2013). Prevalence and onset of regression within autism spectrum disorders: A meta-analytic review. *Journal of Autism & Developmental Disorders, 43*, 817–828.

Baxter, A. J., Brugha, T. S., Erskine, H. E., Scheurer, R. W., Vos, T., & Scott, J. G. (2015). The epidemiology and global burden of autism spectrum disorders. *Psychological Medicine, 45*(3), 601–613. https://doi.org/10.1017/S003329171400172X

Bekhet, A. K., Johnson, N. L., & Zauszniewski, J. A. (2012). Resilience in family members of persons with autism spectrum disorder: A review of the literature. *Issues in Mental Health Nursing, 33*(10), 650–656. doi:10.3109/01612840.2012.671441

Bishop-Fitzpatrick, L., Minshew, N. J., & Eack, S. M. (2013). A systematic review of psychosocial interventions for adults with autism spectrum disorders. *Journal of Autism & Developmental Disorders, 43*, 687–694.

Corcoran, J., Berry, A., & Hill, S. (2015). The lived experience of US parents of children with autism spectrum disorders. *Journal of Intellectual Disabilities, 19*(4), 356–366. doi:10.1177/1744629515577876

Daniels, A. M., & Mandell, D. S. (2014). Explaining differences in age at autism spectrum disorder diagnosis: A critical review. *Autism, 18*(5), 583–597. doi:10.1177/
1362361313480277

Deconinck, N., Soncarrieu, M., & Dan, B. (2013). Toward better recognition of early
predictors for autism spectrum disorders. *Pediatric Neurology, 49*(4), 225–231.
https://doi.org/10.1016/j.pediatrneurol.2013.05.012

DePape, A., & Lindsay, S. (2014). Parents' experiences of caring for a child with autism spectrum disorder. *Qualitative Health Research, 25*(4), 569–583. doi:10.1177/
1049732314552455

Dickinson, A., Jones, M., & Milne, E. (2016). Measuring neural excitation and inhibition in autism: Different approaches, different findings and different interpretations.
Brain Research, 1648, 277–289. doi:10.1016/j.brainres.2016.07.011

Dove, D., Warren, Z., McPheeters, M. L., Taylor, J. L., Sathe, N. A., & Veenstra-
VanderWeele, J. (2012). Medications for adolescents and young adults with autism
spectrum disorders: A systematic review. *Pediatrics, 130*(4), 717–726.

Earle, J. F. (2016). An introduction to the psychopharmacology of children and
adolescents with autism spectrum disorder. *Journal of Child and Adolescent
Psychiatric Nursing, 29*(2), 62–71. doi:10.1111/jcap.12144

Emerson, N. D., Morrell, H. E., & Neece, C. (2016). Predictors of age of diagnosis for
children with autism spectrum disorder: The role of a consistent source of medical
care, race, and condition severity. *Journal of Autism and Developmental Disorders,
46*(1), 127–138. doi:10.1007/s10803-015-2555-x

Farley, M. A., McMahon, W. M., Fombonne, E., Jenson, W. R., Miller, J., Gardner, M.,
Block, H., Pingree, C. B., Ritvo, E. R., Ritvo, R. A., & Coon, H. (2009). Twenty-year
outcome for individuals with autism and average or near-average cognitive abilities.
Autism Research, 2(2), 109–118.

Gates, J. A., Kang, E., & Lerner, M. D. (2017). Efficacy of group social skills interventions
for youth with autism spectrum disorder: A systematic review and meta-analysis.
Clinical Psychology Review, 52, 164–181. doi:10.1016/j.cpr.2017.01.006

Goodman, W. K., Price, L. H., Rasmussen, S. A., Riddle, M. A., & Rapoport, J. L.
(1991). *Children's Yale- Brown obsessive compulsive scale (CY-BOCS)*. New Haven:
Department of Psychiatry, Yale University School of Medicine.

Hancock, G. I., Stokes, M. A., & Mesibov, G. B. (2017). Socio-sexual functioning in autism spectrum disorder: A systematic review and meta-analyses of existing literature. *Autism Research, 10*(11), 1823–1833. doi:10.1002/aur.1831

Hathorn, C., Alateeqi, N., Graham, C., & O'Hare, A. (2014). Impact of adherence to
best practice guidelines on the diagnostic and assessment services for autism spectrum disorder. *Journal of Autism and Developmental Disorders, 44*(8), 1859–1866.
doi:10.1007/s10803-014-2057-2

Hidalgo, N. J., Mcintyre, L. L., & McWhirter, E. H. (2015). Sociodemographic
differences in parental satisfaction with an autism spectrum disorder diagnosis.
Journal of Intellectual and Developmental Disability, 40(2), 147–155. doi:10.3109/
13668250.2014.994171

Hirota, T., Veenstra-Vanderweele, J., Hollander, E., & Kishi, T. (2014). Antiepileptic
medications in autism spectrum disorder: A systematic review and meta-analysis.
Journal of Autism and Developmental Disorders, 44(4), 948–957. doi:10.1007/
s10803-013-1952-2

Hopf, K. P., Madren, E., & Santianni, K. A. (2016). Use and perceived effectiveness of complementary and alternative medicine to treat and manage the symptoms of autism in children: A survey of parents in a community population. *Journal of Alternative and Complementary Medicine, 22*(1), 25–32. https://doi.org/10.1089/acm.2015.0163

Hutsler, J., & Zhang, H. (2010). Increased dendritic spine densities on cortical projection neurons in autism spectrum disorders. *Brain Research, 1309*(1), 83–94.

Ji, X., Kember, R., Brown, C., & Bucan, M. (2016). Increased burden of deleterious variants in essential genes in autism spectrum disorder. *Proceedings of the National Academy of Sciences of the United States of America, 113*(52), 15054–-15059. https://doi.org/10.1073/pnas.1613195113

Kreslins, A., Robertson, A. E., & Melville, C. (2015). The effectiveness of psychosocial interventions for anxiety in children and adolescents with autism spectrum disorder: A systematic review and meta-analysis. *Child and Adolescent Psychiatry and Mental Health, 9*, 22. https://doi.org/10.1186/s13034-015-0054-7

Lai, M. C., Kassee, C., Besney, R., Bonato, S., Hull, L., Mandy, W., Szatmari, P., & Ameis, S. H. (2019). Prevalence of co-occurring mental health diagnoses in the autism population: A systematic review and meta-analysis. *Lancet Psychiatry, 6*(10), 819–829. https://doi.org/10.1016/S2215-0366(19)30289-5

Levy, S., & Hyman, S. (2014). Complementary and alternative medicine treatments for children with autism spectrum disorders. *Child and Adolescent Psychiatry Clinics, 24*(1), 117–143.

Linstead, E., Dixon, D. R., Hong, E., Burns, C. O., French, R., Novack, M. N., & Granpeesheh, D. (2017). An evaluation of the effects of intensity and duration on outcomes across treatment domains for children with autism spectrum disorder. *Translational Psychiatry, 7*(9), e1234. doi:10.1038/tp.2017.207. PMID: 28925999; PMCID: PMC5639250.

Lofthouse, N., Hendren, R., Hurt, E., Arnold, L. E., & Butter, E. (2012). A review of complementary and alternative treatments for autism spectrum disorders. *Autism Research and Treatment, 2012*, 870391. https://doi.org/10.1155/2012/870391

Loomes, R., Hull, L., & Mandy, W. P. (2017). What is the male-to-female ratio in autism spectrum disorder? A systematic review and meta-analysis. *Journal of the American Academy of Child & Adolescent Psychiatry, 56*(6), 466–474. doi:10.1016/j.jaac.2017.03.013

Lord, C., Rutter, M., DiLavore, P. C., Risi, S., Gotham, K., & Bishop, S. (2012). *Autism diagnostic observation schedule* (2nd ed.). Western Psychological Services.

Madden, J. M., Lakoma, M. D., Lynch, F. L., Rusinak, D., Owen-Smith, A. A., Coleman, K. J., . . . Croen, L. A. (2017). Psychotropic medication use among insured children with autism spectrum disorder. *Journal of Autism and Developmental Disorders, 47*, 144–154.

Maenner, M. J., Shaw, K. A., Bakian, A. V., Bilder, D. A., Durkin, M. S., Esler, A., Furnier, S. M., Hallas, L., Hall-Lande, J., Hudson, A., Hughes, M. M., Patrick, M., Pierce, K., Poynter, J. N., Salinas, A., Shenouda, J., Vehorn, A., Warren, Z, Constantino, J. N., . . . Cogswell, M. E. (2021). Prevalence and characteristics of autism spectrum disorder among children aged 8 years: Autism and Developmental Disabilities Monitoring Network, 11 Sites, United States, 2018. *MMWR Surveillance Summaries, 70*(SS-11), 1–16. doi:http://dx.doi.org/10.15585/mmwr.ss7011a1

Maïano, C., Normand, C. L., Salvas, M., Moullec, G., & Aimé, A. (2015). Prevalence of school bullying among youth with autism spectrum disorders: A systematic review and meta-analysis. *Autism Research*, *9*(6), 601–615. doi:10.1002/aur.1568

March, J. S., & Benton, C. M. (2007). *Talking back to OCD: The program that helps kids and teens say "no way"—and parents say "way to go."* New York: Guilford Press.

Matheis, M., Matson, J. L., Burns, C. O., Jiang, X., Peters, W. J., Moore, M., . . . Estabillo, J. (2017). Factors related to parental age of first concern in toddlers with autism spectrum disorder. *Developmental Neurorehabilitation*, *20*(4), 228–235. doi:10.1080/17518423.2016.1211186

Moree, B. N., & Davis, T. E. (2010). Cognitive-behavioral therapy for anxiety in children diagnosed with autism spectrum disorders: Modification trends. *Research in Autism Spectrum Disorders*, *4*(3), 346–354. https://doi.org/10.1016/j.rasd.2009.10.015.

National Autism Center. (2015). *Findings and conclusions: National Standards Project, Phase 2*. National Autism Center.

Ng, M., de Montigny, J., Ofner, M., & Docé, M. (2017). Environmental factors associated with autism spectrum disorder: A scoping review for the years 2003-2013. *Health Promotion of Chronic Diseases Prevention Canada*, *37*(1), 1–23. https://doi.org/10.24095/hpcdp.37.1.01

Oono, I. P., Honey, E. J., & McConachie, H. (2013). Parent-mediated early intervention for young children with autism spectrum disorders (ASD). *Cochrane Database of Systematic Reviews*, *4*, CD009774. https://doi.org/10.1002/14651858.CD009774.pub2

Ramsey, E., Kelly-Vance, L., Allen, J., Rosol, O., & Yoerger, M. (2016). Autism spectrum disorder prevalence rates in the United States: Methodologies, challenges, and implications for individual states. *Journal of Developmental and Physical Disabilities*, *28*(1), 803–820.

Reichow, B. (2012). Overview of meta-analyses on early intensive behavioral intervention for young children with autism spectrum disorders. *Journal of Autism & Developmental Disorders*, *42*, 512–520.

Reichow, B., Servili, C., Yasamy, M. T., Barbui, C., & Saxena, S. (2013). Non-specialist psychosocial interventions for children and adolescents with intellectual disability or low-functioning autism spectrum disorders: A systematic review. *PLoS Medicine*, *10*(12), 1–27.Richards, C., Davies, L., & Oliver, C. (2017). Predictors of self-injurious behavior and self-restraint in autism spectrum disorder: Towards a hypothesis of impaired behavioral control. *Journal of Autism and Developmental Disorders*, *47*, 701–713. https://doi.org/10.1007/s10803-016-3000-5

Risch, N., Hoffman, T. J., Anderson, M., Croen, L. A., Grether, J. K., & Windham, G. C. (2014). Familial recurrence of autism spectrum disorder: Evaluating genetic and environmental contributions. *American Journal of Psychiatry*, *171*(11), 1206–1213.

Rivard, M., Terroux, A., Mercier, C., & Parent-Boursier, C. (2015). Indicators of intellectual disabilities in young children with autism spectrum disorders. *Journal of Autism and Developmental Disorders*, *45*, 127–137. https://doi.org/10.1007/s10803-014-2198-3

Rosenberg, R. E., Landa, R., Law, J. K., Stuart, E. A., & Law, P. A. (2011). Factors affecting age at initial autism spectrum disorder diagnosis in a national survey. *Autism Research and Treatment*, *2011*, 874619. https://doi.org/10.1155/2011/874619

Rossignol, D., Genuis, S. & Frye, R. (2014). Environmental toxicants and autism spectrum disorders: A systematic review. *Translational Psychiatry, 4,* e360. https://doi.org/10.1038/tp.2014.4

Salomone, E., Charman, T., McConachie, H., & Warreyn, P. (2015). Prevalence and correlates of use of complementary and alternative medicine in children with autism spectrum disorder in Europe. *European Journal of Pediatrics, 174*(10), 1277–1285. doi:10.1007/s00431-015-2531-7

Schopler, E., Van Bourgondien, M. E., Wellman, G. J., & Love, S. R. (2010). *Childhood autism rating scale* (2nd ed.). Western Psychological Services.

Schreibman, L., Dawson, G., Stahmer, A. C., Landa, R., Rogers, S. J., McGee, G. G., Kasari, C., Ingersoll, B., Kaiser, A. P., Bruinsma, Y., McNerney, E., Wetherby, A., & Halladay, A. (2015). Naturalistic developmental behavioral interventions: Empirically validated treatments for autism spectrum disorder. *Journal of Autism and Developmental Disorders, 45*(8):2411–2428. doi:10.1007/s10803-015-2407-8. PMID: 25737021; PMCID: PMC4513196.

Schubart, J. R., Camacho, F., & Leslie, D. (2014). Psychotropic medication trends among children and adolescents with autism spectrum disorder in the Medicaid program. *Autism: The International Journal of Research and Practice, 18*(6), 631–637. https://doi.org/10.1177/1362361313497537

Smith, T., & Iadarola, S. (2015). Evidence base update for autism spectrum disorder. *Journal of Clinical Child and Adolescent Psychology, 44*(6), 897–922. https://doi.org/10.1080/15374416.2015.1077448

Steinbrenner, J. R., Hume, K., Odom, S. L., Morin, K. L., Nowell, S. W., Tomaszewski, B., Szendrey, S., McIntyre, N. S., Yücesoy-Özkan, S., & Savage, M. N. (2020). *Evidence-based practices for children, youth, and young adults with autism.* The University of North Carolina at Chapel Hill, Frank Porter Graham Child Development Institute, National Clearinghouse on Autism Evidence and Practice Review Team.

Sukhodolsky, D. G., Bloch, M. H., Panza, K. E., & Reichow, B. (2013). Cognitive-behavioral therapy for anxiety in children with high-functioning autism: A meta-analysis. *Pediatrics, 132*(5), e1341–e1350. https://doi.org/10.1542/peds.2013-1193

Tick, B., Bolton, P., Happé, F., Rutter, M., & Rijsdijk, F. (2016). Heritability of autism spectrum disorders: A meta-analysis of twin studies. *Journal of Child Psychology and Psychiatry, 57*(5), 585–595.

Ung, D., Selles, R., Small, B., & Storch, E. (2015). A systematic review and meta-analysis of cognitive-behavioral therapy for anxiety in youth with high-functioning autism spectrum disorders. *Child Psychiatry & Human Development, 46,* 533–547.

van Schallkwyk, G., Klingensmith, K., & Volkmar, F. (2015). Gender identity and autism spectrum disorders. *Yale Journal of Biology and Medicine, 88*(1), 81–83.

Vierck, E., & Silverman, J. M. (2015). Brief report: Phenotypic differences and their relationship to paternal age and gender in autism spectrum disorder. *Journal of Autism and Developmental Disorders, 45, 1915–1924* https://doi.org/10.1007/s10803-014-2346-9

Wang, S., Parrila, R., & Cui, Y. (2013). Meta-analysis of social skills interventions of single-case research for individuals with autism spectrum disorders: Results from three-level HLM. *Journal of Autism and Developmental Disorders, 43*(7), 1701–1716. doi:10.1007/s10803-012-1726-2

Externalizing Problems

7

Oppositional Defiant Disorder and Conduct Disorder

Samuel Flores, a 12-year-old Latino male, presented to treatment at an outpatient child and adolescent mental health clinic affiliated with an urban hospital, with his mother, Ms. Karla Flores. At intake, Ms. Flores described the presenting problems that had led to referral as being largely related to disciplinary issues at school and a concern that Samuel would be expelled from school because of his behavior. Samuel had been suspended multiple times during the current school year and was at risk of expulsion for what was described as "acting up," frequent fights or threats of aggression toward peers, and defiance toward teachers. Ms. Flores also reported feeling as though she had "no control" over Samuel's behavior at home. She reported that he would come and go from the home as he pleased and refuse to complete schoolwork or help her with tasks around the house when asked.

Samuel was an only child and the first generation in his family born in the United States. His mother had emigrated from Honduras and was primarily Spanish speaking. While Samuel spoke fluent English, all sessions with Ms. Flores required the presence of an interpreter because the clinician only spoke English. Samuel's father was not involved in his life and had moved out of state. As best Ms. Flores knew, he was not regularly working, and during the course of their relationship had not been regularly employed, though he had occasionally worked odd jobs in the construction field. His parents had never been married, and his father had ceased contact with Ms. Flores and Samuel when Samuel was a toddler. Samuel and his mother lived in a predominantly Latino neighborhood of the city and had a close network of extended family nearby who provided support. Ms. Flores worked in corner store owned by a relative and sometimes needed to work evenings and weekends, leaving Samuel unsupervised. The neighborhood the family resided in was characterized by high poverty and gang activity. At intake, Samuel denied involvement in a gang, but his mother expressed concern that he was at risk for going down that path. It became clear to the clinician early on that the culture in the family was highly patriarchal and that Samuel's mother had trouble asserting her authority with Samuel because men in the Flores family, even young men, tended to have a high level of autonomy, and at times authority over women.

Child and Adolescent Mental Health in Social Work. Jacqueline Corcoran and Courtney Benjamin Wolk, Oxford University Press.
© Oxford University Press 2023. DOI: 10.1093/oso/9780197653562.003.0007

OVERVIEW

In the fifth edition of the *Diagnostic and Statistical Manual of Mental Disorders* (DSM-5), oppositional defiant disorder (ODD) and conduct disorder (CD) are placed within a chapter organized around disruptive, impulse-control, and conduct disorders. ODD and CD are discussed together in this chapter because they both feature anger, defiance, rebellion, lying, and school problems (Loeber et al., 2000). ODD is characterized by three dimensions: angry/irritable mood, argumentative/defiant behavior, and vindictiveness. The major distinction between the two disorders is that youths with CD also violate societal norms through aggression, theft or deceit, or destruction of property (American Psychiatric Association [APA], 2022). When a client meets the criteria for both disorders, the DSM advises that, based on the guideline of parsimony, only CD will be diagnosed.

Prevalence

Disruptive behavior disorders are highly prevalent. Studies indicate that among children aged 3 to 17 years, 7.4% had a current behavioral/conduct problem (Ghandour et al., 2019). This rate increased to 10.8% for those who lived under the federal poverty line. ODD is more common than CD, with a lifetime prevalence of 10.2% of the U.S. population (Nock et al., 2006). For preschoolers, estimates for ODD rates range between 4% and 16.8%, and for CD they are between 0% and 4.6% (Egger & Angold, 2006). Males have a higher rate of ODD than do females (APA, 2022; Demmer et al., 2017).

According to the 2016 National Survey on Children's Health, the rates for past-year behavioral/conduct diagnosis were 7.6% in white, 5.5% in Latino, and 10.7% in Black youths (Ghandour et al., 2019). When controlling for socioeconomic status (SES) and neighborhood influences, there is little difference in the prevalence of most conduct problems among Black, Latino, and white youths.

Approximately 40% of youths with ODD go on to develop CD (Egger & Angold, 2006). Antisocial personality disorder in adulthood occurs in 25% of males who had conduct problems as youths (Lemery & Doelger, 2005), whereas borderline personality disorder may be a risk for girls with antisocial behavior (Ehrensaft, 2005). In a systematic review of longitudinal studies that followed youths over at least a 2-year period and assessed outcomes, CD was associated with academic underachievement, mental health, substance use disorders, and illicit drug use (Erskine et al., 2016).

RISK AND PROTECTIVE FACTORS

The current understanding of ODD and CD indicates they arise from an interaction of genetic risk and environmental adversity (Hicks et al., 2009). The biological, psychological, and social risk and protective influences—and how they interact together—are discussed here. Outcomes may partially result from the number of risk influences. In one study, only 2% of youths who had no childhood risk influences showed persistent delinquency in adolescence, compared with 71% of youths who had risk influences in five different areas of life (Frick, 2006).

Biological

About 50% of the variance in the inheritance of CD may be accounted for by genetics (Gelhorn et al., 2006). Children with a biological predisposition toward ODD or CD may demonstrate a difficult temperament as newborns (defined as negative emotionality, intense and reactive responses to stress and frustration, and inflexibility), which predicts later conduct problems (Nigg & Huang-Pollock, 2003). In contrast, an inhibited or approach–withdrawal temperament is protective against antisocial behaviors (Burke et al., 2002; Lahey & Waldman, 2003).

Low IQ, especially verbal deficits, may give rise to the development of antisocial behaviors (Anderson et al., 2016; Hill, 2002; Nigg & Huang-Pollack, 2003; Wachs, 2000). Children who are unable to identify emotions in themselves and others and cannot reason well verbally may react aggressively rather than by talking about their feelings, seeking comfort, or problem-solving.

Male gender is a risk influence for the development of conduct problems. Females may demonstrate more empathy and distress over breaking rules and hurting others at a younger age than boys do (Alvarez & Ollendick, 2003). Girls' communication and social skills are also more developed at a younger age. Other reasons for differences in rates of conduct problems may include gender-specific hormone levels, especially testosterone.

A large-scale British study of 16,000 children showed that among a variety of pregnancy and birth factors examined, only prenatal maternal smoking was highly associated with conduct problems in youths (Murray et al., 2010). Lead exposure further elevates risk for conduct problems (Marcus et al., 2010).

Psychological

More severe and chronic conduct problems and poorer treatment outcomes are associated with several personality traits, such as lack of guilt, empathy, and emotional expression; low harm avoidance; and a preference for novel, exciting, and dangerous activities. These traits are found in about one-third of treatment-referred children with early-onset conduct problems (Frick, 2006). However, the dominant personality profile for CD features impulsivity, low verbal IQ, and a lack of emotional regulation, coupled with higher rates of family problems. Problems with emotional regulation result in impulsive and reactively aggressive behaviors.

A hallmark of ODD/CD is an attributional bias toward seeing the actions of others as hostile and responding in a way that seems justified but is overly reactive (Dodge, 2006). However, youths living in impoverished environments may have exposure to adults who are involved in crime, community violence, gang involvement, availability of drugs, weapon carrying, and aggression. Exposure to this kind of threat may condition youths to view others as hostile and dangerous and may explain why such youths might be at higher risk for the development of a symptom profile that is then diagnosed as CD (Fadus et al., 2020).

Social

Children with a greater genetic predisposition to conduct problems are, unfortunately, more likely to encounter environments that foster antisocial behavior (Loeber et al., 2002). Children predisposed to CD are likely to be raised by ineffective (and sometimes abusive) parents with histories of antisocial behavior, substance use problems, and other psychopathology. Also, the likelihood of persons with particular characteristics selectively partnering and producing children is substantial for antisocial behavior (Ehrensaft, 2005).

Parental psychopathology, particularly bipolar disorder, are risk influences (Ayano et al., 2021). Further, parental rejection of the child, lack of supervision, and lack of involvement in the child's activities increase risk for disruptive disorders. Girls with conduct problems are more likely to come from homes characterized by intense emotional conflict and unstable interpersonal relationships (Ehrensaft, 2005). Conversely, family stability, stable parental relationships, and parental social support are protective. Moreover, child physical abuse and sexual abuse, which often occur in the context of the family, are associated with conduct problems but only in the presence of genetic risk (Jaffee et al., 2005). Living in a married two-parent home is protective for the diagnosis of conduct/behavioral diagnosis (rate of diagnosis is 5.1%) compared with having two parents who are unmarried (10.2%) or living in a single-parent household (12%).

Rates of ODD/CD are significantly higher among children in poverty and on Medicaid (Visser et al., 2016). Children who live in poor and disadvantaged communities experience a variety of risks. These include poverty, unemployment, community disorganization, segregation, overcrowding, poor and unresponsive schools, and lack of access to services—for example, quality early childcare, afterschool programs, and physical and mental health services (Hankin et al., 2005; Hill, 2002; Loeber et al., 2000).

A hallmark of ODD/CD is an attributional bias toward seeing the actions of others as hostile and responding in a way that seems justified. However, youths living in impoverished environments may be exposed to adults involved in crime, community violence, gang involvement, availability of drugs, weapon carrying, and aggression (Fadus et al., 2020). Exposure to this kind of threat may condition youths to view others as hostile and dangerous and may explain why such youths might be at higher risk for the development of a symptom profile that is then diagnosed as CD.

Peer relationships can act as either a risk or a protective mechanism for the onset of and recovery from conduct problems. Deviant peer relationships are a major pathway for adolescent-onset CD (Frick, 2006). Youths with conduct problems display several distortions in the way they perceive and code their social experiences (Dodge, 2003; Kazdin, 2001). These distortions include an inability to produce a variety of strategies to manage interpersonal problems, difficulty figuring out ways to achieve a particular desired outcome, problems identifying the consequences of a particular action and its effects on others, a tendency to attribute hostile motivations to the actions of others, and failure to understand how others feel. The combination of perceived threat and limited options for managing social situations makes antisocial youths more likely to respond with aggression than with prosocial problem-solving strategies. In general, children diagnosed with conduct problems often experience rejection by peers for their aggression and lack of social skills (Miller-Johnson et al., 2002). As a result, delinquent youths often consort together, further reinforcing their conduct problems.

Many of the risks and protective mechanisms associated with recovering from ODD/CD are the same as those associated with the onset of these disorders. In addition, compared with the adolescent onset of ODD/CD, childhood onset results in more severe and chronic problems that may persist into adulthood (Moffit et al., 2002).

ASSESSMENT

Social workers should always engage in a multifaceted approach to ODD and CD, using multiple informants—the child, parents, and school personnel—to obtain reports and using multiple methods—interview, rating scales, and observations of the child—to formulate their assessments (Alvarez & Ollendick, 2003; Fonagy & Kurtz, 2002; McMahon & Frick, 2005). Recognize that transient oppositional behaviors are common. Children tend to downplay their own symptoms (Loeber et al., 2002). Symptom reports from parents and teachers are preferable, although even these sources have their biases. While teachers are more accurate than mothers at identifying a child's attention-deficit/hyperactivity disorder (ADHD) symptoms, parents are more aware of their children's oppositional behavior. For freely available assessment measures, see Table 7.1.

For CD, the DSM-5 includes subtypes based on the age of onset—childhood or adolescent, with age 10 as the marker—and the number and intensity of symptoms, defined as mild, moderate, and severe, which, to some extent, is subjective. CD may go unrecognized in females because of relational or indirect aggressiveness—for example, exclusion of others; threats of withdrawal from relationships; rumor spreading; and efforts to alienate, ostracize, or defame others (Ledingham, 1999; Loeber et al., 2000). Some experts have suggested that the diagnostic criteria for CD should be modified for females to include these variables (Loeber et al., 2000; Ohan & Johnston, 2005), although others have argued there are no gender differences in symptom patterns (Moffit et al., 2001).

Table 7.1 MEASURES OF DISRUPTIVE BEHAVIOR

Psychometric Support	Measure Name	No. of Items	Completed by[a]	Ages[c]	Link to Measure
Excellent	IOWA Conners (Loney & Milich, 1982)	10	P, T	School-aged	https://osf.io/wa5hb/
Excellent	Swanson, Nolan, and Pelham Rating Scale (SNAP-IV; Swanson et al., 2001)	18 or 26 versions	P, T	5–17	http://www.shared-care.ca/toolkits-adhd
Good	Inventory Callous and Unemotional Traits (ICU; Essau et al., 2006)[*]	12 or 24	Y, P, T	3–18	http://labs.uno.edu/developmental-psychopathology/ICU.html
Good	Behavior Problems Inventory—Short Form (BPI-S; Rojahn et al., 2012a, 2012b)[*]	30	P	2+	http://bpi.haoliang.me/pdf/BPI-S/BPI-S%20English.pdf
Good	Disruptive Behavior Disorders Rating Scale (DBDRS; Pelham et al., 1992)[*]	45	P, T	3–13	https://ccf.fiu.edu/about/resources/index.html
Good	Children's Scale of Hostility and Aggression: Reactive/Proactive (C-SHARP; Farmer & Aman, 2009, 2010)[*]	48	P	3–21	https://psychmed.osu.edu/index.php/instrument-resources/c-sharp/
Adequate	Conduct Disorder Rating Scale (CDRS; Waschbusch & Elgar 2007; Fabiana et al., 2006)	12 or 15	P, T	5–12	http://www.midss.org/content/conduct-disorder-rating-scale-teachers-cdrs-t http://www.midss.org/content/conduct-disorder-rating-scale-parents-cdrs-p
Adequate	Modified Overt Aggression Scale (MOAS; Sorgi et al., 1991)	16	P, T	Children and adolescents[d]	https://www.thereachinstitute.org/trainees/ppp-trainees/rating-scales-1
Adequate	Outburst Monitoring Scale (OMS; Kronenberger et al., 2007)	20	P	12–17	http://www.cpack.org/screening-tools-for-kids/
Adequate	Delinquent Activities Scale (DAS; Reavy et al., 2012)	37	Y	Adolescents[d]	http://www.midss.org/sites/default/files/mbq.doc

[a] Completed by: Y = youth, P = parent/caregiver, C = clinician, T = teacher.

[b] Intended clinical use: S = screening, D = diagnostic aid or treatment planning, O = outcome monitoring.

[c] Exact age range for specific forms (e.g., self-report, parent report) may vary.

[d] Exact age range not specified.

* Available in multiple languages.

NOTE: Table adapted from Becker-Haimes, E. M., Tabachnick, A. R., Last, B. S., Stewart, R. E., Hasan-Granier, A., & Beidas, R. S. (2020). Evidence base update for brief, free, and accessible youth mental health measures. *Journal of Clinical Child & Adolescent Psychology, 49*(1), 1–17, reprinted by permission of the publisher (Taylor & Francis Ltd, http://www.tandfonline.com).

References for measures in Table 7.1:

Essau, C. A., Sasagawa, S., & Frick, P. J. (2006). Callous-unemotional traits in a community sample of adolescents. *Assessment, 13*(4), 454–469.

Fabiano, G. A., Pelham Jr, W. E., Waschbusch, D. A., Gnagy, E. M., Lahey, B. B., Chronis, A. M., . . . Burrows-MacLean, L. (2006). A practical measure of impairment: Psychometric properties of the impairment rating scale in samples of children with attention deficit hyperactivity disorder and two school-based samples. *Journal of Clinical Child and Adolescent Psychology, 35*(3), 369–385.

Farmer, C. A., & Aman, M. G. (2010). Psychometric properties of the children's scale of hostility and aggression: Reactive/proactive (C-SHARP). *Research in Developmental Disabilities, 31*(1), 270–280.

Kronenberger, W. G., Giauque, A. L., & Dunn, D. W. (2007). Development and validation of the outburst monitoring scale for children and adolescents. *Journal of Child and Adolescent Psychopharmacology, 17*(4), 511–526.

Milich, R., Loney, J., & Landau, S. (1982). Independent dimensions of hyperactivity and aggression: A validation with playroom observation data. *Journal of Abnormal Psychology, 91*(3), 183–198. https://doi.org/10.1037/0021-843X.91.3.183

Pelham Jr, W. E., Gnagy, E. M., Greenslade, K. E., & Milich, R. (1992). Teacher ratings of DSM-III-R symptoms for the disruptive behavior disorders. *Journal of the American Academy of Child & Adolescent Psychiatry, 31*(2), 210–218.

(continued)

Table 7.1 Continued

Reavy, R., Stein, L. A., Paiva, A., Quina, K., & Rossi, J. S. (2012). Validation of the delinquent activities scale for incarcerated adolescents. *Addictive Behaviors, 37*(7), 875–879.

Rojahn, J., Rowe, E. W., Sharber, A. C., Hastings, R., Matson, J. L., Didden, R., . . . Dumont, E. L. M. (2012). The Behavior Problems Inventory-Short Form for individuals with intellectual disabilities: Part I: development and provisional clinical reference data. *Journal of Intellectual Disability Research, 56*(5), 527–545.

Rojahn, J., Rowe, E. W., Sharber, A. C., Hastings, R., Matson, J. L., Didden, R., . . . Dumont, E. L. M. (2012). The Behavior Problems Inventory-Short Form for individuals with intellectual disabilities: Part II: reliability and validity. *Journal of Intellectual Disability Research, 56*(5), 546–565.

Sorgi, P., Ratey, J., Knoedler, D. W., Markert, R. J., & Reichman, M. (1991). Rating aggression in the clinical setting. A retrospective adaptation of the Overt Aggression Scale: preliminary results. *Journal of Neuropsychiatry and Clinical Neurosciences, 3*(2), S52–S56.

Swanson, J. M., Kraemer, H. C., Hinshaw, S. P., Arnold, L. E., Conners, C. K., Abikoff, H. B., . . . Hechtman, L. (2001). Clinical relevance of the primary findings of the MTA: success rates based on severity of ADHD and ODD symptoms at the end of treatment. *Journal of the American Academy of Child & Adolescent Psychiatry, 40*(2), 168–179.

Waschbusch, D. A., & Elgar, F. J. (2007). Development and validation of the conduct disorder rating scale. *Assessment, 14*(1), 65–74.

ODD is associated with a wide variety of mental disorders manifesting in young adulthood (Copeland et al., 2009). CD increases the risk of many other mental, emotional, and behavioral disorders, such as substance use and mood disorders (Nock et al., 2006). Therefore, it is important to assess for other disorders not only because there is comorbidity but also because other disorders may account for symptom presentation.

ADHD is common in children with ODD and CD. Careful attention needs to be paid to considering a diagnosis of ADHD in minority children. Children from ethnic minority backgrounds are less likely to receive an ADHD diagnosis than are white children, even when the diagnosis is warranted, and are more likely to receive a CD diagnosis (Morgan et al., 2013). This may be because ADHD is seen as more treatable than CD, and children can receive support services.

Providers also must be aware of unconscious biases they may carry. For example, Black people in the United States are more likely to be perceived as "dangerous" (Ballentein, 2019). The DSM cautions that practitioners must be aware that when disruptive behavior disorders are near normative, such as in high crime areas, that the diagnostic label may be potentially misapplied. Context needs to be a consideration when deciding upon a diagnosis (APA, 2022). This reservation may be particularly applicable to ethnic minority youths growing up in high-crime areas. If CD is misdiagnosed, detection of a more accurate diagnosis and treatment may be missed, which may perpetuate the criminalization of Black men (Atkins-Loria et al., 2015; Ballentein, 2019).

For severe ODD and CD where there is extreme overreactivity, aggression, and temper tantrums (at least three of the latter per week), disruptive mood dysregulation disorder (DMDD) is sometimes diagnosed (Center for Behavioral Health Statistics and Quality, 2016). DMDD, a new diagnosis in DSM-5, was developed to address the overdiagnosis of bipolar disorder (BD) in youths when outbursts are assumed to stem from mood issues. Both pediatric BD and DMDD are discussed in Chapter 3. Whereas CD has criminal connotations, DMDD and BD are seen as disorders of mood that can be treated with medication.

Clinical interviews were conducted with Samuel and his mother separately to understand the nature and severity of his symptoms, the family history, and psychosocial risk and protective factors. Samuel's mother reported that he often loses his temper and seems angry, argues frequently with her as well as his teachers, and does not take responsibility for his mistakes. This behavior occurs most days, and this had been the case for at least a year. Ms. Flores reported, "He has been like this for a while, I guess since first or second grade, but it has gotten so much worse over the past year. I don't know why he is causing so much trouble." Ms. Flores stated that it can sometimes be hard to predict what will anger Samuel, but that being asked to do something he doesn't want to do by an adult is often a trigger. Samuel generally refuses to do what he is asked or argues and tries to get out of responsibilities. For example, if told he is not allowed to leave the house, he might yell at his mother and call her names, tell her to "shut up," slam doors, kick the furniture (never to the point of destroying property, per his mother), or simply outright defy her and leave the house anyway. On average, this type of behavior occurs one to two times per week. The exception is when given commands by older male relatives (uncles, cousins); he generally will comply with requests from these individuals. Ms. Flores reported that Samuel has a small group of friends (who also tend to get into trouble and whom she described as "bad influences"), and that other peers seem to either find him annoying or avoid him because he is "one of the bad kids." He often stays out late without permission or sneaks out at night to hang out with friends. Ms. Flores was unclear as to what Samuel does when he sneaks out, but she suspected he may be experimenting with marijuana and alcohol. Samuel has a history of instigating physical fights with peers when he feels they are disrespecting him, and this had led to three suspensions from school in the past 6 months. Ms. Flores did not report any symptoms consistent with ADHD, depression, or mood dysregulation. She reported that Samuel had always done well academically until a year or two ago, when he mostly stopped completing homework and studying. While Samuel had witnessed some neighborhood violence (e.g., witnessing serious fights, hearing gun shots, and seeing blood on the street after—but not actually witnessing the shooting), Ms. Flores did not report any symptoms consistent with post-traumatic stress disorder (PTSD). Ms. Flores reported that the family history was largely unremarkable, with the exception of Samuel's father. While he had never been diagnosed with a mental health disorder to Ms. Flores's knowledge, he had a history of problem drinking and marijuana use, as well as criminal justice involvement related to drugs and theft.

The clinician met individually with Samuel, who largely denied the presence of any symptoms or challenges, stating that his mother was "overreacting" and, "We just have to come here so that school doesn't kick me out." When asked about specific behaviors of concern, including fighting, leaving the house without permission, and refusing to do homework and chores, Samuel said that his teacher "has it in for me and just makes stuff up" and that he doesn't like when adults tell him what to do because "I can make my own decisions." He said he and his friends "just hang out" and denied any substance use or illegal activity.

Particularly given the discrepancies in Samuel and his mother's reports, it was important for the clinician to obtain collateral information. The clinician sent several rating forms home with Ms. Flores for her to complete herself and for her to have a teacher fill out. Given Samuel's reported risk for expulsion, the clinician also arranged a phone call with the school counselor, with Ms. Flores's permission, who corroborated Ms. Flores's account. The school counselor stated that the school was willing to work with the family to maintain Samuel in his current school if he was receiving therapy and if his challenging behaviors did not escalate considerably. The school counselor agreed to apprise the clinician of any changes in behavior or if Samuel's ability to remain in his school came to be in jeopardy. When asked about his goals and plans for the future, Samuel said he would probably just work at his family's store one day.

The clinician determined that a diagnosis of ODD was most appropriate given the constellation of symptoms; Samuel met DSM-5 criteria for ODD because he exhibited the following five symptoms (four or more required for diagnosis): often loses temper, is easily annoyed, is often angry and resentful, often argues with adults, and refuses to comply with requests. The current severity was determined to be "severe" because symptoms were described as present in three settings: at home, at school, and with peers. Samuel also exhibited two of the 15 DSM-5 criteria for conduct disorder (i.e., initiates physical fights and stays out at night despite parental prohibition). Three or more criteria are required for a diagnosis; therefore, a diagnosis of conduct disorder was not given. The clinician noted that Samuel is at risk for conduct disorder, however, and continued to monitor his behavior closely.

INTERVENTION

According to the National Survey of Children's Health, only about half of youths with disruptive behavior disorders received treatment in the past year (53%; Ghandour et al., 2019). However, longitudinal studies indicate that CD is related to numerous poor outcomes, academic underachievement, other mental and substance use disorders, and criminality and violence (Erskine et al., 2016). Therefore, it is important for social workers and other professionals to identify and intervene early.

Psychosocial

The treatments that have received the most research support are individual CBT, parent training, and multicomponent family systems interventions. Individual CBT interventions for disruptive behaviors typically focus on social information processing (Baker & Scarth, 2002), or the way the child goes about reacting to social situations. Instead of reacting with aggression, the child learns how to interpret social situations accurately, figure out options, choose an option that maximizes advantages, and practice the skills in role play (Lochman et al., 2003). The most well-known of these, the Coping Power program, uses a combination of training in social problem-solving, coping with negative emotions, positive play, and group-entry skills and has been demonstrated to be effective with African American youth (Huey & Polo, 2008; Lochman et al., 1993; Lochman & Wells, 2003, 2004).

CBT interventions for adolescents with conduct problems can be effective when delivered with high fidelity (meaning when the therapy is delivered as it was designed to be) (Goense et al., 2016; Lipsey et al., 2007; Wilson & Lipsey, 2007). Battagliese and colleagues (2015) conducted the most recent meta-analysis of 21 randomized controlled trials of CBT and found that it significantly reduces ODD, externalizing, and ADHD symptoms. Parental stress, maternal depression, and parenting skills also improved with CBT. To reduce aggression, CBT had to be delivered to parents and children together.

FAMILY

Behavioral parent training is the most supported intervention for child disruptive behavioral problems. For adolescents, family therapy and its multisystemic variations have also been studied.

Parent Training. Parent training follows the tenets of behavioral theory, which involves the reinforcement and punishment of behavior; parents are taught to positively reinforce prosocial conduct using attention, praise, and point systems and to employ alternative discipline methods to physical discipline, shouting, and threats.

There are many manuals that describe the techniques in detail. For preschool to early elementary school children, there are Helping the Noncompliant Child (ages 3 to 8; Forehand & McMahon, 1981) and the Incredible Years (ages 4 to 8; Webster-Stratton, 2001). Living with Children (renamed Generation PMTO) has the widest age applicability (2 to 18 years; Forgatch, Patterson et al., 2017; Patterson, 1977). For families living in poverty and facing high concrete needs, the addition of a home-visiting component with case management improves outcomes over parent training alone (Lees et al., 2019). The implication is that home-based case management and parent training might improve conduct problems in children of families with greater tangible needs.

In practice, a variety of modalities and methods are used for youths of different ages, but the research has been largely focused on parent training for school-aged children. A meta-review of the meta-analyses on parent training for externalizing disorders found that it is effective, according to both parent and observational reports of externalizing domains (Berg et al., 2020; Mingebach et al., 2018). Further, results are maintained over time (Mingebach et al., 2018) and in real-world settings (Michelson et al., 2013).

To better serve families of color, parent training programs have been culturally adapted by using the following (van Mourik et al., 2017): (1) surface structure adaptations—language, therapist–client ethnic matching, and portraying families of color in treatment materials; and (2) deep structure—making sure that sessions involve cultural and contextual influences on parenting, such as, in some diverse groups, the value of having multiple children or not being emotive. Programs with cultural adaptations were more successful than programs without such adaptations in improving parenting behavior and, to a lesser extent, parental perspectives and child behavior with families of color (van Mourik et al., 2017).

There has also been an increasing interest in technology-assisted parent training programs to increase access to services. In a review of these, most were, on average, short-term (nine sessions), with a completion rate of 69% (Baumel et al., 2017). Compared with no treatment control, technology-assisted programs resulted in significant improvements in child behavior for children younger than 9 years. Programs ranged in how much professional support was involved, but those with reduced contact were not inferior to full-support conditions, and they showed improvement over usual care. Therefore, technology-assisted parent training programs are a promising way to offer services both within the mental health system and perhaps in other settings (school, social service, and medical).

Family Therapy. Family therapy has been supported as an evidence-based approach for adolescents with externalizing problems (McCart et al., 2022). Many models involve purveyor organizations, which may be cost-prohibitive for agencies (Hogue et al., 2017). The core elements of three manualized family therapy approaches were distilled from 302 sessions with 196 youth cases (Hogue et al., 2019). Adolescents were 57% male; 41% Black, 31% white, and 9% Latino. The core elements derived were adolescent engagement, relational emphasis of problems and reframes, and interactional change techniques, which the authors argued represent structural family therapy at its core. For that reason, we present an overview of the theory here and a case application at the end of the chapter.

Developed by Salvador Minuchin (Minuchin, 1974; Minuchin & Fishman, 1981; Minuchin et al., 1967, 1978; Minuchin & Nichols, 1993), structural family therapy has played an influential role in the practice of family work for the past 50 years. As a family systems approach, structural family therapy is bound by certain concepts:

- *Circular causality*: symptoms are not viewed as stemming from linear causes (i.e., by one person's problems) but instead emerge from family interaction patterns.
- *Homeostasis*: symptoms arise to maintain the status quo, as does resistance to change.
- A focus on the *process* of interactions (the pattern) *rather than the content* (what the family is talking about)

The contribution of structural family therapy to family systems approaches is in the name; maintaining a hierarchical *structure*—parents united in taking care of children and in charge of the family in a functional way—formed and maintained through the process of family communications. While every family experiences problems and stress and the difficulties of negotiating new developmental stages, the "normal" family, because of its flexibility and adaptability, can retain its hierarchical structure. Symptoms in a child, therefore, indicate the presence of patterns that have derailed in rigid and nonadaptive ways, indicative of a structural problem (Minuchin, 1974).

A healthy structure means distinct subsystems are in place to enact various functions of the family (Minuchin, 1974). The *parental subsystem* is to care for, protect, and discipline children. Parents have more responsibilities than their children, as well as more rights. Parents are also joined together in the *couple subsystem*, where they spend time being a couple, enacting such functions as giving and receiving affection and handling conflict. The *sibling subsystem* is where children have their first experience of being part of a peer group; they learn how to cooperate, resolve conflict, and negotiate differences. If a parent tries to solve problems for siblings ("Who started it?"), then children do not learn these critical functions. Hierarchical principles still operate within the sibling subsystem. Older siblings enjoy more rights than do their younger siblings; increased responsibility also accompanies these rights.

Boundaries, invisible demarcation lines that regulate hierarchy and proximity of member interactions, separate subsystems. Boundaries are problematic either by being diffuse (weak and blurred) or rigid (impenetrable), which leads to *en-meshment* or *disengagement*, respectively (Minuchin et al., 1967). *Enmeshment* is defined as family members' overinvolvement with each other to the detriment of individual growth and autonomy or to appropriate subsystem functioning. *Disengagement*, on the other hand, is a situation in which individual members are distant and disconnected from other family members and function in isolation from each other.

The central goal of structural family therapy, therefore, is to change the communications in the family in the service of hierarchical organization with clear boundaries around subsystems. These goals are achieved through *enactments*, working with interactions in the session, so that new patterns are formed (Aponte, 2002; Minuchin, 1974). The byproduct of a healthy structure is the amelioration of presenting symptoms.

Family systems therapy and, specifically, structural family therapy are at the heart of other family models that are multicomponent in nature and sometimes involve different system levels beyond the family. Ecological and systems models are routinely offered as frameworks for social work practice. These interventions have been manualized, however, and disseminated through purveyor organizations. An example is multisystemic therapy (MST) (https://www.mstservices.com), in which family preservation, an approach that is popular among child welfare services, is used as the main venue for work with the various systems that are involved with youths. A systematic review of 23 studies of MST indicated that 1 year after the start of treatment, MST improved parent and family outcomes and reduced self-reported delinquency (Littell et al., 2021). Out-of-home placements and arrests were reduced in the United States, but not in other countries. Indeed, the MST condition in non-U.S. countries at 2.5 year follow-up had increased arrest rates over treatment-as-usual (TAU). In the U.S., youth are more likely to be removed from their homes and to be arrested than youth from other countries. Unfortunately, U.S. youth do not receive the same services than similarly-situated youth from other developed countries, which leads to the implication that services as usual should be improved in this country. Other multicomponent models are discussed in Chapter 8 in reference to substance use disorders because the interventions treat both these overlapping concerns.

Medication

As discussed, many youths with ODD or CD will have comorbid ADHD. Stimulants are effective for reducing aggression with this population (Pappadopulos et al., 2006). Systematic reviews of antipsychotic medicine for CD have found some limited efficacy for risperidone in reducing conduct problems and aggression in both children and adolescents in 6- and 12-week trials (Loy et al., 2017). However, weight gain was common, even during this short trial period, and was associated with metabolic impairments. There was insufficient evidence to support the efficacy and safety of other antipsychotics used in clinical practice, including quetiapine and ziprasidone.

In addition, risperidone reduces aggression substantially in youths with CD and below average IQ. Other classes of medication have either not been studied sufficiently or show little evidence of effectiveness. Aggression uncomplicated by ADHD should first be treated with a psychosocial approach, and such an approach should continue even when medications are used.

The clinician conducted individual therapy sessions with Samuel using a CBT framework to guide treatment and behavioral parenting sessions with Samuel's mother. At the outset of treatment planning, the clinician considered the Cultural Treatment Adaptation Framework (Chu & Leino, 2017) and intentionally considered ways to incorporate cultural themes. The clinician reflected on ways that the role of the family and concepts such as machismo and acculturation may be important as well as on how best to incorporate these components into treatment.

Typically, the clinician met with Ms. Flores individually for half the session (and for full sessions as needed) and met with Samuel to help him learn to process social information more accurately and to develop more effective problem-solving strategies. Initially, the clinician had trouble engaging Samuel in individual therapy and so began by using motivational interviewing strategies aimed at enhancing motivation to engage in treatment. They were able to collaboratively identify some things that would be good about therapy, including that it would "get school off my back" and "Uncle Dom told me to give my mom a break. . . . I know he's going to ask her how this is going." They used this as a springboard to agree on a primary treatment goal to "not get kicked out of school" by "not getting into stupid fights—but if someone really disrespects me, I have to, or everyone will think I'm a punk." The clinician didn't challenge this initially because agreeing on a goal to get into less fights was progress, instead deciding to explore the accuracy of this cognition (that people will think he is a punk if he doesn't fight when disrespected) over time.

In addition to this important cognitive restructuring and social processing work, teaching Samuel more effective strategies for problem-solving was a high priority. The clinician worked with Samuel to teach him a structured problem-solving approach in which they began by defining the problem, proceeded to generating solutions (without evaluation at this stage), then evaluated the solutions, chose the best one, and tried it out. Using the method described by Kendall and Hedtke (2006) and consistent with Kazdin and colleagues' (1992) problem-solving approach, the clinician first taught the problem-solving framework and then practiced with Samuel using a nonstressful situation (e.g., you wanted to have waffles for breakfast, but when you opened the freezer you realized you were all out). When he had mastered the skill, they then practiced problem-solving in situations that were more challenging (e.g., a classmate bumps you in the hallway). After engaging in problem-solving and agreeing on a strategy to try, the clinician modeled for Samuel how he might implement it. Then, they role-played implementing the chosen strategy and discussed what Samuel could do if the selected strategy was unsuccessful (e.g., try a different strategy, redefine the problem, and problem-solve it again).

For example, with regard to the problem in which a classmate bumped into him in the hallway, the clinician and Samuel began collaboratively generating potential solutions. They wrote their ideas on a whiteboard. The clinician encouraged Samuel to consider all possibilities (even those that initially seemed unpalatable or unlikely to be successful) and suggested possibilities when he got stuck. This is the list they generated:

1. *Push/bump him back.*
2. *Walk away.*
3. *Tell him to back off.*
4. *Tell a teacher.*
5. *Do nothing in the moment but fight him later.*

Then, the clinician helped Samuel to evaluate each solution. They discussed likely consequences, both positive and negative, for each solution (e.g., pushing him would demonstrate he wasn't a "punk" but might lead to disciplinary issues at school). They also discussed different potential interpretations for the classmate's behavior (e.g., he did it on purpose to test me; it was an accident) and the likely accuracy (e.g., "How would you know if that were true?" and "Are there any other possibilities?") and helpfulness of each interpretation ("What are the downsides to assuming he did it on purpose?"). The clinician was careful to ask questions to help Samuel consider alternatives and reach his own conclusions versus telling him what she thought was likely to be true (Rutter & Friedberg, 1999). Samuel vetoed telling a teacher because, "I'm not a snitch." After weighing pros and cons and determining that pushing/bumping him or fighting him later would both likely lead to more trouble than he could afford to get into at school, they narrowed the candidate solutions down to the following:

1. *Walk away*
2. *Tell him to back off*

Samuel was hesitant to choose walking away as the solution to implement because he was afraid people would see him as weak and "mess with me." The clinician helped Samuel to explore the pros and cons of telling someone to back off or walking away (see Table 7.2).

Table 7.2 Pros and Cons List

Tell him to back off

Pros	Cons
1. I show I'm tough.	1. He might try to fight me.
2. People won't mess with me.	2. A teacher could see, and I'd get in
3. He might back off.	trouble.

Walk away

Pros	Cons
1. I won't get into trouble.	1. He/others might think I'm a punk
2. Mom and Uncle would be proud of me.	and mess with me.

On review of the pros and cons, Samuel agreed to try walking away the next time someone bumped him in the hall. The clinician framed it as an experiment to see how others might react and to learn what the outcome would be of trying this different approach. They agreed to a small reward if Samuel was successful in walking away (a treat from the clinic vending machine). This helped motivate Samuel to try something new. Then, the clinician modeled how to implement this approach while thinking aloud. She pretended she was bumped and then thought (out loud), "I can't believe he just did that. Wait. Slow down and take a breath (demonstrated a breath). Maybe it was an accident, and even if it wasn't, I'm going to get into more trouble than it's worth if I react. Keep your cool and go to class." Then, Samuel participated in role-playing the scenario, first as the kid who bumped him with the therapist playing Samuel, and then playing himself with the therapist bumping him. He agreed to try to walk away the next time a peer bumped into him and to report back to the therapist how it went. Indeed, approximately 1 week later a peer grazed Samuel in the hallway. While he initially started to get mad and react, he was able to catch himself and walk away. They agreed it had been a success and proceeded to practice implementing problem-solving for increasingly challenging situations (e.g., someone tries to start a fight).

Samuel was given specific homework tasks each week to practice the skills from therapy outside of session (e.g., to practice problem-solving or to try out a new way of responding to peers). At the next session, the clinician would check in about homework completion and review how things went, reinforcing the importance of homework completion. Over time, rapport with Samuel improved, and the clinician was able to begin working with him to identify unhelpful or inaccurate patterns in his thinking and processing of social information and to help him challenge these thoughts (i.e., cognitive restructuring) or respond in more helpful ways, for example, by problem-solving a solution.

Parent Training

Behavioral parent training with Ms. Flores included the following components: psychoeducation about ODD and childhood misbehavior, teaching and practicing strategies for positive reinforcement including use of a reward system, consequences for noncompliance, and strategies that could be implemented at home to improve compliance in school.

The clinician provided Ms. Flores with information about why misbehavior in children occurs and, specifically, how behavior is shaped over time and how parents and children can get into negative cycles of interaction.

> **Clinician:** *You've told me about how Samuel often refuses to do what he is asked and that typically there aren't any consequences other than perhaps you might raise your voice. Over time, he has learned that he can get out of doing things he doesn't want to do by simply refusing to follow your directions.*
> **Mother:** *Yeah, probably.*
> **Clinician:** *Similarly, he has learned that, by starting fights at school, kids generally don't mess with him, and worst case, he gets suspended and gets*

to stay home. What happens when he stays home from school because of a suspension? What does he do all day?

Mother: Usually watches TV or plays video games while I'm at work.

Clinician: That probably isn't a very big deterrent, is it? Let's see if we can work together to come up with a strategy in which the consequences are more aversive for misbehavior and where we leverage things he does value, like his cell phone, to motivate him to behave more appropriately.

The clinician and Ms. Flores also discussed the toll that Samuel's behavioral challenges is taking on their relationship.

Clinician: Parenting a child who is frequently misbehaving and acting defiantly can really take a toll on families. Many parents I work with tell me that they feel like they are always yelling, that they don't have as many pleasant or fun interactions with their child as they'd like, and that things always feel so stressful. Does any of that sound familiar?

Mother: It does.

Clinician: One goal of treatment can be for us to work together to identify ways to increase positive interactions between you and Samuel.

Following psychoeducation, the clinician began to work with Ms. Flores on positive reinforcement strategies, namely the use of specific labeled praise and a reward system that would be motivating to change behavior. To break the cycle of negative interactions, the clinician explained to Ms. Flores the importance of catching Samuel when he was exhibiting compliant, prosocial behavior and praising him.

Clinician: For example, if Samuel takes out the trash when asked, saying something like, "I appreciate that you took out the trash when I asked, that was a big help. Thank you."

Mother: Okay.

Clinician: Doing this is important for a couple reasons. Praise from parents can be reinforcing in and of itself, but also you and Samuel have gotten into a pattern in which your communication has become tense or ineffective, and this can be a way to start to break that cycle.

Mother: I understand what you're saying. But he doesn't do a lot of stuff he's supposed to do, so what exactly am I supposed to praise him for?

Clinician: I'm glad you asked. Let's think about the past few days' events and identify some times when praise would have worked. It may feel like we have to look hard to find things to praise at first, but even something simple like Samuel putting his dishes in the sink or brushing his teeth when reminded can be an opportunity.

Mother: I think I see now.

Clinician: As we see how he responds to it, we can continue to look for opportunities to use praise strategically to reinforce behaviors we would like to see more of.

The clinician and Ms. Flores went onto develop a token economy system that would motivate Samuel to achieve behavioral goals. First, they worked together to identify key goals to target first (with the idea that new goals would be added/substituted as progress in these initial goals was demonstrated), including completing homework, obeying curfew, and using words instead of physical aggression. Identified rewards were cell phone access and video game/TV time. These activities had previously been unlimited for Samuel, and the clinician anticipated that shifting to earning those behaviors would be difficult. She asked Ms. Flores to help her understand what would be likely to get in the way of success. Ms. Flores noted that Samuel would most likely refuse to give her his phone or turn off the TV when asked. They discussed strategies that could be used, including the use of parental controls; storing the phone, video game controllers, or cords to the TV in a locked and inaccessible place; or Ms. Flores taking these items to work with her. It also became clear during the problem-solving phase that exerting this type of authority would be difficult for Ms. Flores and would represent a major shift in the parenting dynamic.

COMMUNITY AND CULTURAL RESPONSIVENESS

Recognizing the relevant cultural aspects of the situation, the clinician worked with Ms. Flores to develop a plan in which Samuel's uncle (Ms. Flores's sister's husband, Dom Martinez), who Samuel respected and who lived down the street, would take an active role in helping Ms. Flores to implement this plan. Ms. Flores invited Mr. Martinez to attend a parent session with her, and a plan was developed in which he communicated to Samuel his support of this new plan and regularly checked in with Ms. Flores and Samuel to be sure it was being implemented as intended. Additional strategies for managing noncompliance were also developed in collaboration with Ms. Flores and Mr. Martinez, including loss of enjoyable activities, such as time with peers, for unacceptable behavior like fighting. In developing this plan, it was important to ensure feasibility and develop contingencies. For example, if Samuel gets suspended from school, he must accompany Ms. Flores to work or stay with a relative who can ensure he does not have access to his phone or TV during the day. Mr. Martinez agreed to help implement the plan by doing things such as coming over to help escort Samuel to work with Ms. Flores if needed. He and Ms. Flores also engaged additional extended family members (Mr. Martinez's wife, Samuel's grandmother) in the plan to provide additional support.

Throughout treatment, the clinician maintained communication with the school counselor and integrated school goals into the treatment plans, such as by developing the reward system in a way that Ms. Flores would administer rewards at home for completing homework and exhibiting safe behavior with peers at school. The school counselor, the clinician, and Ms. Flores developed a plan in which the counselor agreed to alert Ms. Flores by 4 p.m. each day if Samuel had not met one or more of his behavioral goals for the day (so that Ms. Flores could respond accordingly at home when administering rewards).

Given that Samuel did not exhibit symptoms consistent with ADHD and had not previously had therapy, the clinician and Ms. Flores collaboratively determined that it was reasonable to try psychotherapy first and that a medication consultation was not warranted at this time. However, they agreed to monitor Samuel's response to therapy and revisit that decision if Samuel's behavior worsened or if progress with psychosocial interventions alone was not satisfactory.

CASE EXAMPLE 2: FAMILY THERAPY

Jamie Saunders, a 15-year-old white male, has been mandated to attend counseling by his probation officer due to shoplifting charges and assaulting his younger brother (he broke his brother's arm). Services will be delivered in the home where Jamie lives with his mother, Sandra Witt, age 42; his brother Kyle, age 11; his maternal grandmother, Betty Clayborne, age 65; and his maternal uncle, Howard Witt, age 38. Divorced from the children's father for 5 years, Sandra says that even though she feels like giving up on Jamie at times, she won't send Jamie to her ex-husband because he was physically abusive to Jamie in the past when the children went to visit him. The children haven't seen their father for 2 years. Sandra says she has been depressed for most of her adult life but that it has worsened in the past 2 years. She currently is prescribed fluoxetine.

Sandra and her children moved from the state they had been living in a year ago to move in with Sandra's mother, Betty Clayborne, who is long divorced from her third husband. Sandra and Howard are the children from Betty's first marriage. Sandra explains that the reason for the move to her mother's house was financial; Sandra is unable to work because of a disability (carpal tunnel syndrome) and is waiting to find out her eligibility for government benefits. Howard Witt lives in the household because of financial problems after a divorce but has recently started a sales position.

Session 1

The site of the first session is Betty Clayborne's house, a two-story rental property located in a quiet neighborhood. The practitioner's previous contact with the family involved a telephone conversation with Jamie's mother to set up the appointment. Ms. Witt said that she was willing to participate and had received counseling in the past for her depression, but that no one else in the family wanted to be part of the family counseling. She said her mother flatly refused to take part. At the time, Ms. Witt said, "She (her mother) is the one who really needs it." Although Ms. Witt stated her willingness to participate, she also expressed her sense of hopelessness about the situation.

To the practitioner's surprise, when she arrives at the home she is ushered in by Ms. Witt, who introduces the practitioner to her mother, Betty Clayborne. Mrs. Clayborne is nicely dressed and made up, as opposed to Sandra, who is unkempt *and has a flat, exhausted expression. Sandra next introduces her brother, Howard, who is tall and looks a little older than his age.*

Grandmother *(to her daughter): Where are the boys?*
Mom: *I told them to come down here.*
Grandmother: *They need to be ready. We're keeping the counselor waiting.*
Mom: *I know, mother (bellows up the stairs): "Jamie, Kyle, come down here!"*

As they wait for the boys to respond, the practitioner compliments Ms. Witt and Mrs. Clayborne on the way the home is decorated. Mrs. Clayborne seems pleased. Suddenly, a thundering of footsteps is heard, and Jamie, a tall, gangly youth, jumps down the last six stairs and stumbles to his feet. Kyle follows behind, giggling.

Mom *(wearily): How many times have I told you not to do that? Jamie, this is—*
But he is off, moving to the dining room.
Jamie *(drawing his grandmother along with him): Okay, Grandma you sit here.*
His grandmother sits at the seat he has chosen for her.
Jamie: *Uncle Howard, you're over there.*
Howard doesn't move. He looks annoyed.
Jamie: *Mom, sit here and—(to practitioner)—I guess there's no room for you.*
Mom: *Jamie, you're not in charge of where everyone sits.*
Jamie: *Yes, I am.*
Mom: *Don't be rude.*
Jamie *(to practitioner): Okay, we'll find you another chair.*
He starts to pull a heavy armchair from the living room.
Mom: *Don't be dragging that over here.*
Jamie: *But we don't have enough seats.*
Kyle sits on the floor, leaning up against the wall.
Mom: *Why don't you sit down there on the floor next to your brother?*
Jamie *(bitterly): Oh, I know he's always perfect.*
Mom: *I didn't say that.*
Jamie *(to his mother with a defiant giggle): Why don't you sit on the floor?*
Howard *(starting to get mad): Don't talk to your mother that way!*
Jamie: *Uncle Howard, you sit there. I'll bring in a chair from the porch.*
Howard: *Jamie, those chairs are chained down. And stop telling everyone where to sit.*

The initial seating arrangements revealed information about the family. In this instance, Jamie's grandmother seemed to do what he wanted. Jamie's mother and Uncle Howard resisted Jamie's commands but remained ineffectual, and a power struggle ensued. In these situations, a structural family therapist might have to lend his or her influence to unfreeze the family from this "stuck" position, by siding with the person who should be the authority over the children.

Note that in the following exchange, Ms. Witt is referred to as "Mom." Parents and other adults involved in caretaking should be referred to by their role ("Mom," "Grandmother," "Uncle") or by their formal title (Ms., Mrs., Mr.) so that their authority is reinforced. Calling a grown-up by his or her first name in front of children tends to put adult and child on the same level.

Practitioner: *Mom, where would you like me to sit?*

The maneuver succeeds, at least partly. Without Mom having to say anything, Jamie gives up his chair and hops to the floor, where he starts to tussle with his younger brother.

Grandmother *(to her daughter): You haven't even offered the counselor anything to drink. (Addressing practitioner): Would you like something to drink? I have some coffee made.*

After a slight hesitation, the practitioner agrees to coffee. Mrs. Clayborne seems to enjoy fussing over its preparation and brings out the coffee in a cup and saucer.

A dilemma underlies the practitioner's hesitation: if she takes Grandmother's offering, this might be seen as acceptance of Grandmother's implicit reprimand of her daughter. On the other hand, this is Grandmother's first involvement in counseling, and she was a reluctant participant, according to Mom. Joining with Grandmother is very important because she plays a key role in the family.

In the joining stage, each family member shares his or her perspective on the family's functioning and what needs changing. In keeping with the structural emphasis, the practitioner asks Mom first to reinforce her parental authority, although Jamie jumps in before Mom can begin talking.

Jamie: *I think counseling's stupid.*
Mom: *Don't talk like that, son.*
Jamie: *It is stupid. (Puts his head in his arms so his voice is muffled.) And boring, too.*
Mom: *That's an example right there. He has no respect for adults. He doesn't listen to anything I say, and it doesn't help when she (indicates her mother) is always sticking up for him. I don't know if you've noticed, but she isn't even speaking to me, hasn't been for 3 days. Do you know what she did? She went out and bought Jamie a new phone. Does she get Kyle anything? No! Does she even acknowledge that he just got straight A's on his last report card? No! While this one (jabs a finger at Jamie) is not even passing!*
Jamie: *I hate that stupid school! It's full of jocks.*
Mom: *Kyle's never here. And I don't blame him. He doesn't want to be around this. He's always off with his friends. And then there's Jamie—he has no friends.*
Jamie *(hotly): I do, too, have friends!*

Mom: *Who?*

Jamie: *Paul!*

Mom: *Paul? (dismissively) He lives in an apartment complex. I don't have very much money right now, but it's very important that my kids don't live in an apartment complex. Paul just comes and goes as he pleases, and his mother doesn't even care.*

Jamie: *You don't know what you're talking about.*

Reframing, attributing a positive intention to behavior, forestalls the argument brewing between Mom and Jamie:

Practitioner: *It sounds like you really care about your son and want the best for him. You feel it's important for him to have a good home, and you are doing something about it—even though it's difficult sometimes.*

Mom *(visibly pleased): I do care about Jamie, even though he's always saying I'm mean. I could just ship him to his father, but I wouldn't do that to him. His father was physically abusive to me, and he was abusive to the boys, too. I'm not going to let them go back to that.*

Now it's Grandmother's turn:

Grandmother: *I just know from my work in sales you've got to build people up if you want them to do things well. You've got to build a boy up, rather than tearing him down all the time.*

Mom *(explosively): I do encourage him, but when he does something wrong, you don't give him the latest phone. And when I set up a punishment, you don't go behind my back and undo it by giving him gifts and special treatment.*

Jamie *(to his mother): Don't you even try to take that phone away from me.*

Howard *(to Jamie): Shut up, Jamie. (To his mother): It's true, Mom, Jamie thinks he can get away with murder the way you go about getting him everything he wants.*

Practitioner: *Let's give Grandmother a chance to finish, and then we'll go around the table until everyone has had a chance to talk.*

Mom *(to her mother): All my life you've downplayed what I've done! You've always totally discounted me, and you reverse everything I do with Jamie, until he knows he doesn't have to follow rules.*

Practitioner *(to Grandmother): Okay, so Mrs. Clayborne, you want there to be more positive reinforcement for what Jamie does right, rather than punishment for what he does wrong? You're right, that can be very effective.*

The practitioner responds to Grandmother's statement, rather than Mom's, for a couple of reasons. The practitioner's responsibility is to provide direction in the session, to make new patterns happen, rather than allowing the family interaction to move in its usual course. The practitioner also must join with each individual in the family and furthers joining by giving Grandmother the opportunity to speak and offering a reframe. Grandmother states her fear that all the negative attention Jamie receives from Mom will "tear him down" and so she "wants to build him up." The phrase, "building a boy up, not tearing him down" will now be tracked across sessions. *Tracking*, noting unique and idiosyncratic phrases the family uses and incorporating them into the practitioner's repertoire, is another part of the joining process so that the practitioner will feel familiar to the family members (Minuchin, 1974).

Next, it's time for Uncle Howard.

Howard: I've never known how to be a dad. Me and my ex-wife didn't have children. I've never been a parent, but I do know that boy is totally out of control. He doesn't listen to anyone, until I get in his face. He doesn't do anything around here. He's failing in school and just got out of jail last week.
Jamie: It wasn't jail—it was juvenile.
Howard: You see how he interrupts and tries to argue? You know why he was locked up? Because he broke his brother's arm. The kid is dangerous, and his mother can't control him.
Mom: How can I control him when I don't have anyone backing me up?
Howard: I back you up. I'm the only one Jamie listens to around here.
Mom: That's because he's scared of you.
Howard: Look who's talking—you get pretty scary yourself sometimes. (To practitioner): I'm the one who spends time with him—all "Buddy Buddy," fixing that old car back there. I don't know why I'm even here at this counseling. I've got my own stuff to deal with. I've just gotten a divorce, financial problems.
Mom: That's what counseling is supposed to help you with. I don't know how many times you've come crying to me about your ex. You could use some help dealing with that.

The practitioner interjects before the focus can get off-track with a summary of Howard's statement, so he knows he's been heard.

Practitioner: So, you are trying to be involved in these kids' lives in a positive way—you fix up old cars with them—
Mom: With Jamie, not Kyle.
Practitioner: And help with enforcing the rules.
Howard: Yeah, but I don't know anything about being a dad.
Practitioner: Who says you have to be?
Howard: I don't know. I know they don't have much of one, and they need a positive male influence.
Practitioner: You don't have to be their dad. You can't be. All you can be is their uncle. And that means not having to set rules, just backing up Sandra's authority as the parent.

ENACTMENTS

In structural family therapy, most of the work involves altering family transactions in the session through *enactments*. Enactments involve allowing family patterns to emerge, but with the practitioner pushing for a different outcome in which parental hierarchy is bolstered. Different techniques are used during the enactment. Habitual patterns are blocked, and the parent is impelled to take command over the child. Changing these patterns may require the practitioner to use *intensity* in applying techniques and to occasionally employ *unbalancing*, siding with one family member over another to shift a "stuck" position in the system. This focus on enactments reflects the assumption that a change in behavior leads to a change in cognitive understanding.

However, to a lesser extent, it is also assumed that change can happen from cognitive understanding delivered through information and reframing. In this case example, Howard's obvious sense of pressure and confusion about fulfilling a father's role is quickly dispelled with a little information about the healthy structure of families, information that the other members also hear.

Practitioner: *Okay, Jamie, it's your turn.*

Jamie feigns snoring. The practitioner realizes that she has succumbed to the family rule that Kyle is ignored by its members.

Practitioner: *Let's go to Kyle then.*

Mom decides to get into a power struggle with Jamie instead.

Mom: *Jamie, answer her when she's talking to you.*
Jamie: *This is so boring. Why do we have to be here?*
Howard: *You've been wanting to talk, Jamie. Now it's your turn. So, go.*
Jamie: *Aren't we done yet? You've been talking the whole time.*
Howard: *We're not the one who broke their brother's arm. You're the one that needs help.*
Jamie *(playfully drumming on Kyle's head): But he forgives me now, don't you?*
Mom: *Jamie, let go of him.*
Practitioner: *Actually, I would like to hear from Kyle.*

Unfortunately, Kyle can't lift his head because of the pummeling he is receiving.

Howard: *Jamie, I'm fixing to come over there and do the same thing to your head. Now let Kyle talk.*
Jamie: *Counseling's boring is all. I've been to counselors ever since I first got put on Ritalin. That's 5 years of counseling. No, wait (counts on fingers)—4. That's too long.*

Practitioner: *This is counseling for the family. What about your family?*
Jamie: *Well, everybody's always fighting.*
Howard: *It's mainly about you.*
Jamie: *That' not true. You've been fighting about the same shit ever since you were my age.*

Howard and Sandra subsequently get lost in a battle about Jamie using a swear word.

Family members usually ascribe causation in a linear fashion (i.e., one person is to blame for the problems). However, from a family systems standpoint, systems are involved in circular causality: interaction patterns maintain the faulty structure. In this view, Jamie's behavior is symptomatic of the family's patterns rather than Jamie causing the family's problems.

Finally, it's Kyle's turn.

Kyle *(ducking his head): Everyone's always fighting. I just want everyone to get along.*

Jamie starts pounding Kyle's head again.

Mom: *Jamie, after what you did to him, I don't want you touching him at all.*
Jamie: *Not even like this?*

Jamie provocatively goes back to his pummeling.

Howard: *Jamie, stop that right now.*

Jamie acts like he hasn't heard.

Howard: *Do you want me to come over there and stop you myself? (Starts to get up.)*
Jamie: *No, no, I'll stop!*
Practitioner: *Mom, what was your reaction to Uncle Howard stopping Jamie?*
Mom: *Thank you, Howard, but sometimes you're damn right scary. I hope you're happy—Jamie's scared of you.*
Howard: *At least he listens to me.*
Practitioner: *I wonder, how can you two work together as a team?*

They look dubious. The practitioner decides on a bold move.

Practitioner: *Kyle, Jamie, why don't you leave for right now? I think I'll just work with the grown-ups.*
Jamie: *We can go?*
Mom: *But he's the one that needs counseling.*
Practitioner: *First, we have to get all the adults working together.*

Mom: I don't want them going off together unsupervised. Jamie's just out of
   juvenile for breaking his brother's arm.

The practitioner's decision to begin work with the parental subsystem
stemmed from the inability of the adult members to work together as a team
with Sandra "at the helm." Forming clear boundaries around a parental subsystem is more challenging in an intergenerational family than in the classic two-
parent household because of the simultaneous roles people employ. Howard and
Sandra are both the children of Betty Clayborne, but Sandra is also a mother to
the two children. In addition, both Howard and Sandra have moved back with
their mother because of financial problems and are now dependent on their
mother for support. It might be difficult for Mom to assume parental control
(and for others to let her) when she is in such a dependent role with her own
mother. However, the rule in structural family therapy is that parents should be
in control of their own children, with other adult relatives and authority figures
enforcing parental rules.

Sandra complains about her mother and brother not backing her up, but when
her brother successfully enforces Sandra's command, Sandra complains about her
brother's "scary" behavior. Understandably, she doesn't want her son to react out
of fear, but she also tends to use punishment to get Jamie into line.

Sandra is also concerned that without Jamie in the session, problems won't
be solved. However, one of the assumptions of structural family therapy is that
problems are not caused by an individual in the family; rather, problems stem
from the family system interaction patterns. In structural family therapy, the
structure of the family system is seen as problematic, which, in turn, has resulted
in Jamie being symptomatic. In addition, the structure of the family is challenged
by multiple stressors, divorce, single-parenthood, financial problems, recent
moves, and disability. The family also faces stress from the many developmental
changes that the family members are simultaneously experiencing: 11-year-old
Kyle, adolescence with Jamie, retirement/growing older (65-year-old Betty), and
divorce (Howard).

As for Sandra's concern that Jamie will hurt Kyle if he is left alone with him, the
assumption of structural family therapy is that the family subsystems should be
strengthened, which includes both the parental and the sibling subsystem. The
two boys being unable to resolve conflict without adult intervention is indicative
of the problematic way in which the sibling subsystem is functioning. If Sandra
continues to intervene between the brothers, without allowing them to work out
their own problems, then paradoxically, Jamie may be more likely to lose control
with his brother in the future.

Mom: You ask, how can we work together as a team? How can we work together when whatever I decide with Jamie, she'll (indicates her mother)
   reverse what I've said? The newest phone? He didn't even pass his exams.
   I told him he wouldn't get to go to [local amusement park] if he didn't pass.
   And she gave him an iPad.

Grandmother: *It's not just for him. It's here in the living room where everyone can use it.*

Mom: *You never said anyone else could use it. Jamie thinks it's his.*

Howard: *Mom, it is Jamie's. You gave it to him.*

Grandmother: *It is Jamie's, but he knows he's supposed to let everyone use it.*

Mom: *But he hasn't let anyone else use it. And what was the point in giving him an iPad? Just so I could look bad? So that I can be the bad guy? He doesn't deserve an iPad. He's got to know if he starts doing something good, then he gets rewards. Why should he work if he gets his rewards anyway?*

Grandmother: *A boy doesn't start to act good unless he feels good about himself.*

Mom: *And is it going to make him feel good about himself when he's done nothing to deserve it?*

Howard (to Sandra): *Why can't you just tell her thank you for buying your son a present? You can't afford to get them anything.*

Mom: *You're in the same position I am—what are you talking about? You wouldn't be here either if you had any money of your own. That's why we're all here. If I could work, you'd think I'd be here?*

Howard: *You could work if you wanted to.*

Mom: *Oh, sure, with these hands? (Holds her hands up helplessly.)*

Howard: *There's some things you could do.*

Mom: *Like what?*

Howard: *You could take tickets in a theater. You could answer phones. You could work in a 7-11.*

Mom (to Howard): *After owning my own business, do you really think I'm going to do anything like that? You haven't heard one word I've told you all summer. I've listened to you for hours about your ex-wife and all about her affair, and you haven't understood one thing I've said.*

Grandmother: *Some people have an anger control problem. And you can't figure out why Jamie has problems with his anger?*

Mom: *So, you finally admit Jamie has an anger control problem. I thought he was perfect.*

Grandmother: *Of course he's got problems. Who wouldn't have problems if someone kept telling him that he was no good?*

Mom: *You can't just reward him when he's bad, mother. (Appeals to practitioner): You know that!*

Howard: *But you can be kind of harsh sometimes.*

Mom (to her brother): *You're the one he's scared of.*

Grandmother (to Sandra): *Well, you can be pretty scary too when you lay into him.*

Practitioner: *What's a way to have both things operating—a mix between letting Jamie face consequences and also building up his self-esteem—because both those things need to happen.*

Mom: *No one else will punish him if I don't. He's already out of control.*

Practitioner: *Can you plan on how gift-giving will fit into some agreed-on rules and consequences?*

Mom: *My mother would never do anything like that. She does all of this completely behind my back.*

Practitioner: *Well, pick one thing you would like everyone to be on the same page about.*

Mom: *The iPad. I think it's ridiculous that Jamie now has one downstairs, although supposedly his younger brother can use it, when he's already got his phone that she—(jabs at Grandmother)—gave him only 6 months ago.*

Grandmother: *Don't be silly, Sandra. That was for his birthday.*

Mom: *She asked us how we were going to be on the same page. I choose the iPad. I want that to be returned and the boys just to have their phones.*

Grandmother: *I can't take the iPad away.*

Mom: *Why not?*

Grandmother: *He'd be heartbroken.*

Mom: *He didn't deserve it in the first place.*

Howard: *See how hard you can be? I think you'd enjoy taking it away from him.*

Practitioner: *Well, let's find out where everyone is at. Sandra, we already know what you want. How about the rest of you?*

Howard: *I don't even care. I don't want any part of it. I just don't want any more fighting.*

Mom: *If you say you give up, you can't argue with me later about it.*

Howard: *When do I ever do that?*

Mom: *Your ex even said you did that—passive-aggressive, she called it. It is very passive-aggressive, Howard.*

Practitioner: *So, Howard, you're saying you don't really care about who has rights and access to the iPad?*

He is red now though and probably hasn't heard the practitioner's last statement. Brother and sister are off, exchanging insults in an escalating fashion.

The reader may feel that the practitioner did not step in as often as needed. However, Minuchin (1974) has suggested that with *disengaged* relationships, in which there is little communication and warmth, as in the case with Sandra and her mother, it is necessary to have conflict occur first.

In the subsequent interaction, the practitioner begins to redirect the sequence of communication. It will be necessary for her to blast through the family's *homeostasis* (the tendency to stay in a steady state and resist change) using the technique of *intensity*, redirection of family interaction through the practitioner's repetition of instruction, use of a loud and emphatic voice tone, or requiring that an interaction endure for longer than families are comfortable (Minuchin & Fishman, 1981). Using a loud tone of voice may be quite acceptable in a family such as this one in which members frequently use raised voices. This also involves *mimesis*, part of the joining process, in which the practitioner purposely mimics the family's affect or style of communication, so that families feel comfortable with the practitioner as part of their system (Minuchin, 1974).

In the session, the practitioner subsequently tries to block the escalating interaction between Sandra and Howard. She repeats herself, louder each time, to break up the argument, and nonverbally uses her arm to block the stream of interaction. But it is not until she has challenged their assumptions by making the comment, "It seems like the adults in this family have just as hard a time listening as the kids" that they finally subside into silence. Although neither Sandra nor Howard responded verbally to this provocative remark, a change in perspective seems to result because the interactions between them thereafter become more contained. The rest of the session is spent discussing the different electronic devices that have been given to one child and not another, on what occasion they were given, the state of repair of the systems, the rules about when they could be used and who could use them, and so forth.

The discussion grinds along so endlessly that a practitioner may feel compelled to solve the problem for the family. However, a structural family therapist must attend to *process*, the sequence of interactions, rather than *content*, the subject matter that is being discussed. If the structural family therapist solves the problem for the family, the family does not find a new process for handling its problems. A family is defined as healthy not by the absence of problems, but by its ability to handle the problems that inevitably come. Problem-solving is assumed to occur as a byproduct of improved structure (Minuchin & Nichols, 1993).

DISCUSSION OF FIRST SESSION

By the end of the first session, much had been learned. From a structural family therapy viewpoint, Jamie's acting out has arisen from a faulty structure in the family. Jamie and his mother bicker like equals; his mother's attempts to establish control are challenged by Jamie until she loses her own temper, and they are both out of control. These behaviors are all indicators of an *enmeshed* relationship.

Ms. Witt's difficulties with managing her son are aggravated by her own mother's usurping of her rules. Grandmother and Jamie have established an *intergenerational coalition* in which she and Jamie are joined against Ms. Witt. *Coalitions* involve alignments of power in a family in which certain members join together (Minuchin et al., 1978). The coalition between Grandmother and Jamie gives Jamie an inappropriate level of power in the family hierarchy. This is seen in his behavior in the session (bossing around the adult members of his family and dominating the session discussion) and in Sandra and Howard's ineffective efforts to establish control.

Evidence of *circular causality* is present with the interactions of Grandmother and Mom regarding Jamie. Grandmother is concerned about the boy's self-esteem, "building a boy up." However, the more she treats Jamie with favoritism, the angrier Ms. Witt becomes, and the harder she is on Jamie. When Ms. Witt comes down on Jamie, Mrs. Clayborne wants to do nice things for him so that he'll feel better. Further, Ms. Witt and Mrs. Clayborne show evidence of a disengaged relationship in that they go for periods of time without speaking to each other and fail to negotiate between them how to handle the children. Each person has a different way of handling the functions of caring for and disciplining the children. They *detour* a lot of their conflict with each other onto Jamie, and Jamie is only too willing to become embroiled in their arguments.

Howard's role is that he fluctuates between playing the parent, thus undermining Sandra's role, and playing the friend, increasing Jamie's power in the family. Howard's alternating alignment with his mother and his sister further illustrate the confused boundaries between family subsystems and each member's role in the household, and how these alternating interactions maintain the balance or the *homeostasis* of the family. *Homeostasis* is further evidenced by the *complementarity* of roles of the two boys: Kyle (good son); Jamie (bad son). The assumption is that if transaction patterns are modified in-session through *enactments*, these new interactions can organize the family in a more functional state of balance in which boundaries between parental and sibling subsystems are more clearly drawn.

Session 2

In the second session, the parental hierarchy continued to be charged with the task of deciding on how they would build "both boys up," as well as give them consequences. *Intensity*, in the form of repeating instructions to talk over what needs to be done about a particular misbehavior of Jamie's, continued to be necessary to prevent members from becoming divided over "building up" and "tearing down."

The technique of *unbalancing* (Minuchin & Fishman, 1981) became necessary when Betty and Sandra were stuck in arguments. In this technique, the practitioner sides with one family member to unblock the "stuck" interaction, being careful to take turns with different family members so that one person doesn't feel "ganged up on." Another technique is to promote healthy complementarity in the family. When Sandra began to report that Jamie seemed less argumentative, she was asked what she was doing to account for his improved behavior. The assumption of circularity is inherent in this question.

To block Howard from continuing to maintain family balance by alternatively siding first with his mother and then his sister, he was challenged as to why he was putting himself in the middle of their arguments. He said he always had felt responsible for helping them get along with each other. When asked how successful his "help" has been, he admitted "not at all." Like his relief at being told that he could not be Jamie's father, Howard was noticeably unburdened to find he held no responsibility for his mother and sister's relationship, and his role in maintaining the family status quo was lessened.

Session 3

By the third session, a tremendous breakthrough occurred. The adults shared with the practitioner a plan they had formulated. It was a much more complex plan than the practitioner could have ever assigned. Each of the adults was to contribute money proportionate to their income to a fund for each child, who would receive certain amounts for reaching agreed-on academic and behavioral standards in school at the end of each grade. Jamie and Kyle could choose to use the money they received in any way they wished. The adults reported this plan with a great deal of enthusiasm, with each person finishing each other's sentences. This manner of interaction was in marked contrast to the bitterness apparent in the first session.

As was appropriate to the parental hierarchy, Mom was selected to report the plan to the children. However, the boys reacted in a low-key way, to the adults' disappointment. The practitioner stressed the importance of the adults working together to come up with a plan. The practitioner also explained the concept of homeostasis, that family members may resist change to maintain the status quo. She suggested the children might have felt uncomfortable with the adults' united front and may have been trying to provoke them into "changing back." The adults were warned to be "on the alert" for the boys' "resistance" and to regard any signs as further evidence of the changes that were occurring in the family system.

This session marked "a turning point," and soon after, the family members decided they had gotten what they needed from the counseling. Somehow, the electronic devices conundrum was resolved, although the practitioner could never track the details of the solution. Ms. Witt began to show more warmth toward Jamie, as well as to Kyle, who even displayed some normal infractions of rules at times. Mom was surprised to discover that although she spent less time refereeing the boys' fights and monitoring Jamie, the boys seemed better able to manage their own problems. On an individual basis, Jamie's behavior, although by no means perfect, seemed generally more compliant. Sandra's affect was altered in the process. Her tired, hopeless air had lifted, and she even considered working toward a mental health degree if she got her disability insurance. She said she wanted to help others as the practitioner had helped her family.

SUMMARY

This chapter reviews the disruptive behavior disorders, namely ODD and CD, which are highly prevalent disorders in youths. Both disorders feature anger and defiance, and ODD is sometimes a precursor to CD. These disorders have genetic and environmental influences and are much more common in youths living in low SES circumstances than in those who are middle to upper class. They also are potentially overdiagnosed in Black youths. Behavioral therapy (parent training) has decades of research support for children and was applied in a case example. The research on treatments for adolescents tends to focus on multicomponent family systems models and structural family therapy; this was demonstrated with an additional case.

REFERENCES

Alvarez, H., & Ollendick, T. (2003). Individual and psychosocial risk factors. In C. A. Essau (Ed.), *Conduct and oppositional defiant disorders: Epidemiology, risk factors, and treatment* (pp. 61–98). Mahwah, NJ: Lawrence Erlbaum.

American Psychiatric Association. (2022). *Diagnostic and statistical manual of mental disorders* (5th ed., Text Revision). Washington, DC: American Psychiatric Association.

Anderson, S., Hawes, D. J., & Snow, P. C. (2016). Language impairments among youth offenders: A systematic review. *Children and Youth Services Review, 65*, 195–203.

Aponte, H. (2002). Structural family therapy. In A. Robers & G. Greene (Eds.), *Social workers' desk reference* (pp. 263–267). New York: Oxford University Press.

Atkins-Loria, S., Macdonald, H., & Mitterling, C. (2015). Young African American men and the diagnosis of conduct disorder: The neo-colonization of suffering. *Clinical Social Work Journal, 43*, 431–441. https://doi-org.proxy.library.upenn.edu/10.1007/s10615-015-0531-8

Ayano, G., Betts, K., Maravilla, J. C., & Alati, R. (2021). A systematic review and meta-analysis of the risk of disruptive behavioral disorders in the offspring of parents with severe psychiatric disorders. *Child Psychiatry & Human Development, 52*(1), 77–95. https://doi.org/10.1007/s10578-020-00989-4

Baker, L. L., & Scarth, K. D. (2002). *Cognitive behavioural approaches to treating children and adolescents with conduct disorder.* Toronto: Children's Mental Health Ontario.

Ballentein, K. (2019). Understanding racial differences in diagnosing ODD versus ADHD using critical race theory. *Families in Society: The Journal of Contemporary Social Services, 100*(3), 282–292.

Baumel, A., Pawar, A., Mathur, N., Kane, J. M., & Correll, C. U. (2017). Technology-assisted parent training programs for children and adolescents with disruptive behaviors. *Journal of Clinical Psychiatry, 78*(8). https://doi.org/10.4088/jcp.16r11063

Burke, J., Loeber, R., & Birmaher, B. (2002). Oppositional defiant disorder and conduct disorder: A review of the past 10 years, part II. *Journal of the American Academy of Child and Adolescent Psychiatry, 41*, 1275–1294.

Center for Behavioral Health Statistics and Quality. (2016). *DSM-5 changes: Implications for child serious emotional disturbance.* Rockville, MD. Retrieved from https://www.ncbi.nlm. nih.gov/books/NBK519708/pdf/Bookshelf_ NBK519708.pdf

Copeland, W. E., Shanahan, L., Costello, E. J., & Angold, A. (2009). Childhood and adolescent psychiatric disorders as predictors of young adult disorders. *Archives of General Psychiatry, 66*(7), 764–772. Retrieved from http://www.archgenpsychiatry.com

Demmer, D. H., Hooley, M., Sheen, J., McGillivray, J. A., & Lum, J. A. (2017). Sex differences in the prevalence of oppositional defiant disorder during middle childhood: A meta-analysis. *Journal of Abnormal Child Psychology, 45*(2), 313–325. https://doi.org/10.1007/s10802-016-0170-8Dodge, K. (2003). Do social information-processing patterns mediate aggressive behavior? In B. Lahey, T. E. Moffitt, & A. Caspi (Eds.), *Causes of conduct disorder and juvenile delinquency* (pp. 254–276). New York: Guilford Press.

Egger, H., & Angold, A. (2006). Common emotional and behavioral disorders in preschool children: Presentation, nosology, and epidemiology. *Journal of Child Psychology and Psychiatry, 47*(3–4), 313–337.

Ehrensaft, M. K. (2005). Interpersonal relationships and sex differences in the development of conduct problems. *Clinical Child and Family Psychology Review, 8*(1), 39–63.

Erskine, H., Norman, R., Ferrari, A., Chan, G., Copeland, W., Whiteford, H. A., & Scott, J. (2016). Long-term outcomes of attention-deficit/hyperactivity disorder and conduct disorder: A systematic review and meta-analysis. *Journal of the American Academy of Child & Adolescent Psychiatry, 55*(10), 841–850. https://doi.org/10.1016/j.jaac.2016.06.016

Fadus, M. C., Ginsburg, K. R., Sobowale, K., Halliday-Boykins, C. A., Bryant, B. B., Gray, K. M., & Squeglia, L. M. (2020). Unconscious bias and the diagnosis of disruptive behavior disorders and ADHD in African American and Hispanic youth. *Acad Psychiatry, 44*, 95–102. https://doi.org/10.1007/s40596-019-01127-6

Fonagy, P., & Kurtz, Z. (2002). Disturbance of conduct. In P. Fonagy, M. Target, D. Cottrell, J. Phillips, & Z. Kurtz (Eds.), *What works for whom? A critical review of treatments for children and adolescents* (pp. 106–192). New York: Guilford Press.

Forehand, R., & McMahon, R. J. (1981). *Helping the noncompliant child: A clinician's guide to parent training.* New York: Guilford Press.

Forgatch, M. S., Patterson, G. R., & Friend, T. (2017). *Raising cooperative kids: Proven practices for a connected, happy family.* Newburyport, MA: Conari Press.

Frick, P. J. (2006). Developmental pathways to conduct disorder. *Child and Adolescent Psychiatric Clinics of North America, 15*, 311–331.

Gelhorn, H., Stallings, M., Young, S., Corley, R., Rhee, S. H., Christian, H., & Hewitt, J. (2006). Common and specific genetic influences on aggressive and nonaggressive conduct disorder domains. *Journal of the American Academy of Child and Adolescent Psychiatry, 45*(5), 570–577.

Ghandour, R. M., Sherman, L. J., Vladutiu, C. J., Ali, M. M., Lynch, S. E., Bitsko, R. H., & Blumberg, S. J. (2019). Prevalence and treatment of depression, anxiety, and conduct problems in US children. *Journal of Pediatrics, 206*, 256–267.

Goense, P. B., Assink, M., Stams, G. -J., Boendermaker, L., & Hoeve, M. (2016). Making "what works" work: A meta-analytic study of the effect of treatment integrity on outcomes of evidence-based interventions for juveniles with antisocial behavior. *Aggression and Violent Behavior, 31*, 106–115. doi:10.1016/j.avb.2016.08.003

Hankin, B. L., Abela, J. R. Z., Auerbach, R. P., McWhinnie, C. M., & Skitch, S. A. (2005). Development of behavioral problems over the life course: A vulnerability and stress perspective. In D. L. Hankin & J. R. Z. Abela (Eds.), *Development of psychopathology: A vulnerability-stress perspective* (pp. 385–416). Thousand Oaks, CA: Sage.

Hicks, B. M., South, S. C., DiRago, A. C., Iacono, W. G., & McGue, M. (2009). Environmental adversity and increasing genetic risk for externalizing disorders. *Archives of General Psychiatry, 66*, 640–648.

Hill, J. (2002). Biological, psychological and social processes in conduct disorders. *Journal of Child Psychology and Psychiatry, 43*(1), 133–164.

Hogue, A., Bobek, M., Dauber, S., Henderson, C., McLeod, B., & Southam-Gerow, M. (2017). Distilling the core elements of family therapy for adolescent substance use: Conceptual and empirical solutions. *Journal of Child & Adolescent Substance Abuse, 26*(6), 437–453. https://doi.org/10.1080/1067828X.2017.1322020

Hogue, A., Bobek, M., Dauber, S., Henderson, C., McLeod, B., & Southam-Gerow, M. (2019). Core elements of family therapy for adolescent behavior problems: Empirical distillation of three manualized treatments. *Journal of Clinical Child and Adolescent Psychology, 48*(1), 29–41. https://doi.org/10.1080/15374416.2018.1555762

Huey, S. J., Jr, & Polo, A. J. (2008). Evidence-based psychosocial treatments for ethnic minority youth. *Journal of Clinical Child and Adolescent Psychology: The Official Journal for the Society of Clinical Child and Adolescent Psychology, American Psychological Association, Division, 53, 37*(1), 262–301. https://doi.org/10.1080/1537441070182017

Jaffee, S. R., Caspi, A., & Moffitt, T. E. (2005). Nature x nurture: Genetic vulnerabilities interact with physical maltreatment to promote conduct problems. *Development and Psychopathology, 17*(1), 67–84.

Kazdin, A. (2001). Treatment of conduct disorders. In J. Hill & B. Maughan (Eds.), *Conduct disorders in childhood and adolescence* (pp. 408–448). New York: Cambridge University Press.Kendall, P. C., & Hedtke, K. (2006). *Cognitive-behavioral therapy for anxious children: Therapist manual* (3rd ed.). Ardmore, PA: Workbook.

Lahey, B., & Waldman, I. (2003). A developmental propensity model of the origins of conduct problems during childhood and adolescence. In B. Lahey, T. E. Moffitt, & A. Caspi (Eds.), *Causes of conduct disorder and juvenile delinquency* (pp. 76–117). New York: Guilford Press.

Ledingham, J. (1999). Children and adolescents with oppositional defiant disorder and conduct disorder in the community: Experiences at school and with peers. In H. Quay & A. Hogan (Eds.), *Handbook of disruptive behavior disorders* (pp. 353–370). New York: Kluwer Academic/Plenum.

Lees, D., Frampton, C. M., & Merry, S. N. (2019). Efficacy of a home visiting enhancement for high-risk families attending parent management programs. *JAMA Psychiatry, 76*(3), 241. doi:10.1001/jamapsychiatry.2018.4183

Lemery, K. S., & Doelger, L. (2005). Genetic vulnerabilities to the development of psychopathology. In B. L. Hankin & J. R. Z. Abela (Eds.), *Development of psychopathology: A vulnerability-stress perspective* (pp. 161–198). Thousand Oaks, CA: Sage.

Lipsey, M. W., Landenberger, N. A., & Wilson, S. J. (2007). Effects of cognitive-behavioral programs for criminal offenders. *Campbell Systematic Reviews, 6.* doi:10.4073/csr.2007.6

Lochman, J. E., & Wells, K. C. (2004). The coping power program for preadolescent aggressive boys and their parents: Outcome effects at the 1-year follow-up. *Journal of Consulting and Clinical Psychology, 72*(4), 571–578.

Lochman, J. E., Barry, T. D., & Pardini, D. P. (2003). Anger control training for aggressive youth. In A. E. Kazdin & J. R. Weisz (Eds.), *Evidence-based psychotherapies for children and adolescents* (pp. 263–281). New York: Guilford.

Lochman, J. E., Coie, J. D., Underwood, M. K., & Terry, R. (1993). Effectiveness of a social relations intervention program for aggressive and nonaggressive, rejected children. *Journal of Consulting and Clinical Psychology, 61*, 1053–1058.

Loeber, R., Burke, J. D., Lagey, B. B., Winters, A., & Zera, M. (2000). Oppositional defiant and conduct disorder: A review of the past 10 years, part I. *Journal of the American Academy of Child and Adolescent Psychiatry, 39*(12), 1468–1484.

Loeber, R., Green, S. M., Lahey, B. B., Frick, P. J., & McBurnett, K. (2002). Findings on disruptive behavior disorders from the first decade of the Developmental Trends Study. *Clinical Child and Family Psychology Review, 3*, 37–60.

Loy, J., Merry, S., Hetrick, S., & Stasiak, K. (2017). Atypical antipsychotics for disruptive behavior disorders in children and youths. *Cochrane Database of Systematic Reviews*, 8, CD008559.

Marcus, D. K., Fulton, J. J., & Clarke, E. J. (2010). Lead and conduct problems: A meta-analysis. *Journal of Clinical Child and Adolescent Psychology*, 39(2), 234–241.

McCart, M. R., Sheidow, A. J., & Jaramillo, J. (2022). Evidence base update of psychosocial treatments for adolescents with disruptive behavior. *Journal of Clinical Child & Adolescent Psychology*, doi:10.1080/15374416.2022.2145566

Michelson, D., Davenport, C., Dretze, J., Barlow, J., & Day, C. (2013). Do evidence-based interventions work when tested in the "real world?": A systematic review and meta-analysis of parent management training for the treatment of child disruptive behavior. *Clinical Child Family Psychology Review*, 16, 18–34. https://doi-org.proxy.library.upenn.edu/10.1007/s10567-013-0128-0

Miller-Johnson, S., Coie, J. D., Maumary-Gremaud, A., & Bierman, K. (2002). Peer rejection and aggression and early starter models of conduct disorder. *Journal of Abnormal Child Psychology*, 30(3), 217–231.

Mingebach, T., Kamp-Becker, I., Christiansen, H., & Weber, L. (2018). Meta-meta-analysis on the effectiveness of parent-based interventions for the treatment of child externalizing behavior problems. *PLOS One*, 13(9). https://doi.org/10.1371/journal.pone.0202855

Minuchin, S. (1974). *Families and family therapy*. Cambridge, MA: Harvard University Press.

Minuchin, S., & Fishman, H. C. (1981). *Family therapy techniques*. Cambridge, MA: Harvard University Press.

Minuchin, S., Montalvo, B., Guerney Jr., B. G., Rosman, B. L., & Schumer, F. (1967). *Families of the slums: An exploration of their structure and treatment*. New York: Basic Books.

Minuchin, S., & Nichols, M. P. (1993). *Family healing: Tales of hope and renewal from family therapy*. New York: Free Press.

Moffitt, T., Caspi, A., Harrington, H., & Milne, B. (2002). Males on the life-course-persistent and adolescence-limited antisocial pathways: Follow-up at age 26 years. *Development and Psychopathology*, 14, 179–207.

Moffitt, T., Caspi, A., Rutter, M., & Silva, P. (2001). *Sex differences in antisocial behavior: Conduct disorder, delinquency, and violence in the Dunedin longitudinal study*. New York: Cambridge University Press.

Morgan, P. L., Staff, J., Hillemeier, M. M., Farkas, G., & Maczuga, S. (2013). Racial and ethnic disparities in ADHD diagnosis from kindergarten to eighth grade. *Pediatrics*, 132(1), 85–93.

Murray, J., Irving, B., Farrington, D. P., Colman, I., & Bloxsom, C. A. J. (2010). Very early predictors of conduct problems and crime: Results from a national cohort study. *Journal of Child Psychology and Psychiatry*, 51(11), 1198–1207. doi:10.1111/j.1469-7610.2010.02287.x

Nigg, J., & Huang-Pollock, C. (2003). An early-onset model of the role of executive functions and intelligence in conduct disorder/delinquency. In B. Lahey, T. E. Moffitt, & A. Caspi (Eds.), *Causes of conduct disorder and juvenile delinquency* (pp. 227–253). New York: Guilford Press.

Nock, M. K., Kazdin, A. E., Hiripi, E., & Kessler, R. C. (2006). Prevalence, subtypes, and correlates of DSM–IV conduct disorder in the National Comorbidity Survey Replication. *Psychological Medicine*, 36(5), 699–710.

Ohan, J., & Johnston, C. (2005). Gender appropriateness of symptom criteria for attention-deficit/hyperactivity disorder, oppositional-defiant disorder, and conduct disorder. *Child Psychiatry and Human Development, 35*, 359–381.

Pappadopulos, E., Woolston, S., Chait, A., Perkins, M., Connor, D. F., & Jensen, P. S. (2006). Pharmacotherapy of aggression in children and adolescents: Efficacy and effect size. *Journal of the Canadian Academy of Child and Adolescent Psychiatry, 15*(1), 27–39.

Patterson, G. R. (1977). *Living with Children: New Methods for Parents and Teachers* (Revised Edition). Champaign, IL: Research Press.

Rutter, J. G., & Friedberg, R. (1999). Guidelines for the effective use of Socratic dialogue in cognitive therapy. In L. Vandecreek, S. Knapp, & T. L. Jackson (Eds.), *Innovations in clinical practice: A sourcebook* (Vol. 17, pp. 481–490). Sarasota, FL: Professional Resource Press.

van Mourik, K., Crone, M. R., de Wolff, M. S., & Reis, R. (2017). Parent training programs for ethnic minorities: A meta-analysis of adaptations and effect. *Prevention Science, 18*(1), 95–105. https://doi.org/10.1007/s11121-016-0733-5

Visser, S. N., Deubler, E. L., Bitsko, R. H., Holbrook, J. R., & Danielson, M. L. (2016). Demographic differences among a national sample of US youth with behavioral disorders. *Clinical Pediatrics, 55*(14), 1358–1362. doi:10.1177/0009922815623229

Wachs, T. (2000). *Necessary but not sufficient.* Washington, DC: American Psychological Association.

Webster-Stratton, C. (2001). The incredible years: Parents, teachers, and children training series. *Residential Treatment for Children & Youth, 18*(3), 31–45.

Wilson, S. J., & Lipsey, M. W. (2007). School-based interventions for aggressive and disruptive behavior: Update of a meta-analysis. *American Journal of Preventive Medicine, 33*(2), S130–S143.

8

Substance Use Disorders

Carly Gomez is a 15-year-old Latina female who was referred for treatment by her school counselor after she and a friend were caught smoking marijuana just off school grounds. Carly presented to treatment accompanied by her mother, Maria Gomez, for an intake evaluation at a community mental health center with an outpatient adolescent substance use program. Carly and her mother live together in a two-bedroom apartment; she does not have any siblings, and her father died while her mother was pregnant with Carly. They do not have any other family in the area, but Ms. Gomez reported a strong support network of friends. Ms. Gomez reported that, before the incident at school, she had suspected Carly had used marijuana because she occasionally smelled an odor of marijuana on her, but Carly had always denied using it herself. Carly had told her mother that some of her friends used it from time to time, but that she did not use it herself. However, after she was found to be using marijuana at school, Ms. Gomez questioned Carly again. Carly admitted that she was using marijuana herself "just once in a while, to unwind." Ms. Gomez reported that she had searched Carly's room after this conversation and found a small baggie of marijuana and a vape pen in Carly's closet.

Based on that and the recommendation from Carly's school, Ms. Gomez scheduled a therapy intake. Ms. Gomez reported that she had also been concerned lately that Carly was "not herself" and described her as seeming to be "in a funk." Carly stated that she was fine and that her marijuana use was "no big deal." She reported that she had only come to the appointment to "get my mom and the school off my back." During the intake appointment, Carly was quiet and mainly looked down at the ground. She responded when spoken to, but her answers were generally short, and she presented as slightly irritable. Ms. Gomez presented as eager to help her daughter but noted that she felt "at a loss" for what to do.

OVERVIEW

Almost 4% of adolescents in the past year met criteria for a substance use disorder (Substance Abuse and Mental Health Services Administration [SAMHSA], 2019). The *Diagnostic and Statistical Manual of Mental Disorders* (DSM) provides

Child and Adolescent Mental Health in Social Work. Jacqueline Corcoran and Courtney Benjamin Wolk, Oxford University Press.
© Oxford University Press 2023. DOI: 10.1093/oso/9780197653562.003.0008

general criteria for *substance-related disorders* rather than separate criteria for each substance, of which 10 categories are included (American Psychiatric Association [APA], 2022). The disorders are characterized as mild, moderate, or severe, depending on the number of symptoms identified, which range from negative consequences of use to compulsive use despite serious consequences, often accompanied by tolerance and withdrawal. Cannabis is the most abused substance among adolescents (SAMHSA, 2019), and opioids are the most common drugs of misuse for adolescent females and the third most common for males (SAMHSA, 2019). Alcohol and tobacco are also commonly misused (Subramaniam & Volkow, 2014). Because of increased prescribing practices of opioids for chronic pain, the use of prescription opioids and the illegal use of opioids have increased drastically. Prescription sales, as well as overdoses from prescription opioids, have quadrupled since 1999 (CDC, 2017). The most common prescription opioids involve methadone, oxycodone (OxyContin), and hydrocodone (Vicodin). A statistically significant increase in the prevalence of prescription opioid misuse occurred among those aged 11 to 30 from 1993 through 2010 (Jordan et al., 2017). Opioids are currently the most common cause of accidental death in the United States, and between 1999 and 2006 opioid overdoses increased more sharply among adolescents than any other age group (Edlund et al., 2015); the increased availability of fentanyl, which is highly potent, has been identified as one reason for this (King et al., 2014).

Of note, this chapter focuses on adolescent substance use. While substance use disorders can and do occur in childhood, the rates of childhood substance use disorders are low. The prevalence and burden of substance use disorders increases considerably during the adolescent period and into adulthood; rates of substance use begin to increase notably during the middle school years (Gallimberti et al., 2015). Additionally, the empirical literature on the treatment of substance use in youths is focused predominantly on adolescents because of the low base rate in childhood (Erskine et al., 2014).

RISK AND PROTECTIVE FACTORS

Biological

Heritability is an estimate of the genetic contribution to individual differences within a population. A review of twin and adoption studies indicates that adolescent substance use is moderately heritable, with genetic factors explaining 45% of the variance in risk for alcohol dependence and 37% for marijuana dependence (Hopfer et al., 2003). The Collaborative Study on the Genetics of Alcoholism indicates that the gene GABRA2 is related to alcohol dependence (Edenberg et al., 2004). The neurotransmitter system most associated with addiction is the dopamine system and its associated genes. Cravings are experienced when people want to experience the same level of dopamine that has been stimulated by substance.

To explain the onset of substance misuse in adolescents, a *dual systems model* has been discussed in the literature (Hogue et al., 2018). First, there is maturation in the adolescent brain's motivation and reward system that is associated with pleasure-seeking. At the same time, alterations in the cognitive control system and its related executive functions make adolescence a period of potential risky behavior. Changes in the brain have been observed following treatment. According to a systematic review, "cortical and subcortical brain regions involved in cognition, emotion regulation, decision-making, reward, and self-reference are associated with treatment response in addicted youth" (Hammond et al., 2019).

While some experimentation with substances is normative in adolescence, early use of substances is a risk factor for the development of problem use (Hingson et al., 2006). For example, 15.2% of people who start drinking by age 14 eventually develop alcohol abuse/dependence, compared with only 2.1% of those who wait until they are at least 21 years old (McCabe et al., 2007).

Psychological

One factor that protects against the development of substance use disorders is not having another mental disorder (Armstrong & Costello, 2002). A systematic review looking at prospective risk for substance-related disorders found 37 studies involving 762,187 participants. Childhood attention-deficit/hyperactivity disorder (ADHD), oppositional defiant disorder (ODD), conduct disorder (CD), and depression (but not anxiety) increased the risk for development of a substance use disorder (Groenman et al., 2017; Nawi et al., 2021) and for relapse following treatment (Chung & Maisto, 2006; Hogue et al., 2018).

Early externalizing problems raise the risk of developing a substance use disorder later. In treatment, most adolescents with substance use disorder will have another mental health disorder (Hawke et al., 2018). Other psychological risk factors have been identified, including impulsivity, rebelliousness and risk-taking, lack of emotional regulation, and more screen time (Nawi et al., 2021).

Social

At the social level, peers who use substances place an individual at risk, whereas friends who do not support such use are protective against the development of alcohol and drug problems. Consorting with non–substance-using peers after treatment also protects a youth against relapse (Cheng, 2006). Sports participation in high school apparently reduces illicit drug use but not alcohol use (Kwan et al., 2014).

Several parenting and family factors are related to substance misuse in youths. Lack of parental monitoring and a parenting style that is either warm without holding children accountable or strict without warmth (Bahr & Hoffmann, 2010), parental provision of alcohol, and parental drinking are positively associated with risk. Along the same lines, parental monitoring, positive parent–child relationship, parental support, and parental involvement are protective qualities (Yap et al., 2017). A relationship with a caring adult who instills goals and cultural values is a protective factor against substance use disorders for American Indian/Alaskan Native youths, who have higher rates of substance use disorders compared with other ethnic groups (Woods et al., 2022).

Youth who have experienced trauma (child maltreatment; Nawi et al., 2021) and LGBTQ youths are at particularly high risk for substance misuse. In the National Comorbidity Replication Survey—Adolescent Supplement, experiencing traumatic events before age 11 was associated with higher risk for use of marijuana, cocaine, and prescription drugs (Carliner et al., 2016). A systematic review indicated that lesbian, gay, and bisexual youths have 190% higher odds for use compared with heterosexual youths (Marshal et al., 2008). This has been attributed to the increased social stigma, discrimination, and psychosocial stressors experienced by LGBTQ youths.

Neighborhood factors can also provide risk or protection. Availability of substances is associated with abuse (Nawi et al., 2021). A literature base on the effect of new state policies governing the legality of cannabis and the impact on adolescents has developed. A systematic review of U.S. medical marijuana laws found that laws did not increase the prevalence of adolescent marijuana use (Sarvert et al., 2018), although recent research suggests that while smoking marijuana declined in adolescents following legalization, other modes of ingestion increased (e.g., edibles, dabbing; Tormohlen et al., 2019). An analysis showed that the proximity and density of medical marijuana dispensaries was not related to adolescents' current use or susceptibility to use marijuana (Shi et al., 2018). Medical marijuana legislature was associated with declines in use among male, Black, and Latino adolescents (Coley et al., 2019). Decriminalization predicted significant declines in marijuana use among Latino adolescents and significant increases among white adolescents. Neither medical marijuana nor decriminalization policies were significantly associated with frequency of use or heavier marijuana use (Coley et al., 2019).

ASSESSMENT

Before discussing the assessment of adolescents for substance use disorders, the clinician should recognize the critiques of the DSM criteria. A primary concern is whether the physiologic change domain is relevant for adolescents. Winters, Martin, and Chung (2011) asserted that symptoms, such as tolerance (i.e., needing more of the substance to get the same high), may be developmentally normative for adolescents and young adults as they move from experimental use to regular use, whereas symptoms of withdrawal (i.e., physical symptoms experienced when use of the substance is stopped) may be a relatively rare phenomenon in this age group because of the time required to become physically dependent.

Table 8.1 CRITERIA COMMON ACROSS MANY OF THE DSM SUBSTANCE
USE DISORDERS

Cognitive, behavioral, and physiologic symptoms denoting use despite significant
substance-related problems (at least two):

A. Impaired control
   1. Taking larger amounts/over a longer period
   2. Persistent desire to cut down use but unsuccessful
   3. A lot of time devoted to getting the substance
   4. Cravings
B. Social impairment due to use
   1. At major role obligations
   2. Persistent/recurrent interpersonal conflict
   3. Important social, occupational, or recreational activities are sacrificed
C. Risky use when
   1. Physically hazardous
   2. It causes physical or psychological problems
D. Pharmacologic
   1. Tolerance—need for increased dose
   2. Withdrawal

One way to screen for alcohol use disorders is the DSM-IV two-item instrument: (1) In the past year, have you sometimes been under the influence of alcohol in situations where you could have caused an accident or gotten hurt? (2) Have there often been times when you had a lot more to drink than you intended to have? Adolescents who answer yes to at least one of the two items are eightfold more likely to be diagnosed with a disorder, according to a systematic review (Newton et al., 2017).

Although cannabis is widely used, it remains unclear which consumption patterns are more likely to produce future consequences (risky/hazardous use) or current damage (problematic/harmful use). According to a systematic review on this topic, definitions identified in articles and official websites varied considerably (Casajuana et al., 2016), and the recommendation is to use "weekly cannabis use" as a cutoff for problematic use and to have youths take the Cannabis Abuse and Screening Test (Bastiani et al., 2017). See Table 8.1 for some typical questions to ask in a clinical interview, Table 8.2 for a list of freely available measures, and Box 8.1 for potential goals to work on.

A method for identifying and enhancing motivation to reduce substance misuse and to seek treatment is the screening, brief intervention, and referral to treatment (SBIRT) approach, although empirical support for its use with adolescents is not yet conclusive (Gwin Mitchell et al., 2013; Yuma-Guerrero et al., 2012). See https://psattcelearn.org/courses/4hr_sbirt/ for a free training course on this approach.

The social worker met separately with Carly and her mother to conduct clinical interviews to understand Carly's current symptoms and functioning and relevant

Table 8.2 Measures of Addiction in Youth

Psychometric Support	Measure Name	No. of Items	Completed by[a]	Ages[c]	Link to Measure
Excellent	Hooked on Nicotine Checklist (HONC; DiFranza et al., 2002)	10	Y	12+	https://cancercontrol.cancer.gov/brp/tcrb/guide-measures/honc.html
Good	Fagerstrom Test for Nicotine Dependence (FTND; Prokhorov et al., 1996; Heatherton et al., 1991)	7	Y	Adolescents[d]	http://bit.ly/FTND_inst
Good	Car-Relax-Alone-Forget-Family-and-Friends-Trouble (CRAFFT; Farrell et al., 1999)*	9	Y, C	14–18	https://crafft.org/get-the-crafft/
Good	Cannabis Use Problems Identification Test (CUPIT; Bashford et al., 2010)	16	Y	13+	http://www.massey.ac.nz/massey/learning/departments/school-of-psychology/research/cupit/clinicians/clinicians_home.cfm
Good	Adolescent Cannabis Problems Questionnaire (CPQ-A; Gates & Swift, 2006)	12 and 27	Y	14–18	http://bit.ly/CPQ-A_inst; https://cannabissupport.com.au/files/media/4564/adolescent-cannabis-problems-questionnaire.pdf
Adequate	CAGE—Adapted to Include Drugs (AID; Couwenbergh et al., 2009; Brown et al., 1995)	4	Y, P	18–Dec	http://bit.ly/CAGE-AID_inst
Adequate	Severity Dependence Scale (SDS; Gossop et al., 1995)*	5	Y	14+	http://adai.washington.edu/instruments/pdf/Severity_of_Dependence_Scale_397.pdf
Adequate	Cannabis Use Disorder Identification Test—Revised (CUDIT-R; Loflin et al., 2018)	8	Y	Adolescents[d]	http://bit.ly/CUDIT_inst

			[a]	[b][c]	
Adequate	Brief Screener for Tobacco Alcohol and Other Drugs (BSTAD; Kelly et al., 2014; Levy et al., 2014)	11	Y	12–17	https://www.drugabuse.gov/nidamed-medical-health-professionals/screening-tools-resources/screening-tools-for-adolescent-substance-use
Adequate	TCU Drug Screen (Knight et al., 2014)*	15	Y	13–19	https://ibr.tcu.edu/forms/drug-use-and-crime-risk-forms-adol/s
Adequate	Rutgers Alcohol Problem Index (RAPI; White & Labouvie, 1989)	10, 18, or 23	Y, C	12–18+	http://bit.ly/RAPI_inst
Adequate	Risks and Consequences Questionnaire (RCQ; Stein et al., 2010)	26	Y	14–19	http://www.midss.org/content/risks-and-consequences-questionnaire-rcq
Adequate	Adolescents' Need for Smoking Scale (ANSS; Richardson et al., 2007)	35	Y	Adolescents[d]	http://www.chrisgrichardson.ca/anss/about-the-anss/get-the-anss/

[a] Completed by: Y = youth, P = parent/caregiver, C = clinician, T = teacher.
[b] Intended clinical use: S = screening, D = diagnostic aid or treatment planning, O = outcome monitoring.
[c] Exact age range for specific forms (e.g., self-report, parent report) may vary.
[d] Exact age range not specified.
* Available in multiple languages.

NOTE: Table adapted from Becker-Haimes, E. M., Tabachnick, A. R., Last, B. S., Stewart, R. E., Hasan-Granier, A., & Beidas, R. S. (2020). Evidence base update for brief, free, and accessible youth mental health measures. *Journal of Clinical Child & Adolescent Psychology*, *49*(1), 1–17, reprinted by permission of the publisher (Taylor & Francis Ltd, http://www.tandfonline.com).

(continued)

Table 8.2 Continued

References for measures in Table 8.2:

Bashford, J., Flett, R., & Copeland, J. (2010). The Cannabis Use Problems Identification Test (CUPIT): Development, reliability, concurrent and predictive validity among adolescents and adults. *Addiction, 105*(4), 615–625.

Brown, R. L., & Rounds, L. A. (1995). Conjoint screening questionnaires for alcohol and other drug abuse: Criterion validity in a primary care practice. *Wisconsin Medical Journal, 94*(3), 135–140.

Couwenbergh, C., Van Der Gaag, R. J., Koeter, M., De Ruiter, C., & Van den Brink, W. (2009). Screening for substance abuse among adolescents: Validity of the CAGE-AID in youth mental health care. *Substance Use & Misuse, 44*(6), 823-834.

DiFranza, J. R., Savageau, J. A., Fletcher, K., Ockene, J. K., Rigotti, N. A., McNeill, A. D., . . . Wood, C. (2002). Measuring the loss of autonomy over nicotine use in adolescents: The DANDY (Development and Assessment of Nicotine Dependence in Youths) study. *Archives of Pediatrics & Adolescent Medicine, 156*(4), 397–403.

Gossop, M., Darke, S., Griffiths, P., Hando, J., Powis, B., Hall, W., & Strang, J. (1995). The Severity of Dependence Scale (SDS): Psychometric properties of the SDS in English and Australian samples of heroin, cocaine and amphetamine users. *Addiction, 90*(5), 607–614.

Heatherton, T. F., Kozlowski, L. T., Frecker, R. C., & Fagerstrom, K. O. (1991). The Fagerström test for nicotine dependence: A revision of the Fagerstrom Tolerance Questionnaire. *British Journal of Addiction, 86*(9), 1119–1127.

Kelly, S. M., Gryczynski, J., Mitchell, S. G., Kirk, A., O'Grady, K. E., & Schwartz, R. P. (2014). Validity of brief screening instrument for adolescent tobacco, alcohol, and drug use. *Pediatrics, 133*(5), 819–826.

Knight, D. K., Blue, T. R., Flynn, P. M., & Knight, K. (2018). The TCU drug screen 5: Identifying justice-involved individuals with substance use disorders. *Journal of Offender Rehabilitation, 57*(8), 525–537.

Knight, J. R., Shrier, L. A., Bravender, T. D., Farrell, M., Vander Bilt, J., & Shaffer, H. J. (1999). A new brief screen for adolescent substance abuse. *Archives of Pediatrics & Adolescent Medicine, 153*(6), 591–596.

Levy, S. J., & Williams, J. F. (2016). Substance use screening, brief intervention, and referral to treatment. *Pediatrics, 138*(1), e20161211.

Loflin, M., Babson, K., Browne, K., & Bonn-Miller, M. (2018). Assessment of the validity of the CUDIT-R in a subpopulation of cannabis users. *American Journal of Drug and Alcohol Abuse, 44*(1), 19–23.

Martin, G., Copeland, J., Gilmour, S., Gates, P., & Swift, W. (2006). The adolescent cannabis problems questionnaire (CPQ-A): Psychometric properties. *Addictive Behaviors, 31*(12), 2238–2248.

Prokhorov, A. V., Pallonen, U. E., Fava, J. L., Ding, L., & Niaura, R. (1996). Measuring nicotine dependence among high-risk adolescent smokers. *Addictive Behaviors, 21*(1), 117–127.

Richardson, C. G., Johnson, J. L., Ratner, P. A., Zumbo, B. D., Bottorff, J. L., Shoveller, J. A., & Prkachin, K. M. (2007). Validation of the Dimensions of Tobacco Dependence Scale for adolescents. *Addictive Behaviors, 32*(7), 1498–1504.

Stein, L. A., Lebeau, R., Clair, M., Rossi, J. S., Martin, R. M., & Golembeske, C. (2010). Validation of a measure to assess alcohol- and marijuana-related risks and consequences among incarcerated adolescents. *Drug and Alcohol Dependence, 109*(1–3), 104–113.

White, H. R., & Labouvie, E. W. (1989). Towards the assessment of adolescent problem drinking. *Journal of Studies on Alcohol, 50*(1), 30–37.

Box 8.1

ASSESSMENT QUESTIONS FOR ADOLESCENT SUBSTANCE USE DISORDERS

1. Examine patterns of use, including onset, frequency, quantity, drugs of choice, tolerance or withdrawal symptoms, and craving. Note that the pattern of drinking in youths is often not so much one of high frequency as it is binge drinking (Miranda & Treloar, 2016).
2. Examine attributions for use (e.g., the thrill of risky behavior, depression), "triggers," and contexts of use.
3. Review consequences of substance use in the physical (might include physical examination), psychological, relationship, legal, financial, and educational realms.
4. Assess motivation for treatment, including the perceived advantages and disadvantages of use, and consider client's possible goals (e.g., reduced drinking) that align with the level of motivation. See SBIRT (screening, brief intervention, and referral to treatment).
5. Review major life events that may contribute to substance use.
6. Assess the possible coexistence of other disorders, including the relationship between the onset and progression of the other symptoms and their association with substance use. Conduct disorder may be considered if used for thrills, involves experimentation with peers, and occurs in the context of behaviors, such as sneaking out of the house, vandalism, and so forth. Depression may be considered if used for feelings of stress, emotional pain, and so forth.
7. Consider the client's strengths and coping skills and inquire about periods of abstinence or reduced use.
8. Assess the client's social support networks.
9. Assess suicide risk.

---

history. Ms. Gomez reported that she herself has struggled with depression off and on over the years, especially following the death of Carly's father in a car accident when she was pregnant with Carly. Ms. Gomez reported that was a difficult time for her because "I was pregnant and now my baby wouldn't have her father." Ms. Gomez received a great deal of support from her mother during Carly's childhood, but Carly's grandmother had passed away 4 years earlier, which was a difficult time for both Carly and Ms. Gomez. Carly's paternal relatives all live in Mexico, and Ms. Gomez does not have any siblings or extended family in the area. Ms. Gomez reported a strong connection to some other Mexican American families in their neighborhood and a strong social support network of friends. Ms. Gomez works in the office of a car repair shop and occasionally helps a friend clean houses for extra money on weekends. Carly often accompanies her mother to clean.

Carly is currently a sophomore in high school and reports that she would like to be a nurse one day. Carly generally earns good grades, although recently (about

2 weeks ago) she failed a midterm exam, which has caused considerable stress. Carly's academic attendance is consistent. Carly has several close friends her age and a best friend, Jess, whom she has been friends with since first grade. She maintains a friendship with her former boyfriend, whom she broke up with several months ago after he was unfaithful to her. This breakup has been an additional source of stress for Carly.

Carly has never been in therapy before or received any other mental health or substance use treatment. Carly's medical history is unremarkable. Her mother reported that Carly receives regular routine medical care and noted that she was evaluated for a thyroid abnormality within the past 6 months, after her mother had mentioned to the pediatrician during a routine physical exam that Carly had seemed "a little down," and that the results of these tests were unremarkable.

Carly's mother was unsure how long Carly had been using marijuana or the frequency of her use. She noted that Carly has seemed "down" for several months and more tired than usual but was unsure whether the changes in mood were related to or coincided with marijuana use. Ms. Gomez did not endorse any additional areas of concern for Carly.

Carly was initially quiet and denied any concerns, but as the interview progressed, she warmed up a bit and started to disclose additional information. She did not volunteer many details but was able to respond to specific questions when asked and appeared to be doing so in an open and honest manner. Carly reported that she had used marijuana for the first time about 1 year earlier with a boy she liked at the time. At first, she said she would only use marijuana once or twice a month when with a particular group of friends; however, in the past 3 months she has begun buying it for herself from a classmate's older sibling. This increase in use reportedly coincided with finding out that her first boyfriend, whom she dated for 2 months, had cheated on her at a party. She stated she usually uses with friends after school, and lately this has been happening most days. Over the past month, she has also started to use on her own some days in the evenings or on weekends (two to three times per week) when her mother is working or out of the house. Carly reported, "Smoking weed just helps me relax. I'm not really sure what the big deal is—it's just weed. Everyone does it." She stated that she could stop using at any time but had no desire to stop, other than she doesn't like getting in trouble at school or upsetting her mother. She denied symptoms of tolerance or withdrawal. In addition to getting in trouble at school, Carly reported that her best friend Jess doesn't like that Carly uses marijuana and has told her she thinks, "It's trashy" and has asked, "Why are you into that?" Carly reported that she and Jess have spent much less time together over the past month than they used to because Jess does not like to be around marijuana or the friends from school that Carly sometimes uses it with. Carly also noted that after a stressful day she just wants to "go smoke so I can take my mind off things and chill." She noted that when she wants to smoke at home, she will sneak out her bedroom window and climb up the fire escape to the roof to smoke even though her mother has forbidden her from using the fire escape except in the event of an emergency.

Based on Carly's report, the clinician determined Carly met criteria for a diagnosis of cannabis use disorder (mild severity). Carly denied any other drug use and reported that she had tried alcohol on a few occasions with friends, drinking two or three drinks on each of those occasions.

Carly also reported experiencing several depressive symptoms; however, it was unclear during the intake whether these symptoms were independent of Carly's marijuana use or related. Specifically, Carly reported she has been experiencing depressed mood and loss of interest in previously pleasurable activities for several weeks. Additional symptoms reported included insomnia (difficulty falling asleep for approximately 1.5 hours nightly despite being tired unless she has recently used marijuana) and fatigue. Carly also reported that approximately 2 weeks ago, after she was caught by a school employee using marijuana near the school, she began thinking that it would be better if she were dead. Carly reported that while thinking about being better off dead she "caught myself," and realized she didn't actually want to die. She stated she would never harm herself because she has hope that things will improve in the future. She has never made a plan for suicide or had any suicide attempts. The social worker decided not to assign a major depressive disorder (MDD) diagnosis at the time because the symptoms were occurring solely in the context of increased cannabis use, but to closely monitor the symptoms and consider whether additional interventions for depression would be needed.

INTERVENTION

Adolescents who access care for substance use concerns are often clients in other intervention systems, such as child welfare, juvenile justice, primary care, emergency departments, and mental health (Merikangas et al., 2011). The needs of each young person may consequently be managed by multiple agencies, and providing quality treatment often requires the social worker's navigation across these systems (Kraft et al., 2006).

Among the approximately 1.7 million adolescents in the United States meeting substance use disorder diagnostic criteria annually, only 7% receive specialized alcohol or drug abuse treatment, and only 25% receive any kind of mental health services (U.S. Department of Health and Human Services, 2011). Unfortunately, the evidence-based treatments that are discussed in this section are not delivered to most of the youths in need of services (Hogue et al., 2018), but it is important for social workers to know what the evidence supports so that they can provide leadership to their agencies and treatment settings.

Most adolescents (80%) receive substance use disorder treatment on an outpatient basis (Hogue et al., 2018). Cannabis may be easier than alcohol or other drugs to treat on an outpatient basis (Tanner-Smith et al., 2013). Other settings involve intensive outpatient treatment (three to five times a week), inpatient hospital stays, day treatment, residential placement, and, at times, incarceration. For further guidance on appropriate placement, social workers should be aware of the American Society of Addiction Medicine (ASAM) criteria (2020) [https://www.asam.org/asam-criteria/about].

Box 8.2

TEMPLATE OF GOALS FOR ADOLESCENT SUBSTANCE USE DISORDERS

1. Reduce or eliminate substance use. Lifelong abstinence might not be a necessary goal given the age of the child (Miranda & Treloar, 2016), but abstinence for a time period may be necessary.
2. Improve psychological and social functioning by mending disrupted relationships, reducing impulsivity, building social and vocational skills, and maintaining employment.
3. Prevent relapse.
4. Improve family communication.
5. Help parents develop skills for providing proper guidance and limit-setting.
6. Recognize and, if possible, treat addiction patterns in the parents.
7. Help adolescents and their families develop substance use–free lifestyles.

Although the goals of treatment should be collaboratively derived with the client, the template of goals in Box 8.2 may be useful as a starting point (Bukstein et al., 2005; Larimer et al., 1999). Regarding interventions that will help adolescents reach their goals, we will focus on psychosocial treatment because the research on medications for adolescent substance use disorders is scarce and has tended to comprise null findings (Miranda & Treloar, 2016). When comorbid conditions are present, the integration of substance use interventions with other evidence-based interventions (e.g., for comorbidities like depression) is recommended (SAMHSA, 2020). However, there has been limited research to date specifically examining the integration or sequencing of evidence-based substance use and mental health interventions among youth samples (e.g., Rohde et al., 2014). More research is needed.

Individual Therapy

MOTIVATIONAL INTERVIEWING

Motivational interviewing (MI) is a person-centered, collaborative method for exploring ambivalence and enhancing motivation to change (Miller & Rollnick, 2012). MI delivered in a single session does not have much impact on drug use (Li et al., 2016), but Tanner-Smith and Lipsey (2015) analyzed 24 adolescent studies and found that MI was moderately effective in reducing alcohol consumption and related problems among adolescents, with effects maintained up to 1 year. More recently, MI was studied in relation to problematic cannabis use. In teens, MI was helpful for the outcome of abstinence (no longer using) but not for the outcome of reduction of use (Calomarde-Gómez et al., 2021). According to this systematic review, outcomes for adults were more positive overall than for adolescents. In Hogue et al.'s (2018) analysis, motivational interviewing warranted a classification

Table 8.3 COGNITIVE-BEHAVIORAL THERAPY TECHNIQUES

Technique	Description
Functional analysis of behavior problems	Identifying the typical scenarios in which substance misuse occurs and antecedents ("triggers"), analyzing positive and negative outcomes (i.e., decisional balancing, cost–benefit analysis)
Prosocial activity sampling	Restructuring everyday environments "stimulus control" to (a) avoid high-risk persons and situations and (b) seek new outlets for social and recreational activities
Cognitive monitoring and restructuring	Monitoring cognitions and gaining awareness of how cognitions and core beliefs influence emotions and behaviors; learning to view events or behaviors in a new light, to use reason, or to consider alternatives
Emotion regulation training	Anger management and relaxation training
Problem-solving training	Identifying stressors, breaking them down into manageable problems, brainstorming solutions, analyzing and weighing the advantages and disadvantages, and selecting an option to use
Communication training	Active listening, suggesting possible solutions, role-playing effective communication

of "probably efficacious," which means there were at least two group-design studies that showed MI was superior to wait-list controls. In sum, MI seems to be a promising approach to use with adolescents with substance use disorders.

Cognitive-behavioral therapy (CBT) is another treatment that has been researched for adolescent substance use disorders and often delivered in a brief timeframe (five to 12 sessions). MI is sometimes used as a part of CBT treatments, either in the initial session or imparted as needed. Hogue et al. (2020) have distilled six core practice elements of CBT (see Table 8.3). According to the American Psychological Association Division 12 Task Force, both group and individual CBTs have been classified as "well-established" treatments (Godley et al., 2011; Hogue et al., 2018).

Family Therapy

Family therapy models are generally ecological in nature, given the biopsychosocial risk factors that are involved in the development of adolescent substance use disorders. All the models discussed in Table 8.4 are managed by purveyor organizations that provide implementation support internationally. Treatment fidelity, or the clinician implementing the intervention as intended (also sometimes referred to as adherence), is critical to treatment success (Hartnett et al., 2017); purveyor approaches are one method sometimes used to support fidelity (Hogue

Table 8.4 Description of Family Therapy Models

Name of Model	Theory	Techniques	Length
Family Behavioral Treatment (Donohue & Azrin, 2001; Donohue, Azrin, Allen, Romero, Hill, et al., 2009)	Behavioral	Assessment to understand factors that reinforce substance use. Youths taught strategies to avoid/manage triggers, contracting with parents to supervise child's therapeutic homework and to provide rewards for positive child activities	16–20 sessions that may range in time from 1–2 hours and are spread out over as long as a 1-year period
Multidimensional Treatment Foster Care (Chamberlain & Smith, 2003)	Social learning theory	Youths live in specially trained foster parent homes and receive individual therapy and behavioral support outside the home	Youths are placed one per foster home for 6–9 months and given intensive support and treatment in the foster home setting involving a daily token reinforcement system Individual weekly therapy sessions (problem-solving skills, anger expression, social skills development, and educational or vocational planning once or twice a week (2–6 hours per week) with behavioral support specialists
Functional Family Therapy (Alexander & Parsons, 1982)	Cognitive/behavioral and family systems	Techniques include changing beliefs, cognitions, expectations, and reactions between family members. Interactions between family members rather than the behavior of the adolescent are the focus of intervention.	Involves 8–12 sessions for mild cases and up to 30 hours of direct service
Multidimensional Family Therapy (Liddle et al., 2001)	Cognitive/behavioral and risk factors	Multicomponent intervention targeting individual (communication skills, social competence, and abstinence-related skills), peer, school, and family risk factors	Can be delivered from one to three times per week over the course of 3–6 months depending on the treatment setting and the severity of adolescent problems and family functioning

(continued)

Table 8.4 Continued

Name of Model	Theory	Techniques	Length
Multisystemic therapy	Bronfenbrenner's (1979) social-ecological model: systems surrounding individuals influence their behavior in both direct and indirect ways. The microsystems (the most direct systems that impact the child, such as immediate and extended family) and mesosystems (more distal influences that the child and his or her microsystems are embedded within, such as the school or neighborhood) affect the child and are affected by the child in a systemic fashion. Systems that affect and are affected by delinquent behavior include the child's own intrapersonal system (i.e., cognitive ability, social skills), the parent–child system, the family system, the school system (interactions with teachers), and the child–peer system (e.g., Henggeler, 1991).	Interventions target the different system levels, typically with family systems and cognitive-behavioral therapy.	Families are seen 2–3 times a week in intensive services that last for about 4–6 months.

et al., 2018). Table 8.4 includes descriptions of the various "multicomponent" family therapy models.

Family therapy appears to be more effective than treatment as usual, according to a review and meta-analysis of 24 studies (Baldwin et al., 2012), with no significant differences observed between the various family therapy models (Baldwin et al., 2012). Another systematic review focusing only on outpatient treatment also found that family therapy was more effective than models without a family component (Tanner-Smith et al., 2013).

Carly presented at a center that had several substance use treatment options for adolescents. Based on Carly's intake evaluation, the social worker recommended to Carly and her mother that Carly enroll in the adolescent cannabis program, which uses both individual and group treatment sessions. The program follows the five-session motivational enhancement training (MET) and CBT program outlined in the Cannabis Youth Treatment (CYT) Series, which consists of two individual MET sessions followed by three group CBT sessions (Sampl & Kadden, 2001). Carly was scheduled for an initial MET appointment with the program leader, with the plan that Carly may continue to work with the social worker she met with during her intake appointment if she needed additional support for her substance use or depressive symptoms following the five-session individual and group MET/CBT program.

Carly's initial MET sessions focused on generating motivation to change her marijuana use. Additionally, the therapist used these individual meetings to prepare Carly for the CBT group sessions and to introduce functional analysis and the concept of triggers. Session 1 began with introductions, and the therapist endeavored to build rapport with Carly. The therapist focused first on informal conversations about topics such as school and Carly's interests, then reviewed Carly's intake evaluation results and asked about what had brought Carly to treatment. Throughout, the therapist was careful to listen for opportunities to begin to use MET strategies and to avoid giving advice or telling Carly she had a problem. They discussed how Carly's use of marijuana had started and her current patterns of use as well as what her goals were for treatment. Carly stated, "I'm here because I got caught at school and the school freaked my mom out, so I'm just doing what I need to do so everyone will just chill out because it's just some weed. It's not that big of a deal." In response, the therapist employed the MET strategy of rolling with resistance. He stated, "So you're here because of your school and your mom. You don't want them making this into a big deal. Some teens in our program find that participating helps them get more information and get a better sense of whether using weed is a big deal or not for them."

During this initial conversation, the therapist also identified a couple of opportunities to help Carly develop discrepancy between where her life was at present and where she wanted it to be. For example, by stating, "I'm hearing you like smoking weed but also that you don't want to worry your mom." Additionally, Carly mentioned her friend Jess and that their relationship had been strained as of late because Jess did not like Carly's marijuana use. The therapist reflected these concerns back to Carly as, "You'd like to continue your friendship with Jess, she has been your best friend for many years, but smoking weed is straining that friendship."

In addition to establishing rapport and orienting Carly to treatment, a major focus of the first session involved reviewing Carly's personalized feedback report, which had been prepared in advance based on her intake evaluation. As they reviewed Carly's report, there were opportunities for discussion and for the therapist to employ MET strategies when appropriate. The personalized feedback report included the following information: substances used/primary substance, extent of use, problems encountered because of use, reasons for quitting, patterns of use (e.g., where, with whom), and confidence about ability to abstain. The report had been precompleted with information from the intake where available, and the review of the report included opportunities for discussion as well as for Carly to provide additional information to round out the report. Throughout the review of the report, the therapist used MET to demonstrate acceptance, develop discrepancy, and help Carly develop self-efficacy for change.

To conclude the session, the therapist summarized the main things he had heard Carly say and inquired about her readiness for change. "It sounds like you've noticed that using has caused some problems at school, with your mom, and with your friend Jess, and you recognize that quitting weed would solve some of the problems you are having now. What do you think about this?" Carly was able to set a goal that she would like to "cut back" on her use and stop using alone. "Maybe just now and then with friends but less so I can get everyone off my back." The therapist did not try to move Carly toward a commitment to total abstinence; rather, he thanked her for her hard work in session and asked for her reactions to the session before concluding their meeting. Carly stated, "This wasn't as bad as I thought it would be. I thought you were just going to tell me I had to quit completely and that I couldn't see my friends anymore." The therapist told Carly they would continue discussing these issues when they met again next week and scheduled their next individual session.

In session 2, the therapist began by asking Carly generally how the past week had gone. They then discussed specifically how often Carly had used in the past week (twice) and the circumstances of that use, as well as how Carly thought and felt about her use. The therapist praised that Carly had been successful in cutting back some, consistent with her goal. The therapist and Carly then spent time in session developing more specific, measurable, and actionable goals. They discussed that many people are most successful in reducing their substance use when they can identify situations that they may be more likely to use in and plan for how to reduce the occurrence of such situations. Carly wrote down her goal (to use no more than once a week) and the ideas they generated. Ideas Carly identified included hanging out with Jess after school (a non-using friend) instead of her friends who smoke and having her mom drop her off at school on her way to work instead of walking where she would be more likely to run into her friends who smoke and be tempted to use with them. They also discussed that stress and boredom are triggers for use for Carly and identified ways for Carly to distract herself until the urge to smoke subsides, such as by texting Jess, watching a movie, or helping her mom around the house.

Following the goal-setting exercise, they moved on to exploring the function that using marijuana was serving for Carly. Together, they explored triggers of use, including the friends that Carly was most likely to use with and when, as well as other *times and situations (e.g., stressed, bored). Some of this information had already been discussed, so the conversation focused mainly on helping Carly to connect antecedents, behaviors, and consequences. The therapist asked Carly how she felt and what she thought the last time she used, and what Carly did in response to recent triggers. Additionally, they discussed what is positively reinforcing about smoking for Carly (e.g., "I feel more relaxed") and what are the negative consequences of use she has experienced.*

Finally, because this was their last individual session before starting CBT groups, they also discussed what to expect in groups, including the format, composition of the group members, and topics, which would include discussing problems related to marijuana use, developing and practicing coping skills, and planning for how to employ coping strategies between sessions. Carly expressed some nervousness about the group sessions because she was worried about what the other participants would think of her but agreed to try them.

Following these two MET sessions, Carly transitioned to the CBT groups, which lasted approximately 75 minutes each and focused on developing coping skills that would provide alternatives to marijuana use. Carly's group included five other teens—four boys and one other girl. Each of the three group sessions focused on a particular skill: the first on marijuana refusal skills, with opportunities for behavioral rehearsal; the second on enhancing one's social support network, including increasing pleasant events; and the third on coping with unanticipated high-risk situations and relapse. Throughout, the therapist also needed to be attentive to group dynamics by setting ground rules, monitoring and giving feedback to participants as needed, and ensuring that the experience felt supportive and safe for all participants.

In session 3 (the first group CBT session), the group began with brief introductions, review of progress since beginning treatment, and progress over the past week toward their goals and in response to plans established in session 2. Then, the group transitioned to a discussion of marijuana refusal skills with opportunities to practice/role-play. Specific discussion points included how, as marijuana use increases, people tend to socialize more and more with other users. While it is best to avoid others whom one is more likely to use with, that cannot always be done, and thus it is important to develop tools to handle pressures to use. The need to practice these skills was also emphasized. For Carly, this session helped her to develop a stronger sense of the importance of avoiding peers she usually smokes with and bolstering relationships with non-using peers like Jess. She also developed some language to use when asked to smoke, including that she could say, "No thanks, I'm not smoking anymore," "I'd love to hang out but not if people are going to be smoking," and "I can't risk getting into any more trouble at school, so I'm not smoking."

Session 4 focused on social support and pleasant activity scheduling. Before the start of the group, members were asked to provide urine samples for drug testing. Like in session 3, the group reviewed individual progress and practice exercises completed since the last session. Then, they moved to a discussion of social support. The therapist explained that social support can increase confidence in one's ability to cope and can even help one quit or reduce use. They discussed who might be able to support them and what types of support would be most helpful. They also discussed how to actively take steps to increase their social network or optimize the supports in their life, including in their relationships with family and friends. Carly was able to identify her friendship with Jess as one that was helpful and would be important to work toward restrengthening. She also identified a few other friends and peers in her community who were outside of the circle of friends she usually smoked with whom she would like to spend more time with. Additionally, Carly recognized her mother as an important support and identified a desire to rebuild her mother's trust. The group also identified ways to increase positive activities. Members brainstormed activities that could be fun instead of using marijuana, including activities that they enjoyed doing while using and were unsure if they would be fun if done without substances. They each identified activities to try over the next week.

Carly decided to schedule an activity with Jess and invite her over to watch a movie and order pizza, to attend a community event with her mother and a few other families, and to accompany her mother to clean houses over the weekend because she suspected her mother would appreciate that and it would also provide some distraction. Carly's drug test results were negative, and she reported she had not used since session 1.

The final group CBT session, session 5, focused on coping in unanticipated risky situations and how to deal with relapse. As with the other group sessions, session 5 included a review of practice and out-of-session practices. Most of the time in the session was spent planning for potential emergencies and high-risk situations, as well as relapse. The group discussed being prepared for challenging situations and developing coping plans in advance. It was noted that even when one endeavors to avoid risky situations, it is not always possible to anticipate or avoid risk. They brainstormed as a group about potential situations that could lead to a relapse, such as running into a friend they used with unexpectedly, failing an exam, or experiencing a breakup. They discussed problem-solving and worked as a group to problem-solve how one might cope in several high-risk situations. Then, each group member developed a personal emergency plan, which included things to do and not to do in an emergency and people to turn to for help. The group concluded with a discussion about termination, which included reflections about what they had learned, opportunities to provide one another feedback, and a summary of their post-treatment goals. At the conclusion of the group, Carly had been abstinent from marijuana for 4 weeks. Both she and her mother reported her mood had been much more positive. All parties agreed that further treatment was not needed at this time, and the family was invited to contact the clinic if additional support is needed in the future.

SUMMARY

Adolescent substance use disorders are usually part of a behavioral profile of dysregulated, antisocial, and aggressive behaviors, and therefore, the material in this chapter overlaps with information presented in Chapter 7. In almost all cases, co-occurring diagnoses will be present, including ADHD and depression. Effective treatments have been identified for this population of youths, but most presenting for services do not receive them, and many more youths never receive intervention. Social workers' intersection with this population may occur in mental health treatment, specialized addiction services, and other social service settings, such as child welfare, juvenile justice, and the school system, where they can promote the implementation of empirically supported interventions.

REFERENCES

Alexander, J., & Parsons, B. V. (1982). *Functional family therapy*. Pacific Grove, CA: Brooks/Cole.

American Psychiatric Association. (2022). *Diagnostic and statistical manual of mental disorders* (5th ed., Text Revision). Washington, DC: American Psychiatric Association.

Armstrong, T., & Costello, J. (2002). Community studies on adolescent substance use, abuse, or dependence and psychiatric comorbidity. *Journal of Consulting and Clinical Psychology, 70*, 1224–1239.

Bahr, S. J., & Hoffmann, J. P. (2010). Parenting style, religiosity, peers, and adolescent heavy drinking. *Journal of Studies on Alcohol and Drugs, 71*(4), 539–543.

Bastiani, L., Potente, R., Scalese, M., Siciliano, V., Fortunato, L., & Molinaro, S. (2017). The Cannabis Abuse Screening Test (CAST) and its applications. In V. R. Preedy (Ed.), *Handbook of cannabis and related pathologies: Biology, pharmacology, diagnosis, and treatment* (pp. 971–980). Elsevier Academic Press. https://doi.org/10.1016/B978-0-12-800756-3.00117-4

Bronfenbrenner, U. (1979). *The ecology of human development: Experiments by nature and design*. Cambridge, MA, and London: Harvard University Press.

Bukstein, O. G., Cornelius, J., Trunzo, A. C., Kelly, T. M., & Wood, D. S. (2005). Clinical predictors of treatment in a population of adolescents with alcohol use disorders. *Addictive Behaviors, 30*, 1663–1673.Carliner, H., Keyes, K. M., McLaughlin, K. A., Meyers, J. L., Dunn, E. C., & Martins, S. S., (2016). Childhood trauma and illicit drug use in adolescence: A Population-Based National Comorbidity Survey Replication–Adolescent Supplement study. *Journal of the American Academy of Child & Adolescent Psychiatry, 55*, 701–708.

Chamberlain, P., & Smith, D. K. (2003). Antisocial behavior in children and adolescents: The Oregon multidimensional treatment foster care model. In A. E. Kazdin & J. R. Weisz (Eds.), *Evidence-based psychotherapies for children and adolescents* (pp. 282–300). New York: Guilford Press.

Chung, T., & Maisto, S. A. (2006). Relapse to alcohol and other use in treated adolescents: Review and reconsideration of relapse as a change point in clinical course. *Clinical Psychology Review, 26*, 149–161.

Coley, R. L., Hawkins, S. S., Ghiani, M., Kruzik, C., & Baum, C. F. (2019). A quasi-experimental evaluation of marijuana policies and youth marijuana use. *American Journal of Drug and Alcohol Abuse, 45*(3), 292–303. doi:10.1080/00952990.2018.1559847.

Donohue, B., Azrin, N., Allen, D. N., Romero, V., Hill, H. H., Tracy, K., Lapota, H., Gorney, S., Abdel-Al, R., Caldas, D., Herdzik, K., Bradshaw, K., Valdez, R., & Van Hasselt, V. B. (2009). Family behavior therapy for substance abuse and other associated problems: A review of its intervention components and applicability. *Behavior Modification*, *33*(5), 495–519. https://doi.org/10.1177/0145445509340019

Edenberg, H. J., Dick, D. M., Xuei, X., Tian, H., Almasy, L., Bauer, L. O., & Begleiter, H. (2004). Variations in GABRA2, encoding the alpha 2 subunit of the GABA(A) receptor, are associated with alcohol dependence and with brain oscillations. *American Journal of Human Genetics*, *74*(4), 705–714.

Edlund, M. J., Forman-Hoffman, V. L., Winder, C. R., Heller, D. C., Kroutil, L. A., Lipari, R. N., & Colpe, L. J. (2015). *Opioid abuse and depression in adolescents*: Results from the National Survey on Drug Use and Health. *Drug and Alcohol Dependence*, *152*, 131–138.

Erskine, H. E., Moffitt, T. E., Copeland, W. E., Costello, E. J., Ferrari, A. J., Patton, G., Degenhardt, L., Vos, T., Whiteford, H. A., & Scott, J. G. (2014). A heavy burden on young minds: The global burden of mental and substance use disorders in children and Youth. *Psychological Medicine*, *45*(7), 1551–1563. https://doi.org/10.1017/s0033291714002888

Godley, S. H., Garner, B. R., Smith, J. E., Meyers, R. J., & Godley, M. D. (2011). A large-scale dissemination and implementation model for evidence-based treatment and continuing care. *Clinical Psychology: Science and Practice*, *18*, 67–83.

Groenman, A. P., Janssen, T. W. P., & Oosterlaan, J. (2017). Childhood psychiatric disorders as risk factor for subsequent substance use: A meta-analysis. *Journal of the American Academy of Child & Adolescent Psychiatry*, *56*(7), 556–559. https://doi.org/10.1080/01926188808250729

Hawke, L. D., Koyama, E., & Henderson, J. (2018). Cannabis use, other substance use, and co-occurring mental health concerns among youth presenting for substance use treatment services: Sex and age differences. *Journal of Substance Abuse Treatment*, *91*, 12–19. https://doi.org/10.1016/j.jsat.2018.05.001Hogue, A., Bobek, M., MacLean, A., Miranda, R., Wolff, J. C., & Jensen-Doss, A. (2020). Core elements of CBT for adolescent conduct and substance use problems: Comorbidity, clinical techniques, and case examples. *Cognitive and Behavioral Practice*, *27*(4), 426–441. https://doi.org/10.1016/j.cbpra.2019.12.002

Hogue, A., Henderson, C. E., Ozechowski T. J., & Robbins, M. S. (2018). Evidence base on outpatient behavioral treatments for adolescent substance use: Updates and recommendations, 2007–2013. *Journal of Clinical Child & Adolescent Psychology*, *43*(5), 695–720. doi:10.1080/15374416.2014.915550

King, N. B., Fraser, V., Boikos, C., Richardson, R., & Harper, S. (2014). Determinants of increased opioid-related mortality in the United States and Canada, 1990–2013: A systematic review. *American Journal of Public Health*, *104*(8), e32 e42. https://doi.org/10.2105/AJPH.2014.301966

Kraft, K., Schubert, K., Pond, A., & Aguirre-Molina, M. (2006). Adolescent treatment services: The context of care. In H. A. Liddle & C. L. Rowe (Eds.), *Adolescent substance abuse: Research and clinical advances* (pp. 174–188). New York: Cambridge University Press.

Larimer, M., Palmer, R., & Marlatt, A. (1999). Relapse prevention: An overview of Marlatt's cognitive-behavioral model. *Alcohol Research and Health*, *23*, 151–160.

Liddle, H. A., Dakof, G. A., Parker, K., Diamond, G. S., Barrett, K., & Tejeda, M. (2001). Multidimensional family therapy for adolescent drug abuse: Results of a randomized clinical trial. *American Journal of Drug and Alcohol Abuse*, *27*, 651–688.McCabe, S.

E., West, B. T., Morales, M., Cranford, J. A., & Boyd, C. J. (2007). Does early onset of non-medical use of prescription drugs predict subsequent prescription drug abuse and dependence? Results from a national study. *Addiction, 102*(12), 1920–1930.

Miranda, R., & Treloar, H. (2016). Emerging pharmacologic treatments for adolescent substance use: Challenges and new directions. *Current Addiction Reports, 3*, 145–156. https://doi.org/10.1007/s40429-016-0098-7

Mitchell, S. G., Gryczynski, J., O'Grady, K. E., & Schwartz, R. P. (2013). SBIRT for adolescent drug and alcohol use: Current status and future directions. *Journal of Substance Abuse Treatment, 44*(5), 463–472. https://doi.org/10.1016/j.jsat.2012.11.005

Nawi, A. M., Ismail, R., Ibrahim, F., Hassan, M. R., Manaf, M. R., Amit, N., Ibrahim, N., & Shafurdin, N. S. (2021). Risk and protective factors of drug abuse among adolescents: A systematic review. *BMC Public Health, 21*(1). https://doi.org/10.1186/s12889-021-11906-2

Newton, A. S., Soleimani, A., Kirkland, S. W., & Gokiert, R. J. (2017). A systematic review of instruments to identify mental health and substance use problems among children in the emergency department. *Academic Emergency Medicine, 24*(5), 552–568. https://doi.org/10.1111/acem.13162

Rohde, P., Waldron, H. B., Turner, C. W., Brody, J., & Jorgensen, J. (2014). Sequenced versus coordinated treatment for adolescents with comorbid depressive and substance use disorders. *Journal of Consulting and Clinical Psychology, 82*(2), 342–348. https://doi.org/10.1037/a0035808

Sampl, S., & Kadden, R. (2001). *Motivational enhancement therapy and cognitive behavioral therapy for adolescent cannabis users: 5 Sessions, Cannabis Youth Treatment (CYT) series* (Vol. 1). Rockville, MD: Center for Substance Abuse Treatment, Substance Abuse and Mental Health Services Administration.

Shi, Y., Cummins, S. E., & Zhu S. (2018). Medical marijuana availability, price, and product variety and adolescents' marijuana use. *Adolescent Health, 63*, 88–93.

Subramaniam, G. A., & Volkow, N. D. (2014). Substance misuse among adolescents: To screen or not to screen? *JAMA Pediatrics, 168*(9), 798–799. https://doi.org/10.1001/jamapediatrics.2014.958

Substance Abuse and Mental Health Services Administration (SAMHSA). (2020). *Substance use disorder treatment for people with co-occurring disorders.* Treatment Improvement Protocol (TIP) Series, No. 42. SAMHSA Publication No. PEP20-02-01-004. Rockville, MD: Center for Behavioral Health Statistics and Quality.

Tanner-Smith, E. E., & Lipsey, M. W. (2015). Brief alcohol interventions for adolescents and young adults: A systematic review and meta-analysis. *Journal of Substance Abuse Treatment, 51*, 1–18. https://doi.org/10.1016/j.jsat.2014.09.001

Tormohlen, K. N., Schneider, K. E., Johnson, R. M., Ma, M., Levinson, A. H., & Brooks-Russell, A. (2019). Changes in prevalence of marijuana consumption modes among Colorado high school students from 2015 to 2017. *JAMA Pediatrics, 173*(10), 988–989. doi:10.1001/jamapediatrics.2019.2627

Internalizing Problems

Anxiety Disorders and Obsessive-Compulsive Disorder

Justin Russo is a 15-year-old male who lives with his biological parents and two siblings. His family identifies as Italian American and lives in a low- to middle-income urban neighborhood. Justin and his parents self-referred to a hospital-affiliated anxiety specialty clinic after reading an article about the clinic online. Justin's parents, John and Tina Russo, reported that they sought treatment for Justin at the clinic because of his worries, social anxiety, and school-related anxiety. Justin reported that he was also interested in receiving treatment and was motivated to work on his anxiety. The clinic was largely staffed by clinicians in training, and Justin was assigned to work with a social work field placement student. The student clinician saw clients at a reduced fee and was closely supervised by a licensed social worker with extensive experience with cognitive-behavioral treatments for anxiety.

At the time of intake Justin was enrolled in cyber-school and scheduled to enter the 11th grade at a local parochial high school in the fall. Justin's parents reported that Justin has always been an "outstanding" student and had been at the top of his class since elementary school. Before 10th grade, Justin had been a top student and won many awards for his academic performance. According to his parents, Justin had always been very well liked by his classmates and teachers. For example, Justin had been invited to be a peer mediator at his school.

Justin's parents reported that approximately 1½ years earlier, Justin began struggling in school, and his grades and attention were affected. Justin's parents noted that Justin would state, "I don't feel like myself." Justin's difficulties with anxiety continued to increase over the summer break, and in August before 10th grade, Justin expressed that he was terrified to go back to high school where he would have to interact with new people. His parents did enroll him in 10th grade, and he attempted to attend classes; however, his anxiety was highly distressing, and he stopped going to school. Additionally, during this time, Justin ceased communicating with his extended family and friends because of his intense anxiety, and he had trouble sleeping. Justin's parents took him to see multiple other professionals, including a psychologist they were referred to by the school counselor and a social worker affiliated with his pediatrician's office, to help him cope with his anxiety. He also received a psychiatric

Child and Adolescent Mental Health in Social Work. Jacqueline Corcoran and Courtney Benjamin Wolk, Oxford University Press.
© Oxford University Press 2023. DOI: 10.1093/oso/9780197653562.003.0009

evaluation and began a trial of sertraline (Zoloft). Sertraline was discontinued after 1 month because of side effects—Justin's parents reported that "it made him feel funny." No other medications were prescribed. Later in the year, Justin enrolled in the local public high school and tried going for 1 day. He was unable to attend, and at that point began attending cyber-school. He completed cyber-school instruction from home for the 10th-grade year. Both Justin and his parents noted that one of their main treatment goals was for Justin to be able to get back into a traditional "brick-and-mortar" school setting.

Mr. and Mrs. Russo reported that Justin used to have more friends than most teenagers his age; however, during the 10th grade year he "cut everybody out of his life" and at intake no longer had any close friends. His parents reported that they believed this was because Justin worried about getting into trouble and felt anxious when his friends experimented with activities that he did not want to engage in (e.g., drinking). Justin's parents reported that he felt like "he doesn't fit in" with his friends anymore. Justin used to enjoy playing basketball, going to the movies, and playing poker with his friends in the neighborhood. However, he stopped seeing his friends, although they continued to attempt to reach out to him. For example, if a friend knocked on the door, Justin would ask his mother to "tell him I'm not here." Justin continued to play basketball, which he reportedly excels at. Justin's parents said that he continued to be able to enjoy basketball despite his impairing anxiety.

OVERVIEW

Anxiety disorders are distinguished from commonplace and transient fears during developmental stages, such as the following: in infancy, being startled and being exposed to strangers; for toddlers, separation from caregivers; for school-aged children, the supernatural, physical well-being, and natural disasters; and for adolescents, social and existential worries. Anxiety disorders are characterized by intense, almost unbearable fears, worry, and avoidance that disrupt a person's capacity for social functioning. The fourth edition of the *Diagnostic and Statistical Manual of Mental Disorders* (DSM-IV) devoted one chapter to the anxiety disorders, but DSM-5 has spread them among three chapters to group them according to shared features. They now fall into the following categories: (1) anxiety disorders; (2) obsessive-compulsive disorder (OCD) and related disorders; and (3) trauma and stressor-related disorders (discussed in Chapter 13). There are seven different anxiety disorders. Most of the research that we draw on generalizes to anxiety as a whole, which is justified given shared features of somatic, cognitive, and emotional symptoms. We will exclude simple phobia from our discussion mainly because in social work settings, clients generally have more severe presentations. The ones most salient for children are *separation anxiety disorder* (excessive anxiety about separating from a major attachment figure), *social anxiety* (fears of social humiliation and rejection around performance, observation, and interaction; Kodal et al., 2017), and *generalized anxiety disorder* (pervasive worry and nervousness; see Table 9.1). Social anxiety disorder, generalized

Table 9.1 DSM Criteria

Separation Anxiety

Developmentally inappropriate and excessive fear concerning separation from individuals to whom the person is attached with at least three persistent and recurrent symptoms of the following for 4 weeks:

a. Excessive distress when anticipating or experiencing separation from home or caregivers
b. Worry about losing major attachment figures or harm coming to them
c. Worry about something bad happening
d. Reluctance/refusal to go out, away from home, to school, to work
e. Fear/reluctance about being alone or without major figure
f. Reluctance/refusal to sleep away from home or to go to sleep without being near major figure
g. Nightmares involving separation
h. Complaints of physical symptoms (e.g., headaches, stomachaches, nausea, vomiting)

Social Anxiety

a. The individual experiences marked fear or anxiety about one or more social situations that involve exposure to possible scrutiny in peer settings.
b. The individual fears that he or she will act in a way or show anxiety symptoms that will be negatively perceived.
c. The social situations almost always provoke fear or anxiety.
d. The social situations are avoided or endured with intense fear or anxiety.
e. The fear or anxiety is out of proportion to the actual threat posed by the social situation.
f. The fear, anxiety, or avoidance is persistent, typically lasting for 6 months or more.
g. Fear causes clinically significant distress or impairment in social, occupational, or other important areas of functioning.

Generalized Anxiety

Excessive anxiety and worry occurring more days than not for at least 6 months, about various events or situations, that is difficult to control. Only one of the following items required for diagnosis in children:

a. Restlessness or feeling keyed up or on edge
b. Being easily fatigued
c. Difficulty concentrating or mind going blank
d. Irritability
e. Muscle tension
f. Sleep disturbance (difficulty falling or staying asleep, or restless, unsatisfying sleep)

Obsessive-Compulsive Disorder

Obsessions or compulsions, or both, are present and are time-consuming (e.g., ≥1 hour/day) or cause significant distress or impairment.

Obsessions defined by:

a. Persistent thoughts, urges, or images that are intrusive and unwanted
b. Attempts by the individual to ignore or suppress such thoughts, urges, or images

Compulsions defined by:

a. Individual feels drawn to complete repetitive behaviors or mental acts.
b. Behaviors or mental acts are aimed at preventing or reducing anxiety or distress.

anxiety disorder, and separation anxiety disorder are often researched jointly (e.g., Kendall et al., 2008; Walkup et al., 2008), have been hypothesized to share an underlying anxiety construct (Pine & Grun, 1998), and are highly comorbid with one another (e.g., Essau et al., 2018; Hankin et al., 2016). We also touch on OCD, which involves obsessive (recurrent, intrusive thoughts that cause distress) and compulsive (repetitive behaviors to reduce the distress of the obsessive thinking or preventing a dreaded event) components; the risk and protective factors, as well as the treatment approaches, are like those of the other anxiety disorders. Additionally, school refusal, although not classified as a DSM-5 disorder, often involves anxiety as the underlying feature. Afflicted children and adolescents may be diagnosed with unspecified anxiety disorder if their presentation is one of anxiety rather than defiant reasons for truancy. School refusal may also occur within the context of other anxiety disorders. For example, children with social anxiety may refuse to attend school because of social evaluation concerns.

Prevalence

The point prevalence of different anxiety disorders among children and adolescents varies, but 7% to 8% report being severely impaired by at least one type of anxiety disorder (Ghandour et al., 2019; Merikangas et al., 2010). Specific to teens, rates of 11% for social anxiety disorder and 9% for separation anxiety disorder have been established (Merikangas et al., 2010). The OCD 12-month prevalence rate is 0.6% to 7.1% (Costello et al., 2005). In the general population, the prevalence of school refusal is between 1% and 2% (Costello, Egger, & Angold, 2005).

RISK AND PROTECTIVE FACTORS

A consistent theme across the book has been the biopsychosocial experience of each mental disorder through the lens of both challenges and strengths. The course of anxiety disorders over time was studied in the Child/Adolescent Anxiety Multimodal Extended Long-term Study (CAMELS; Ginsburg et al., 2018). Rates and predictors of stable anxiety remission (across 4 follow-up years) were examined. In the original study, the multisite Child/Adolescent Anxiety Multimodal Study (CAMS; Walkup et al., 2008), youth participants diagnosed with separation, social, or generalized anxiety disorder were randomized to 12 weeks of medication, cognitive-behavioral therapy (CBT), their combination, or pill placebo. Almost 22% of youths were in stable remission, 30% were chronically ill, and 48% showed a relapsing pattern at long-term follow-up. Rapid treatment responders were less likely to be in the chronically ill group. Treatment type was not associated with remission status across the follow-up. Several variables (e.g., male gender) predicted stable remission from anxiety disorders.

Biological

A predisposition to anxiety is genetically based but modestly so, accounting for 30% to 40% of the variance (Hettema et al., 2001). OCD is slightly more heritable, at a range of 45% to 65%, according to a review of twin studies (van Grootheest et al., 2005). A systematic review of neural activity indicates that anxiety involves "hyperactivity" of the amygdala (Ashworth et al., 2021). Other biological risk factors include physical illness (Hayward et al., 2008; Remes et al., 2016) and temperament. *Low self-directedness, anxiety sensitivity* (the tendency to respond fearfully to anxiety symptoms), *temperamental sensitivity* (including a range of emotional reactions toward negativity, such as fear, sadness, self-dissatisfaction, hostility, and worry), and *harm avoidance and behavioral inhibition* (timidity, shyness, emotional restraint, and withdrawal from unfamiliar situations) are associated with anxiety (Bosquet & Egeland, 2006; Essex et al., 2010; Liotta, 2013). Conversely, an extroverted temperament exerts a protective influence (Bosquet & Egeland, 2006).

Psychological

Psychological theories about the development of anxiety are dominated by the concept of *conditioning*, which is the process of developing patterns of behavior through responses to certain environmental stimuli or behavioral consequences (Kazdin, 2001). An initially neutral stimulus comes to produce a conditioned response after being paired with a conditioned stimulus. For instance, if individuals have an embarrassing experience speaking in front of a classroom, they may then generalize this experience to all public speaking situations. As well as direct experience, conditioning may play a role through vicarious learning (watching another person experience a bad experience) or warnings about danger from parents. Contemporary theories consider these learning histories along with the temperamental predisposition toward anxiety, such as behavioral inhibition, which may result in a person's perception of uncontrollability (Mineka & Zinbarg, 2006). For children and adolescents, fear of uncertainty has a strong association with both anxiety and worry (Osmanağaoğlu et al., 2018). Principles of reinforcement are also important. For OCD, the compulsions to reduce anxiety are negatively reinforcing, making it more likely that a person will perform the particular compulsion in the future in response to the obsession. In other anxiety disorders, parents and school personnel may permit children to avoid anxiety-provoking experiences; however, avoidance leads to a reduction in anxiety, which again is negatively reinforcing. In this way, anxiety can be cyclical and self-reinforcing.

Another self-perpetuating cycle can result from the formation of maladaptive schemas, which have also been linked to youth anxiety (Tariq et al., 2021). Schemas are the underlying belief structures, originating early in life in response to experience, that orient a person's outlook. The main schemas, according to Young et al. (2003), for youth anxiety typically involve the following:

- *Disconnection/rejection*: "an expectation of insecure and unstable relationships with excessive feelings of isolation and inferiority
- *Impaired autonomy/performance*: "feelings of incompetence, failure and greater vulnerability to harm and catastrophic situations"
- *Other-directed*: "beliefs associated with excessive sacrifice and compromise for others at the expense of one's own needs"

Comorbidity is high among individuals with anxiety. The most common co-morbid patterns are other anxiety disorders and depressive disorders, with co-morbidity rates ranging from 50% to 72%. Among those with both anxiety and depression, up to 75% reported the first onset of anxiety before that of depression (Essau et al., 2014). Comorbid disorders are associated with less positive outcomes (Storch et al., 2008). For children with OCD, frequently diagnosed comorbid conditions include anxiety disorders, tic disorders, and depression, but also attention-deficit/hyperactivity disorder (ADHD) and oppositional defiant disorder or conduct disorder, according to a review by Gryczkowski and Whiteside (2014).

When psychosocial outcomes at age 30 were analysed separately by the age at which anxiety disorders begin, adolescent-onset predicted worse outcome in terms of overall adjustment, employment, family relationships, chronic stress, and poor coping skills (Essau et al., 2014). Hypotheses for this phenomenon included the biological changes of puberty coupled with the fact that the developmental period is one of taking on critical roles and responsibilities. The anxiety might have impaired functioning in key domains, meaning that teens did not acquire the necessary roles of adulthood.

Social

Girls present with more fears than boys and generally have higher rates of anxiety disorders, starting during adolescence and continuing through the life span; whether the gender difference is due to biological factors (such as genetic predispositions), social factors (such as increased rates of sexual abuse), or a combination of the two is unknown (Ozer et al., 2003; Remes et al., 2016). One hypothesis involves the way males and females react to biological and social changes at puberty (Cyranowski et al., 2000; Hankin et al., 2007 as cited in Essau et al., 2014). Starting around puberty, girls demonstrate an increased need for interpersonal affiliation; anxiety may result if interpersonal needs are not met (Essau et al., 2014).

Family-related influences may affect the onset of anxiety disorders. These include stressful, negative, or traumatic life events, including disruptions of relationships (Bandelow et al., 2002; Phillips et al., 2005). Anxious attachment patterns in children are another family-related risk factor. Anxious attachment is characterized by an infant's becoming distressed and frantically seeking comfort from the attachment figure through clinging and crying when faced with something the child fears (Hanklin et al., 2005). Subsequent contact with the caregiver, however, does not seem to help the child experience a sense of security or reduce the anxiety. In a study that tracked children from infancy to adolescence, youths with an anxious attachment pattern were more likely to suffer from an anxiety disorder as teenagers than those who were securely attached or showed avoidant attachment (Warren et al., 1997). The means by which insecure attachment history exerts its influence on adolescent anxiety appeared to be related to the negative internalized representations of the relationship in childhood (Bosquet & Egeland, 2006).

Other interpersonal patterns are seen in families of children with anxiety disorders, particularly parental overcontrol (McLeod et al., 2007), but also overprotection and criticism (Donovan & Spence, 2000). In addition to having a genetic risk, children of anxious parents may be more likely to observe anxiety in their parents and learn faulty interpretations of neutral events (Subar & Rozenman, 2021), and to have fearful behavior reinforced by their parents (Bandelow et al., 2002). Despite the number of possible family factors involved, family variables in total explain only a modest amount (4%) of the variance in anxiety (McLeod et al., 2007).

Family factors are also associated with recovery. Parental anxiety is a risk factor for persistent child anxiety. If a parent is anxiety free, the child may have more positive outcomes from treatment (Kendall et al., 2008). Relatedly, family accommodation of anxiety maintains anxiety in children. Accommodation involves caregiver reinforcement of the anxiety by allowing the child to avoid triggers, by accommodating or participating in compulsions, and by providing excessive reassurance. Family accommodation is important to assess and target in treatment because its reduction results in better treatment response (Murphy & Flessner, 2015).

Finally, socioeconomic status (SES) and its link to anxiety for youths aged 10 to 15 years was studied in a systematic review (Lemstra et al., 2008). The lower the SES, the higher the rate of anxiety. Therefore, social workers need to be able to recognize anxiety in their low-SES young clients and appropriately screen and assess.

ASSESSMENT

A thorough and comprehensive clinical assessment of anxiety should be undertaken (Bernstein & Shaw, 1997; Stein et al., 2010). Box 9.1 provides a summary of key assessment components. See Table 9.2 for clinical self-report measures that have been validated. See Table 9.3 for other diagnoses that might mimic symptoms of anxiety for the purpose of differential diagnosis.

The social work student and the supervising clinician jointly completed a clinical interview with Justin and his parents, meeting individually with Mr. and Mrs. Russo first, then individually with Justin. During the interview, Justin kept his head down and did not make eye contact with the clinicians. He spoke softly and succinctly

Box 9.1

GUIDELINES FOR ASSESSMENT

   I. History of the onset, development, frequency, and nature of the symptoms

  II. Family history of anxiety

 III. Any coexisting psychiatric disorders

 IV. A general medical history and review of a person's medications, including a physical examination to search for a possible physical basis for the anxiety. If there is a physical basis for the symptoms, the appropriate diagnosis is anxiety disorder due to a general medical condition. For medication- or substance-induced anxiety, the appropriate diagnosis is substance-induced anxiety disorder.

  V. The client's response to life transitions, major life events, and stressor or trauma

 VI. Social and school functioning

VII. An investigation of times when the anxiety symptoms are not present or are more manageable and what is different about those times

VIII. Parenting styles (overprotective, controlling, accommodating) that might contribute to anxiety

 IX. Any anxiety disorders in parents

  X. Broad anxiety screening questions might include: "Do you feel worried or anxious a lot of time?" "Are there specific things you are afraid of or nervous about?" "Do you often find that there are thoughts in your head that you can't get rid of?" "Do you have trouble controlling or managing your worries?" More in-depth screening for particular anxiety disorders can then take place.

 XI. A "fear thermometer" or other visual analogue tool is useful for assessing the range of anxious feelings or strength of those feelings. A fear thermometer can be drawn and labeled as follows: "10" for "extremely anxious—can't think about anything else," "5" for "thinking anxious thoughts a lot," and "1" for "barely worried at all."

XII. When the client is a child, separate interviews with parents and child are recommended (Velting et al., 2004). Children frequently report fewer symptoms than their parents and tend to be less reliable than parents in reporting details about the onset and duration of anxiety symptoms. For OCD, parent–child agreement about symptoms is often low, and many children lack insight and attempt to conceal their symptoms (see review, Gryczkowski & Whiteside, 2014).

---

but did answer questions when asked. Mr. and Mrs. Russo expressed great concern and motivation to help Justin overcome his anxiety. Results of the intake interview suggested that Justin's symptoms at the time were best conceptualized under the diagnoses of social anxiety disorder and generalized anxiety disorder. He was also assigned a "rule out" diagnosis of persistent depressive disorder.

Table 9.2 MEASURES OF ANXIETY

Psychometric Support	Measure Name	No. of Items	Completed by[a]	Ages[c]	Link to Measure
Excellent	Spence Children's Anxiety Scale (SCAS; Spence 1998)*	38	Y, P	7–19	https://www.scaswebsite.com/
Excellent	Screen for Child Anxiety-Related Emotional Disorders (SCARED; Birmaher et al., 1999)*	41	Y, P	7–17	https://www.pediatricbipolar.pitt.edu/resources/instruments
Excellent	Revised Child Anxiety and Depression Scale (RCADS/RCADS-P; Chorpita et al., 2005)*	47/25	Y, P	Grade 3–12[d]	https://www.childfirst.ucla.edu/resources/
Good	Short OCD Screener (SOCS; Uher et al., 2007)	7	Y	9–19	https://primarycare.ementalhealth.ca/index.php?m=survey&ID=14
Good	Penn State Worry Questionnaire—Child Version (PSWQ-C; Chorpita et al., 1997)*	14	Y	7–17	https://www.childfirst.ucla.edu/resources/
Good	School Anxiety Scale—Teacher Report (SAS-TR; Lyneham et al., 2008)*	16	T	5–12	https://www.mq.edu.au/research/research-centres-groups-and-facilities/healthy-people/centres/centre-for-emotional-health-ceh/resources
Good	Child Anxiety Life Interference Scale—Parent/Child, Form and Preschool Version (CALIS/CALIS-PV; Lyneham et al., 2013)*	19, 10, 18	Y, P	3–17	https://www.mq.edu.au/research/research-centres-groups-and-facilities/healthy-people/centres/centre-for-emotional-health-ceh/resources
Good	Preschool Anxiety Scale—Revised (PAS; Edwards et al., 2010)*	28	P	3–5	https://www.mq.edu.au/research/research-centres-groups-and-facilities/healthy-people/centres/centre-for-emotional-health-ceh/resources
Adequate	Social Worries Questionnaire (SWQ; Spence 1995)	10	Y, P, T	8–17	http://www.scaswebsite.com/index.php?p=1_57

(continued)

Table 9.2 Continued

Psychometric Support	Measure Name	No. of Items	Completed by[a]	Ages[c]	Link to Measure
Adequate	Hamilton Anxiety Rating Scale—A (Hamilton 1959)*	14	C	Adolescents[d]	https://dcf.psychiatry.ufl.edu/files/2011/05/HAMILTON-ANXIETY.pdf
Adequate	Patient-Reported Outcomes Measurement Information System (PROMIS Anxiety; DeWalt et al., 2015)*	15	Y, P	8–17	http://www.healthmeasures.net/administrator/components/com_instruments/uploads/15-09-01_02-00-50_Neuro-QOLv1.0-PediatricAnxietySF_03-14-2014.pdf
	Childhood Yale-Brown Obsessive Compulsive Scale (CY-BOCS) (iocdf.org: International OCD Foundation [IOCDF], 2018).	19	Y, P	6–17	https://iocdf.org/wp-content/uploads/2016/04/05-CYBOCS-complete.pdf

[a] Completed by: Y = youth, P = parent/caregiver, C = clinician, T = teacher.

[b] Intended clinical use: S = screening, D = diagnostic aid or treatment planning, O = outcome monitoring.

[c] Exact age range for specific forms (e.g., self-report, parent report) may vary.

[d] Exact age range not specified.

* Available in multiple languages.

NOTE: Table adapted from Becker-Haimes, E. M., Tabachnick, A. R., Last, B. S., Stewart, R. E., Hasan-Granier, A., & Beidas, R. S. (2020). Evidence base update for brief, free, and accessible youth mental health measures. *Journal of Clinical Child & Adolescent Psychology, 49*(1), 1–17, reprinted by permission of the publisher (Taylor & Francis Ltd, http://www.tandfonline.com).

References for measures in Table 9.2:

Birmaher, B., Brent, D. A., Chiappetta, L., Bridge, J., Monga, S., & Baugher, M. (1999). Psychometric properties of the Screen for Child Anxiety Related Emotional Disorders (SCARED): A replication study. *Journal of the American Academy of Child & Adolescent Psychiatry, 38*(10), 1230–1236.

Chorpita, B. F., Moffitt, C. E., & Gray, J. (2005). Psychometric properties of the Revised Child Anxiety and Depression Scale in a clinical sample. *Behaviour Research and Therapy, 43*(3), 309–322.

Chorpita, B. F., Tracey, S. A., Brown, T. A., Collica, T. J., & Barlow, D. H. (1997). Assessment of worry in children and adolescents: An adaptation of the Penn State Worry Questionnaire. *Behaviour Research and Therapy, 35*(6), 569–581.

DeWalt, D. A., Gross, H. E., Gipson, D. S., Selewski, D. T., DeWitt, E. M., Dampier, C. D., . . . Varni, J. W. (2015). PROMIS(®) pediatric self-report scales distinguish subgroups of children within and across six common pediatric chronic health conditions. *Quality of Life Research, 24*(9), 2195–2208. doi:10.1007/s11136-015-0953-3

Edwards, S. L., Rapee, R. M., Kennedy, S. J., & Spence, S. H. (2010). The assessment of anxiety symptoms in preschool-aged children: The revised Preschool Anxiety Scale. *Journal of Clinical Child & Adolescent Psychology, 39*(3), 400–409.

Goodman, W. K., Price, L. H., Rasmussen, S. A., Riddle, M. A., & Rapoport, J. L. (1991). *Children's Yale-Brown obsessive compulsive scale (CY-BOCS).* New Haven: Department of Psychiatry, Yale University School of Medicine.

Hamilton, M. A. X. (1959). The assessment of anxiety states by rating. *British Journal of Medical Psychology, 32*(1), 50–55.

Lyneham, H. J., Sburlati, E. S., Abbott, M. J., Rapee, R. M., Hudson, J. L., Tolin, D. F., & Carlson, S. E. (2013). Psychometric properties of the child anxiety life interference scale (CALIS). *Journal of Anxiety Disorders, 27*(7), 711–719.

Lyneham, H. J., Street, A. K., Abbott, M. J., & Rapee, R. M. (2008). Psychometric properties of the school anxiety scale—Teacher report (SAS–TR). *Journal of Anxiety Disorders, 22*(2), 292–300.

Spence, S. H. (1995). The social worries questionnaire. Social skills training: Enhancing social competence with children and adolescents. Windsor: NFER-Nelson.

Spence, S. H. (1998). A measure of anxiety symptoms among children. *Behaviour Research and Therapy, 36*(5), 545–566.

Uher, R., Heyman, I., Mortimore, C., Frampton, I., & Goodman, R. (2007). Screening young people for obsessive-compulsive disorder. *British Journal of Psychiatry, 191*(4), 353–354.

Table 9.3 DIFFERENTIAL DIAGNOSIS: MENTAL DISORDERS THAT SHARE
SYMPTOMS WITH ANXIETY DISORDERS

Diagnosis	Symptoms
Attention-deficit/hyperactivity disorder	Distractibility, restlessness
Depression	Distractibility, insomnia, somatic complaints
Bipolar disorder	Distractibility, restlessness, irritability, insomnia
Obsessive-compulsive disorder	Intrusive thoughts, avoidance, reassurance seeking
Psychotic disorders	Restlessness, agitation, social withdrawal, distractibility
Autism spectrum disorder	Social withdrawal, social skills deficits, distractibility
Learning disorders	Worries about school performance

SOURCE: Adapted from Walter et al. (2020).

According to his parents' report, Justin met diagnostic criteria for social anxiety disorder. Justin's parents said that Justin worried that he would embarrass himself in front of peers and that one of the main reasons he worried about attending school was meeting new teens and interacting with them. Justin's parents endorsed social anxiety symptoms in the classroom setting and regarding interacting with other youths. Justin's parents also reported that he had great anxiety about public eating, and he had requested that he be able to eat in a teacher's office in the upcoming year rather than the cafeteria so that other youths could not see him eat. Justin's parents also noted that he had difficulty asking friends over and was unable to go to parties with other youths, although he used to be able to do both things.

Justin also endorsed meeting the necessary diagnostic criteria to warrant a diagnosis of social anxiety disorder. He reported that the primary reason he had not been able to attend school was concerns of social evaluation, primarily from peers. While in a regular academic environment at the beginning of 10th grade, Justin reported being unable/unwilling to answer questions in class, give an oral report or read in front of the class without mumbling, ask the teacher for help in front of peers, write on the board in front of the class, participate in group work, participate to his best ability in gym class, and initiate or join in on a conversation with peers. Justin reported feeling especially anxious during unstructured portions of the school day or when there was a change in routine. He also endorsed evaluative concerns outside of school. He did not answer the phone unless he could see on the caller ID that it was a family member or other person with whom he felt comfortable speaking. He reported he would not be able to invite a friend over and had not done this in nearly a year. He avoided socializing with friends because he was concerned they might engage in behavior he was uncomfortable with. He had not been to a party since eighth grade graduation and tried to get out of having his picture taken if possible. He tried to avoid going to places where there would be a lot of people, like grocery stores, because of concerns about social evaluation. Justin experienced physiologic arousal in social situations, including a racing heart, tightness in his chest, and difficulty breathing.

According to his parents' report, Justin also met criteria for a diagnosis of generalized anxiety disorder. Justin's parents described Justin as an "excessive worrier" and noted that Justin was incredibly distressed that he was not able to go to school. They described "an ongoing argument" in his head regarding whether he could return to school. Justin's parents reported he worried across several areas daily. Justin worried about returning to school, his grades, and his performance. According to Justin's parents, he also worried about returning to school because of the possibility of getting in trouble, the confusion that he may feel with a new schedule, and because classes would be in a new part of the building (e.g., he might get lost while switching classes). Justin also worried about social/interpersonal matters and "little things," especially saying the wrong thing. He worried about his own health and the health of loved ones and family issues, such as if his parents have enough money. Justin's parents reported that while money was sometimes tight, there was no reason for Justin to be especially worried about family finances. Justin's parents also said that he worried frequently about world issues (e.g., climate change). He reportedly had great difficulty when he was not in control of a situation and when unsure about what he needed to do (e.g., knowing how to order food at the cafeteria). Justin's parents reported that Justin had been worrying daily for more than 6 months without being able to stop and endorsed numerous physical symptoms of generalized anxiety disorder. They stated that Justin's worrying was interfering because it kept him from socializing and attending school.

Justin also endorsed enough symptoms to warrant a diagnosis of generalized anxiety disorder. He stated that he often worried about his grades in school and worried a great deal about making a good impression and what others thought of him. Justin also endorsed worries about little things or small mistakes he had made. He described several perfectionistic concerns, especially regarding school and being on time. He stated that if he knew he had somewhere to be the next day he would often start thinking about it the day before and begin planning what he needed so that he would be sure to be ready on time. Justin also endorsed concerns about his own health and the health of family members. He also reported worrying about family matters and things going on in the world. He reported worrying most days since age 12 or 13. When worried, Justin reported experiencing trouble relaxing, fatigue, impaired concentration, irritability, tension in his neck and back or feelings that his arms and legs were unusually heavy, and difficulty sleeping.

According to his parents' report, Justin also experienced distressing and interfering mood-related symptoms at the time of intake that may have indicated persistent depressive disorder. This "low-grade sadness" began a little over 1 year earlier. There had not been a period of 2 months or longer since onset when Justin did not experience a depressed mood. Justin's parents endorsed the following symptoms: eating less, trouble sleeping, feeling tired, and feeling hopeless. Justin's parents believed that he felt this way because of his anxiety and that if his anxiety ameliorated, he would be much happier and could function as he did before. According to Justin's report he had not experienced any depressive episodes. He reported feeling sad more often than he felt happy during the short time he was enrolled in 10th grade at the brick-and-mortar school; however, he did not endorse sufficient depressive symptoms to warrant a mood disorder diagnosis based on his report.

INTERVENTION

Sixty percent of youths with anxiety get treatment of some kind, leaving a substantial number without intervention (Ghandour et al., 2019). Anxiety, including OCD, is important to identify and treat in children because it can become chronic. A meta-analysis indicated that a childhood diagnosis of separation anxiety disorder significantly increases the risk of not only panic disorder but also any anxiety disorder in adulthood (Kossowsky et al., 2013). Further, the presence of a childhood anxiety disorder predicts a range of difficulties in adolescence and young adulthood including separation anxiety, generalized anxiety, social anxiety, panic attacks, conduct disorder, depression, oppositional defiant disorder, and ADHD (Bittner et al., 2007; Cummings et al., 2014). Effective treatment can protect against negative sequalae (Benjamin et al., 2013), including future cases of substance use and drug disorder in adulthood (Essau et al., 2014) and suicidality (Wolk et al., 2015). CBT has the most research support for treating anxiety in youths but is not widely available in community settings.

Psychosocial

CBT has been evaluated more than any other psychosocial intervention type (James et al., 2020). See Table 9.4 for a list of treatment components found in most CBT child anxiety protocols. A recent development involves a Unified Protocol that is labeled "transdiagnostic," meaning that it can be used for anxiety and other disorders, such as depression (Ehrenreich-May et al., 2017). The Unified Protocol may be a good choice for youths with comorbidities or emotion regulation difficulties (Ehrenreich et al., 2009; Seager et al., 2014). A systematic review of CBT treatment for separation anxiety disorder found that school-aged and adolescent clients improved most following treatment that had a transdiagnostic approach, and preschool children with a separation anxiety disorder had better outcomes following treatment guided by a separation anxiety–specific protocol (Giani et al., 2022).

   Exposure is a key component of CBT for child anxiety. It is typically conducted in a graduated fashion, in which the practitioner helps the client to construct a hierarchy of situations from least to most feared and then to work through these in order, conquering smaller fears before going on to bigger ones in a process called *systematic desensitization*. The point of these exercises is for the client to learn that the situation is not dangerous and that, without avoidance, the anxiety will naturally dissipate (Worden & Tolin, 2014). Research indicates that exposure is the most critical component of effective anxiety treatment (Abramowitz, 2013; Higa-McMillan et al., 2016).

Table 9.4 Components of Cognitive-Behavioral Treatment for Anxiety Disorders

Component	Description	Other Considerations
Psychoeducation	Providing information about the nature of anxiety and how it can be controlled	
Monitoring	Frequency and duration of symptoms and triggers	Fear thermometer
Cognitive restructuring	Identifying, challenging, and changing maladaptive belief systems that contribute to anxiety	
Relaxation training	Mind–body exercises that help control physiologic symptoms are taught as ways to cope and can be effective for anxiety on their own (Borquist-Conlon et al., 2019).	a. Breathing control (deep breathing) b. Progressive muscle relaxation (alternately tightening and relaxing certain muscle groups) c. Mindfulness (cultivating a practice of accepting and detaching from thoughts instead of letting them become consuming)
Problem-solving	Generating and implementing a variety of practical solutions to stressors	
Exposure	A process in which the client learns to face feared objects or situations; research suggests this is the most important component of effective anxiety treatment.	For OCD, this features prolonged and repeated exposure to the situation that triggers the need to perform the compulsion. The client is coached to refrain from avoiding the stimulus or engaging in ritualistic behavior. A parent may be involved as a support person for response prevention.

SOURCES: March & Mulle (1998); Stein et al. (2010); Velting, Setzer, & Albano (2004).

For children, parents and other caregivers should be involved in exposure planning and execution because it is important for them to refrain from accommodation and avoidance and instead to provide support, encouragement, and positive reinforcement for the child's efforts (Gryczkowski & Whiteside, 2014). Some parents may need additional assistance because of their own distress at watching their child go through anxiety, and they may need coaching to refrain from expressing frustration or criticism or from accommodating to the disorder.

The most well-known manual for child anxiety treatment is Kendall and Hedtke's (2006) *Coping Cat* program for youths ages 7 to 14 years. *Coping Cat* is designed for use with a variety of anxiety disorders, including separation anxiety, generalized anxiety, and social anxiety. Adaptations of this program include the C.A.T. project for adolescents (Kendall et al., 2002) and multiple international translations. Beidas and colleagues (2010) have also discussed how to adapt the manual for younger children and adolescents, as well as for those who have co-morbid conditions, such as attention problems and depression. Recently, discussion has centered on adaptations involving reducing the number of sessions and meeting for concentrated blocks of time (Öst & Ollendick, 2017). Even though CBT is considered a brief model with 12 to 16 sessions, the duration might not make it feasible for certain settings or families. However, single-session CBT holds a lot of promise, having performed well for reducing anxiety in youths compared with wait-list controls (Bertuzzi et al., 2021).

For early childhood anxiety, the strongest empirical support is for family-involved CBT and not individual treatment (Comer et al., 2019). An overview of the systematic reviews of child and adolescent CBT for anxiety disorders (Bennett et al., 2016) found that CBT was more effective compared with wait-list controls. A recent meta-analysis indicated that complete recovery rates for anxiety from CBT ranged from 48% to 66% compared with up to 21% in both wait-list and active control conditions (Warwick et al., 2017). Different modalities of CBT may be comparably efficacious. School refusal treatment has also been subject to meta-analysis; most studies were of CBT protocols (Maynard et al., 2015). According to a pooled estimate of eight studies, active treatment for school refusal was more effective than attention control.

For adolescents, CBT treatment, either individually or in groups, has been shown to be very effective at 4-year follow-up (Kodal et al., 2018). In the majority of cases (63%), youths no longer met criteria for the principal anxiety disorder that brought them to treatment. Social anxiety disorder had lower odds of recovery compared with separation anxiety disorder and generalized anxiety disorder (Evans et al., 2021; Kodal et al., 2018).

Similarly for OCD, CBT has been shown to be more effective than no intervention and comparable to use of selective serotonin reuptake inhibitors (SSRIs) and SSRIs plus CBT, based on two meta-analyses (Öst et al., 2016; Uhre et al., 2019). While CBT alone may not be the appropriate initial treatment for children with a family history of OCD, even for these children, CBT may provide benefits when combined with an SSRI compared with using an SSRI by itself (Turner et al., 2018). OCD symptom severity, higher initial impairment, depressive symptoms, comorbidity, and family accommodation predict a worse outcome after CBT (Turner et al., 2018). See Chapter 6 for an illustration of OCD treatment in a youth with autism.

A promising mode of delivery of CBT involves computer assistance, according to a review of seven studies of anxiety disorders (Rooksby et al., 2015;

Wickersham et al., 2022) and for OCD (Babiano et al., 2019). The authors suggest that computer-assisted delivery may be a helpful alternative when there are barriers to access, when people prefer this mode, or as a first-line intervention. Social workers could play a coaching role in this mode of delivery (Rooksby et al., 2015). Another promising mode of delivery is single-session treatment, which appears to perform well against no treatment control and multisession treatment (Bertuzzi et al., 2021). Social workers in settings like schools where a single contact might be the norm can therefore consider using a single-session CBT protocol.

Medication

The past 30 years have seen an increased use of medications initially developed as antidepressants to treat anxiety disorders. An overview of systematic reviews for children indicated that four types of SSRI (fluoxetine, fluvoxamine, paroxetine, and sertraline) and one type of serotonin and norepinephrine reuptake inhibitor (SNRI; venlafaxine) show benefits over placebo for reducing anxiety in youths (Bennett et al., 2016). However, head-to-head comparisons between the effects of different medications are needed. Antidepressants appear to produce better effects for anxiety over placebo than for depression in youths (Locher et al., 2017). At the same time, antidepressants increased the risk of suicidal ideation and attempts. In a more recent systematic review, CBT and medication were compared and found equivalent, and their combination was even more effective for anxiety (Sigurvinsdóttir et al., 2020). Because of the potential side effects of psychotropic medications, and to support children and adolescents in developing long-term coping skills, psychosocial interventions are generally recommended when medication is used (Bernstein & Shaw, 1997).

For anxiety, in the CAMS trial, the largest randomized trial to date comparing CBT to sertraline to combination treatment (CBT plus sertraline), both monotherapies were effective in reducing anxiety symptoms, and combination treatment outperformed either monotherapy (Piacentini et al., 2014; Walkup et al., 2008). Two systematic reviews have demonstrated that, for youths with OCD, SSRIs performed better than placebo for OCD (Ivarsson et al., 2015; Khan, 2020). Fluoxetine and sertraline were more effective than fluvoxamine (Khan, 2019). Adding CBT to SSRI treatment was found effective for nonresponders and partial responders, but, interestingly, adding SSRI to CBT did not add benefits. Another systematic review showed that combined CBT plus medication was more effective than either alone for OCD, and found support for escitalopram (Lexapro) over other SSRIs (Tao et al., 2022). Taking the results together, both medication and CBT can be effective for OCD.

Justin began treatment with the student clinician, who met weekly with her supervisor to review Justin's progress. Justin participated in a total of 17 sessions of a cognitive-behavioral treatment program. Treatment was guided by the C.A.T. Project manual, the adolescent version of *Coping Cat (Kendall et al., 2002). The goals for treatment, developed in collaboration with the family, were to give Justin skills to better manage his anxiety, including effective education, coping skills, relaxation training, and problem-solving skills training, and to practice using these skills in real-life situations (i.e., exposure). Throughout treatment, Justin worked on better understanding his worries and bodily reactions to anxiety-provoking situations, challenging his anxious thoughts in these situations, approaching (rather than avoiding) anxiety-provoking situations, and helping himself cope effectively in situations in which he feels anxiety.*

Treatment was divided into two segments: psychoeducation and exposures. During the psychoeducation phase, Justin and the clinician worked to identify his somatic symptoms of anxiety (i.e., racing heart, tightness in his chest, difficulty breathing) and to understand the negative thoughts he has when in anxiety-provoking situations. Justin was able to share his common anxious cognitions: "I will make a mistake and embarrass myself" and "I will get into trouble." Justin was taught a series of skills to use in situations that make him nervous, including relaxation techniques, coping thoughts, and problem-solving. After the psychoeducation phase was complete Justin began the exposure phase of treatment, which was the bulk of Justin's work in therapy.

Justin worked his way through a hierarchical list of anxiety-provoking situations both in and out of session, collaboratively developed between Justin and the clinician and with input from his parents (see Figure 9.1). These exposures included

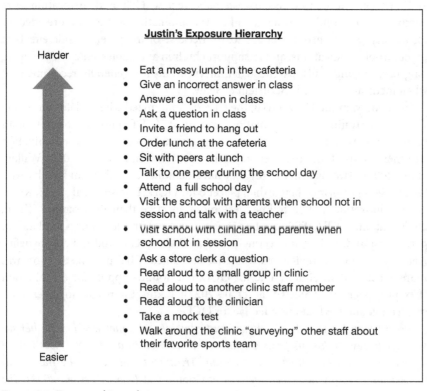

Justin's Exposure Hierarchy

Harder

- Eat a messy lunch in the cafeteria
- Give an incorrect answer in class
- Answer a question in class
- Ask a question in class
- Invite a friend to hang out
- Order lunch at the cafeteria
- Sit with peers at lunch
- Talk to one peer during the school day
- Attend a full school day
- Visit the school with parents when school not in session and talk with a teacher
- Visit school with clinician and parents when school not in session
- Ask a store clerk a question
- Read aloud to a small group in clinic
- Read aloud to another clinic staff member
- Read aloud to the clinician
- Take a mock test
- Walk around the clinic "surveying" other staff about their favorite sports team

Easier

Figure 9.1 Exposure hierarchy.

conducting surveys, reading in front of new people, talking to store clerks, visiting school before beginning the new academic year, and taking mock tests. Out of session, Justin worked to use his coping skills to attend school consistently, talk to new people at school, order lunch from the cafeteria, attend school social events, and socialize with peers outside of school. For each exposure, Justin and the clinician would collaboratively define the exposure task, and Justin would engage in the task (with modeling and support from the therapist as needed and only to the extent required to support Justin in moving up his exposure hierarchy). During the exposure, the clinician asked Justin to rate his anxiety periodically and then plotted these ratings for review after the exposure. After the exposure was completed, Justin and the clinician would process how Justin felt he did, discuss what he had learned, and review his anxiety ratings. Then, they would agree on exposure activities for Justin to engage in outside of session for homework, including his parents as appropriate, and then would determine the exposure task for the subsequent session. Sometimes they would repeat an exposure several times or at varying intensities before moving up the hierarchy. Other times Justin quickly learned that his feared outcomes were not realized, and he was able to move rapidly to a more challenging exposure.

Throughout treatment Justin was encouraged to approach situations that made him anxious rather than avoid them (e.g., "I know this is hard, but you can do it!"). These situations provided him with opportunities to practice his coping skills. Justin was engaged throughout treatment and willingly attempted all exposure tasks, even those that he was very afraid of. Throughout treatment Justin appeared to become more confident in his abilities to manage anxiety and stress in his life. Justin appeared proud of his accomplishments both in and out of session, particularly attending school, which he began doing around session 10.

The student clinician and her supervisor jointly met with Justin and his mother to determine whether treatment termination was warranted following 17 sessions of CBT. Mrs. Russo reported that Justin is "not experiencing anxiety" and that he is doing "above and beyond all expectations." Justin's mother reported progress in all the anxiety-related areas that prompted Justin's treatment. Justin's mother reported that Justin no longer experiences much social anxiety and greatly enjoys school. He had not missed any school days because of anxiety this academic year. Justin's mother reported hardly noticing any anxiety exhibited by Justin and believes that the anxiety she is aware of is normative. For example, Justin has indicated some anxiety about going to the school dance but also expresses excitement and eagerness to attend. Justin stated that he is no longer nervous about attending or staying in school. He endorsed no clinically significant anxiety in any social situations. Moreover, Justin stated that he now enjoys attending school regularly, is looking forward to participating in a school talent show, and is planning to run for class president.

Additionally, Justin and his mother indicated no excessive worry or depressive symptoms. Mrs. Russo reported that Justin exhibits some concern over his grades and tends to be a perfectionist. However, she specified that Justin does not worry about these things but simply "wants to do well." She described his concern over his performance as "just enough for him to stay on top of things." The family was extremely proud of Justin's remarkable turnaround and also expressed frustration that the previous clinicians Justin had met with before coming to the clinic had not utilized exposure, which had been instrumental in Justin's recovery.

SUMMARY

Anxiety disorders are the most common mental health diagnoses in youths and are even more prevalent in youths living in low-SES circumstances. For youths, the most common types are typically separation anxiety disorder, social anxiety disorder, and generalized anxiety disorder. Depressive disorders are often comorbid. Anxiety disorders in youths are treatable, and effective early intervention can prevent anxiety disorders in adulthood as well as common sequelae such as risk for substance misuse and suicide. Therefore, practitioners who work with young people should know how to screen for anxiety and its common comorbidities and refer children and adolescents to appropriate treatment. If there are a lack of clinicians trained in evidence-based treatment (i.e., exposure therapy) in the community, social workers can potentially undertake the work themselves with the *Coping Cat* or another evidence-based CBT manual.

REFERENCES

Abramowitz, J. S. (2013). The practice of exposure therapy: Relevance of cognitive-behavioral theory and extinction theory. *Behavior Therapy, 44*(4), 548–558.

American Psychiatric Association. (2022). *Diagnostic and statistical manual of mental disorders* (5th ed., Text Revision). Washington, DC: American Psychiatric Association.

Ashworth, E., Brooks, S. J., & Schiöth, H. B. (2021). Neural activation of anxiety and depression in children and young people: A systematic meta-analysis of fMRI studies. *Psychiatry Research Neuroimaging, 311*, 111272. https://doi.org/10.1016/j.pscychresns.2021.111272

Babiano-Espinosa, L., Wolters, L. H., Weidle, B., Op de Beek, V., Pedersen, S. A., Compton, S., & Skokauskas, N. (2019). Acceptability, feasibility, and efficacy of Internet cognitive behavioral therapy (iCBT) for pediatric obsessive-compulsive disorder: A systematic review. *Systematic Reviews, 8*(1), 284. https://doi.org/10.1186/s13643-019-1166-6

Bandelow, B., Spath, C., Tichauer, A., Broocks, A., Hajak, G., & Ruther, E. (2002). Early traumatic life events, parental attitudes, family history, and birth risk factors in patients with panic disorder. *Comprehensive Psychiatry, 43*, 269–278.

Beidas, R. S., Benjamin, C. L., Puleo, C. M., Edmunds, J. M., & Kendall, P. C. (2010). Flexible applications of the Coping Cat program for anxious youth. *Cognitive and Behavioral Practice, 17*(2), 142–153. http://doi.org/10.1016/j.cbpra.2009.11.002

Benjamin, C. L., Harrison, J. P., Settipani, C. A., Brodman, D. M., & Kendall, P. C. (2013). Anxiety and related outcomes in young adults 7 to 19 years after receiving treatment for child anxiety. *Journal of Consulting and Clinical Psychology, 81*(5), 865–876. doi:10.1037/a0033048

Bernstein, G., & Shaw, K. (1997). Practice parameters for the assessment and treatment of children and adolescents with anxiety disorders. *Journal of the American Academy of Child and Adolescent Psychiatry, 36*(Suppl. 10), 69S–84S.

Bertuzzi, V., Fratini, G., Tarquinio, C., Cannistrà, F., Granese, V., Giusti, E. M., Castelnuovo, G., & Pietrabissa, G. (2021). Single-Session therapy by appointment for the treatment of anxiety disorders in youth and adults: A systematic review of the literature. *Frontiers in Psychology, 12*, 721382.

Bittner, A., Egger, H. L., Erkanli, A., Jane Costello, E., Foley, D. L., & Angold, A. (2007). What do childhood anxiety disorders predict? *Journal of Child Psychology and Psychiatry, 48*, 1174–1183. https://doi.org/10.1111/j.1469-7610.2007.01812.x

Bosquet, M., & Egeland, B. (2006). The development and maintenance of anxiety symptoms from infancy through adolescence in a longitudinal sample. *Development and Psychopathology, 18*, 517–550.

Comer, J. S., Hong, N., Poznanski, B., Silva, K., & Wilson, M. (2019). Evidence base update on the treatment of early childhood anxiety and related problems. *Journal of Clinical Child & Adolescent Psychology, 48*(1), 1–15. https://doi.org/10.1080/15374 416.2018.1534208

Costello, E., Egger, H., & Angold, A. (2005). 10-year research update review: The epidemiology of child and adolescent psychiatric disorders: I. Methods and public health burden. *Journal of the American Academy of Child & Adolescent Psychiatry, 44*(10), 972–986.

Cummings, C. M., Caporino, N. E., & Kendall, P. C. (2014). Comorbidity of anxiety and depression in children and adolescents: 20 years after. *Psychological Bulletin, 140*(3), 816–845. https://doi.org/10.1037/a0034733

Cyranowski, J. M., Frank, E., Young, E., & Shear, M. K. (2000). Adolescent onset of the gender difference in lifetime rates of major depression: A theoretical model. *Archives of General Psychiatry, 57*(1), 21–27. https://doi.org/10.1001/archpsyc.57.1.21

Donovan, C., & Spence, S. (2000). Prevention of childhood anxiety disorders. *Clinical Psychology Review, 20*, 509–531.

Ehrenreich, J. T., Goldstein, C. R., Wright, L. R., & Barlow, D. H. (2009). Development of a unified protocol for the treatment of emotional disorders in youth. *Child & Family Behavior Therapy, 31*(1), 20–37.

Ehrenreich-May, J., Kennedy, S. M., Sherman, J. A., Bennett, S. M., & Barlow, D. H. (2017). *Unified protocol for transdiagnostic treatment of emotional disorders in adolescents: Workbook*. New York: Oxford University Press.

Essau, C. A., Lewinsohn, P. M., Olaya, B., & Seeley, J. R. (2014). Anxiety disorders in adolescents and psychosocial outcomes at age 30. *Journal of Affective Disorders, 163*, 125–132.

Essau, C. A., Lewinsohn, P. M., Lim, J. X., Ho, M. R., & Rohde, P. (2018). Incidence, recurrence and comorbidity of anxiety disorders in four major developmental stages. *Journal of Affective Disorders, 228*, 248–253. https://doi.org/10.1016/ j.jad.2017.12.014

Essex, M. J., Klein, M. H., Slattery, M. J., Goldsmith, H. H., & Kalin, N. H. (2010). Early risk factors and developmental pathways to chronic high inhibition and social anxiety disorder in adolescence. *American Journal of Psychiatry, 167*(1), 40–46.

Evans, R., Clark, D. M., & Leigh, E. (2021). Are young people with primary social anxiety disorder less likely to recover following generic CBT compared to young people with other primary anxiety disorders? A systematic review and meta-analysis. *Behavioural and Cognitive Psychotherapy, 49*(3), 352–369. https://doi.org/10.1017/ s135246582000079x

Ghandour, R. M., Sherman, L. J., Vladutiu, C. J., Ali, M. M., Lynch, S. E., Bitsko, R. H., & Blumberg, S. J. (2019). Prevalence and treatment of depression, anxiety, and conduct problems in US children. *The Journal of Pediatrics, 206*, 256–267.e3. https://doi. org/10.1016/j.jpeds.2018.09.021

Giani, L., Caputi, M., Forresi, B., et al. (2022). Evaluation of cognitive-behavioral therapy efficacy in the treatment of separation anxiety disorder in childhood and adolescence: A systematic review of randomized controlled trials. *International Journal of Cognitive Therapy, 15*, 57–80. https://doi.org/10.1007/s41811-021-00129-3

Ginsburg, G. S., Becker-Haimes, E. M., Keeton, C., Kendall, P. C., Iyengar, S., Sakolsky, D., Albano, A. M., Peris, T., Compton, S. N., & Piacentini, J. (2018). Results from the Child/Adolescent Anxiety Multimodal Extended Long-Term Study (CAMELS): Primary Anxiety Outcomes. *Journal of the American Academy of Child and Adolescent Psychiatry, 57*(7), 471–480. https://doi.org/10.1016/j.jaac.2018.03.017

Gryczkowski, M. R., & Whiteside, S. P. H. (2014). Pediatric obsessive-compulsive disorder. In E. A. Storch & D. McKay (Eds.), *Obsessive-compulsive disorder and its spectrum: A life-span approach* (pp. 37–57). Washington, DC: American Psychological Association.

Hankin, B. L., Mermelstein, R., & Roesch, L. (2007). Sex differences in adolescent depression: Stress exposure and reactivity models. *Child Development, 78*(1), 279–295. http://www.jstor.org/stable/4139225

Hanklin, B., Kassel, J. D., & Abela, J. R. (2005). Adult attachment dimensions and specificity of emotional distress symptoms: Prospective investigations of cognitive risk and interpersonal stress generation as mediating mechanisms. *Personality and Psychology Bulletin, 31*, 136–151.

Hayward, C., Wilson, K. A., Lagle, K., Kraemer, H. C., Killen, J. D., & Taylor, C. B. (2008). The developmental psychopathology of social anxiety in adolescents. *Depression and Anxiety, 25*, 200–206. doi:10.1002/da.20289

Hettema, J. M., Neale, M. C., & Kendler, K. S. (2001). A review and meta-analysis of the genetic epidemiology of anxiety disorders. *American Journal of Psychiatry, 1574*, 1568–1578.

Ivarsson, T., Skarphedinsson, G., Kornør, H., Axelsdottir, B., Biedilæ, S., Heyman, I., Asbahr, F., Thomsen, P. H., Fineberg, N., March, J., & Accreditation Task for the Canadian Institute for Obsessive Compulsive Disorders. (2015). The place of and evidence for serotonin reuptake inhibitors (SRIs) for obsessive compulsive disorder (OCD) in children and adolescents: Views based on a systematic review and meta-analysis. *Psychiatry Research, 227*(1), 93–103. doi:10.1016/j.psychres.2015.01.015

James, A., Reardon, T., Soler, A., James, G., & Creswell, C. (2020). Cognitive behavioural therapy for anxiety disorders in children and adolescents. *Cochrane Database of Systematic Reviews, 11*, CD013162. doi:10.1002/14651858.CD013162.pub2

Kazdin, A. (2001). Treatment of conduct disorders. In J. Hill & B. Maughan (Eds.), *Conduct disorders in childhood and adolescence* (pp. 408–448). New York: Cambridge University Press.

Kendall, P. C., Choudhury, M., Hudson, J., Webb, A. (2002). *The CAT project manual.* Ardmore, PA: Workbook Publishing.

Kendall, P. C., & Hedtke, K. (2006) *Cognitive-behavioral therapy for anxious children: Therapist manual* (3rd ed.). Ardmore, PA: Workbook Publishing.

Kendall, P. C., Hudson, J., Gosch, E., Flannery-Schroeder, E., & Suveg, C. (2008). Child and family therapy for anxiety-disordered youth: Results of a randomized clinical trial. *Journal of Consulting and Clinical Psychology, 76*, 282–297.

Khan, A. M. (2020). 27.3 the effectiveness of SSRIs for treatment of OCD in children and adolescents: A systematic review and meta-analysis. *Journal of the American Academy of Child and Adolescent Psychiatry, 59*(10), S202–S202. https://doi.org/ 10.1016/j.jaac.2020.09.006

Kodal, A., Fjermestad, K., Bjelland, I., Gjestad, R., Öst, L. G., Bjaastad, J., Haugland, B., Havik, O., Heiervang, E., & Wergeland, G. (2018). Long-term effectiveness of cognitive behavioral therapy for youth with anxiety disorders. *Journal of Anxiety Disorders, 53*, 58–67.

Kossowsky, J., Pfaltz, M., Schneider, S., Taeymans, J., Locher, C., & Gaab, J. (2013). *American Journal of Psychotherapy, 170*, 768–781.

Lemstra, M., Neudorf, C., D'Arcy, C., Kunst, A., Warren, L. M., & Bennett, N. R. (2008). A systematic review of depressed mood and anxiety by SES in youth aged 10-15 years. *Canadian Journal of Public Health, 99*(2), 125–129.

Liotta, M. (2013). Relationship between temperament and anxiety disorders: a systematic review. *Mediterranean Journal of Clinical Psychology, 1*(1), 1–25.

March, J. S., & Mulle, K. (1998). *OCD in children and adolescents: A cognitive behavioral therapy manual.* New York: Guilford Press.

Maynard, B., Heyne, D., Brendel, K., Bulanda, J., Thompson, A., & Pigott, T. (2015). Treatment for school refusal among children and adolescents: A systematic review and meta-analysis. *Research on Social Work Practice, 28*, 56–67.

McLeod, B., Weisz, J., & Wood, J. (2007). Examining the association between parenting and childhood depression: A meta-analysis. *Clinical Psychology Review, 27*, 986–1003.

Merikangas, K. R., He, J., Burstein, M., Swanson, S. A., Avenevoli, S., Cui, L., Benjet, C., Georgiades, K., & Swendsen, J. (2010). Lifetime prevalence of mental disorders in U.S. adolescents: Results from the National Comorbidity Study-Adolescent Supplement (NCS-A). *Journal of the American Academy of Child and Adolescent Psychiatry, 49*(10), 980–989.

Mineka, S., & Zinbarg, R. (2006). A contemporary learning theory perspective on the etiology of anxiety disorders: It's not what you thought it was. *American Psychologist, 61*, 1–25.

Murphy, Y. E., & Flessner, C. A. (2015). Family functioning in pediatric obsessive compulsive and related disorders. *British Journal of Clinical Psychology, 54*, 414–434.

Osmanağaoğlu, N., Creswell, C., & Dodd, H. F. (2018). Intolerance of uncertainty, anxiety, and worry in children and adolescents: A meta-analysis. *Journal of Affective Disorders, 225*, 80–90. https://doi.org/10.1016/j.jad.2017.07.035

Öst, L. G., & Ollendick, T. H. (2017). Brief, intensive and concentrated cognitive behavioral treatments for anxiety disorders in children: A systematic review and meta-analysis. *Behaviour Research and Therapy, 97*, 134–145. https://doi.org/10.1016/ j.brat.2017.07.008

Öst, L. G., Riise, E. N., Wergeland, G. J., Hansen, B., & Kvale, G. (2016). Cognitive behavioral and pharmacological treatments of OCD in children: A systematic review and meta-analysis. *Journal of Anxiety Disorders, 43*, 58–69. https://doi.org/10.1016/j.janxdis.2016.08.003

Ozer, E., Best, S., Lipsey, T., & Weiss, D. (2003). Predictors of posttraumatic stress disorder and symptoms in adults: A meta-analysis. *Psychological Bulletin, 129*, 52–73.

Phillips, N. K., Hammen, C. L., Brennan, P. A., Najman, J. M., & Bor, W. (2005). Early adversity and the prospective prediction of depressive and anxiety disorders in adolescents. *Journal of Abnormal Child Psychology, 33*, 13–24.

Piacentini, J., Bennett, S., Compton, S. N., Kendall, P. C., Birmaher, B., Albano, A. M., March, J., Sherrill, J., Sakolsky, D., Ginsburg, G., Rynn, M., Bergman, R. L., Gosch, E., Waslick, B., Iyengar, S., McCracken, J., & Walkup, J. (2014). 24- and 36-week outcomes for the Child/Adolescent Anxiety Multimodal Study (CAMS). *Journal of the American Academy of Child and Adolescent Psychiatry, 53*(3), 297–310. https://doi.org/10.1016/j.jaac.2013.11.010

Remes, O., Brayne, C., Linde, R., & Lafortune, L. (2016). A systematic review of reviews on the prevalence of anxiety disorders in adult populations. *Brain and Behavior, 6*(7).

Rooksby, M., Elouafkaoui, P., Humphris, G., Clarkson, J., & Freeman, R. (2015). Internet-assisted delivery of cognitive-behavioural therapy (CBT) for childhood anxiety: Systematic review and meta-analysis. *Journal of Anxiety Disorders, 29*, 83–92.

Seager, I., Rowley, A. M., & Ehrenreich-May, J. (2014). Targeting common factors across anxiety and depression using the unified protocol for the treatment of emotional disorders in adolescents. *Journal of Rational-Emotive & Cognitive-Behavior Therapy, 32*(1), 67–83.

Sigurvinsdóttir, A. L., Jensínudóttir, K. B., Baldvinsdóttir, K. D., Smárason, O., & Skarphedinsson, G. (2020). Effectiveness of cognitive behavioral therapy (CBT) for child and adolescent anxiety disorders across different CBT modalities and comparisons: A systematic review and meta-analysis. *Nordic Journal of Psychiatry, 74*(3), 168–180. https://doi.org/10.1080/08039488.2019.1686653

Stein, M., Goin, M., Pollack, M., Roy-Byrne, P., Sareen, J., Simon, N., & Campbell-Sills, L. (2010). Practice guideline for the treatment of patients with panic disorder, 2nd ed. Washington, DC: American Psychiatric Association.

Storch, E. A., Merlo, L. J., Larson, M. J., Geffken, G. R., Lehmkuhl, H. D., Jacob, M. L., Murphy, T. K., & Goodman, W. K. (2008). Impact of comorbidity on cognitive-behavioral therapy response in pediatric obsessive-compulsive disorder. *Journal of the American Academy on Child and Adolescent Psychiatry, 47*(5), 583–592.

Subar, A. R., & Rozenman, M. (2021). Like parent, like child: Is parent interpretation bias associated with their child's interpretation bias and anxiety? A systematic review and meta analysis. *Journal of Affective Disorders, 291*, 307–314. https://doi.org/10.1016/j.jad.2021.05.020

Tao, Y., Li, H., Li, L., Zhang, H., Xu, H., Zhang, H., Zou, S., Deng, F., Huang, L., Wang, Y., Wang, X., Tang, X., Fu, X., & Yin, L. (2022). Comparing the efficacy of pharmacological and psychological treatment, alone and in combination, in children and adolescents with obsessive-compulsive disorder: A network meta-analysis. *Journal of Psychiatric Research, 148*, 95–102. https://doi.org/10.1016/j.jpsychires.2022.01.057

Tariq, A., Quayle, E., Lawrie, S. M., Reid, C., & Chan, S. W. Y. (2021). Relationship between Early Maladaptive Schemas and Anxiety in Adolescence and Young Adulthood: A systematic review and meta-analysis. *Journal of Affective Disorders, 295*, 1462–1473. https://doi.org/10.1016/j.jad.2021.09.031

Turner, C., O'Gorman, B., Nair, A., & O'Kearney, R. (2018). Moderators and predictors of response to cognitive behaviour therapy for pediatric obsessive-compulsive disorder: A systematic review. *Psychiatry Research, 261*, 50–60.

Van Grootheest, D. S., Cath, D. C., Beekman, A. T., & Boomsma, D. I. (2005). Twin studies on obsessive-compulsive disorder: A review. *Twin Research and Human Genetics, 8*(5), 450–458. http://dx.doi.org.proxy.library.vcu.edu/10.1375/twin.8.5.450

Velting, O., Setzer, N., & Albano, A. M. (2004). Update on and advances in assessment and cognitive-behavioral treatment of anxiety disorders in children and adolescents. *Professional Psychology: Research and Practice, 35*, 42–54.

Walkup, J. T., Albano, A. M., Piacentini, J., Birmaher, B., Compton, S. N., Sherrill, J. T., Ginsburg, G. S., Rynn, M. A., McCracken, J., Waslick, B., Iyengar, S., March, J. S., & Kendall, P. C. (2008). Cognitive behavioral therapy, sertraline, or a combination in childhood anxiety. *New England Journal of Medicine, 359*(26), 2753–2766. https://doi.org/10.1056/NEJMoa0804633

Warren, S., Huston, L., Egeland, B., & Sroufe, L. A. (1997). Child and adolescent anxiety disorders and early attachment. *Journal of the American Academy of Child and Adolescent Psychiatry, 36*, 637–644.

Warwick, H., Reardon, T., Cooper, P., Murayama, K., Reynolds, S., Wilson, C., & Creswell, C. (2017). Complete recovery from anxiety disorders following Cognitive Behavior Therapy in children and adolescents: A meta-analysis. *Clinical Psychology Review, 52*, 77–91.

Wickersham, A., Barack, T., Cross, L., & Downs, J. (2022). Computerized cognitive behavioral therapy for treatment of depression and anxiety in adolescents: Systematic review and meta-analysis. *Journal of Medical Internet Research, 24*(4), e29842. https://doi.org/10.2196/29842

Wolk, C. B., Kendall, P. C., & Beidas, R. S. (2015). Cognitive-behavioral therapy for child anxiety confers long-term protection from suicidality. *Journal of the American Academy of Child and Adolescent Psychiatry, 54*(3), 175–179. https://doi.org/10.1016/j.jaac.2014.12.004

Worden, B., & Tolin, D. F. (2014). Obsessive-compulsive disorder in adults. In E. A. Young, A. S., Klap, R., Sherbourne, C. D., & Wells, K. B. (2001). The quality of care for depressive and anxiety disorders in the United States. *Archives of General Psychiatry, 58*, 55–61.

Young, J. E., Klosko, J. S., & Weishaar, M. E. (2003). Schema therapy. New York: Guilford.

Depressive Disorders

Jessica Anderson is a 17-year-old Black female who presented to treatment with her grandmother, Ms. Monet Anderson, because of concerns that Jessica's performance in school had been declining, she had been withdrawing from family and friends, and according to Ms. Anderson, she seemed "sad all the time." Jessica lives with her grandmother and younger sister, 12-year-old Janay. Jessica and Janay's father had died several years earlier from a drug overdose. According to Ms. Anderson, he had "never really been in picture." Their mother has also struggled with substance use for most of her children's lives, namely crack cocaine. Occasionally, when sober, she lives with her daughters and her mother, Ms. Anderson; however, she has been largely absent through Jessica's teenage years. Ms. Anderson stated that Jessica and Janay's mother had shown signs of recovery about 6 months ago and had briefly reintegrated with the family but quickly relapsed, and they have had little contact with her since. This latest relapse "hit Jessica hard" according to Ms. Anderson and may have triggered the onset of Jessica's current symptoms. Jessica attends 11th grade at a large urban high school. According to Ms. Anderson, and corroborated by Jessica, Jessica has always been a top student who is well liked by her peers. This semester, her grades have declined noticeably, prompting the school counselor to refer Jessica for an evaluation with the social worker who provides mental health services through a satellite outpatient clinic on the high school's campus. The social worker met with Jessica and Ms. Anderson separately to determine whether Jessica would be eligible for school-based mental health services.

OVERVIEW

The depressive disorders that pertain to youths are (1) *major depressive disorder* (MDD): at least a 2-week period during which a person experiences a depressed mood or loss of interest in nearly all life activities, with five or more symptom categories being represented; (2) *persistent depressive disorder*: chronic, ongoing symptoms that are similar to, but less intense than, those of major depression; and (3) *disruptive mood dysregulation disorder*: (DMDD); a 12-month pattern of behavior characterized by an almost daily display of irritable and angry mood, erupting into temper outbursts, starting before the age of 10 (see Table 10.1)

Child and Adolescent Mental Health in Social Work. Jacqueline Corcoran and Courtney Benjamin Wolk, Oxford University Press. © Oxford University Press 2023. DOI: 10.1093/oso/9780197653562.003.0010

Table 10.1 DSM Criteria for Depression Disorders

Major Depressive Disorder
At least five of the following in a 2-week period:
1. Depressed mood most of the day, nearly every day
2. Diminished interest or pleasure in almost all activities most the of the day, nearly every day
3. Significant weight loss when not dieting or weight gain
4. Insomnia or hypersomnia nearly every day
5. Psychomotor agitation or retardation nearly every day
6. Fatigue or loss of energy nearly every day
7. Excessive feelings of worthlessness or guilt
8. Diminished ability to think or concentrate nearly every day
9. Recurrent thoughts of death and suicidal ideation

Persistent Depressive Disorder
Depressed mood with at least two of the following occurring most days for 1 year (for youths):
1. Poor appetite or overeating
2. Insomnia or hypersomnia
3. Low energy or fatigue
4. Low self-esteem
5. Poor concentration or difficulty making decisions
6. Feelings of hopelessness

(APA, 2022). Suicidality is one of the symptoms of MDD, but we have covered the range of self-harm/suicidal thoughts and behaviors in Chapter 12.

DMDD is a new diagnosis in the fifth edition of the *Diagnostic and Statistical Manual of Mental Disorders* (DSM-5) created to curb the overused practice of diagnosing children with bipolar disorder (Stebbins & Corcoran, 2014). Irritability of this early onset and pervasiveness is considered a mood because such children can remain in this state for long periods, sometimes without an apparent cause. The DMDD criteria were created so that this pervasive irritability was distinguished from the discrete manic episodes of bipolar disorder (Vidal-Ribas et al., 2016). DMDD does not yet have a strong evidence basis to guide psychosocial treatment, a criterion of ours for including certain disorders in this book. Additionally, psychiatrists will generally be performing the diagnoses in these cases because they will probably be prescribing a mood stabilizer, which justifies a more severe diagnosis. For these reasons, we cover these briefly in Chapter 3 and only because they are diagnosed in practice settings where social workers are trained and employed.

PREVALENCE

Depression in children is relatively rare (2.8% of elementary school–aged children, according to Costello et al., 2006), but in adolescence, new cases spike to lifetime and 12-month prevalence rates of 11% and 7.5%, respectively (Avenevoli et al., 2015). Depression is on the increase among 12- to 17-year-olds compared with every other age group (Weinberger et al., 2018). A systematic review of global prevalence has found a point prevalence rate of 34% among adolescents 10 to 19 years (Shorey et al., 2022). Subthreshold levels of major depression are even more common and important to identify because they are associated with high rates of comorbid disorders, functional impairment, and suicidality (Carrellas et al., 2017). The recent report of the Centers for Disease Control (CDC) annual Youth Behavior Survey has indicated high self-reported depression; 42% of respondents reported persistent feelings of sadness or hopelessness in 2021, which was the second year of the worldwide pandemic (CDC, 2023). The majority of females endorsed these feelings (57%). In the survey, Latinx and multi-racial students were more likely to report these feelings than any other racial group.

RISK AND PROTECTIVE FACTORS

The theories that explain the onset of depression and the factors that influence its occurrence are discussed here from a biopsychosocial perspective.

Biological

Nantel-Vivier and Pihl (2008) explored neurobiological origins of depression, which are various in nature and include structural and functional brain anomalies, hormonal changes, and neurotransmitter systems, as well as the interaction between biological vulnerabilities and environmental stress. More recently, a systematic review involving 68 longitudinal studies was conducted on neurobiological markers of the onset and course of youth depression (Toenders et al., 2019). Although results varied, the most consistent evidence involved blunted reward-related activity as a potential biological marker for both MDD onset and course. Elevated morning cortisol has been identified as a risk factor for depression in adolescence, signaling that the hypothalamic-pituitary system is overreactive (Zajkowska et al., 2022).

Major depression tends to run in families, which supports, at least in part, a process of genetic transmission. Genes can predispose individuals to MDD in various ways. They help control the metabolism of neurotransmitters, the types of neurons and their connections, the intracellular transmission of neuron signals, and the speed with which all these activities take place in response to environmental stressors.

The serotonin transporter gene is the most studied in MDD. A shorter variation of this gene is believed to slow down the synthesis of the serotonin transporter, which reduces the speed at which serotonin neurons can adapt to changes in environmental stimulation. Given that an acute stressor increases serotonin release, this variation may influence a person's sensitivity to stress (aan het Rot et al.,

2009). Dunn et al. (2011) looked at 16 studies, focusing on gene–environment interactions for the risk of child and adolescent depression, and found at least one significant gene–environment association in 80% of studies. Further, stressful life events may increase the reactivity of the hypothalamic-pituitary-adrenal (HPA) axis and the release of cortisone, which, over time, may lead to structural changes in the brain (aan het Rot et al., 2009).

Based on a meta-analysis of five twin studies, the variance explaining the heritability for major depression is significant, in the range of 31% to 42% (Sullivan et al., 2000). Interestingly, when Lau and Eley (2008) reviewed genetic studies involving youths and depression, they found that adoption studies have not replicated the family and twin studies. Therefore, the biology of depression involves a complex and reciprocal process of interrelated systems of the brain, about which much remains unknown.

Another systematic review sheds light on neurocognitive factors associated with depression. Compared with healthy controls, youths with depression have more neurocognitive deficits in terms of ability to focus, verbal reasoning, and recalling previously provided information. They also demonstrated lower IQ (Goodall et al., 2018). Causality cannot be inferred because of the cross-sectional nature of these studies. Therefore, it is not known from this research whether neurocognitive deficits increase risk of depression, whether depression produces deficits, or if some other factors confer risk for both depression and neurocognitive deficits. Nonetheless, there are treatment implications. Neurocognitive deficits likely affect the way youths engage with treatment for depression, especially cognitive interventions. Therefore, treatment may need to be adapted so that youths can best understand, focus on, remember, and apply information.

Germane to the discussion of biological risk factors, Cairns, Yap, Pilkington, and Jorm (2014) conducted a systematic review of longitudinal studies to identify risk and protective factors for adolescent depression that are modifiable. Risk factors associated with the biological level included substance use (alcohol, tobacco, cannabis, other illicit drugs, and polydrug use), dieting, and being overweight. Biological protective factors involved healthy diet and sleep (Cairns et al., 2014). Sleep seems to play a critical role in depression. Teenagers reporting five or fewer hours per night were 71% more likely to suffer from depression and 48% more likely to think about committing suicide than those who reported getting 8 hours of nightly sleep (Gangwisch et al., 2010).

Psychological

At the psychological level, theories of depression have centered on cognitive factors; these include attributional theory, Beck's cognitive theory of depression, and stress and coping theory (Abela & Hankin, 2009). Increased vulnerability for depression may occur in adolescence because it is a time of life when the capacity for personal reflection, abstract reasoning, and formal operational thought develops. At this stage, youths can first consider causality for the events in their lives, and they may develop a depressive attributional style (Abramson et al., 1978). This style attributes negative events to internal, stable, and global attributions ("I failed the test because I was stupid"), while positive outcomes are ascribed to external, transient, and specific reasons ("I passed the test because it was easy"). Adolescence is also a time in development when a future orientation develops; with this ability, the adolescent may experience hopelessness about the future (Abela et al., 2002).

Another theory of depression involves Beck's conceptualization of the role of thoughts and beliefs in the development of depression and how cognitions affect feelings and behavior. Beck identified the "cognitive triad" of depression: thoughts about the self as worthless, the world as unfair, and the future as hopeless (Beck et al., 1979). In individuals experiencing these thought patterns, depression may arise and become entrenched. People can become aware of these thinking patterns and learn to shift them to be more realistic and helpful; treatment models arising out of cognitive theory are discussed later.

Compas and colleagues (2017) integrated stress and coping theory along with the role of emotion regulation and identified both helpful and unhelpful coping mechanisms. Their work suggests that, for situations that are not in a person's control, temporary distraction and acceptance of a negative situation, maintaining an optimistic yet realistic outlook, or reappraisal of the stressor can be beneficial (Schäfer et al., 2016). Rumination and searching for reasons behind negative emotions can be problematic. Rumination is defined as the tendency to focus on the symptoms of a poor mood, mulling over the reasons for its occurrence in incessant, passive ways rather than in an active, problem-solving manner (Nolen-Hoeksema, 2002). One of the factors involved with emotion regulation is being aware of one's emotions. A lack of ability to identify emotions has been associated with depression, especially for children younger than 12 (Sendzik et al., 2017).

Social

Social factors involved in depression include family, gender, ethnicity, sexual identity, childhood adversity, and social media use. Family factors include family functioning and parent–child relationship, as well as maternal depression. Insecure attachment is a risk factor for depression (Herstell et al., 2021). Rudolph (2009) discussed insecure attachment and maternal depression as setting the stage for poor interpersonal functioning and subsequent depression. Depression, in turn, leads to further interpersonal problems and risk for recurrence. A recent systematic review on family risk found that depression in youths was associated with conflict between parents, lack of parental warmth and aversiveness, overinvolvement, and both lack of ability to provide autonomy to children and lack of adequate monitoring (Yap et al., 2014). Parental support is a protective factor for recovery from depression in a systematic review of longitudinal studies (Shore et al., 2018).

Abuse is discussed in this section because it usually occurs in the context of the family. A meta-analysis by Infurna et al. (2016) estimated the associations between depression and different types of childhood maltreatment, finding that psychological abuse and neglect were most strongly associated with the outcome of depression. Depression in mothers is a particular risk factor for youth depression for many possible reasons (note that paternal depression also plays a role, but there are far less studies on paternal depression). First, genetic factors may be involved (Goodman, 2007). Other biological factors may include the abnormal neuroendocrine functioning found in women who are depressed during pregnancy. As a result, the fetus may be exposed to increased cortisol levels and reduced blood flow, leading to slower growth and less movement. Psychosocial explanations have also been posited (Goodman, 2007). Mothers may be emotionally unavailable and feel a sense of helplessness amid parenting challenges. Parents may model depressive affect, thinking patterns, and behaviors for their children and then reinforce their children's depressive behaviors. Depressed parents also tend to see their children's behavior in a negative light, using low rates of reward and high rates of punishment or responding indiscriminately to the child's behavior.

ETHNICITY

While rates vary by study (Merikangas et al., 2009), a replicated finding is that Latino ethnicity is associated with a greater risk of depression compared with other U.S. ethnic groups (Allen & Astuto, 2009). The recent report of the Centers for Disease Control (CDC) annual Youth Behavior Survey indicated that Latinx (46%) and multi-racial students (49%) were more likely to endorse persistent sadness and hopelessness feelings than other racial groups. Hypotheses suggested for these higher rates include the stress of acculturation; language barriers; being raised by parents who are immigrants and who may suffer from poverty, unemployment, and depression themselves; and cultural factors, such as fatalism and an external locus of control (Allen & Astuto, 2009). In a study of risk and protective factors for Latino adolescent depression, males who were more oriented toward mainstream culture were possibly more vulnerable to the effects of discrimination (Umana-Taylor & Updegraff, 2007). Conversely, a high level of involvement in Latino culture may act in a protective way, in that discrimination may not affect their feelings of self-worth and contribute to depression. Acculturation was highlighted in another study by Cespedes and Huey (2008). Specifically, the authors found that a discrepancy between gender role expectations among Latino teenagers and their parents was associated with depression, particularly among girls.

GENDER

Another consistent finding is the greater risk for depression in females that emerges in adolescence (about age 13) and persists throughout the life span (Merikangas & Knight, 2009). Hilt and Nolen-Hoeksema (2009) reviewed the 2:1 difference in depression between females and males that starts at about age 13. Not only did females experience a higher incidence of depression, but episodes were also more chronic (Essau et al., 2010; Shore et al., 2018). Similarly, in the CDC Youth Behavior Survey, the majority of females endorsed feeling persistent sadness and hopelessness (57%) (CDC, 2023).

Various reasons, including biological and psychosocial, have been hypothesized for gender disparities in depression. Biological factors include reproductive hormonal development in girls—specifically estradiol, the primary female sex hormone, which influences the neurotransmitter and HPA axis. The main function of the HPA axis is to maintain homeostasis of various bodily processes, particularly the regulation of stress. One theory is that people undergoing chronic stress may develop poorly regulated neuroendocrine systems, so that exposure to even minor stress later may cause the HPA axis to become reactive and result in difficulty returning to homeostasis.

Another hypothesis is that hormonal changes interact with psychosocial factors. Role changes associated with reproductive events in societies that devalue women's roles may result in depression. Although, in general, having positive peers is associated with less depression in adolescence (Gutman & Sameroff, 2004), for teen girls interpersonal stress may contribute to the onset of depression. Adolescent girls invest more than boys in relationships and tend to be more concerned about others' approval, which is associated with self-worth (Girgus & Nolen-Hoeksema, 2006). These tendencies lead to greater sensitivity and reactivity to interpersonal stress (Rudolph, 2002), which may place them further at risk for relationship problems, which, in turn, can result in distress. Social reasons for depression may include the higher rate of sexual abuse in females than in males (Barth et al., 2013); experiencing abuse leads to risk for depression. At the psychological level, girls may be more likely to use the coping strategy of rumination, which, as discussed, is problematic (Nolen-Hoeksema, 2002). When they are 12 years old, males and females diverge in their use of rumination, with girls showing higher rumination, and depression differences emerge about a year later (Jose & Brown, 2008).

Peers
Having supportive peers is associated with less depression in adolescence (Gutman & Sameroff, 2004; Shore et al., 2018), whereas bullying (being either a perpetrator or a victim) is associated with depression, with higher frequencies of bullying (physical, verbal, or relational) having a linear relationship to levels of depression (Wang et al., 2011). For girls, relational victimization, when paired with genetic vulnerability, is also predictive of depression (Benjet et al., 2010).

Sexual Minorities
According to a systematic review of 22 studies, sexual minority youths reported higher rates of depressive symptoms and depressive disorder compared with heterosexual young people (Lucassen et al., 2017). Female sexual minority adolescents were more at risk than males. Another systematic review examined risk and protective factors for depression and found that internalized oppression, stress from hiding a socially stigmatized identity, maladaptive coping, parental rejection, abuse and other trauma, negative interpersonal interactions, negative religious experiences, school bullying, and being a victim of violence are associated with depression. Protective factors included a positive LGBQ identity, self-esteem, peer social support, and family support (Hall, 2018).

Screen Time and Social Media Use

There is emerging evidence to link increased time spent using screens for leisure and entertainment with heightened depressive symptoms and psychological distress among children and adolescents. In a recent meta-analysis of 22 articles containing 197,673 participants, both children and adolescents, Zhou et al. (2021) examined time spent watching TV, being on the computer, videogaming, and phone/tablet use separately. For TV, depression was low when time spent watching was less than an hour and a half each day but beyond 4.5 hours a day of TV was associated with higher risk of depression. The optimal period for computer time was 30 minutes a day; above that and depression risk rose. The risk of depression increased when videogaming was beyond two hours a day, and for phone time beyond 30 minutes a day. The results of this meta-analysis therefore has some clear implications for the specific types of sedentary behaviors: TV should be limited to an hour and a half; computer time should be limited to 30 minutes; videogaming to two hours; and phone use less than 30 minutes a day. This finding lends empirical support to the American Academy of Pediatrics guideline of limiting screen use to 2 hours a day.

Community Disadvantage and Socioeconomic Status

Socioeconomic status (SES) and its link to depression for youths aged 10 to 15 years was studied in a systematic review (Lemstra et al., 2008) that established a negative association between the two variables. That is, the lower the SES, the higher the rate of depression.

ASSESSMENT

Although DSM criteria for depressive disorders are similar for youths and adults, there are a few differences. Irritable mood is a criterion for youths but not for adults. The weight loss criterion is not used with children because children and adolescents are continuing to develop physically; instead, they may meet this criterion by not sustaining normal standards of growth and weight (American Psychiatric Association, 2022). In addition to some of the special considerations noted in the DSM, a greater reliance on collateral reports from parents and teachers may be necessary (Waslick et al., 2002). A symptom may be counted as present if either the parent or the child reports its existence. Because depression is an internal experience, it is sometimes not easily recognized by others. The use of validated self-report measures can therefore help elucidate the youth's experience. Freely available screening and progress monitoring tools are presented in Table 10.2.

A systematic review was conducted to understand how childhood major depression can be distinguished from bipolar disorder (Uchida et al., 2015). Findings from the four studies located indicated that bipolar disorder could be differentiated by greater depression severity; impairment; comorbid disorders of oppositional defiant disorder, conduct disorder, and anxiety disorders; and a family history of mood and

Table 10.2 MEASURES OF DEPRESSION

Psychometric Support	Measure Name	No. of Items	Completed by:[a]	Ages[b]	Link to Measure
Excellent	Mood and Feelings Questionnaire (MFQ; Angold et al., 1995)*	13 or 33	Y, P	6–17	https://devepi.duhs.duke.edu/measures/the-mood-and-feelings-questionnaire-mfq/
Excellent	Patient Health Questionnaire-9 (PHQ-9; Johnson, Harris, Spitzer, & Williams, 2002)*	9	Y	13+	https://www.amerihealthcaritasla.com/pdf/provider/behavioral-health/depression-toolkit-adolescent-questionnaire.pdf See phqscreeners.com for translations
Excellent	Positive and Negative Affect Scale for Children (PANAS-C; Laurent et al., 1999)	27	Y	9–17	https://www.phenxtoolkit.org/protocols/view/180502#Source
Excellent	Revised Child Anxiety and Depression Scale (RCADS/RCADS-P; Chorpita et al., 2005)*	47/25	Y, P	Grades 3–12[c]	https://www.childfirst.ucla.edu/resources/
Good	Center for Epidemiological Studies-Depression Scale for children (CES-DC; Faulstich et al., 1986)	20	Y	6–18	https://www.brightfutures.org/mentalhealth/pdf/professionals/bridges/ces_dc.pdf
Good	Depression Self-Rating Scale (DSRS; Birelson, 1981)*	18	Y	8–14	http://www.childrenandwar.org/projectsresources/measures/
Good	Hopelessness Scale for Children (HSC/HPLS; Kazdin, Rodgas, & Colbus, 1986)	17	Y, C	6–13	https://www.phenxtoolkit.org/protocols/view/640601#Source
Good	Hospital Anxiety and Depression Scale (HADS; Snaith, 2003)	14	Y	12+	https://www.svri.org/sites/default/files/attachments/2016-01-13/HADS.pdf
Good	Kutcher Adolescent Depression Scale (KADS; Brooks, Krulewicz, & Kutcher, 2003)*	6 or 11	Y	12–17	6-item: https://teenmentalhealth.org/wp-content/uploads/2014/09/6-KADS.pdf 11-item: https://teenmentalhealth.org/wp-content/uploads/2014/08/CAPN_11Item_KADS.pdf

(continued)

Table 10.2 CONTINUED

Psychometric Support	Measure Name	No. of Items	Completed by:[a]	Ages[b]	Link to Measure
Good	Preschool Feelings Checklist (PFC; Luby et al., 2004)[d]	16	P	3–6	https://medicine.tulane.edu/centers-institutes/tecc/provider-resources/problem-screens
Adequate	Depression Anxiety and Stress Scale (DASS-21; Henry & Crawford, 2005)*	21	Y	12+	http://www2.psy.unsw.edu.au/dass/
Adequate	Mental Health Problems Self Report Questionnaire (SRQ-20; Beusenberg & Orley, 1994)*	20	Y	Adolescents	https://www.infontd.org/content/srq-self-reporting-questionnaire
Adequate	PROMIS Depression (DeWalt et al., 2015)*	8	Y, P	5–17	http://www.healthmeasures.net/index.php?Itemid=992

[a] Completed by: Y = youth, P = parent/caregiver, C = clinician.

[b] Exact age range for specific forms (e.g., self-report, parent report) may vary.

[c] Exact age range not specified.

[d] A 20-item version of this measure exists with more psychometric support (particularly for outcome monitoring) but was not identified as freely or accessibly available.

* Available in multiple languages.

NOTE: Table adapted from Becker-Haimes, E. M., Tabachnick, A. R., Last, B. S., Stewart, R. E., Hasan-Granier, A., & Beidas, R. S. (2020). Evidence base update for brief, free, and accessible youth mental health measures. *Journal of Clinical Child & Adolescent Psychology, 49*(1), 1–17, reprinted by permission of the publisher (Taylor & Francis Ltd, http://www.tandfonline.com).

References for measures in Table 1C.2:

Beusenberg, M., Orley, J. H., & World Health Organization. (1994). A user's guide to the self reporting questionnaire (SRQ (No. WHO/MNH/PSF/94.8. Unpublished). Geneva: World Health Organization.

Birleson, P. (1981). The validity of depressive disorder in childhood and the development of a self-rating scale: A research report. *Journal of Child Psychology and Psychiatry*, 22(1), 73–88.

Brooks, S. J., Krulewicz, S. P., & Kutcher, S. (2003). The Kutcher Adolescent Depression Scale: Assessment of its evaluative properties over the course of an 8-week pediatric pharmacotherapy trial. *Journal of Child and Adolescent Psychopharmacology*, 13(3), 337–349.

Chorpita, B. F., Moffitt, C. E., & Gray, J. (2005). Psychometric properties of the Revised Child Anxiety and Depression Scale in a clinical sample. *Behaviour Research and Therapy*, 43(3), 309–322.

DeWalt, D. A., Gross, H. E., Gipson, D. S., Selewski, D. T., DeWitt, E. M., Dampier, C. D., . . . Varni, J. W. (2015). PROMIS® pediatric self-report scales distinguish subgroups of children within and across six common pediatric chronic health conditions. *Quality of Life Research*, 24(9), 2195–2208.

Faulstich, M. E. (1986). Depression–Pediatric. *Psychiatry*, 143, 1024–1027.

Henry, J. D., & Crawford, J. R. (2005). The short-form version of the Depression Anxiety Stress Scales (DASS-21): Construct validity and normative data in a large non-clinical sample. *British Journal of Clinical Psychology*, 44(2), 227–239.

Johnson, J. G., Harris, E. S., Spitzer, R. L., & Williams, J. B. (2002). The patient health questionnaire for adolescents: Validation of an instrument for the assessment of mental disorders among adolescent primary care patients. *Journal of Adolescent Health*, 30(3), 196–204.

Kazdin, A. E., Rodgers, A., & Colbus, D. (1986). The Hopelessness Scale for Children: Psychometric characteristics and concurrent validity. *Journal of Consulting and Clinical Psychology*, 54(2), 241.

Laurent, J., Catanzaro, S. J., Joiner Jr, T. E., Rudolph, K. D., Potter, K. I., Lambert, S., . . . Gathright, T. (1999). A measure of positive and negative affect for children: scale development and preliminary validation. *Psychological Assessment*, 11(3), 326.

Luby, J. L., Heffelfinger, A., Koenig-McNaught, A. L., Brown, K., & Spitznagel, E. (2004). The preschool feelings checklist: A brief and sensitive screening measure for depression in young children. *Journal of the American Academy of Child & Adolescent Psychiatry*, 43(6), 708–717.

Messer, S. C., Angold, A., Costello, E. J., Loeber, R., Van Kammen, W., & Stouthamer-Loeber, M. (1995). Development of a short questionnaire for use in epidemiological studies of depression in children and adolescents: Factor composition and structure across development. *International Journal of Methods in Psychiatric Research*, 5, 251–262.

Snaith, R. P. (2003). The hospital anxiety and depression scale. *Health and Quality of Life Outcomes*, 1(1), 29.

disruptive behavior disorders in first-degree relatives. Although we discuss suicide and self-harm in Chapter 11, suicidal ideation is itself a symptom of MDD and is even more common in bipolar disorder (Crescenzo et al., 2017).

The social worker conducted a clinical interview with Jessica to assess DSM-5 mood symptoms and to rule out anxiety, trauma, and behavioral and developmental concerns. She also met with Ms. Anderson to understand her observations of Jessica's symptoms and the psychosocial history. Finally, the social worker had Jessica and her grandmother complete the youth and caregiver report versions of the Revised Child Anxiety and Depression Scale (RCADS; Chorpita et al., 2005).

Based on the social worker's assessment, Jessica met DSM-5 diagnostic criteria for MDD. Specifically, Jessica reported that she feels sad and down most of the day, has lost interest in schoolwork and social activities, and has had a decreased appetite, trouble falling asleep at night, and trouble getting up for school in the morning. She sometimes falls asleep in class and has been having noticeable trouble concentrating on her schoolwork. Symptoms have been present for about 5 months, and impairment in academic performance was reported, which was a drastic change from Jessica's previous high achievement in school. Additionally, Jessica stated that most of her friends have stopped reaching out to her because she has been largely ignoring their efforts to socialize. Jessica stated that she thinks often about her mother's relapse and that she could have done more to help her mom stay sober. "I was so busy with school and my friends, and I didn't spend as much time with her as I should have when she came back around, and if I had maybe she'd have stayed clean." Ms. Anderson corroborated Jessica's report, and self and caregiver scores on the RCADS were consistent with elevated depression symptoms.

The social worker carefully assessed for suicidal thoughts and behavior using the Columbia Suicide Severity Rating Scale (C-SSRS); Jessica denied experiencing thoughts of wanting to harm herself or any previous attempts to harm herself, and Ms. Anderson agreed that she had not ever seen or heard anything from Jessica that made her concerned in this domain. Jessica did say that she sometimes feels like "this will never get better—what's the point" but was clear in her report that she was not experiencing any recurrent thoughts about death or any thoughts of suicide. As part of the comprehensive assessment, the social worker also ruled out mania, substance use, and attention-deficit/hyperactivity disorder.

Based on the results of the assessment, Jessica met criteria for MDD and was eligible to receive ongoing therapy services with the social worker in her school, which she began the next week. A significant stressor had occurred before the onset of symptoms; however, because Jessica met criteria for MDD, the social worker determined that was the more appropriate diagnosis to assign versus adjustment disorder with depressed mood (which would only have been appropriate if Jessica's symptoms did not meet the threshold for MDD).

INTERVENTION

Most adolescents with depression have received past-year treatment (Ghandour et al., 2020), but only a minority obtain treatment designed for depression or delivered from the mental health sector (Avenevoli et al., 2015). For this reason, it is important for social workers to know the empirical evidence for various treatment approaches. This section covers psychosocial treatment (psychotherapy) and medication, followed by studies that assess combining psychotherapy with medication.

Psychosocial

Psychosocial treatment models that have been tested for depression in youths primarily include cognitive-behavioral therapy (CBT), interpersonal psychotherapy, and family therapy. We describe these models next and then discuss the systematic reviews of the research.

COGNITIVE-BEHAVIORAL THERAPY

Interventions based on CBT models include: (1) behavioral models that focus on the development of coping skills, especially in the domain of social skills and choosing pleasant daily activities, so that the youths receive more reinforcement from their environments, and (2) cognitive models that assess and change the distorted thinking that people with depression exhibit, in which they cast everyday experiences in a negative light. A few of the representative treatments are discussed here.

One representative treatment for teens is the Adolescent Coping With Depression course (Clarke et al., 1990), which includes the following components delivered over 15 to 16 sessions: (1) cognitive restructuring, (2) social skills training (how to make and maintain friendships), (3) communication and social problem-solving (how to share feelings and resolve conflict without alienating others), (4) progressive relaxation training (to ease stress and tension), and (5) structuring mood-boosting activities into daily life. Some versions include concurrent parent groups that involve sharing information about the topics and skills being taught in the adolescent group. The Adolescent Coping With Depression course is freely downloadable for practitioners (see resources at the end of the chapter).

Behavioral activation is another type of behaviorally based treatment that can be used with teens (Dimidijian et al., 2011). Behavioral activation focuses on helping individuals to structure their daily life with tasks and pleasant activities to experience mastery and pleasure, respectively (Tindall et al., 2017).

For younger youths (ages 4 to 15), Primary and Secondary Control Enhancement Training (PASCET) involves training in skills to modify problematic environmental factors that are distressing (primary control) and to change subjective responses to situations that cannot be changed (secondary control; Weisz et al., 1999).

INTERPERSONAL PSYCHOTHERAPY

Interpersonal psychotherapy (IPT) is a brief (12 to 16 sessions) intervention focusing on how current interpersonal relationships have contributed to depression and helping teens repair these conflicts (Mufson et al., 2004a). The general goals of IPT are to decrease depressive symptoms and to improve interpersonal functioning in the areas of grief, conflict, changing relationships and life circumstances, and social isolation. The IPT therapist helps children and adolescents identify areas within which to build skills to improve relationships and decrease depressive symptoms. IPT has been adapted for adolescents (IPT-A); this adapted version addresses common developmental issues in adolescents such as romantic relationships. Sessions are primarily individual, although parents may be involved as appropriate. IPT-A has been shown to be effective in individual and group formats and for both prevention and intervention (Gunlicks-Stoessel & Mufson, 2016; Gunlicks-Stoessel et al., 2010; Hall & Mufson, 2009; Mufson et al., 2004b; Spence et al., 2016; Young et al., 2006).

FAMILY TREATMENT

Family-based treatment comprises a wide array of interventions, including psychoeducation, therapy, and parent training. Family psychoeducation may show promise as a first-line intervention (Jones et al., 2018). One family therapy model has been developed specifically for suicide in adolescents: attachment-based family therapy (Diamond et al., 2013). It relies on attachment and family system theories as a basis and is designed to improve the quality of relationships in the family of the adolescent with depression. An awareness of the influence of trauma has burgeoned in mental health circles. Attachment-based family therapy focuses on increasing the extent to which the adolescent can discuss trauma events with parents and for parents to respond in a warm and supportive manner (see also Chapter 13). Research suggests that family-based interventions produce a small benefit, but it is not yet established which interventions are most effective (Dippel et al., 2022).

SYSTEMATIC REVIEWS OF THERAPY

The most recent systematic review of the body of psychosocial treatment studies on depression in youths involved 55 studies (Eckshtain et al., 2020). The overall effect size was 0.36 at post-treatment and 0.21 at an average of 42-week follow-up, with effects significantly larger for interpersonal therapy than for CBT, which translates into "a probability of 60% that a randomly selected youth receiving psychotherapy would be better off after treatment than a randomly selected youth in a control condition." The benefits, though modest, were found across individual and group modalities, which indicates that group, a more cost-effective modality, can be used effectively. This result for group modalities was confirmed by Keles and Idsoe (2016).

Eckshtain et al. (2020) found that the following components produced higher effects: behavior activation, the "challenging thinking" part of cognitive restructuring, and involvement of parents (the latter particularly with children younger than 12). Therefore, these components deserve emphasis. However, a systematic review only of treatment outcome studies involving children 12 and under ($N = 7$) did not find support that interventions, mostly CBT, were better than no treatment for this younger age group (Forti-Buratti et al., 2016).

PREVENTION: MINDFULNESS-BASED STRESS REDUCTION

Mindfulness-based stress reduction (MBSR) involves the cultivation of self-awareness and an attitude of openness and acceptance, with the goal of helping people calm their minds and body and enhance coping ability (Chi et al., 2018). MBSR has been adapted for adolescents, such as the Learning to BREATHE (L2B) curriculum. L2B is a six-session, 50-minute course delivered weekly. It is a universal school-based prevention program for adolescents to reduce emotional problems and strengthen emotional regulation. The researchers assessed the literature in a systematic review of the effectiveness of MBSR in adolescents and young adults and located 18 randomized controlled trials involving more than 2,042 participants. MBSR had a moderate effect over control groups on depressive symptoms at post-test but not at follow-up, although few studies examined follow-up. The authors argued that this finding was generally consistent with previous reviews finding that MBSR is moderately efficacious in treating mood disorders, including depression among children and adolescents in clinical and nonclinical settings (Zenner et al., 2014; Kallapiran et al., 2015).

Medication

Antidepressants are currently being used by 3.2% of the U.S. adolescent population (Jonas et al., 2013). Systematic reviews of antidepressant treatment indicate that selective serotonin reuptake inhibitors (SSRIs) and serotonin and norepinephrine reuptake inhibitors (SNRIs) are more effective than tricyclic antidepressants (TCAs; Qin et al., 2014) and placebo, but effect sizes are small, and there is an increased risk of suicidal ideation with SSRIs (Hetrick et al., 2012). Fluoxetine (Prozac) is often the first-line treatment because it has been researched the most in youths with depression (Bridge et al., 2007; Usala et al., 2008; Whittington et al., 2004). Sertraline (Zoloft) has also received support for use in adolescents, but not children. More recently, there has been support for escitalopram (Lexapro) and nefazodone (Trazadone) for depression in youths (Teng et al., 2022). Prozac and CBT combined may be more effective for depression than single treatment (Xiang et al., 2022).

Jessica's treatment consisted of individual CBT and psychoeducation about depression with Jessica and Ms. Williams. Individual CBT components included psychoeducation, behavioral activation, cognitive restructuring, and social problem-solving. The social worker also assessed for suicidal ideation at each encounter.

Psychoeducation

Treatment began with psychoeducation with both Jessica and her grandmother. The social worker explained the diagnosis of MDD, provided an overview of CBT treatment, and answered their questions and concerns. The social worker also described the evidence for antidepressant medication; both Jessica and her grandmother preferred to try psychotherapy first, and the social worker agreed this was a reasonable treatment plan for Jessica.

The social worker explained the CBT model and the connection between thoughts, feelings, and behavior. The social worker then tied the specific treatment components of behavioral activation, cognitive restructuring, and social problem-solving to the CBT model, underscoring the rationale for why they would use those intervention strategies.

> **Clinician:** *Depression can cloud the way we see the world and how we interpret what's happening in our lives, often in ways that can be inaccurate and unhelpful. In CBT we will examine your thinking to identify your thoughts, check their accuracy and helpfulness, and shift them toward more accurate and helpful ways of thinking. We also will look at your current activities, or behaviors, and experiment with trying to find things that bring you a sense of pleasure or accomplishment and ways we can increase those types of activities in your life.*
> **Jessica:** *Nothing really feels fun anymore.*
> **Clinician:** *That must be tough to feel that nothing is fun anymore. This is a common experience that people with depression report. Would you be willing to try a few experiments in therapy to explore if it really is true that nothing can bring you pleasure anymore?*
> **Jessica:** *Sure, I guess I'll try anything. I just don't want to feel like this anymore.*
> **Clinician:** *Do you have any other questions or concerns about treatment?*
> **Jessica:** *Well, I guess one thing I worry about is even if I get better, I think my friends all hate me now because I've been blowing them off for months. So, I may not even have any friends left to hang out with even if I do feel like doing stuff again.*
> **Clinician:** *I'm so glad you brought this concern up to me Jessica, I think it sounds very important to make sure we address this in our work together. As part of our work, I think we should spend some time problem-solving strategies for reintegrating with your friends, and we can think through what you could say or do and how to navigate those situations. I have some ideas.*

Behavioral Activation

After psychoeducation and introduction to the CBT model, the clinician decided to initiate behavioral activation. This intervention strategy was selected because Jessica was reporting considerable anhedonia. Additionally, behavioral activation can lead to rapid improvement in mood symptoms. For some clients, a course of behavioral activation is effective; for other clients it is a helpful strategy to use in conjunction with cognitive interventions.

The clinician and Jessica began by discussing the cyclical nature of depression and avoidance, in which stressful events (i.e., mom's relapse) lead to negative emotions (e.g., sadness), which in turn lead to actions such as avoiding friends and staying in bed. These actions then lead to more negative emotions, which lead to increased avoidance.

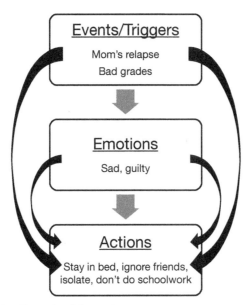

Figure 10.1 Mapping the cycle of depression.
Note: Figure adapted from University of Michigan. Behavioral Activation for Depression. Retrieved from https://medicine.umich.edu/sites/default/files/content/downloads/Beh avioral-Activation-for-Depression.pdf on July 24, 2020.

This cycle can even then lead to increased negative or stressful events (e.g., failing courses, peer rejection). The clinician and Jessica mapped out this cycle together (see Figure 10.1).

Next, the clinician and Jessica moved on to activity monitoring, which is a strategy for tracking one's activities throughout the day to understand how actions correspond with mood. The social worker gave Jessica a blank weekly schedule (see Figure 10.2) and explained that throughout the next week Jessica would record each activity she engaged in, including where she was, who she was with, and what she did. For each activity she would also note her mood using a 0 to 10 scale, with 0 being in a very down/ low mood to 10 being in a good mood. As practice, they completed the record form together for the current day, retrospectively noting each activity Jessica had engaged in thus far and her mood rating. The clinician explained that going forward Jessica should complete the record in as close to real time as possible. They brainstormed together how Jessica could remember to complete her activity monitoring sheet (Jessica set periodic reminders for herself on her phone) and where she would keep it so that it would be accessible. They agreed that Jessica would complete the activity monitoring form over the next week and bring it to their next session to review.

> **Jessica:** *Am I supposed to be doing anything different this week? This is kind of a lot.*
>
> **Clinician:** *You don't need to make any changes in your activities this week, just complete this activity monitoring worksheet as best you can, noting the things you are already doing.*

Directions: Note each activity you engaged in. Then, in parenthesis after each activity, note your mood on a 0 to 10 scale, where 0 = low and 10 = high.
For example, *I walked to school (3)*.

	Sunday	Monday	Tuesday	Wednesday	Thursday	Friday	Saturday
7–8am							
8–9am							
9–10am							
10–11am							
11am–12pm							
12–1pm							
1–2pm							
2–3pm							
3–4pm							
4–5pm							
5–6pm							
6–7pm							
7–8pm							
8–9pm							
9–10pm							
11pm–12am							
12am–7am							

Figure 10.2 Sample activity monitoring worksheet

Jessica: *That's good.*
Clinician: *I wonder too if it would be helpful for your grandmother to know about this plan so that she can help you remember and stay motivated to complete it. What do you think?*
Jessica: *That might help. Maybe we can call her and tell her about it now?*
Clinician: *Great idea! Let's do that now.*

At the next session, Jessica and the social worker reviewed the activity monitoring record form. The social worker praised Jessica for having completed it most days. As they reviewed the form, they made note of which activities Jessica had engaged in over the past week that had been associated with a lower mood rating and which had been associated with a higher mood rating.

Jessica: *It looks like when I was with my family my mood was a little better than when I was alone in my room, even when we weren't really doing anything, just eating dinner together or something.*
Clinician: *What do you make of that?*
Jessica: *Well, I guess I'm a little surprised because I know I told you I felt bad all the time, but I guess sometimes things aren't as bad as others and its worse when I'm alone in my room.*
Clinician: *That's an insightful and important observation, Jessica.*

The next step, the clinician explained, would be for them to work together to plan or schedule some activities that Jessica would engage in over the next week. They worked together to develop a list of activities that would be relevant for Jessica, including activities with the potential to bring her pleasure, lead to a feeling of accomplishment or mastery, or are consistent with her values. To help Jessica generate a list of meaningful activities, the clinician queried about activities that Jessica had previously enjoyed doing or had done often before the onset of her depression. She also asked Jessica about her values and what was most important to her and identified positive peer and familial relationships and academic achievement as key areas of importance to her. They also discussed that not all activities needed to lead to feelings of pleasure; rather, some simple activities such as washing the dishes or folding the laundry can contribute to feelings of success or mastery when completed. The social worker helped Jessica to generate a list of activities ranging from simple things she could do on her own (e.g., take a walk, pick out my clothes for school the next day) to more complex activities or those that involved other people (e.g., text a friend to say hi, play a board game with her grandmother, complete a homework assignment). The social worker ensured that the list included social activities, self-care activities (e.g., take a bath), and physical activities (e.g., take a walk, dance) so that Jessica would have a range of choices that did not always rely on others or specific circumstances to implement. After the list had been generated, they selected two or three activities for Jessica to "schedule" for herself each day. Using the same activity monitoring form, they prepopulated some activities that Jessica agreed to try, and Jessica was instructed to record her mood after each activity. They agreed to check in mid-week to see how Jessica was doing with implementing the planned activities; the social worker knew this would be a challenge for Jessica and didn't want her to go an entire week without checking in, in case she encountered difficulties with motivation.

Jessica was generally successful in implementing planned activities. Each week she and the social worker would review her worksheet, noting which activities were associated with higher mood ratings. In subsequent weeks they worked to increase the scheduled pleasant activities and homed in on activities that Jessica was most likely to complete and that led to the best mood. Throughout this work, Jessica's mood overall began to improve. Ms. Anderson, Jessica's grandmother, also noted improvements in Jessica's mood, stating, "She's not completely her old self, but I am seeing more and more of the old, happier Jessica. She comes out of her room more, and she's eating and sleeping better."

Cognitive Restructuring

Jessica's improvement with behavioral activation alone was considerable, although she continued to report feeling guilty at times about her mother's relapse and thinking that her friends would never forgive her for ignoring them over the past several months. Jessica and the social worker worked together to identify the common cognitive distortions that Jessica was experiencing, and Jessica practiced noticing when she was having these thoughts throughout the week. Common cognitive distortions Jessica shared included, "It's my fault mom relapsed," and "My friends all hate me—I'm such a loser." Using curious, nondirective and nonjudgmental questions, the social worker helped Jessica explore the accuracy and helpfulness of these thoughts. For example, the clinician asked, "Have your friends told you they are angry?" Jessica replied, "No, I guess not." In fact, when they explored the issue, Jessica became less certain that this was true, and with the social worker's help was able to identify that most of her friends' correspondences had expressed concern or a desire to maintain a relationship (e.g., "Are you ok?" and "I miss you, lets hang out"). Similarly, Jessica was eventually able to identify that her mother's relapse had likely not been her fault given her mother's previous relapses that she did not attribute to herself. Over time, Jessica became more adept and independent in identifying cognitive distortions, exploring their accuracy and helpfulness, and reframing them.

Social Problem-Solving

The final key component to Jessica's treatment involved using principles of social problem-solving, another CBT strategy. Specifically, the social worker and Jessica problem-solved strategies Jessica could employ to communicate to her friends how she had been feeling and implement steps to repair her relationships. They decided that Jessica would start by explaining how she had been feeling to her best friend Kim, in a way that Jessica felt comfortable with. Jessica decided to reach out to Kim by text message first and say, "Hey, I'm sorry I haven't been in touch lately, I haven't felt like myself and I've been going through some stuff but I'm starting to feel better. Can we hang out soon?" Jessica sent the initial text with support from the therapist during one of their appointments, and Kim quickly responded positively that she would like to find a time to meet up. They made plans for a simple activity, walking to school together the next morning, and Jessica and the therapist problem solved what they could talk about and how Jessica could respond if Kim expressed frustration or asked her to share more about how she had been feeling than Jessica was comfortable with. After a successful walk to school with Kim, Jessica became more confident, and she and the social worker worked to extend her interactions to other peers and increase her social activities in a similar manner. Jessica's treatment consisted of 16 sessions overall, and by termination her mood symptoms had improved to the point that she no longer met criteria for current major depression, her grades were steadily improving, and she was no longer isolating. Jessica reported feeling "like myself" again, and Ms. Anderson noted considerable improvement as well.

SUMMARY

Depression is a serious problem that is rare in childhood and increases dramatically in adolescence. Family history and genetics influence the development of depression, but so do stressful environments. Therefore, those who work with teenagers should be aware of the signs of depression and demonstrate the capacity to screen and assess for symptoms in youths. (Refer again to Table 10.1.) This is particularly important in settings such as child welfare and foster care, juvenile justice, and the school because youths will typically not self-identify as *depressed*, and symptoms are not always noticeable by adults. Social workers should be knowledgeable about evidence-based interventions, make referrals, and advocate to ensure that adolescents with depression receive optimal treatment. Social workers should also address circumstances that are contributing to depression so that youths experience relief.

REFERENCES

aan het Rot, M., Mathew, S. J., & Charney, D. S. (2009). Neurobiological mechanisms in major depressive disorder. *Canadian Medical Association Journal, 180*(3), 305–313.

Abela, J. R. Z., Brozina, K., & Haigh, E. P. (2002). An examination of the response styles theory of depression in third-and seventh-grade children: A short-term longitudinal study. *Journal of Abnormal Child Psychology, 30*(5), 515–527.

Abela, J. R. Z., & Hankin, B. L. (2009). Cognitive vulnerability to depression in adolescents: A developmental psychopathology perspective. In S. Nolen-Hoeksema & L. M. Hilt (Eds.), *Handbook of depression in adolescents* (pp. 335–376). New York: Routledge, Taylor & Francis.

Abramson, L. Y., Seligman, M. E., & Teasdale, J. D. (1978). Learned helplessness in humans: Critique and reformulation. *Journal of Abnormal Psychology, 87*, 49–74.

Allen, L., & Astuto, J. (2009). Depression among racially, ethnically, and culturally diverse adolescents. In S. Nolen-Hoeksema & L. M. Hilt (Eds.), *Handbook of depression in adolescents* (pp. 75–110). New York: Routledge, Taylor & Francis.

American Psychiatric Association. (2022). *Diagnostic and statistical manual of mental disorders (5th ed., Text Revision)*. Washington, DC: American Psychiatric Association.

Avenevoli, S., Swendsen, J., He, J. P., Burstein, M., & Merikangas, K. R. (2015). Major depression in the national comorbidity survey-adolescent supplement: Prevalence, correlates, and treatment. *Journal of the American Academy of Child & Adolescent Psychiatry, 54*(1), 37–44.

Barican, J. L., Yung, D., Schwartz, C., Zheng, Y., Georgiades, K., & Waddell, C. (2021). Prevalence of childhood mental disorders in high-income countries: A systematic review and meta-analysis to inform policymaking. *Evidence Based Mental Health,* *25*(1), 36–44. https://doi.org/10.1136/ebmental-2021-300277

Barth, J., Bermetz, L., Heim, E., Trelle, S., & Tonia, T. (2013). The current prevalence of child sexual abuse worldwide: A systematic review and meta-analysis. *International Journal of Public Health, 58*, 469. https://doi.org/10.1007/s00038-012-0426-1.

Beck, A., Rush, A., Shaw, B., & Emery, G. (1979). *Cognitive therapy of depression.* New York: Guilford.

Benjet, C., Thompson, R., J., & Gotlib, I. H. (2010). 5-HTTLPR moderates the effect of relational peer victimization on depressive symptoms in adolescent girls. *Journal of Child Psychology and Psychiatry, 51*(2), 173–179. https://doi.org/10.1111/j.1469-7610.2009.02149.x

Bentley, K. J., & Walsh, J. (2006). *The social worker and psychotropic medication: Toward effective collaboration with mental health clients, families and providers* (3rd ed.). Monterey, CA: Brooks/Cole-Thomson.

Berg, R. C., Johansen, T. B., Jardim, P. S. J., Forsetlund, L., & Nguyen, L. (2020). Interventions for children and youth with behavioral problems or criminal behavior: an overview of reviews. *Norwegian Institute of Public Health.* Retrieved from https://www.fhi.no/en/publ/2020/Interventions-for-children-and-youth-with-behavioral-problems-or-criminal-behavior/

Bowman, M. A., & Daws, L. C. (2019). Targeting serotonin transporters in the treatment of juvenile and adolescent depression. *Frontiers in Neuroscience, 13*, 156.

Brent, D. A. (2007). Clinical response and risk for reported suicidal ideation and suicide attempts in pediatric antidepressant treatment: A meta-analysis of randomized controlled trials. *Journal of the American Medical Association, 297*(15), 1683–1696.

Bridge, J. A., Iyengar, S., Salary, C. B., Barbe, R. P., Birmaher, B., Pincus, H. A., & Brent, D. A. (2007). Clinical response and risk for reported suicidal ideation and suicide attempts in pediatric antidepressant treatment: a meta-analysis of randomized controlled trials. *Journal of the American Medical Association, 297*(15), 1683–1696.

Brown, R. T., Antonuccio, D. O., Dupaul, G. J., Fristad, M. A., King, C. A., Leslie, L. K., McCormick, G. S., Pelham Jr., W. E., Piacentini, J. C., & Vitiello, B. (2007). *Childhood mental health disorders: Evidence-base and contextual factors for psychosocial, psychopharmacological, and combined interventions.* Washington, DC: American Psychological Association.

Cairns, K. E., Yap, M. B. H., Pilkington P. D., & Jorm, A. F. (2014). Risk and protective factors for depression that adolescents can modify: A systematic review and meta-analysis of longitudinal studies. *Journal of Affective Disorders, 169*, 61–75.

Carellas, N., Diederman, J., & Uchida, M. (2017). How prevalent and morbid are subthreshold manifestations of major depression in adolescents? A literature review. *Journal of Affective Disorders, 210*, 166–173.

Centers for Disease Control and Prevention. (2023). Youth risk behavior survey: Data summary and trends report 2011–2021. Retrieved from https://www.cdc.gov/healthyyouth/data/yrbs/pdf/YRBS_Data-Summary-Trends_Report2023_508.pdf

Cespedes, Y. M., & Huey, S. J. (2008). Depression in Latino adolescents. *Cultural Diversity and Ethnic Minority Psychology, 14*(2), 168–172.

Chi, X., Bo, A., Liu, T., Zhang, P., & Chi, I. (2018). Effects of mindfulness-based stress reduction on depression in adolescents and young adults: A systematic review and meta-analysis. *Frontiers in Psychology.* Retrieved from https://link-gale-com.

proxy.library.upenn.edu/apps/doc/A543862356/AONE?u=upenn_main&sid=
AONE&xid=b002c27b

Clarke, G. N., Lewinsohn, P. M., & Hops, H. (1990). Adolescent coping with depression course. *Kaiser Permanente*. Retrieved from http://www.kpchr.org/acwd/acwd.html.

Compas, B. E., Jaser, S. S., & Benson, M. A. (2009). Coping and emotion regulation: Implications for understanding depression during adolescence. In S. Nolen-Hoeksema & L. M. Hilt (Eds.), *Handbook of depression in adolescents* (pp. 419–439). New York: Routledge, Taylor & Francis.

Compas, B., Jaser, S., Bettis, A., Watson, K., Gruhn, M., Dunbar, J., Williams, E. & Thigpen, J. (2017). Coping, emotion regulation, and psychopathology in childhood and adolescence: A meta-analysis and narrative review. *Psychological Bulletin, 14*(9), 939–991. doi:10.1037/bul0000110

Costello, E. J., Erkanli, A., & Angold, A. (2006). Is there an epidemic of child or adolescent depression? *Journal of Child Psychology and Psychiatry and Allied Disciplines, 47*, 1263–1271.

Cox, G. R., Callahan, P., Churchill, R., Hunot, V., Merry, S. N., Parker, A. G., & Hetrick, S. E. (2014). Psychological therapies versus antidepressant medication, alone and in combination for depression in children and adolescents. *Cochrane Database of Systematic Reviews, 11*, CD008324.

Diamond, G., Diamond, G., & Levy, S. (2013). *Attachment-based family therapy for depressed adolescents*. Washington, DC: American Psychological Association.

Dimidjian, S., Barrera, M., Martell, C., Muñoz, R. F., & Lewisohn, P. M. (2011). The origins and current status of behavioral activation treatments for depression. *Annual Review of Clinical Psychology, 7*, 1–38, https://doi.org/10.1146/annurev-clinpsy-032210-104535

Dippel, N., Szota, K., Cuijpers, P., Christiansen, H., & Brakemeier, E. L. (2022). Family involvement in psychotherapy for depression in children and adolescents: Systematic review and meta-analysis. *Psychology and Psychotherapy: Theory, Research and Practice, 95*(3), 656–679. https://doi.org/10.1111/papt.12392

Dunn, E. C., Uddin, M., Subramanian, V. S., Smoller, J. W., Galea, S., & Koenen, K. C. (2011). Research review: Gene-environment interaction research in youth depression—a systematic review with recommendations for future research. *Journal of Child Psychology and Psychiatry, 52*(12), 1223–1238.

Eckshtain, D., Kuppens, S., Ugueto, A., Ng, M. Y., Vaughn-Coaxum, R., Corteselli, K., & Weisz, J. R. (2020). Meta-analysis: 13-year follow-up of psychotherapy effects on youth depression. *Journal of the American Academy of Child and Adolescent Psychiatry, 59*, 45–63.

Emslie, G. J., Mayes, T., Porta, G., Vitiello, B., Clarke, G., Wagner, K. D., Asarnow, J. R., Spirito, A., Birmaher, B., Ryan, N., Kennard, B., DeBar, L., McCracken, J., Strober, M., Onorato, M., Zelazny, J., Keller, M., Iyengar, S., & Brent, D. (2010). Treatment of resistant depression in adolescents (TORDIA): Week 24 outcomes. *American Journal of Psychiatry, 167*(7), 782–791.

Essau, C. A., Lewinsohn, P. M., Seeley, J. R., & Sasagawa, S. (2010). Gender differences in the developmental course of depression. *Journal of Affective Disorders, 127*(1–3), 185–190.

Forti-Buratti, M. A., Saika, R., Wilkinson, E., & Ramchandani, P. (2016). Psychological treatments for depression in pre-adolescent children (12 years and younger): Systematic review and meta-analysis of randomised controlled trials. *European Child & Adolescent Psychiatry, 25*, 1045–1054.

Gangwisch, J. E., Babiss, L. A., Malaspina, D., Turner, J. B., Zammit, G. K., & Posner, K. (2010). Earlier parental set bedtimes as a protective factor against depression and suicidal ideation. *Sleep, 33*(1), 97–106. https://doi.org/10.1093/sleep/33.1.97

Gillham, J. E., & Reivich, K. J. (1999). Prevention of depressive symptoms in school children: Update. *Psychological Science, 10*, 461–462.

Girgus, J., & Nolen-Hoeksema, S. (2006). Cognition and depression. In C. L. Keyes & S. H. Goodman (Eds.), *Women and depression: A handbook for the social, behavioral, and biomedical sciences* (pp. 147–175). New York: Cambridge University Press.

Goodall, J., Fisher, C., Hetrick, S., Phillips, L., Parrish, E., & Allot, K. (2018). Neurocognitive functioning in depressed young people: A systematic review and meta-analysis. *Neuropsychology Review, 28*, 216–231.

Goodman, S. H. (2007). Depression in mothers. *Annual Review of Clinical Psychology, 3*, 107–135.

Gunlicks-Stoessel, M., Mufson, L., Bernstein, G., Westervelt, A., Reigstad, K., Klimes-Dougan, B., Cullen, K., Murray, A., & Vock, D. (2019). Critical decision points for augmenting interpersonal psychotherapy for depressed adolescents: A pilot sequential multiple assignment randomized trial. *Journal of the American Academy of Child & Adolescent Psychiatry, 58*(1), 80–91.

Gunlicks-Stoessel, M., & Mufson, L. (2016). Innovations in practice: A pilot study of interpersonal psychotherapy for depressed adolescents and their parents. *Child and Adolescent Mental Health, 21*(4), 225–230.

Gunlicks-Stoessel, M., Mufson, L., Jekal, A., & Turner, J. B. (2010). The impact of perceived interpersonal functioning on treatment for adolescent depression: IPT-A versus treatment as usual in school-based health clinics, *Journal of Consulting and Clinical Psychology, 78*(2), 260–267. https://doi.org/10.1037/a0018935

Gutman, L. M., & Sameroff, A. J. (2004). Continuities in depression from adolescence to young adulthood: Contrasting ecological influences. *Development and Psychopathology, 16*, 967–984.

Hall, E. B., & Mufson, L. (2009). Interpersonal psychotherapy for depressed adolescents (IPT-A): A case illustration. *Journal of Clinical Child and Adolescent Psychology, 38*(4), 582–593. https://doi.org/10.1080/15374410902976338

Hall, W. (2018). Psychosocial risk and protective factors for depression among lesbian, gay, bisexual, and queer youth: A systematic review. *Journal of Homosexuality, 65*(3), 263–316. doi:10.1080/00918369.2017.1317467

Herstell, S., Betz, L. T., Penzel, N., Chechelnizki, R., Filihagh, L., Antonucci, L., & Kambeitz, J. (2021). Insecure attachment as a transdiagnostic risk factor for major psychiatric conditions: A meta-analysis in bipolar disorder, depression and schizophrenia spectrum disorder. *Journal of Psychiatric Research, 144*, 190–201. https://doi.org/10.1016/j.jpsychires.2021.10.002

Hetrick, S. E., McKenzie, J. E., Cox, G. R., Simmons, M. B., & Merry, S. N. (2012). Newer generation antidepressants for depressive disorders in children and adolescents. *Cochrane Database of Systematic Reviews, 11*, CD004851.

Hilt, L. M., & Nolen-Hoeksema, S. (2009). The emergence of gender differences in depression in adolescence. In S. Nolen-Hoeksema & L. M. Hilt (Eds.), *Handbook of depression in adolescents* (pp. 111–136). New York: Routledge, Taylor & Francis.

Hollis, C., Falconer, C., Martin, J., Whittington, C., Stockton, S., Glazebrook, C., & Davies, E.B. (2017). Annual research review: Digital health interventions for children and young people with mental health problems—a systematic and meta-review. *Journal of Child Psychology and Psychiatry, 58*, 474–503.

Infurna, M. R., Reichl, C., Parzer, P., Schimmenti, A., Bifulco, A., & Kaess, M. (2016). Associations between depression and specific childhood experiences of abuse and neglect: A meta-analysis. *Journal of Affective Disorders, 190*, 47–55.Johnson, D., Dupuis, G., Piche, J., Clayborne, Z., & Colman, I. (2018). Adult mental health outcomes of adolescent depression: A systematic review. *Depression & Anxiety, 35*, 700– 716. https://doi-org.proxy.library.upenn.edu/10.1002/da.22777

Jonas, B., Gu, Q., & Albertorio-Diaz, J. (2013). Psychotropic medication use among adolescents: United States, 2005–2010. *National Center for Health Statistics, Data Brief No. 135.*

Jones, R., Thapar, A., Stone, Z., Thapar, A., Jones, I., Smith, D., & Simpson, S. (2018). Psychoeducational interventions in adolescent depression: A systematic review. *Patient Education and Counseling, 101*, 804–816.

Jose, P., & Brown, I. (2008). When does the gender difference in rumination begin? Gender and age differences in the use of rumination by adolescents. *Journal of Youth & Adolescence, 37*(2), 180–192.

Kaslow, N. J., Robbins Broth, M., Cowles Arnette, N., & Collins, M. H. (2009). Family-based treatment for adolescent depression. In S. Nolen-Hoeksema & L. M. Hilt (Eds.), *Handbook of depression in adolescents* (pp. 531–570). New York: Routledge, Taylor & Francis.

Keles, S., & Idsoe, T. (2016). A meta-analysis of group cognitive behavioral therapy (CBT) interventions for adolescents with depression. *Journal of Adolescence, 67*, 129–139.

Kennard, B. D., Clarke, G. N., Weersing, V. R., Asarnow, J. R., Shamseddeen, W., Porta, G., Berk, M., Hughes, J. L., Spirito, A., Emslie, G. J., Keller, M. B., Wagner, K. D., & Brent, D. A. (2009). Effective components of TORDIA cognitive-behavioral therapy for adolescent depression: Preliminary findings. *Journal of Consulting and Clinical Psychology, 77*(6), 1033–1041.

Lau, J. Y. F., & Eley, T. C. (2008). New behavioral genetic approaches to depression in childhood and adolescence. In J. R. Z. Abela & B. L. Hankin (Eds.), *Handbook of depression in children and adolescents* (pp. 124–148). New York: Guilford Press.

Lemstra, M., Neudorf, C., D'Arcy, C., Kunst, A., Warren, L. M., & Bennett, N. R. (2008). A systematic review of depressed mood and anxiety by SES in youth aged 10–15 years. *Canadian Journal of Public Health, 99*(2), 125–129.

Lucassen, M. F., Stasiak, K., Samra, R., Frampton, C. M., & Merry, S. N. (2017). Sexual minority youth and depressive symptoms or depressive disorder: A systematic review and meta-analysis of population-based studies. *Australian & New Zealand Journal of Psychiatry, 51*(8), 774–787. https://doi.org/10.1177/0004867417713664

McLaughlin, K. (2009). Universal prevention for adolescent depression. In S. Nolen-Hoeksema & L. M. Hilt (Eds.), *Handbook of depression in adolescents* (pp. 661–689). New York: Routledge, Taylor & Francis.

Merikangas, K. R., & Knight, E. (2009). The epidemiology of depression in adolescents. In S. Nolen-Hoeksema & L. M. Hilt (Eds.), *Handbook of depression in adolescents* (pp. 53–73). New York: Routledge, Taylor & Francis.

Merikangas, K. R., Nakamura, E. F., & Kessler, R. C. (2009). Epidemiology of mental disorders in children and adolescents. *Dialogues in Clinical Neuroscience, 11*(1), 7–20.

Mufson, L., Dorta, K. P., Moreau, D., & Weissman, M. M. (2004a). *Interpersonal psychotherapy for depressed adolescents* (2nd ed.). New York: Guilford Press.

Mufson, L. H., Dorta, K. P., Olfson, M., Weissman, M. M., & Hoagwood, K. (2004b). Effectiveness research: Transporting Interpersonal Psychotherapy for Depressed Adolescents (IPT-A) from the lab to school-based health clinics. *Clinical Child and Family Psychology Review, 7*, 251–261. https://doi.org/10.1007/s10567-004-6089-6

Nantel-Vivier, A., & Pihl, R. O. (2008). Biological vulnerability to depression. In J. R. Z. Abela & B. L. Hankin (Eds.), *Handbook of depression in children and adolescents* (pp. 103–123). New York: Guilford Press.

Nilsen, T. S., Eisemann, M., & Kvernmo, S. (2013). Predictors and moderators of outcome in child and adolescent anxiety and depression: A systematic review of psychological treatment studies. *European Child & Adolescent Psychiatry, 22*(2), 69–87.

Nolen-Hoeksma, S. (2002). Gender differences in depression. In I. H. Gotlib (Ed.), *Handbook of depression* (pp. 492–509). New York: Guilford Press.

Olfson, M., & Marcus, S. (2009). National patterns in antidepressant medication treatment. *Archives of General Psychiatry, 66*, 848–856.

Oud, M., de Winter, L., Vermeulen-Smit, E., Bodden, D., Nauta, M., Stone, L., van den Heuvel, M., Taher, R., de Graaf, I., Kendall, T., Engels, R., & Stikkelbroek, Y. (2019). Effectiveness of CBT for children and adolescents with depression: A systematic review and meta-regression analysis. *European Psychiatry, 57*, 33–45. https://doi.org/10.1016/j.eurpsy.2018.12.008

Qin, B., Zhang, Y., Zhou, X., Cheng, P., Liu, Y., Chen, J., Fu, Y., Luo, Q., & Xie, P. (2014). Selective serotonin reuptake inhibitors versus tricyclic antidepressants in young patients: A meta-analysis of efficacy and acceptability. *Clinical Therapeutics, 36*(7), 1087–1095.

Rudolph, K. (2002). Gender differences in emotional responses to interpersonal stress during adolescence. *Journal of Adolescent Health, 30*, 3–13.

Rudolph, K. D. (2009). The interpersonal context of adolescent depression. In S. Nolen-Hoeksema & L. M. Hilt (Eds.), *Handbook of depression in adolescents* (pp. 377–418). New York: Routledge, Taylor & Francis.

Schäfer, J. Ö., Naumann, E., Holmes, E. A., Tuschen-Caffier, B., & Samson, A. C. (2017). Emotion regulation strategies in depressive and anxiety symptoms in youth: A meta-analytic review. *Journal of Youth and Adolescence, 46*(2), 261–276.

Sendzik, L., Ö Schäfer, J., Samson, C., Andrea, Naumann, E., & Tuschen-Caffier, B. (2017). Emotional awareness in depressive and anxiety symptoms in youth: A meta-analytic review. *Journal of Youth and Adolescence, 46*(4), 687–700. doi:http://dx.doi.org.proxy.library.upenn.edu/10.1007/s10964-017-0629-0

Shore, L., Toumbourou, J. W., Lewis, A. J., & Kremer, P. (2018). Longitudinal trajectories of child and adolescent depressive symptoms and their predictors—a systematic review and meta-analysis. *Child and Adolescent Mental Health, 23*(2), 107–120.

Shorey, S., Ng, E. D., & Wong, C. H. (2021). Global prevalence of depression and elevated depressive symptoms among adolescents: A systematic review and meta-analysis. *British Journal of Clinical Psychology, 61*(2), 287–305. https://doi.org/10.1111/bjc.12333

Spence, S. H., O'Shea, G., & Donovan, C. L. (2016). Improvements in interpersonal functioning following interpersonal psychotherapy (IPT) with adolescents and their association with change in depression. *Behavioural and Cognitive Psychotherapy*, *44*(3), 257–272. https://doi.org/10.1017/S1352465815000442

Stebbins, M. B., & Corcoran, J. (2016). Pediatric bipolar. *Journal of Child and Adolescent Social Work*, *33*, 115. doi:10.1007/s10560-015-0411-7.

Sullivan, P. F., Neale, M. C., & Kendler, K. S. (2000). Genetic epidemiology of major depression: Review and meta-analysis. *American Journal of Psychiatry*, *157*(10), 1552–1562.

TADS Team. (2007). The treatment of adolescents with depression study (TADS): Long-term effectiveness and safety outcomes. *Archives of General Psychiatry*, *64*(10), 1132–1144.

Tindall, L., Mikocka-Walus, A., McMillan, D., Wright, B., Hewitt, C., & Gascoyne, S. (2017). Is behavioural activation effective in the treatment of depression in young people? A systematic review and meta-analysis. *Psychology and Psychotherapy Theory, Research and Practice*, *90*(4), 770–796.

Toenders, Y. J., van Velzen, L. S., Heideman, I. Z., Harrison, B. J., Davey, C. G., & Schmaal, L. (2019). Neuroimaging predictors of onset and course of depression in childhood and adolescence: A systematic review of longitudinal studies. *Developmental Cognitive Neuroscience*, *39*, 100700.

Twenge, J. M., & Nolen-Hoeksema, S. (2002). Age, gender, race, socioeconomic status, and birth cohort difference on the children's depression inventory: A meta-analysis. *Journal of Abnormal Psychology*, *111*(4), 578–588.

Uchida, M., Serra, G., Zayas, L., Kenworthy, T., Faraone, S., & Biederman, J. (2015). Can unipolar and bipolar pediatric major depression be differentiated from each other? A systematic review of cross-sectional studies examining differences in unipolar and bipolar depression. *Journal of Affective Disorders*, *176*, 1–7.

Umaña-Taylor, A., & Updegraff, K. (2007). Latino adolescents' mental health: Exploring the interrelations among discrimination, ethnic identity, cultural orientation, self-esteem, and depressive symptoms. *Journal of Adolescence*, *30*(4), 549–567.

Usala, T., Clavenna, A., Zuddas, A., & Bonati, M. (2008). Randomised controlled trials of selective serotonin reuptake inhibitors in treating depression in children and adolescents: A systematic review and meta-analysis. *European Neuropsychopharmacology*, *18*(1), 62–73.

U.S. Food and Drug Administration. (2004). *Suicidality in children and adolescents being treated with antidepressant medications. FDA public health advisory*. Rockville, MD: U.S. Food and Drug Administration.

Wang, J., Nansel, T. R., & Iannotti, R. J. (2011). Cyber and traditional bullying: Differential association with depression. *Journal of Adolescent Health*, *48*(4), 415–417. https://doi.org/10.1016/j.jadohealth.2010.07.012

Waslick, B. D., Kandel, R., & Kakouros, A. (2002). Depression in children and adolescents: An overview. In D. Shaffer & B. D. Waslick (Eds.), *The many faces of depression in children and adolescents* (pp. 1–36). Washington, DC: American Psychiatric Publishing.

Weinberger, A., Gbedemah, M., Martinez, A., Nash, D., Galea, S., & Goodwin, R. (2018). Trends in depression prevalence in the USA from 2005 to 2015: Widening disparities in vulnerable groups. *Psychological Medicine, 48*(8), 1308–1315. doi:10.1017/S0033291717002781

Weisz, J. R., Weersing, V. R., Valeri, S. M., & McCarty, C. A. (1999). *Therapist's manual for PASCET: Primary and secondary control enhancement training program.* Los Angeles: University of California.

Werner-Seidler, A., Perry, Y., Calear, A., Newby, J., & Christensen, H. (2017). School-based depression and anxiety prevention programs for young people: A systematic review and meta-analysis. *Clinical Psychology Review, 51,* 30–47.

Whittington, C. J., Kendall, T., Fonagy, P., Cottrell D., Cotgrove, A., & Boddington, E. (2004). Selective serotonin reuptake inhibitors in childhood depression: systematic review of published versus unpublished data. *Lancet, 363*(9418), 1341–1345.

Xiang, Y., Cuijpers, P., Teng, T., Li, X., Fan, L., Liu, X., Jiang, Y., Du, K., Lin, J., Zhou, X., & Xie, P. (2022). Comparative short-term efficacy and acceptability of a combination of pharmacotherapy and psychotherapy for depressive disorder in children and adolescents: A systematic review and meta-analysis. *BMC Psychiatry, 22*(1), 139. https://doi.org/10.1186/s12888-022-03760-2

Yap, M. B. H., Pilkington, P. D., Ryan, S. M., & Jorm, A. F. (2014). Parental factors associated with depression and anxiety in young people: A systematic review and meta-analysis. *Journal of Affective Disorders, 156,* 8–23.

Young, J., F., Mufson, L., & Davies, M. (2006). Efficacy of Interpersonal Psychotherapy—Adolescent Skills Training: An indicated preventive intervention for depression. *Journal of Child Psychology and Psychiatry, 47*(12), 1254–1262. https://doi.org/10.1111/j.1469-7610.2006.01667.x

Zhou, X., Hetrick, S. E., Cuijpers, P., Qin, B., Barth, J., Whittington, C. J., Cohen, D., Del Giovane, C., Liu, Y., Michael, K. D., Zhang, Y., Weisz, J. R., & Xie, P. (2015). Comparative efficacy and acceptability of psychotherapies for depression in children and adolescents: A systematic review and network meta-analysis. *World Psychiatry, 14*(2), 207–222. http://doi.org/10.1002/wps.20217

Zhou, X., Michael, K. D., Liu, Y., Del Giovane, C., Qin, B., Cohen, D., Gentile, S., & Xie, P. (2014). Systematic review of management for treatment-resistant depression in adolescents. *BMC Psychiatry, 4,* 340. http://dx.doi.org/10.1186/s12888-014-0340-6

Nonsuicidal Self-Injury and Suicidal Thoughts and Behaviors

JACQUELINE CORCORAN, SAMANTHA SCHINDELHEIM, AND COURTNEY BENJAMIN WOLK ■

Sara is a 15-year-old Dominican American, cisgender, bisexual female who presented to dialectal behavior therapy for adolescents (DBT-A) treatment following a 2-week inpatient hospitalization for self-harming without suicidal intent. She had never been in treatment before, but according to reports from her biological father and her inpatient hospitalization treatment team, she had been self-harming for the past 6 months. Sara's best friend found her cutting her thigh with a razorblade in the school bathroom and told a teacher, who called 911. Sara then spent 2 weeks in the inpatient facility.

Sara lives with her father and 12-year-old brother. She doesn't have a close relationship with her biological mother who has lived in the Dominican Republic since Sara was 2 years old. Sara's parents immigrated to the United States when they were adolescents with their respective families, and Sara's mother returned there permanently. According to Sara's father, her mother calls occasionally but only visited the family once when Sara was 4 years old.

Sara's father works at a barbershop in their neighborhood and reports that their formerly close relationship became tense as she entered the teenage years. Jessica reports that she rarely speaks to her younger brother and finds him "annoying" and "a know it all."

Sara attends 10th grade at an urban charter school. According to Sara's father, she is a very hard worker and a "perfectionist," further describing that she recently received Bs on two separate exams and became very upset, "yelling, crying, and screaming." He reports that her school is demanding, the school hours are long, and he worries that this reinforces her "desire to always excel at everything." He also shares that she seems to have difficulty sleeping and is easily startled.

The school offered Sara support through one-on-one tutoring when they noticed that her grades were dropping, but Sara refused the additional help, stating "I just want to do it all on my own." Sara does not receive any in-school mental health counseling, but several teachers have verbalized concern to her father, and one teacher referred her to the school's mental health counselor because of concerns about her irritability and withdrawing from peers. However, Sara refused to attend these sessions. Sara disclosed during her inpatient hospitalization to a social worker that a male peer at a party sexually assaulted her about 9 months ago and stated that she has not told anyone else about it.

OVERVIEW

This chapter discusses both nonsuicidal self-injury (NSSI) and suicidal thoughts and behavior because of their interrelationship and their high occurrence rates in adolescents. NSSI is defined as "intentional and non-socially acceptable behaviors that are intended to cause destruction or impairment of bodily tissues but only minor or moderate physical harm, performed without any conscious suicidal intention, self-directed, and used to reduce psychological distress" (International Society for the Study of Self-Injury, 2018). The most common method is "cutting" (layperson nomenclature for NSSI), followed by head banging, scratching, hitting, and burning (Gillies et al., 2018).

In previous versions of the *Diagnostic and Statistical Manual of Mental Disorders* (DSM), NSSI was captured as an "impulse control disorder not otherwise specified," but in the DSM-5, NSSI disorder is classified as "a condition requiring further study" (section 3; American Psychiatric Association [APA], 2022).

Other definitions pertinent to this chapter include *self-injury* (a term that includes NSSI and any behavior such as exposing oneself to violent situations) and *deliberate self-harm* (which includes NSSI behavior and intentional drug overdoses). Despite the numerous variations in the definitions of these clinical populations, the prevalence of these various behaviors tends to be stable (Grandclerc et al., 2016).

Prevalence

Suicide is the second leading cause of death among 15- to 29-year-olds globally (Centers for Disease Control and Prevention, 2018). In the United States, the suicide rate for persons aged 10 to 14 years tripled from 2007 to 2017, and for 15- to 19-year-olds it increased 10% per year from 2014 to 12% in 2017 (Heron, 2019). While 68% of all youth suicide deaths occurred without a previous suicide attempt, death was strongly related to self-injurious thoughts and behaviors. Additionally, attempts were associated with prior self-injurious thoughts and behaviors (Castellví et al., 2017), and suicidal ideation commonly precedes repetitive self-harm (Witt et al., 2019). A systematic review of adolescent self-harm from community-based studies spanning 597,548 adolescent participants from 41 countries over 25 years (1990 through 2015) found a lifetime prevalence of 16.9% (Gillies et al., 2018). Increases in rates for recent cohorts were found. Suicidal ideation and attempts were significantly higher in adolescents who self-harmed more frequently. Finally, individuals who may have no history of suicidal intent but engage in NSSI may accidentally injure themselves more seriously than they intended (Newman, 2009), underscoring the importance of identifying and treating NSSI.

RISK AND PROTECTIVE FACTORS

Biological

Despite the increasing recognition of NSSI as a clinical problem, the neurobiological underpinnings of the behaviors are still poorly understood. There are several theories of multiple neurobiological factors potentially at work, including genetics, functional differences in the brain, and deficiencies in neurochemistry. Several genes have been identified as potentially influential in NSSI behaviors, but the research has been inconsistent (Evens et al., 2000; Hankin et al., 2011; Joyce et al., 2006). Advances in the field of neuroimaging have given neuroscientists the opportunity to conduct several studies of brain morphology and functional neuronal activity. In particular, functional magnetic resonance imaging has shown that the amygdala and anterior cingulate cortex in the limbic system are hyperaroused in individuals with borderline personality disorders (BPD) or NSSI, as summarized in the review by Groschwitz and Plener (2012).

Additionally, several neurochemicals in the brain have been linked to NSSI. These neurochemicals include the neurotransmitters serotonin and dopamine as well as the hormone cortisol and endogenous opioids (Groschwitz & Plener, 2012). Reduced levels of cortisol and endogenous opioids are consistently associated with increased NSSI and indicate the possibility of an atypical stress response in those who engage in NSSI behaviors (Groschwitz & Plener, 2012). Low levels of endogenous opioids could explain why NSSI behaviors can have an addictive quality; when an individual engages in NSSI behaviors, the expected neurochemical response would be the release of endogenous opioids (Nixon et al., 2002). Habitually low levels of endogenous opioids not only are associated with repeated NSSI behaviors but also are present in individuals who experienced childhood abuse and neglect (Sher & Stanley, 2009; Stanley, 2010).

Lack of sleep is a biological factor that has been linked to suicide risk in prospective studies of youths (Kearns et al., 2020). The authors argue that sleep makes a good target for prevention because it is easy to assess in medical settings and relatively easy to treat compared with other aspects of a teen's life. Most teens (75%) do not receive the recommended 8 to 10 hours of sleep.

Psychological

Psychological and social factors have been emphasized in the development of NSSI and suicide risk. NSSI is most common among adolescents and young adults, and the age of onset often occurs in early adolescence (12 to 14 years). By older adolescence and young adulthood, the rate decreases. Most cases of NSSI (81%) involve other disorders (Carballo et al., 2020; Hawton et al., 2013), usually depression (Moller et al., 2022) followed by anxiety (Hawton et al., 2013). Additionally, depression severity and recurrence increase risk (Moller et al., 2022). Internalizing or externalizing disorders increase the odds of later suicide attempts (Soto-Sanz et al., 2019). NSSI may be a maladaptive way to cope with distress or an expression of the symptoms of the underlying disorder. For instance, self-harm is a symptom of BPD, and hopelessness is a symptom of depression, but hopelessness itself is a risk factor for self-harm (Witt et al., 2019). A reduction in hopelessness is also important for recovery (Adrian et al., 2019). The implication is that clinicians should take an active role in managing hopelessness by providing psychoeducational information about how it may influence outcomes, helping teens connect problem-solving efforts to goals attainment, supporting them in applying coping skills to daily challenges, conveying optimism about the benefits of treatment, and thus, instilling hope (Asarnow & Mehlum, 2019).

Problematic substance use is also associated with suicide risk in youths (Carballa et al., 2021; Moller et al., 2022). A systematic review examined the directionality of this relationship. Most studies found that substance use predicted later suicide risk, but there is a bidirectional nature to the association. Implications are that mental health and substance use disorders should be treated early so that a comorbid problem does not develop.

The most frequent reason cited for NSSI is relief from a negative state (Gillies et al., 2018). Nock and Prinstein (2004) developed the four-factor model of NSSI, focusing on the stimulus and consequences that initiate and then maintain the behavior. The four processes include: (1) automatic negative reinforcement, where NSSI serves to reduce aversive internal states; (2) automatic positive reinforcement, where NSSI acts to increase positive feelings; (3) social negative reinforcement, where NSSI serves to avoid interpersonal demands; and (4) social positive reinforcement, where NSSI serves to gain attention, or increase social support.

Social

Many social factors have been linked to the development of NSSI, including adversity, family influences, gender, ethnicity, sexual minority status, school and peer variables, and Internet use. Multiple family factors, in addition to adversity occurring within the family context, have been implicated in NSSI and suicide risk (Arbuthnott & Lewis, 2015). The interpersonal theory of suicide has been formulated involving the concepts of "thwarted belongingness" and the perception of being "a burden" (Joiner, 2009; Van Orden et al., 2010). These two constructs encapsulate interpersonal risk factors and intrapersonal factors. For instance, family conflict, child maltreatment, or poverty may cause youth to feel they are a burden to the family and have no worth. Hopelessness about these states is also part of the theory, as is the capability to die by suicide, which includes habituation to the pain of self-harm and the fear of suicide.

FAMILY FACTORS

Family conflict is a risk factor, and sometimes a specific trigger, for adolescent NSSI and suicidal behavior (Grimmond et al., 2019); family cohesion serves as a protective factor (Clarke et al., 2019). Lower attachment to parents is associated with NSSI and suicide attempts (Woo et al., 2022). Additionally, insecure attachment in the form of either a preoccupied or an avoidant style predicts future suicide attempts. Conversely, a secure attachment is negatively associated with NSSI and suicide attempts. Strengthening the parent–child relationship and improving family functioning are critical, therefore, when working with youths who are self-harming or suicidal (Arbuthnott & Lewis, 2015; Clarke et al., 2019). The goal is for adolescents to be able to go to their parents if they are experiencing intense distress and crisis and receive support and access to professional help.

ADVERSITY

Adversity generally (Ferrigno et al., 2015; Serafini et al., 2015) and childhood maltreatment (Cipriano et al., 2017), particularly sexual abuse (Serafini et al., 2015), are predictive of NSSI among adolescents. In 28 studies, a positive dose–response relationship was observed between the number of adversities or negative life events experienced and youth suicidal behavior (Serafini et al., 2015). Similarly, individuals who have been in the care of the child welfare system are at an elevated risk. The estimated prevalence of suicidal ideation was 24.7% in children and young people in care compared with 11.4% in noncare populations (Evans et al., 2017). Parental education, as a proxy socioeconomic status (SES) measure, is associated with risk. According to a worldwide systematic review, lower parental education was correlated with an increased risk of youth suicide attempts in Northern America and suicidal ideation in high- income countries.

GENDER

NSSI is more common in girls (Gillies et al., 2018), and adolescent and young adult females exhibit more suicide attempts (Miranda-Mendizabal et al., 2019); girls are more likely to experience sexual abuse, at a rate of 27% by age 17 (Finkelhor et al., 2014). In the most recent Youth Behavior Survey in 2021, 13% of females had attempted suicide (CDC, 2023). Adolescent and young adult males have higher risk for death from suicide attempts. Specific risk factors have also been identified. In a review of 67 studies (Miranda-Mendizabal et al., 2019), female-specific risk factors for suicide attempts include eating disorder, post-traumatic stress disorder (PTSD), bipolar disorder, depressive symptoms, dating violence, interpersonal problems, and previous abortion. Male-specific factors for suicide attempt include disruptive behavior/conduct problems, hopelessness, parental separation/ divorce, friend's suicidal behavior, and access to lethal means. Males with drug abuse, an externalizing disorder, or access to firearms are also at higher risk for suicide death.

RACE AND ETHNICITY

The Centers for Disease Control and Prevention Youth Risk Behavior Surveillance System (2017), which includes data from 1991 through 2017, demonstrated that American Indian/Alaskan, Asian, and Pacific Islander high school youths have the highest rates of past-year serious thoughts of suicide and suicide plans compared with other ethnic groups. Black high school youth exhibited a higher rate of past-year suicide attempts and past-year attempts requiring medical treatment in this study, though they did not report persistent feelings of sadness and hopelessness at the same rate (CDC, 2023)

SCHOOL AND SOCIAL NETWORKS

The school and peer environment play a role in the development of NSSI. School failure Castellví et al., 2020) and lack of connection to school are associated with reports of suicidal ideation and suicide attempts for the general population of adolescents and high-risk groups (Marraccini & Brier, 2017). Bullying, including cyberbullying (Glendenning et al., 2018), is associated with self-harm, as are peer conflict, rejection, isolation, and romantic disappointment (Grimmond et al., 2019).

Moreover, the influence of the social network is seen in the correlation between NSSI/suicidal behaviors in individuals and that of their peers and family members. The authors of this systematic review of 86 papers published internationally speculated that rather than a "copycat" effect, it may be instead that people with preexisting vulnerabilities gravitate to those that appear similar to themselves (e.g., Goth or Emo subgroups; Quigley et al., 2016, 2017). Peers may also undergo similar stressors, such as the suicide of a friend, which may result in vulnerability to suicidal ideation.

SEXUAL MINORITY IDENTIFICATION

Systematic reviews have indicated that LGBTQ youths exhibit increased risk for suicidal ideation, behaviors, and self-harm (Liu et al., 2019; Marshal et al., 2011; Pompili et al., 2014). Fear of family and peer reactions to their coming out, bullying, and discrimination are speculated as adding increased stress for these youths. Connection to the school can help reduce risk (Arraccini & Brier, 2017).

INTERNET USE

Most young people spend a considerable amount of time online daily ("almost constantly" is the modal response). According to a systematic review of 52 publications, Internet sites about self-harm and suicidal behavior, which may include normalization of this type of behavior, triggering, competition between users, and a source of contagion and harmful information for vulnerable individuals

(Marchant et al., 2017), may cause harm. However, there could also be benefits to Internet use, such as information-seeking on a sensitive and stigmatized topic; the potential for anonymity; the creation of support and reduced isolation; and support during a crisis.

ASSESSMENT

While the evidence does not conclusively support universal screening of young people for suicide risk and self-harm (Morken et al., 2019), there is also no evidence that asking about suicidal thoughts and behaviors increases suicidal ideation (a common concern expressed by clinicians). In a review of 13 studies of youths and adults, none found that suicidal ideation increased at a statistically significant level among participants who were asked about their suicidal thoughts (Dazzi et al., 2014). Given the extent to which youths at risk for suicide or engaging in NSSI might have experienced adversity and trauma, the importance of a trauma-informed approach to suicide/self-harm screening and care is emphasized. It is important to assess for and consider current and past exposure to traumatic stress. (See https://ncsacw.samhsa.gov/userfiles/files/SAMHSA_Trauma.pdf.) Since most youths with NSSI or experiencing a suicidal crisis have another disorder, it is also important to conduct a comprehensive assessment so that appropriate treatment can follow.

A systematic review of assessment tools found, unfortunately, that no single tool was suitable for predicting a higher risk of suicide or self-harm in adolescent populations (Harris et al., 2019). A list of freely accessible measures is available in Table 11.1. There are also online resources available for training on screening and risk assessment (see https://www.nimh.nih.gov/research/research-conducted-at-nimh/asq-toolkit-materials/index.shtml and https://cssrs.columbia.edu/training/training-options/).

Part of assessment is determining the youth's reasons for feeling suicidal or self-injurious. In a synthesis of qualitative studies, teens state that it is because of their difficulties expressing emotion, their need to establish control over a situation that they experienced as not controllable, distraction from a negative state (often associated with self-loathing and feelings of worthlessness, or anger), and their desire to punish themselves or others (Grimmond et al., 2019).

During her inpatient hospitalization, a social worker conducted a clinical interview with Sara to assess for DSM-5 mood and anxiety symptoms, as well as rule out symptoms of psychosis and behavioral and developmental concerns. Sara's father participated in a separate collateral interview to gather further information about his observations of Sara's symptoms, psychosocial history, and overall concerns. Sara's father provided written consent for the social worker to speak with Sara's school principal, who shared that Sara has had trouble focusing over the past few months, confirmed that her grades have dropped (which has been considerable given that Sara "has always been an A student"), and reported that Sara has appeared less socially engaged with peers lately. Sara's principal mentioned that Sara used to have

Table 11.1 Measures of Nonsuicidal Self-Injury and Suicidality

Psychometric Support	Measure Name	No. of Items	Completed by:[a]	Ages[b]	Link to Measure
Excellent	Alexian Brothers Urge to Self-Injure Scale (ABUSI; Washburn et al., 2010)	5	Y	Adolescents[c]	https://itriples.org/measures/
Good	Columbia Suicide Screen Severity Rating Scale (C-SSRS; Posner et al., 2008)*	19	C	5–18	http://cssrs.columbia.edu/
Adequate	Ask Suicide—Screening Questions (ASQ; Horowitz et al., 2012)*	4	C	10–24	https://www.nimh.nih.gov/research/research-conducted-at-nimh/asq-toolkit-materials/index.shtml
Adequate	Depressive Symptom Inventory Suicidality Subscale (DSI-SS; Joiner et al., 2002)	4	Y	15+	https://psy.fsu.edu/~joinerlab/resources.html
Adequate	Suicidal Behaviors Questionnaire—Revised (SBQ-R; Osman et al., 2001)	4	C	Older adolescents[c]	https://www.integration.samhsa.gov/images/res/SBQ.pdf
Adequate	Functional Assessment of Self-Mutilation (FASM; Lloyd-Richardson et al., 2007)	40	Y	Adolescents[c]	https://itriples.org/measures/

[a] Completed by: Y = youth, P = parent/caregiver, C = clinician, T = teacher.

[b] Exact age range for specific forms (e.g., self-report, parent report) may vary.

[c] Exact age range not specified.

* Available in multiple languages.

NOTE: Table adapted from Becker-Haimes, E. M., Tabachnick, A. R., Last, B. S., Stewart, R. E., Hasan-Granier, A., & Beidas, R. S. (2020). Evidence base update for brief, free, and accessible youth mental health measures. *Journal of Clinical Child & Adolescent Psychology*, 49(1), 1–17, reprinted by permission of the publisher (Taylor & Francis Ltd, http://www.tandfonline.com).

References for measures in Table 11.1:

Australian National General Practice Youth Suicide Prevention Project. *Behaviour Research and Therapy, 40*(4), 471–481.

Horowitz, L. M., Bridge, J. A., Teach, S. J., Ballard, E., Klima, J., Rosenstein, D. L., . . . Joshi, P. (2012). Ask Suicide-Screening Questions (ASQ): A brief instrument for the pediatric emergency department. *Archives of Pediatrics & Adolescent Medicine, 166*(12), 1170–1176.

Joiner Jr, T. E., Pfaff, J. J., & Acres, J. G. (2002). A brief screening tool for suicidal symptoms in adolescents and young adults in general health settings: Reliability and validity data from Klonsky, E. D., & Muehlenkamp, J. J. (2007). Self-injury: A research review for the practitioner. *Journal of Clinical Psychology, 63*(11), 1045–1056.

Osman, A., Bagge, C. L., Gutierrez, P. M., Konick, L. C., Kopper, B. A., & Barrios, F. X. (2001). The Suicidal Behaviors Questionnaire—Revised (SBQ-R): Validation with clinical and nonclinical samples. *Assessment, 8*(4), 443–454.

Posner, K., Brent, D., Lucas, C., Gould, M., Stanley, B., Brown, G., . . . Mann, J. (2008). Columbia-suicide severity rating scale. New York: Columbia University.

Washburn, J. J., Juzwin, K. R., Styer, D. M., & Aldridge, D. (2010). Measuring the urge to self-injure: Preliminary data from a clinical sample. *Psychiatry Research, 178*(3), 540–544.

a perfect attendance record but over the past few months has missed several days of school in a row without written permission.

To assess mood and anxiety symptoms, the Patient Health Questionnaire-9 (PHQ-9) was administered by the social worker, and the Difficulties in Emotion Regulation Scale (DERS) and Screen for Child Anxiety Related Disorders (SCARED) were completed by Sara and her father. Even though children cannot be diagnosed with a personality disorder before age 18, Sara also completed the Borderline Symptom List 23 (BSL-23) to assess traits of BPD and to help inform which treatment modality would be the most useful at this time. To better understand Sara's trauma symptoms, Sara completed the UCLA Posttraumatic Stress Disorder Reaction Index (UCLA PTSD-RI). The social worker assessed for suicidal thoughts and behaviors using the Columbia Suicide Severity Rating Scale (C-SSRS); Sara denied experiencing thoughts of wanting to die when self-harming but endorsed frequent engagement in NSSI behaviors. To further understand her engagement in NSSI, the social worker completed the Inventory of Statements about Self-Injury (ISAS) with Sara. Sara reported that, over the past 6 months, she has attempted to harm herself without suicidal intent through severe scratching, cutting with a knife and razorblade, interfering with wound healing, and burning her skin with a cigarette lighter. She also reported that she has an urge to self-harm almost daily and wants to stop engaging in this behavior. She has self-harmed in multiple places, including while at school, in her bedroom, in her apartment bathroom, and at a friend's home. She endorsed the following functions of the self-harm behavior: to calm herself down, to punish herself, to let others know the extent of her emotional pain, and to signify the emotional distress she experiences. Based on these functions, it was clear that the function of this behavior is ego-dystonic, conflicting with Sara's desire to get better. The comprehensive assessment also involved ruling out symptoms of mania, substance use, attention-deficit/hyperactivity disorder, and psychosis.

The inpatient social worker determined that Sara met DSM-5 diagnostic criteria for major depressive disorder and PTSD. Based on the interviews and assessments with both Sara and her father, it was clear that Sara has experienced depressed and irritable mood for most of the time, has lost interest in spending time with her family and friends, and engages minimally in daily living skills, such as bathing and eating regular meals. It was also clear from the collateral interview with both Sara's father and her school principal that there has been a distinct shift from her previous functioning. They reported that she appears more restless and has expressed feelings of worthlessness and shame about her outward appearance. Sara reported in the assessment that she feels down most of the day, has trouble concentrating, finds it challenging to fall and stay asleep, has lost interest in academic work and activities with peers, and often feels "not worthy of love and happiness," which she copes with by cutting herself "to take the pain away." Sara also meets criteria for a trauma disorder related to the sexual assault she experienced and has considerable feelings of abandonment related to the absence of her mother. Sara disclosed in the interview that her mother's absence has caused her to feel "not worthy of being loved by anyone" and is something she thinks about frequently. Since her sexual assault more than 9 months ago, she endorses avoiding school so that she did not have to see her abuser, is highly reactive to sudden movements, particularly around males, and has flashbacks almost daily of memories of the event. She also reports cutting herself "with anything I can get my hand on that's sharp, usually a razorblade or knife" on her wrists and thighs whenever she has a flashback.

Based on the results of the assessment and final diagnoses of major depressive disorder and PTSD, it was determined that Sara could benefit from dialectical behavior therapy for adolescents (DBT-A; Miller & Rathus, 2014), which involves weekly individual psychotherapy, a skills group in which Sara and her father would participate for a minimum of 6 months, and phone coaching to help with generalizing skills learned in treatment outside of therapy sessions. A recommendation was also made for Sara to receive a psychopharmacology assessment to determine whether she could benefit from medication with a selective serotonin reuptake inhibitor (SSRI).

INTERVENTION

Adolescents often do not disclose NSSI; about 50% of adolescents will seek help (Gillies et al., 2018). When they do, it is most often from a friend. In this section, we first discuss safety planning and means restriction to prepare social workers in all settings for this critically important work. Then, we focus on psychosocial interventions that have received empirical study. We also refer the reader to the information on medication for depression in Chapter 10 because there are limited research recommendations specific to medication interventions for NSSI or suicidal thoughts and behaviors. Careful monitoring is needed with antidepressants, as well as other medicines, because rarely they have been associated with the emergence of suicidal ideation (Asarnow & Mehlum, 2019).

Psychiatric Hospitalization and Safety Planning

Psychiatric hospitalization is considered when an adolescent is determined to be at high risk of imminent suicidal behavior, but the highest rates of suicide death are in the first 3 months after discharge (Chung et al., 2017). These findings suggest that hospitalization is not an adequate intervention for lowering risk for subsequent suicidal behavior; however, it may be essential for ensuring safety in the short term and may pave the way for better compliance with outpatient treatment (Rufino et al., 2019). Partial hospitalization following in-patient treatment may allow more time for stabilization and to address current stressors (Shaffer & Pfeffer, 2001).

For youth who are at risk for suicide but do not require hospitalization, the Safety Planning Intervention is an excellent choice for a brief, evidence-based intervention strategy. The Safety Planning Intervention typically takes 20 to 45 minutes to complete. It is a six-step intervention designed to help individuals identify specific coping strategies and support contacts to engage when self-harm thoughts emerge (Stanley & Brown, 2009). Safety planning has replaced no-suicide contracts, which involve the clinician asking patients to promise or contract not to harm themselves (not an effective, evidence-based strategy) as standard practice (Clarke et al., 2019). Stanley and Brown's safety planning template is available online (see https://www.sprc.org/sites/default/files/resource-program/Brown_St anleySafetyPlanTemplate.pdf). A protocol for children ages six to 12 has also been developed with modifications for family involvement (Itzhaky & Stanley, 2022).

In safety planning, the social worker helps the client with the following:

1. Recognizing warning signs (triggers) of another suicidal crisis
2. Identifying "internal coping strategies" such as distraction, and any barriers involved, so that adolescents learn that suicidal urges can be mastered.
3. Using social contacts as a means of distraction from suicidal thoughts, not necessarily revealing suicidal distress
4. Choosing supportive family members to help resolve the crisis
5. Providing contact information for mental health professionals or agencies, any local 24-hour emergency facility, and local or national support services that handle emergency calls, such as national Suicide Prevention Lifeline: 988 or 800-273-8255 (TALK).
6. Problem-solving on reducing potential use of lethal means, such as locking up firearms and sharp objects and throwing away expired or risky medications.

Slovak et al. (2008) surveyed 697 social workers about their attitudes, knowledge, and behaviors regarding client firearm assessment and safety counseling and found only 34% routinely assessed for firearm ownership within the past 2 years of practice. Barriers to such assessment included lack of training and awareness of risks, feeling discomfort regarding this topic in their practice, and lack of time. Despite social worker reluctance, conversations about means restriction with families are critical to keep at-risk adolescents safe.

A safety planning intervention for adolescents was evaluated in an emergency room setting in a small randomized controlled trial (Bettis et al., 2020). The safety planning intervention was more effective for reducing depression than the enhanced treatment as usual control condition. The other outcomes for hopelessness, suicidal ideation, and alcohol use trended positive but they were not statistically different than the control condition.

Hospitalization and Treatment Engagement

Engaging youths experiencing NSSI or suicide risk can be challenging. Rufino et al. (2019) examined risk and protective factors related to treatment compliance in suicidal adolescents. Female gender, having a diagnosis of major depressive disorder, and having parents who expressed a need for treatment were associated with better engagement. Ethnic minority status and a diagnosis of conduct disorder were associated with less engagement.

A review by Yuan and colleagues (2019) explored factors associated with engaging in four or more sessions of treatment (Yuan et al., 2019). Therapy that used a specific psychotherapy model was associated with better engagement. In the next section, we discuss the specific psychological therapy of DBT because it has received the most research validation to date.

Psychotherapeutic Interventions

Studies and systematic reviews have been conducted recently on effective treatments for these populations. The studies that have been conducted vary widely in their inclusion criteria, ranging from youths exhibiting repeated self-harm within the context of other symptoms of borderline personality to those experiencing self-harm in past month, suicidality and substance abuse, suicide attempts and self-harm, or suicidal ideation and attempts (Flaherty, 2018). The most up-to-date meta-analysis found, overall, that specific psychological therapies did slightly better than treatment as usual in decreasing suicidal ideation and depressive symptoms but were not significantly better than treatment as usual for reducing self-harm (Kothgassner et al., 2020).

DBT is an intensive intervention based on cognitive-behavioral and social learning theories originally developed for BPD (Linehan, 1993; Rizvi et al., 2013, Robins & Chapman, 2004). The term *dialectical* refers to the challenge of balancing one's needs for both self-acceptance and change as well as the premise that BPD is a product of biological and environmental influences. The goal of treatment is to help the client engage in functional, life-enhancing behaviors even when intense emotions are present. Practitioners of DBT view client behaviors as natural reactions to environmental reinforcers. In the case of BPD, one of the most frequent dialectical tensions is that a behavior such as self-injury is both functional (short-term stress reduction) and dysfunctional (negative effects on health and interpersonal functioning in the long term.) This tension is resolved by finding a synthesis—validating the client's need to relieve stress while helping the client use skills to reduce stress in the long run. Intervention focuses on shaping and reinforcing more adaptive behaviors while also providing clients with a validating environment. Practitioners pay attention to the factors that maintain dysfunctional behaviors, such as reinforcers of self-injurious behaviors and aversive consequences of more appropriate behavior.

DBT-A was developed to reduce NSSI by addressing the common skill deficits among adolescents and their families (Mehlum et al., 2014). Treatment includes 2 hours of multi-family group sessions and 1 hour a week of individual sessions. Individual sessions focus on skill application to real-life situations. The four skill areas of focus in DBT-A are described in Table 11.2. Telephone consultations are included between sessions to reinforce therapeutic goals (Flaherty, 2018).

Table 11.2 SKILLS TRAINING

Module	Description
Core mindfulness	To diminish identity confusion and self-dysregulation, including teaching mindfulness skills to enhance emotional control
Interpersonal effectiveness	To enable interpersonal problem-solving through assertiveness training and for the adolescent to be mindful of goals in these situations
Distress tolerance	Teaching acceptance and tolerance of painful situations with self-soothing and distraction
Emotion regulation skills	Identification of emotions
	Reduction of emotional vulnerability
	Increase positive events

SOURCE: Adapted from Flaherty et al. (2018).

DBT has been categorized in the *Journal of Clinical Child and Adolescent Psychology* Evidence Base Update as a *well-established* intervention for reducing deliberate self-harm (a composite measure of nonsuicidal and suicidal self-injury) and suicide ideation in youths in two trials and as *probably efficacious* for reducing NSSI and suicide attempts (i.e., Mehlum et al., 2014, 2016; Glenn Esposito et al., 2019). The journal uses a five-level ranking system (Southam-Gerow & Prinstein, 2014), adapted from the APA Division 12 Task Force on the Promotion and Dissemination of Psychological Procedures to evaluate intervention efficacy (Chambless et al., 1998). After this evidence-based update, the 3-year follow-up of Melhum and colleagues' study was published (Mehlum et al., 2019). No between-group differences at the 3-year follow-up emerged between DBT-A and treatment as usual on suicidal ideation, hopelessness, depressive symptoms, and borderline personality symptoms. However, adolescents who received DBT did report reduced self-harm behavior compared with those receiving treatment as usual. The overall conclusion was that DBT-A was more effective than treatment as usual for NSSI.

A critique of DBT is that it may be more intense than some adolescents and their families need, considering its multicomponent nature and the length of treatment (although one trial was shortened to 19 weeks; Clarke et al., 2019). Another critique is that the intensive nature of the treatment might tie up youths' time, and so they may not be as available for sports, recreation, socializing, or other activities that might also help them feel better (Asarnow et al., 2019). Further, DBT might be expensive for an agency or treatment facility to adopt. DBT requires mandatory and costly training of its clinicians and involves considerable staffing to deliver (an individual therapist, a group skills trainer, and a consultant team).

The research has begun to consider the characteristics of adolescents and their families to determine whether certain factors are associated with better outcomes. For example, DBT has been shown to be more effective than supportive therapy for Latino families and among adolescents and parents who struggled with emotion dysregulation at baseline (McCauley et al., 2019). Stepped care approaches that match treatment intensity to level of risk may prove helpful for identifying the most cost-effective treatment delivery strategies (Clarke et al., 2019), saving the most expensive or least accessible models for adolescents and their families who are most in need (Kothgassner et al., 2020). Computer applications are also available for monitoring and deterring self-harm (Witt et al., 2017).

At this point in the research, there are few interventions besides DBT that have been evaluated in more than one trial, although other promising treatments exist (e.g., Glenn et al., 2019). Many youths with NSSI or suicidality receive medication, and polypharmacy is common. However, there is a lack of research on pharmacotherapy, most likely because of the variation in comorbid conditions presenting with NSSI (Asarnow & Mehlum, 2019). Additionally, because of the increase in self-injurious thoughts and behaviors among preadolescents, interventions that are inclusive of this age group should be further investigated (Clarke et al., 2019).

Finally, working with youths who are self-harming and suicidal can be stressful for practitioners, who may experience secondary trauma. Awareness of signs and symptoms of trauma and burnout and the importance of self-care are critical for clinicians to ensure they can provide optimal services to youths and their families (Asarnow & Mehlum, 2019; SAMHSA, 2014).

PRETREATMENT: ORIENTATION AND COMMITMENT TO DBT-A TREATMENT

The social worker met with Sara and her father in an outpatient treatment clinic following discharge from the inpatient facility to assess their commitment to engaging in the comprehensive DBT-A treatment model. The social worker explained Sara's diagnosis, the reasons that Sara could benefit from DBT-A, and the structure of this treatment and commitment timeline. The social worker also explained that the DBT multi-family skills group is not a family therapy group because it specifically focuses on learning adaptive strategies in five modules: mindfulness (being present in the moment and understanding signs of unregulated emotions), distress tolerance (recognizing urges to cope in ineffective ways such as cutting), emotion regulation (coping with difficult situations by building strategies to decrease emotional extremes), interpersonal effectiveness (learning to interact more effectively with others), and walking the middle path (learning how to validate, compromise, and negotiate between parents and adolescents). The social worker also shared information about antidepressant medication and how it could be useful in combination with DBT-A treatment. Sara expressed motivation to try a medication to improve her mood and anxiety symptoms, but her father was less eager. However, he agreed to meet with a psychiatrist to learn more about medication options.

The social worker informed Sara and her father that DBT-A is an intensive, highly structured program that was originally designed for adults but has been specifically adapted for adolescents with extreme emotional instability or dysregulation, including self-harm and suicidal ideation. The social worker also explained, "The 'D' in DBT means 'dialectical' because the therapy strives to help people deal with two things that might seem contradictory: acceptance of feelings and learning to use thoughts to change how we feel." The goal of DBT-A was described as a treatment to teach adolescents techniques to help them understand their emotions and to give them skills and strategies to manage those emotions and change behaviors in ways that will make their lives worth living. She also explained that there are central dialectical dilemmas, or behavioral problems, experienced by adolescents and their families that occur, causing them to shift to different extremes to regulate emotional states. The treatment targets that Sara will learn about in her individual therapy sessions will help her decrease her maladaptive behaviors that develop from these dilemmas.

Sara and her father learned the treatment structure of DBT-A. Sara's social worker shared, "To participate in this treatment, Sara would have to commit to meeting with me once weekly, and both Sara and her father would need to attend a weekly multi-family skills group where they will learn DBT skills with other families." Sara and her father were informed by the social worker that family members are considered partners in treatment, working out a plan together regarding how best to respond to the adolescent engaging in self-harm behaviors. The social worker explained to Sara's father that this treatment can be helpful in providing parents with psychoeducation around empathy and validation and nonjudgmental communication strategies that help parents remain emotionally connected to their child after a dramatic change in the child's behavior (i.e., sudden disclosure of self-harm). They were also informed that the social worker would be on a DBT consultation team, which is a group of providers who meet every week to help one another manage the high stress and burnout of treating clients engaged in high-risk behaviors. If Sara and her father agreed to medication, they would also need to attend medication management sessions where frequency would be determined by the psychiatrist.

After laying out the components of DBT-A treatment, the social worker said, "I'm interested in what you are both thinking after hearing Sara's treatment plan. Do think you can commit to coming to treatment every week, attending multi-family skills group every week, and attending psychiatry appointments if there is an agreed-on plan to start medication?" Sara's father stated, "This sounds like it could be really helpful for my daughter, but it's a lot. I'm worried about making it to group since I work late every day and we really need the money." The therapist validated Sara's father by stating, "Many parents in the group have had similar difficulties with meeting the demands of this program." She also reminded him that the commitment would be a fixed amount of time (around 6 months) if they are able to participate consistently, and they problem-solved ways other parents have been able to make it work, such as providing Sara's father with a letter to excuse him from work for the time he will spend commuting and attending the group. The therapist also pointed out the severity of Sara's self-harm behaviors as a way to demonstrate the importance of addressing high-risk behaviors before they get worse. Sara's father agreed to speak with his boss. Sara had similar concerns with commitment given that she participates in after-school activities, and the therapist attended to this by validating her concerns (acceptance) and helping her to problem-solve (change) around her schedule.

SAFETY PLANNING

Because of the extent of Sara's self-harming behaviors and concern for ongoing risk concerns, the social worker collaboratively developed a plan for safety with Sara during their first session. While the Stanley and Brown (2012) Safety Planning Intervention is evidence-based for suicide prevention and not NSSI, the social worker used that framework to guide the creation of a written document with Sara to help keep her safe. They collaboratively determined a specific set of coping strategies and supports Sara could contact when self-harm thoughts emerge. The first step of the safety plan involves identifying triggers and warning signs that often occur before self-harming incidences. After, Sara and her social worker brainstormed a predetermined set of coping skills that she would commit to trying before acting on any self-harm urges. Sara stated, "I find it really helpful to listen to music when I have a trauma flashback or get into an argument with my dad. I also like to take a long walk outside or call my best friend, Katherine." The social worker took a collaborative approach to build rapport with Sara and assist with problem-solving barriers together that may develop when she uses her safety plan. The social worker explained, "Those are great strategies to distract you when you are upset. What type of music do you find most helpful to listen to during these times?" To decrease Sara's dysregulation during these moments, the social worker encouraged her to listen to upbeat, cheerful lyrics and suggested that she create a favorite music list of specific songs and artists that she can automatically direct herself to once she recognizes that she is upset. The social worker and Sara completed all steps of the Safety Plan and then invited Sara's father to join the end of the session to review the plan, which Sara consented to. The social worker explained to Sara's father that with Sara's permission, it would be helpful to remind Sara to try her safety plan when he notices that she is having a difficult time keeping herself safe. He was also shown the list of emergency contact numbers on her Safety Plan, which he and Sara can contact if they become concerned about her safety.

The social worker also engaged Sara's father separately in a means-restriction intervention to help him brainstorm items in their apartment that Sara may have access to for engaging in self-harm behaviors. The social worker recommended that Sara's father go through the home and look for objects that she has previously used such as razorblades, knives, and cigarette lighters. He was also encouraged to go around the home to look for anything else that may be sharp or easily accessible to Sara to harm herself. The social worker suggested, "You can either throw away these items or lock them in a place that Sara cannot easily access, such as a high kitchen cupboard or high closet shelf." She further explained, "The less access Sara has to these harmful objects, the more she is able to attempt to use helpful coping strategies instead. It is important that you search through the entire apartment, but I recommend that you ask Sara for permission before going through her room. When Sara is regulated, you can ask her to do this together." It was also recommended that Sara's father buy a lockbox, which the social worker also recognized could be an expensive investment. Lastly, she explained to Sara's father, "I understand that this may seem like Sara is being punished. As Sara becomes able to start using safer coping strategies, we can gradually allow her to shower with a razorblade without permission and return kitchen knives to the kitchen countertop. Right now, it is very important that we keep her safe in her home so that she does not have to return to the hospital." Sara's father responded, "Thank you for these suggestions. I want to keep my daughter safe. I am going home now and will plan to go through our apartment tonight." The social worker asked, "Would it be okay if I call you later to check in to see what you were able to do? I can also help you problem-solve if there are any challenges that you come across when I call." He replied, "Sure. That would be fine."

Developing a DBT Target Hierarchy

Sara's individual sessions with the social worker started the following week. Sara was informed that the structure and focus of sessions would be determined based on a target hierarchy (see Figure 11.1). The therapist shared, "Adolescents who receive DBT-A typically have multiple problems that require treatment. DBT-A uses a hierarchy of treatment targets to help the therapist determine in which order the problems should be addressed." The social worker explained that the target 1 behaviors are called "life-interfering behaviors," behaviors that could lead to the client's death. The social worker asked Sara if she engages in any behaviors in target 1. Sara replied, "Yes, I cut myself and sometimes burn my skin with a cigarette lighter." Target 2 behaviors, called "therapy-interfering behaviors," were addressed next, which included examples such as coming late to sessions, cancelling last minute, or not showing up at all, and not participating or collaborating in treatment sessions. The social worker informed Sara that therapist-interfering behaviors can also be addressed in target 2 and gave examples, such as if Sara feels invalidated or

Figure 11.1 Sara's target hierarchy.

not heard by the social worker, the social worker arrives to Sara's session late or does not show at all, or the social worker seems preoccupied or inattentive in sessions. Finally, target 3 was described as "quality-of-life behaviors," which are any other behaviors that interfere with Sara's functioning and impair her ability to achieve a reasonable quality of life, such as psychosocial stressors, interpersonal conflicts, and mood and anxiety symptoms. The social worker asked Sara to brainstorm behaviors that could be helpful to address within this target, and Sara stated, "Arguments with my dad, not wanting to go to school, my PTSD symptoms, and I guess conflicts with friends." The therapist praised Sara for identifying appropriate behaviors for this target and explained, "It is really important that we focus on your trauma. However, we will first need to focus on decreasing your life-interfering behaviors so that you have the skills to help yourself regulate when we begin processing what has happened to you." Trauma is addressed in DBT-A treatment after clients master stabilization and are able to move out of DBT-A stage 1.

Sara was informed that there are four stages of treatment in DBT-A. She explained, "Sara, right now you are in stage 1, which is focused on getting be-havioral control and stopping life-threatening behaviors by replacing them with adaptive skills. In stage 2, we will begin to process your past trauma along with maladaptive thoughts and behaviors associated with this. Stage 3 is aimed at solving problems of everyday living or working toward a life that is worth living, and stage 4 is focused on building a capacity for joy." While discussing target be-havior hierarchies and the stages of DBT-A, Sara was asked, "What are your life-worth-living goals? In other words, what are your goals that keep you motivated to live a meaningful life?" with the purpose of assessing her level of commitment in doing the work in treatment while also determining her level of safety and pro-tective factors. Sara stated, "I do want to get better because I want to be a marine biologist, and I don't want my brother or dad to worry about me anymore. I also want to live to be able to buy my dad a house one day because he has worked so hard for our family and cares a lot about me."

DBT-A: DIARY CARD

In Sara's second individual session, the social worker introduced the DBT-A diary card, a strategy to track daily behavioral urges, levels of emotions, and any skills Sara used during the week (see Figure 11.2). Sara was provided with a blank diary card and informed that she is to complete it daily and must bring it completed to session each week. The social worker explained, "The primary aim of the diary card is to in-crease your awareness of vulnerable urges and emotions. It is also used as a tool each week in treatment to identify behavior patterns and triggers that occur in your life." The therapist went through each section of the diary card, editing it to add specific behavioral targets that would be helpful for Sara to focus on. The following week, the social worker started the session by praising Sara and asking for her to help set the agenda by stating, "Thank you for completing your diary card this week. You did a nice job filling out all the sections. Now, what do you notice about your diary card?" The social worker then had Sara identify target 1, 2, and 3 behaviors to address in the session.

Dialectical Behavior Therapy Adolescent Diary Card	First Name			Filled out in session? Y/ N		How often did you fill out this section?___Daily ___ 2-3x ___ Once								Date started		

(Diary card form — columns: Day, Self Harm (Urge 0-5, Actions Yes/No), Suicidal (Thoughts 0-5, Actions Yes/No), Meds (Taken as Prescribed? Yes/No), School (Cut class/school Yes/No), Risky/Sex, Other; Emotions (Anger 0-5, Fear 0-5, Happy 0-5, Anxious 0-5, Sad 0-5, Shame 0-5, Lying Yes/No, Skills 0-7); Notes)

USED SKILLS
0=Not thought about or used
1=Thought about, not used, didn't want to
2=Thought about, not used, wanted to
3=Tried but couldn't use them

4= Tried, could do them but they didn't help
5= Tried, could use them, helped
6= Didn't try, used them, didn't help
7= Didn't try, used them, helped

Rating Scale for Emotions and Urges:
0=Not at all 1=A bit 2=Somewhat 3=Rather Strong 4=Very Strong 5=Extremely Strong
Urge to harm self: ____   Urge to quit therapy: ____   Misery Index: ____

Instructions: Circle the days you worked on each skill

(Skills list with days Mon–Sun, grouped by Core Mindfulness, Interpersonal Effectiveness, Distress Tolerance, Walking the Middle Path)

1. Wise mind
2. Observe (Just notice what's going on inside)
3. Describe (Put words on the experience)
4. Participate (Enter into the experience)
5. Don't Judge (Non-judgemental stance)
6. Stay Focused (One mindfully, in-the-moment)
7. Do what works (Effectiveness)
12. Identifying and labeling emotions
13. PLEASE (Reduce vulnerability to emotion mind)
14. MASTER (Building mastery, feeling effective)
15. Engaging in pleasant activities
16. Working toward long-term goals
17. Building structure // time, work, play
22. Acting opposite to current emotion

8. DEAR MAN (Getting what you want)
9. GIVE (Improving the relationship)
10. FAST (Feeling effective & keeping your self-respect)
11. Cheerleading statements for worry thoughts
18. ACCEPTS (Distract)
19. Self-soothe (5 senses)
20. Pros and cons
21. Radical Acceptance
23. Positive reinforcement
24. Validate self
25. Validate someone else
26. Think dialectically (non black and white)
27. Act dialectically (walk the middle path)

Miller, Rathus, & Linehan, 2004

Figure 11.2 Dialectical behavior therapy for adolescents diary card.
Retrieved from https://www.signnow.com/jsfiller-desk18/?requestHash=9ad7b3e107fb
e25a59c2013bced00da286fae73307a0ef8a14e8cdd6df88a7a1&et=l2f&projectId=555830
726#d8d8aade95087c34cebd37f13c7d6cd4 on October 9, 2020.

BEHAVIOR CHAIN ANALYSIS

In this session, Sara endorsed cutting herself with a kitchen knife on her thigh on one occasion over the past week. She rated her urge at a "5" and denied suicidal intent. Sara and her social worker identified that this was a target 1 behavior to focus on in the session. Sara also indicated that she cut class one day and had very high anxiety every day. Sara and her therapist added these to the agenda as target 3 behaviors. The therapist introduced a behavior chain analysis, a technique designed to help someone understand the function of a particular behavior (see Figure 11.3; Rizvi & Ritschel, 2014). With help from the social worker, Sara was led through a process of discovering all the links in the chain that ultimately resulted in the problem behavior of cutting. Sara was informed that behavior chain analysis could be used for problem

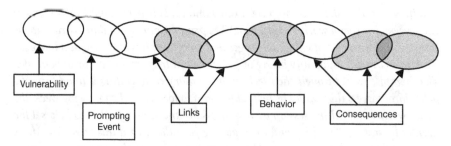

Figure 11.3 Behavior chain analysis.
Retrieved from https://spaciousmindcounselling.com/how-can-dbt-be-useful-over-the-
holidays/behavior-chain-analysis-practicing-wisdom-blog/ on October 9, 2020.

behaviors in any of the three target groups. The behavior chain analysis is divided into five parts: vulnerability factors, prompting event, links, problem behavior, and consequences. Her social worker explained the purpose: "Sara, the goal of this exercise is to increase your awareness of all of the factors that may put you at risk for the problem behavior to occur as well as to identify skills you can use early on to prevent the behavior from occurring in the future. Today, we are going to use this exercise to better understand why you cut yourself."

The social worker filled out the chain while Sara shared what happened, providing her with a helpful visual and a tool that she can look back on in the future to remind her of skills that she can use the next time a similar problem behavior occurs. Sara stated, "I cut myself after I got into an argument with my dad. My dad got a call from the assistant principal asking why I was absent yesterday. He was really disappointed. I just couldn't get myself out of bed to go to school yesterday. He got so mad at me, and I felt like I needed to punish myself." Her social worker responded with validation, "I imagine that it must have been really hard to hear dad share his disappointment on top of struggling with getting yourself out of bed to go to school." Sara stated, "It really was." Her social worker explained the next step in the behavior chain analysis process. "To understand what happened, let's go through the behavior and what occurred before and afterward so that you have a better idea about how to help yourself the next time you have an urge to hurt yourself."

They identified vulnerability factors that may have influenced the problem behavior. Sara mentioned, "I only slept 3 hours the night before, so it was already really hard to get out of bed, and then I barely ate the whole day because I just didn't feel like it and I didn't go to school." Together they also identified that the prompting event that started her on the chain to her problem behavior was when her father got upset that she didn't go to school and stated his disappointment.

The social worker continued, "Sara, I'm wondering how you felt when your dad stated that he was disappointed with you." Sara shared, "I felt a lot of shame. He didn't understand how hard it was to get up that day." The social worker responded, "You felt shame, and it sounds like you were also thinking about how dad doesn't understand what you were going through when you tried to get out of bed but couldn't." Sara stated, "Yes, exactly." Together they went through the links leading up to the problem behavior and Sara labeled her emotions and thoughts for each section of the chain, another important step toward helping Sara increase her awareness of the problem behavior. Sara stated, "As I was cutting myself, I felt so angry. I couldn't stop thinking about how I keep messing up and that I needed to punish myself. I couldn't just sit with that feeling."

Sara's social worker made sure that she validated Sara's emotions and thoughts while leading her through the chain and before switching to finding solutions to the problem behavior. Validating a client's experience can help them feel more motivated to make helpful changes. The social worker stated, "It sounds like you were in a lot of pain yesterday. Can you tell me more about how you think you are messing up?" Sara continued, "I used to be so good at everything, and now it's even harder for me to get out of bed in the morning. My dad reminds me a lot about how lucky I am to get a good education because he didn't have the same opportunities as I do now when he was growing up in the Dominican Republic." The social worker responded, "I want to recognize that it's understandable that you feel this way and how invalidating it must feel that dad is having a hard time understanding the distress you are in. You have been through a lot of pain. It sounds like this is something we could work on together: tolerating your distress when you experience anger toward yourself as well as communicating effectively with dad. The strategies that you will learn with me and in the DBT multi-family skills group will help you manage your distress so that it doesn't get worse. I think there are many helpful communication skills that you and dad can benefit from, so I am glad he is attending multi-family skills group sessions with you. Before we get to problem-solving though, let's continue to understand what happened."

They then went through the consequences of Sara's cutting behavior. Sara shared, "I felt shame yesterday after I cut. I also now have to deal with cleaning my wound, and there is definitely going to be a scar, which will constantly remind me of what I did. I have to work hard at hiding my cuts. And I've had to tell a few friends that I do this because they've seen the cuts a few times when I wasn't being careful about hiding them. I hate having to do that. I know my dad is really worried about me too. I don't want to upset him anymore." The social worker helped Sara identify whether the consequences were short or long term and assessed if they were significant enough to encourage Sara to remain committed to stopping this problem behavior. The social worker asked, "Sara, I'm noticing that there are several consequences that happen when you cut yourself. I'm wondering if you could commit to engaging in a skill before acting on your urge to self-harm." Sara agreed, and together they brainstormed where in the chain Sara could have used DBT skills to avoid cutting herself. Sara remembered a new skill that she learned in the DBT multi-family skills group the other day called "ACCEPTS," a distress tolerance skill that adolescents can use to distract themselves when they are in heightened emotional states. Each letter in the acronym stands for a different skill. For example, the "A" in "ACCEPTS" is "activities." Sara shared, "After speaking with my dad and noticing that I was feeling shame toward myself, I could have distracted my emotions by watching a funny YouTube clip or by taking a really cold shower."

Sara and her therapist went through each part of the chain again, starting with vulnerability factors, and brainstormed DBT skills that Sara could use the next time a similar self-harm urge occurred. Her social worker also encouraged her to use skills earlier in the chain, such as improving her sleep hygiene to avoid vulnerability factors. Over time, as Sara went through the DBT modules in her skills group, she learned effective interpersonal skills to help her maintain her self-respect and get what she needs, such as telling her dad when she is having a challenging time rather than cutting school and suffering the consequences. She also reminded Sara, "A good time for you to reach out for phone coaching is if you are not successful with using your skills either because you don't know which skill to use or because the skill isn't working. Where in the chain do you think you could have reached out for phone coaching?" Sara responded, "Right before I started to cut, like maybe when the thought entered my mind that I wanted to harm myself?" Sara's social worker agreed and assessed whether Sara could commit to reaching out to her social worker *for phone coaching the next time she has an urge to cut herself. Her social worker also explained, "You can also reach out if you tried using skills and they weren't effective, such as when you were trying to get out of bed and go to school. That's another great opportunity for you to call me for phone coaching." Sara and her social worker spent the entire session going through the behavior chain analysis of this problem behavior. While Sara had target 2 and 3 behaviors to discuss in the session, they only were able to get to target 1. Sara stated, "I still want to talk about an argument that I had with my friend. It made me feel really anxious." However, because there was not enough time, the social worker reminded her, "We always need to get through the life-interfering behaviors before we can move through the agenda we set. We will definitely get to that next week if you are able to keep yourself safe and do not have any target 1 behaviors that we need to go over first." Sara responded, "Okay. I'm going to try to use skills this week so that we can get to the other things I want to talk about."*

DBT-A: STAGE 2 AND BEYOND

Sara consistently engaged in individual sessions with her social worker following this model, which helped Sara build increased awareness of her emotions and effective skill use throughout each week. She used behavior chain analysis to address target behaviors whenever indicated, and together they identified ways Sara could generalize skill use in her everyday life. Her social worker also worked with Sara throughout treatment on her commitment to use skills and her ability to remain in therapy. For example, a few sessions into treatment, Sara stated, "I'm done with this. I don't think this is working. DBT is too much work." Her social worker responded, "This is a lot of work Sara, and I hear that you don't want to continue with treatment." She then proceeded to use DBT commitment strategies such as playing the devil's advocate to move Sara further toward the commitment side of this dialectical dilemma. Her social worker responded, "I'm going to play devil's advocate. So if you don't go to treatment anymore, you're more likely to continue to struggle with cutting yourself because you haven't yet learned strategies that you can use to replace this behavior, which will cause your dad and your friends to worry about you more, and there is a chance that if you don't stop hurting yourself, you'll have to return to the hospital so that you can be safe." Being offered this alternative helped Sara see the value of remaining in treatment as opposed to quitting right now.

Sara and her father actively participated in the multi-family skills group weekly for 6 months, and Sara and her father agreed to start medication to treat her depression. By the time she graduated from the multi-family skills group, Sara had stopped harming herself for 2 months, developed a core set of distress tolerance skills to replace cutting herself when she became highly dysregulated, improved her relationship with her father through effectively expressing her needs, and started to regulate her emotional patterns through attending to her activities of daily living.

Because of this progress, Sara was able to enter stage 2 of DBT-A treatment with her social worker. In stage 2 of DBT-A treatment, Sara began to process her past trauma and develop strategies to decrease avoidance of painful emotions and memories associated with the sexual assault. DBT skills were reviewed in every session so that Sara could continue to generalize them in her daily life, especially when she experienced

PTSD symptoms. Sara was also given the option to join a graduate skills group, which was run by a therapist at the clinic just for adolescents who had completed multi-family skills group and would like to continue to get support from peers through reviewing DBT skills and problem-solving target behaviors. Sara's social worker continued to follow the DBT-A model for treatment until Sara graduated from high school and went away to college, a natural break where both Sara and her social worker agreed that Sara was ready to end DBT-A treatment. Sara remained in therapy in college to work on emerging adulthood goals, including maintaining a healthy sexual relationship with her new college boyfriend and academic and career goals.

SUMMARY

This chapter discusses both NSSI and suicidal thoughts and behavior because of their inter-relationship and their high rates of occurrence in adolescents.

Suicide is the second leading cause of death among 15- to 29-year-olds globally. Depression and other comorbid conditions are often present. Risk factors have been identified, such as low SES, early adversity, bullying, and family conflict, as well as a sense of hopelessness. A structured safety planning intervention can be undertaken for cases that do not require hospitalization. Social workers are also urged to discuss firearm safety with parents. DBT-A has been developed to treat adolescents and their families who deal with serious dysregulation, but a stepped-care approach needs research so that less intensive programs are available for those who do not require or cannot access DBT.

REFERENCES

Adrian, M., McCauley, E., Berk, M. S., Asarnow, J. R., Korslund, K., Avina, C., Gallop, R., & Linehan, M. M. (2019). Predictors and moderators of recurring self-harm in adolescents participating in a comparative treatment trial of psychological interventions. *Journal of Child Psychology and Psychiatry, 60,* 1123–1132. doi:10.1111/jcpp.13099

Arbuthnott, A. E., Lewis, S. P. (2015). Parents of youth who self-injure: A review of the literature and implications for mental health professionals. *Child and Adolescent Psychiatry and Mental Health, 9,* 35. https://doi.org/10.1186/s13034-015-0066-3

Asarnow, J. R., & Mehlum, L. (2019). Practitioner review: Treatment for suicidal and self-harming adolescents—advances in suicide prevention care. *Journal of Child Psychology and Psychiatry, 60*(10), 1046–1054. doi:10.1111/jcpp.13130

Bettis, A. H., Donise, K. R., MacPherson, H. A., Bagatelas, P., & Wolff, J. C. (2020). Safety planning intervention for adolescents: Provider attitudes and response to training in the emergency services setting. *Psychiatric Services (Washington, D.C.), 71*(11), 1136–1142. https://doi.org/10.1176/appi.ps.201900563

Castellví, P., Miranda-Mendizábal, A., Alayo, I., Parés-Badell, O., Almenara, J., Alonso, I., Blasco, M. J., Cebrià, A., Gabilondo, A., Gili, M., Lagares, C., Piqueras, J. A., Roca, M., Rodríguez-Marín, J., Rodríguez-Jimenez, T., Soto-Sanz, V., & Alonso, J. (2020). Assessing the relationship between school failure and suicidal behavior in adolescents and young adults: A systematic review and meta-analysis of longitudinal studies. *School Mental Health*, 12(3), 429–441. https://doi.org/10.1007/s12 310-020-09363-0

Chambless, D. L., Baker, M. J., Baucom, D. H., Beutler, L. E., Calhoun, K. S., Crits-Christoph, P., Daiuto, A., DeRubeis, R., Detweiler, J., Haaga, D., Johnson, S., McCurry, S., Mueser, K., Pope, K., Sanderson, W., Shoham, V., Stickle, T., Williams, D., & Woody, S. R. (1998). Update on empirically validated therapies, II. *Clinical Psychologist*, 51(1), 3–16.

Clarke, S., Allerhand, L., A., & Berk, M., S. (2019). Recent advances in understanding and managing self-harm in adolescents. *F1000 Research*, 8, F1000 Faculty Rev-1794. https://doi.org/10.12688/f1000research.19868.1

Dazzi, T., Gribble, R., Wessely, S., & Fear, N. T. (2014). Does asking about suicide and related behaviours induce suicidal ideation? What is the evidence? *Psychological Medicine*, 44(16), 3361-3363.

Finkelhor, D., Shattuck, A., Turner, H. A., Hamby, S. L. (2014). The lifetime prevalence of child sexual abuse and sexual assault assessed in late adolescence. *Journal of Adolescent Health, 55*, 329–333. doi:10.1016/j.jadohealth.2013.12.026

Flaherty, H. B. (2018). Treating adolescent nonsuicidal self-injury: A review of psychosocial interventions to guide clinical practice. *Child and Adolescent Social Work Journal, 35*(1), 85–95. doi:10.1007/s10560-017-0505-5

Gillies, D., Christou, M. A., Dixon, A. C., Featherston, O. J., Rapti, I., Garcia-Anguita, A., Villasis-Keever, M., Reebye, P., Christou, E., Al Kabir, N., & Christou, P. A. (2018). Prevalence and characteristics of self-harm in adolescents: Meta-analyses of community-based studies 1990–2015. *Journal of the American Academy of Child & Adolescent Psychiatry, 57*(10), 733–741. doi:10.1016/j.jaac.2018.06.018

Glendenning, A. C., Marchant, A., Montgomery, P., Stewart, A., Wood, S., Lloyd, K., & Hawton, K. (2018). Self-harm, suicidal behaviours, and cyberbullying in children and young people: Systematic review. *Journal of Medical Internet Research*, 20(4). doi:10.2196/jmir.9044

Glenn, C. R., Esposito, E. C., Porter, A. C., & Robinson, D. J. (2019). Evidence-base update of psychosocial treatments for self-injurious thoughts and behaviors in youth. *Journal of Clinical Child and Adolescent Psychology*, 48(3), 357–392.

Grandclerc, S., De Labrouhe, D., Spodenkiewicz, M., Lachal, J., & Moro, M. R. (2016). Relations between nonsuicidal self-injury and suicidal behavior in adolescence: A systematic review. *PLoS One*, 11(4), e0153760. doi:10.1371/journal. pone.0153760

Groschwitz, R., & Plener, P. (2012). The neurobiology of non-suicidal self-injury (NSSI): A review. *Suicidology Online, 2012*(3), 24–32.

Harris, I. M., Beese, S., & Moore, D. (2019). Predicting repeated self-harm or suicide in adolescents and young adults using risk assessment scales/tools: A systematic review protocol. *Systematic Reviews*, 8(1), 87. https://doi.org/10.1186/s13643-019-1007-7Hawton, K., Saunders, K., Topiwala, A., & Haw, C. (2013) Psychiatric disorders in patients presenting to hospital following self-harm: A systematic review. *Journal of Affective Disorders, 151*(3):821–830. doi:10.1016/j.jad.2013.08.020. Epub 2013 Sep 7. PMID: 24091302.

Heron M. (2019). Deaths: Leading causes for 2017. *National Vital Statistics Reports*, 68(6). Hyattsville, MD: National Center for Health Statistics.

In-Albon, T., Ruf, C., & Schmid, M. (2013). Proposed diagnostic criteria for the DSM-5 of nonsuicidal self-injury in female adolescents: Diagnostic and clinical correlates. *Psychiatry Journal, 2013*, 159208. doi:10.1155/2013/159208

International Society for the Study of Self-Injury. (2018, May). What is self-injury? Retrieved from: https://itriples.org/about-self-injury/what-is-self-injury

Itzhaky, L., & Stanley, B. (2022). The Safety Planning Intervention for Children (C-SPI): Rationale and Case Illustration. *Cognitive and Behavioral Practice.* Online in press, https://doi.org/10.1016/j.cbpra.2022.10.001

Kearns, J. C., Coppersmith, D. D. L., Santee, A. C., Insel, C., Pigeon, W. R., & Glenn, C. R. (2020). Sleep problems and suicide risk in youth: A systematic review, developmental framework, and implications for hospital treatment. *General Hospital Psychiatry, 63*, 141–151. https://doi.org/10.1016/j.genhosppsych.2018.09.011

King, C. A., Gipson, P. Y., Horwitz, A. G., & Opperman, K. J. (2015). Teen options for change: An intervention for young emergency patients who screen positive for suicide risk. *Psychiatric Services, 66*(1), 97–100. https://doi.org/10.1176/appi.ps.201300347

Kothgassner, O. D., Robinson, K., Goreis, A., Ougrin, D., & Plener, P. L. (2020). Does treatment method matter? A meta-analysis of the past 20 years of research on therapeutic interventions for self-harm and suicidal ideation in adolescents. *Borderline Personality Disorder and Emotion Dysregulation, 7*(1), 1–16. doi:10.1186/s40479-020-00123-9

Linehan, M. (1993). *Cognitive behavioral treatment of borderline personality disorder.* New York: Guilford Press.

Liu, R. T., Sheehan, A. E., Walsh, R. F. L., Sanzari, C. M., Cheek, S. M., & Hernandez, E. M. (2019). Prevalence and correlates of non-suicidal self-injury among lesbian, gay, bisexual, and transgender individuals: A systematic review and meta-analysis. *Clinical Psychology Review, 74*, 101783. doi:10.1016/j.cpr.2019.101783

Marchant, A., Hawton, K., Stewart, A., Montgomery, P., Singaravelu, V., Lloyd, K., Purdy, N., Daine, K., & John, A. (2017). A systematic review of the relationship between internet use, self-harm and suicidal behaviour in young people: The good, the bad and the unknown. *Plos One, 13*(3). doi:10.1371/journal.pone.0193937

Marraccini, M. E., & Brier, Z. M. F. (2017). School connectedness and suicidal thoughts and behaviors: A systematic meta-analysis. *School Psychology Quarterly, 32*(1), 5–21. https://doi.org/10.1037/spq0000192

Journal of Adolescent Health, 49(2), 115–123. doi:10.1016/j.jadohealth.2011.02.005

Mehlum, L., Ramberg, M., Tørmoen, A. J., Haga, E., Diep, L. M., Stanley, B. H., Miller, A. L., Sund, A. M., & Grøholt, B. (2016). Dialectical behavior therapy compared with enhanced usual care for adolescents with repeated suicidal and self-harming behavior: Outcomes over a one-year follow-up. *Journal of the American Academy of Child and Adolescent Psychiatry, 55*(4), 295–300. doi:10.1016/j.jaac.2016.01.005

Mehlum, L., Tørmoen, A. J., Ramberg, M., Haga, E., Diep, L. M., Laberg, S., Larsson, B. S., Stanley, B. H., Miller, A. L., Sund, A. M., & Grøholt, B. (2014). Dialectical behavior therapy for adolescents with repeated suicidal and self-harming behavior: A randomized trial. *Journal of the American Academy of Child & Adolescent Psychiatry, 53*, 1082–1091.

Moller, C. I., Davey, C. G., Badcock, P. B., Wrobel, A. L., Cao, A., Murrihy, S., Sharmin, S., & Cotton, S. M. (2022). Correlates of suicidality in young people with depressive disorders: A systematic review. *Australian & New Zealand Journal of Psychiatry*, 000486742210864. https://doi.org/10.1177/00048674221086498

Morken, I. S., Dahlgren, A., Lunde, I., & Toven, S. (2019). The effects of interventions preventing self-harm and suicide in children and adolescents: An overview of systematic reviews. *F1000Research*, *8*, 890. https://doi.org/10.12688/f1000resea rch.19506.2

Newman, C. F. (2009). Cognitive therapy for nonsuicidal self-injury. In M. K. Nock (Ed.), *Understanding nonsuicidal self-injury: Origins, assessment, and treatment* (pp. 201–219). Washington, DC: American Psychological Association.

Nixon, M. K., Cloutier, P. F., & Aggarwal, S. (2002). Affect regulation and addictive aspects of repetitive self- injury in hospitalized adolescents. *Journal of the American Academy of Child and Adolescent Psychiatry*, *41*, 1333–1341.

Nock, M. K., & Prinstein, M. J. (2004). A functional approach to the assessment of self-mutilative behavior. *Journal of Consulting and Clinical Psychology*, *72*(5), 885–890. doi:10.1037/0022-006x.72.5.885

Rizvi, S. L., & Ritschel, L. A. (2014). Mastering the art of chain analysis in dialectical behavior therapy. *Cognitive and Behavioral Practice*, *21*(3), 335–349.

Rizvi, S. L., Steffel, L. M., & Carson-Wong, A. (2013). An overview of dialectical behavior therapy for professional psychologists. *Professional Psychology: Research and Practice*, *44*(2), 73–80. doi:10.1037/a0029808

Robins, C. J., & Chapman, A. L. (2004). Dialectical behavior therapy: Current status, recent developments, and future directions. *Journal of Personality Disorders*, *18*(1), 73–89. doi:10.1521/pedi.18.1.73.32771

Slovak, K., Brewer, T. W., & Carlson, K. (2008). Client firearm assessment and safety counseling: The role of social workers. *Social Work*, *53*(4), 358–366

Southam-Gerow, M. A., & Prinstein, M. J. (2014). Evidence base updates: The evolution of the evaluation of psychological treatments for children and adolescents. *Journal of Clinical Child and Adolescent Psychology*, *43*(1), 1–6. doi:10.1080/15374416.2013.855128

Stanley, B., & Brown, G. K. (2012). Safety planning intervention: A brief intervention to mitigate suicide risk. *Cognitive and Behavioral Practice*, *19*(2), 256–264.

Witt, K., Spittal, M. J., Carter, G., Pirkis, J., Hetrick, S., Currier, D., Robinson, J., & Milner, A. (2017). Effectiveness of online and mobile telephone applications ('apps') for the self-management of suicidal ideation and self-harm: A systematic review and meta-analysis. *BMC Psychiatry*, *17*(1).

Witt, K., Townsend, E., Arensman, E., Gunnell, D., Hazell, P., Sailsbury, T. T., & Hawton, K. (2019). Psychosocial interventions for people who self-harm: Methodological issues involved in trials to evaluate effectiveness. Archives of Suicide Research, 1–81.

Woo, J., Wrath, A. J., & Adams, G. C. (2022). The relationship between attachment and self-injurious behaviors in the child and adolescent population: A systematic review of the literature. Archives of Suicide Research, 26(2), 406–427. doi:10.1080/13811118.2020.1804024

Eating Disorders

**DAWN EICHEN, JACQUELINE CORCORAN,
AND COURTNEY BENJAMIN WOLK ▓**

Jenny is a 16-year-old bisexual female who is currently living in a residential treatment facility. Jenny was born in a small rural town in Taiwan; her family immigrated to America when Jenny was 2 years old. Jenny is an only child and has no close relatives in the United States. She reports that her family has always been very poor and has just "scraped by." When Jenny was 12 years old, her father walked out on the family, and she hasn't seen him since. Jenny and her mother moved to a rental apartment in an impoverished urban neighborhood with a high crime rate. Jenny's mother, who speaks little English, began work as a seamstress and works 12 to 18 hours a day, 7 days a week, which leaves Jenny alone for many hours of the day. At age 15, she started hanging out with peers in her neighborhood and began smoking marijuana and drinking alcohol. She ate irregular meals and mainly consumed "junk food"—cookies, potatoes chips, fast food, and so on. Jenny gained approximately 10 pounds over the course of a few months. She began taking over-the-counter diet pills or amphetamines she obtained from her friends to try to manage her weight. On a few occasions, after binge eating, she would purge in secret. Eventually, Jenny was using substances about five to six times a week. Jenny said she was so desperate to obtain alcohol and drugs that she began engaging in sexual acts with peers in exchange for drugs or money. She eventually contracted a sexually transmitted disease. Four months ago, she was arrested for drinking when underage and prostitution. Jenny was put on probation for these crimes with a condition that she enter residential treatment to address her substance and alcohol use. Since she has been at the residential treatment program, Jenny has had only occasional contact with her mother because of her mother's work schedule and the language division between them.

OVERVIEW

Feeding and eating disorders are characterized by disturbances in a person's eating behaviors and perceptions of body weight and shape (American

Psychiatric Association, 2022). The focus of this chapter is on anorexia nervosa, bulimia nervosa, and, new to the fifth edition of the *Diagnostic and Statistical Manual of Mental Disorder* (DSM-5), binge eating disorder. *Anorexia nervosa* (AN) is characterized by self-induced restriction of energy intake resulting in significantly low body weight coupled with fears of being overweight, with two diagnostic subtypes: restricting and binge–purge types. *Bulimia nervosa* (BN) is characterized by binge eating (i.e., discrete episodes of eating large amounts of food while experiencing a sense of loss of control) and recurrent compensatory behaviors with either purging or nonpurging (e.g., fasting or overexercise) methods with self-evaluation tied to shape or body weight. *Binge eating disorder* (BED) is characterized by regular binge eating without compensatory behaviors with marked distress, occurring at least once a week for 3 months. *Avoidant/restrictive food intake disorder* is a new diagnosis in the feeding and eating disorders chapter of the DSM-5 and involves low interest in food or eating, avoidance based on the sensory characteristics of food, and concern about possible aversive consequences of eating. Avoidant/restrictive food intake disorder will not be a focus of this chapter because of the lack of research at this time (Bryant-Waugh, 2019). It is also important to note that a category of other specified feeding or eating disorder (OSFED) exists that represents presentations that have clinically significant impairments without meeting criteria for one of the "threshold" eating disorders (AN, BN, BED), and clinicians should specify why the presentation doesn't meet one of the other categories such as atypical AN, BN, or BED of low frequency or limited duration, purging disorder, or night eating syndrome. This category is important because although understudied, many patient presentations will fall into this category, particularly among children and adolescents.

Lifetime DSM-5 eating disorder prevalence estimates obtained from a community sample of 496 adolescent females by conducting annual diagnostic interviews for 8 years were: 0.8% for AN, 2.6% for BN, 3.0% for BED, 2.8% for atypical AN, 4.4% for subthreshold BN, 3.6% for subthreshold BED, and 3.4% for purging disorder (Stice et al., 2013). In total, 13.1% of females met criteria for at least one eating disorder (including OSFED) over the 8 years, with 5.2% meeting criteria for AN, BN, or BED at some point and 11.5% meeting criteria for OSFED. A study using survey data distributed to adolescents in Australia estimated the rates of any eating disorder at 22.2%, with 6.2% meeting criteria for AN, BN, or BED, while 11.2% met OSFED criteria (Mitchison et al., 2020). Lifetime prevalence for experiencing any eating disorder by age 40 is nearly 1 in 7 for males and nearly 1 in 5 for females (Ward et al. 2019).

Eating disorders cause a significant burden because they are costly, contribute to mortality and disability, and significantly affect quality of life (Erkine et al., 2016; Treasure et al., 2020; van Hoeken & Hoek, 2020). Similar patterns of comorbidity, suicidality, impairment, and distress arise among OSFED and subthreshold diagnoses (Stice et al., 2013; Swanson et al., 2011). Further, many individuals with eating disorders transition across clinical presentations (Castellini et al., 2011; Stice et al., 2013), highlighting the importance of diagnosing and effectively treating the spectrum of eating disorders.

RISK AND PROTECTIVE FACTORS

For the purposes of examining the risk and protective mechanisms for the onset of eating disorders, AN, BN, and BED will be considered together because the field has accepted a "transdiagnostic" approach that highlights the shared symptoms and overlapping risk factors (Balakar et al., 2015; Fairburn et al., 2003; Levinson et al., 2018). It is widely accepted that eating disorders have a complex etiology related to interactions among biological, psychological, and sociocultural factors (Culbert et al., 2015).

Biological

The role of genetic factors in eating disorders has been established through family, twin, and molecular genetic studies. Eating disorders are moderately to highly heritable (Bulik et al., 2022; Culbert et al., 2015; Watson et al., 2019; Yilmaz et al., 2015). Specific studies have focused on evaluating genes related to dopamine, serotonin, and brain-derived neurotrophic factor (BDNF; Balakar et al., 2015). Larger genome-wide association studies (GWAS) have begun to emerge for eating disorders, with most focusing on AN, largely owing to increased research funding in this area (Bulik et al., 2021). It is expected that as genetic research continues to advance over the next decade or so, it will continue to expand our understanding of eating disorders and possibly inform future treatment targets.

Age and pubertal status are believed to affect the genetic expression of eating disorders, particularly among females, with female risk of developing an eating disorder increasing in mid to late adolescence and mid to late puberty (Balakar et al, 2015; Culbert et al., 2015; Klump et al., 2012). Relatedly, early onset of puberty confers particular risk for the development of eating disorders in late adolescence (Baker et al., 2012; Klump, 2013). Since female reproductive hormones appear to play a role in the development of some eating disorders, this at least partially explains why adolescence is a developmental stage in which females are particularly vulnerable to developing eating disorders.

Neurobiological research in eating disorders has further highlighted the biological basis of these disorders. Much of the research has focused on reward processing and self-regulatory neurocircuitry that are related to neurotransmitters implicated in genetic studies (Balakar et al., 2015; Wierenga et al., 2014). Specific neurocognitive traits that have been investigated and implicated in the development of eating disorders include cognitive flexibility, inhibitory control, and reward/punishment sensitivity (Balakar et al., 2015; Culbert et al., 2015; Wierenga et al., 2014).

Psychological

Several psychological factors have been implicated in the development of eating disorders, namely temperament and personality traits (Lilenfeld et al., 2006;

Paganini et al., 2021). Specifically, perfectionism has been associated with the development and maintenance of eating disorders (Bardone-Cone et al., 2007; Hilbert et al., 2014; Holland et al., 2013). Some research suggests perfectionism may be stronger in certain eating disorder diagnoses like AN, but others find it serves as a risk factor across diagnoses (Balakar et al., 2015; Hilbert et al., 2014). Negative emotionality, which suggests a propensity to experience negative affect, and difficulties with emotion regulation have persistently been associated with risk of developing eating disorders and appears to be more present across diagnoses (Balakar et al., 2015; Culbert et al., 2015; Henderson et al., 2019; Lavender et al, 2015). Impulsivity, specifically negative urgency (i.e., the tendency to act impulsively while under negative emotions like distress; Whiteside & Lynam, 2001), is another personality trait identified as a risk factor for binge eating and purging behaviors (Balakar et al., 2015; Culbert et al., 2015; Fischer et al., 2008).

The co-occurrence of eating disorders with other psychiatric disorders is well established (Bahji et al., 2019; Balakar et al., 2015; Hudson et al., 2007; Swanson et al., 2011). Similarly is the link between suicidal ideation and suicidal behaviors with eating disorders (Smith et al., 2020; Swanson et al., 2011). While some consider comorbidity a risk factor for the development of eating disorders, it is more likely that shared genetic vulnerabilities and neurobiological bases are contributing to multiple psychiatric disorders.

Social

The idealization of thinness, particularly for women in Westernized cultures, is a widely agreed on risk factor for eating disorders (Keel & Forney, 2013; Stice et al., 2013; Thompson & Stice, 2001). Media exposure, including social media, may contribute to the development of eating disorders because individuals more susceptible to the internalization of the idealization of thinness are more likely to experience increased body dissatisfaction following exposure to these images (Hausenblas et al., 2013; Saul et al., 2022). Higher weight status (Larsen et al., 2015) as well as dieting (Balakar et al., 2015; Lowe & Timko, 2004) are associated with increased eating disorder behaviors. Further, children criticized by their parents or who experience weight-related teasing may be at greater risk (Balakar et al., 2015; Larsen et al., 2015). This is likely due to the connection with increased idealization of thinness. Additionally, both male and female athletes, particularly those who participate in sports that have more focus on body shape and weight (e.g., wrestling, cheerleading, gymnastics), may be at greater risk of developing eating disorders (Striegel-Moore & Cachelin, 1999; Sundgot-Borgen & Torstveit, 2004). However, despite the ubiquitousness of the thin idealization, particularly among Westernized cultures, most individuals (including those who diet or have higher weight status) do not develop eating disorders, so this is likely not sufficient to lead to the development of an eating disorder.

Demographic factors may be related to the presence of eating disorders. Although it is true that eating disorders are more prevalent among females, it is dangerous to neglect that eating disorders are still present among males and that, among certain diagnoses (e.g., BED), prevalence is more equivalent across the sexes. Further, sexual minorities have greater prevalence rates of eating disorders (AN, 1.7%; BN, 1.3%; and BED, 2.2%) compared with heterosexual cisgender adults (Kamody et al., 2020). Body dissatisfaction may be particularly increased among transgender people (Nagata et al., 2020). Significant ethnic differences have been documented for BN, with Latino adolescents reporting the highest prevalence. Additionally, trends toward ethnic minorities reporting more BED have been observed, and white adolescents tend to report more AN (Swanson et al., 2011). Unlike many other mental disorders, high socioeconomic status (SES) does not confer protection against the development of eating disorders (Balakar et al., 2015). The common belief is that females of middle and upper SES populations may be more vulnerable because of increased demands for social compliance and perfectionism. However, Lock and colleagues (2015) reported that measures of SES, including parental education, household income, and parental/surrogate marital status, were not significantly associated with any eating disorder presentation. Social workers, therefore, need to be aware that clients living in poverty may also be at risk for eating disorders and should be screened accordingly. In fact, food insecurity has been related to binge eating behaviors (Rasmusson et al., 2019).

Child maltreatment and other trauma and abuse are related to the presence of eating disorders (Caslini et al., 2016; Molendijk et al., 2017). Further, a recent review found that family-related nonabuse adverse life events were related to eating disorders and that AN may be less affected by these than BN or BED (Grogan et al., 2020). Understanding adverse life events, including history of trauma and abuse, may be important in understanding eating disorder risk.

Taken together, there are a multitude of risk factors associated with developing an eating disorder. Many individuals are exposed to several of these risk factors and do not develop an eating disorder. Thus, it cannot be denied that there is a strong biological basis related to the development of eating disorders. Although understanding this biological basis may help some individuals and families feel relief and that they are not to be blamed, others may feel hopeless to overcome their biology, or some parents may feel they are to blame because of the genetic link. It is important to ensure that patients and families understand that (1) there is not a single known factor that is both necessary and sufficient to cause eating disorders; (2) eating disorders arise from the combined effects of genes as well as one's environment and experiences, and (3) individuals inherit a vulnerability to eating disorders, not an eating disorder (Bulik et al., 2019).

ASSESSMENT

People with eating disorders tend to be underdiagnosed and undertreated. Screening for the possibility of an eating disorder should routinely be done during the assessment of adolescents in medical and mental health settings (Lock et al.,

2015) because both health (Johnston et al., 2007) and mental health professionals (Hudson et al., 2007) often overlook eating disorders. Initial brief screening may first help identify whether an eating disorder may be present, whereas more detailed assessment may help tease apart the specific eating disorder diagnosis and co-occurring conditions to help determine appropriate treatment. For example, it is recommended that all mental health clinicians ask preteens and adolescents about eating patterns and body satisfaction as well as obtaining height and weight (Lock et al., 2015). The SCOFF (Morgan et al., 2000) is a five-item brief questionnaire that can quickly be completed by patients. A positive response to any question from this brief assessment may indicate that further assessment for eating disorders is warranted. The established cutoff of two positive responses on the SCOFF resulted in 100% sensitivity for AN and BN and 87.5% specificity, suggesting that while there are some false positives, it captured all individuals with one of those diagnoses.

Assessment guidelines involve the following components (Lock et al., 2015; Mizes & Palermo, 1997; Zucker et al., 2009):

1. **Clinical interview**. As part of a clinical interview, it is important to assess general social and developmental history and family psychiatric history in addition to a thorough assessment of eating disorder symptoms and concurrent psychiatric disorders. It is important to gather current height and weight as well as a weight history including significant changes in weight. Obtaining height and weight history plotted on developmental curves from the physician could also be very helpful, especially for children and adolescents. To assess eating pathology, understanding body image concerns, eating patterns, presence of weight control behaviors including dieting, calorie counting, and exercise behaviors is needed. Additionally, specific assessment of binge eating as well as any compensatory behaviors including purging and nonpurging methods are essential. Understanding frequency and duration of all behaviors is essential. Assessment of concurrent psychiatric conditions is important, and care should be taken to ensure that the concurrent condition was present before and the symptoms are not a result of the eating disorder. For example, in AN, starvation may produce the depression, irritability, obsessiveness, and anxiety that is often present. Best practice is to treat AN symptoms first and then reassess for comorbid conditions as the client's eating disorder improves (e.g., client reestablishes a healthier body weight, exhibits decreased disordered thinking and behaviors related to eating; Lock, 2019). However, other concurrent conditions such as substance/alcohol use disorders and trauma may need specific intervention during the course of eating disorder treatment and should not be delayed.

2. **Medical evaluation.** To understand the medical impact of the eating disorder and help establish appropriate level of care for treatment it is recommended that, in addition to a routine checkup, additional labs

and medical tests are conducted to assess for problems due to significant weight loss or malnutrition and purging behaviors (e.g., amenorrhea, bone density, heart arrhythmias, electrolyte imbalance).

3. **Standardized measures** of eating disorders, body image, and related problems. See Table 12.1 for measures that are freely available.

4. **Motivation** to overcome the disorder (an important predictor of treatment) and **goals** for the future and interests outside the eating disorder. Due to the ego syntonic nature of some eating disorders, treatment motivation is commonly low. Children may only seek treatment because of parental concern. Thus, it is important to assess treatment motivation to inform treatment planning.

Considerations for Assessment of Eating Disorders

Unlike most other psychiatric disorders, eating disorders can have very significant medical comorbidities and consequences, so the medical evaluation is essential to ensure the client is able to be seen in an outpatient setting and does not need a higher level of care (e.g., hospitalization to ensure medical stabilization). Further, it is important to consider the developmental level of the child. In general, children may have difficulties separating emotional body signals and may describe the physical sensation like stomach discomfort versus identifying it as anxiety. Additionally, unique challenges regarding assessing binge eating persist in children. A sense of loss of control over eating, rather than the amount of food consumed, may be more relevant for assessing binge eating episodes in children and adolescents because younger children generally cannot gain access to large amounts of food. Relatedly, research demonstrates that pathology is similar among children with loss of control regardless of the amount consumed (Shomaker et al., 2010). Further, unlike other disorders, many individuals with eating disorders may not wish to be in treatment because some of their symptoms may produce relief and comfort (e.g., rigid rules around food restriction may reduce guilt and provide comfort and help the client feel in control). Early diagnosis is key; a better prognosis exists for individuals who seek treatment closer to the start of their illness because they have had less time for their eating disorders to become severe and entrenched (Lock et al., 2015). Lastly, it is important to involve the family in the assessment process given the expected developmental limitations, possible lack of insight, and ego syntonic nature of some eating disorders. However, speaking individually to the client is still important because many eating disorder behaviors may occur in secret.

When asked by the social worker at intake how she feels, Jenny responded, "fat and worthless." She said she cries daily and often thinks about committing suicide and had attempted to do so on one occasion about 9 months ago by taking about 10 aspirin and drinking. At intake, Jenny denied current purging and minimized her history of purging and binge eating but only reported her concerns about shape and weight.

Table 12.1 Measures of Eating Disorders in Youths

Psychometric Support	Measure Name	No. of Items	Completed by[a]	Ages[b]	Link to Measure
Excellent	Eating Disorder Diagnostic Scale (EDDS; Stice et al., 2000)	22	Y	13+	http://www.ori.org/sticemeasures
Excellent	Bulimic Investigatory Test, Edinburgh (BITE; Henderson & Freeman, 1987)	33	Y	12+	http://www.wales.nhs.uk/sitesplus/866/opendoc/224740
Good	Ideal Body Stereotype Scale-Revised (IBSS-R; Stice, 2001)*	6	Y	Adolescents[c]	http://www.ori.org/sticemeasures
Good	Children's Eating Attitudes Test (ChEAT; Maloney et al., 1988)	26	Y	8–13	http://www.1000livesplus.wales.nhs.uk/sitesplus/documents/1011/ChEAT.pdf
Good	Eating Attitudes Test (EAT; Garner et al., 1982)	26 or 40	Y	13+	https://www.eat-26.com/
Good	Body Checking Questionnaire (BCQ; Netemeyer & Williamson, 2002)	23	Y	15+	https://www.phenxtoolkit.org/toolkit_content/supplemental_info/mhr_eating_disorders/measures/Body_Checking_Questionnaire.doc
Adequate	Eating Disturbances in Youth Questionnaire (EDY-Q; Kurz et al., 2015)*	14	Y	8–13	http://ul.qucosa.de/api/qucosa%3A14486/attachment/ATT-0/
Adequate	Clinical Impairment Assessment (CIA; Bohn et al., 2008)	16	Y	Adolescents[c]	http://www.wales.nhs.uk/sitesplus/documents/866/CIA.pdf
Adequate	Physical Appearance State and Trait Anxiety Scale (PASTAS; Reed et al., 1991)	17	Y	13+	https://sites.google.com/site/bodyimageresearchgroup/measures/physical-appearance-state-and-trait-anxiety-scale---state-and-trait-versions-pastas
Adequate	Dimensional Yale Food Addiction Scale for Children 2.0 (YFAS-C; Gearhardt et al., 2013)	25	Y	13+	https://fastlab.psych.lsa.umich.edu/yale-food-addiction-scale/
Adequate	Sociocultural Attitudes Towards Appearance Questionnaire—4 (SATAQ-4; Thompson et al., 2000)	30	Y	Adolescents[c]	https://sites.google.com/site/bodyimageresearchgroup/measures

a Completed by: Y = youth.

b Exact age range for specific forms (e.g., self-report, parent report) may vary.

c Exact age range not specified.

★ Available in multiple languages.

NOTE: Table adapted from Becker-Haimes, E. M., Tabachnick, A. R., Last, B. S., Stewart, R. E., Hasan-Granier, A., & Beidas, R. S. (2020). Evidence base update for brief, free, and accessible youth mental health measures. *Journal of Clinical Child & Adolescent Psychology, 49*(1), 117, reprinted by permission of the publisher (Taylor & Francis Ltd, http://www.tandfonline.com).

References for measures in Table 12.1:

Bohn, K., & Fairburn, C. G. (2008). The clinical impairment assessment questionnaire (CIA) (pp. 315–317. In C. G. Fairburn (Ed.), *Cognitive Behavioral Therapy for Eating Disorders*. New York: Guilford Press.

Cattarin, J. A., Thompson, J. K., Thomas, C., & Williams, R. (2000). Body image, mood, and televised images of attractiveness: The role of social comparison. *Journal of Social and Clinical Psychology, 19*(2), 220–239.

Gearhardt, A. N., Roberto, C. A., Seamans, M. J., Corbin, W. R., & Brownell, K. D. (2013). Preliminary validation of the Yale Food Addiction Scale for children. *Eating Behaviors, 14*(4), 508–512.

Henderson, M., & Freeman, C. P. L. (1987). A self-rating scale for bulimia the 'bite.' *British Journal of Psychiatry, 150*(1), 18–24.

Kurz, S., Van Dyck, Z., Dremmel, D., Munsch, S., & Hilbert, A. (2015). Early-onset restrictive eating disturbances in primary school boys and girls. *European Child & Adolescent Psychiatry, 24*(7), 779–785.

Maloney, M. J., McGuire, J. B., & Daniels, S. R. (1988). Reliability testing of a children's version of the Eating Attitude Test. *Journal of the American Academy of Child & Adolescent Psychiatry, 27*(5), 541–543.

Reed, D. L., Thompson, J. K., Brannick, M. T., & Sacco, W. P. (1991). Development and validation of the physical appearance state and trait anxiety scale (PASTAS). *Journal of Anxiety Disorders, 5*(4), 323–332.

Reas, D. L., Whisenhunt, B. L., Netemeyer, R., & Williamson, D. A. (2002). Development of the body checking questionnaire: A self-report measure of body checking behaviors. *International Journal of Eating Disorders, 31*(3), 324–333.

Stice, E., Chase, A., Stormer, S., & Appel, A. (2001). A randomized trial of a dissonance-based eating disorder prevention program. *International Journal of Eating Disorders, 29*(3), 247–262.

Stice, E., Telch, C. F., & Rizvi, S. L. (2000). Development and validation of the Eating Disorder Diagnostic Scale: A brief self-report measure of anorexia, bulimia, and binge-eating disorder. *Psychological Assessment, 12*(2), 123.

When screened for depressive symptoms at intake, Jenny scored in the moderate to severe range. Jenny's mother (through the assistance of an interpreter) confirmed Jenny's preoccupation with her weight and poor and irregular eating patterns. She also corroborated observing Jenny's depression. Jenny was referred to the psychiatrist for a medication evaluation. The treatment team decided to observe Jenny's eating behaviors to evaluate whether additional eating disorder treatment was needed outside of the standard therapy provided by the residential treatment.

One month after Jenny was admitted to the residential treatment program, one of the other residents at the program came forward and told the staff that Jenny had been purging after meals. When the staff approached Jenny, she broke down and said she had been doing this since she arrived at the program. At meals, Jenny would try to limit her intake to a salad and some vegetables to help control her weight, and then would return to her room where she had stashed away candy and always ends up "eating like a pig." Jenny reported that she usually feels as if she can't control how much she eats and likened it to a ball rolling down the hill—once she starts—she can't stop. After these binges, she would ask the staff if she could take a shower and then when the water was running, she would force herself to vomit in the toilet or in the shower. She did this at least three times a week.

Jenny stated that she initially starts eating to try to soothe her depression. However, she quickly feels very guilty about eating too much food. Jenny reported that she feels "better" after she purges her food and believes that if she were skinny, she would not have any problems. Jenny constantly talked about how fat she is to others and compared herself to her peers. She admitted that she thinks about her body weight most of the day. Jenny is about 10 pounds overweight. Jenny stated that she just wishes she would "die," although she doesn't have a specific plan. She reported that there is no reason for her to live because she is "stupid, ugly, and fat."

INTERVENTION

Although treatment goals should be individualized, some standard priorities follow (Yager et al., 2012). The first involves weight restoration and achieving medical stabilization (if applicable). A second is to reduce the number of binge eating or compensatory behavior episodes. Early response of these indicators has been identified repeatedly as a predictor of good treatment outcome. An implication is that the practitioner, aware of this fact, can encourage and promote rapid progress by focusing on these areas. (Graves et al., 2017; Linardon et al., 2016; Vall & Wade, 2015). Unfortunately, the factors related to having an early response have not been elucidated (Linardon et al., 2016).

Although most adolescents with an eating disorder sought some form of treatment, only a minority received treatment specifically for their eating or weight problems (Lock et al., 2015). Treatment of eating disorders often involves a multidisciplinary team of providers including a psychotherapist, pediatrician, dietitian, and possibly child psychiatrist who should have experience treating children and adolescents with eating disorders (Lock et al., 2015). *Outpatient* treatment is recommended as a first-line treatment for children and adolescents (Lock et al., 2015), as long as the patient is medically appropriate for outpatient care. Only if that is unsuccessful should more intensive intervention settings such as partial hospitalization/day treatment, residential treatment, or psychiatric hospitalization be used. In *partial hospitalization*, clients spend 6 to 10 hours a day between 3 and 7 days a week and receive meals, group therapy, individual therapy, and dietetic and medication management (Friedman et al., 2016). *Residential treatment* involves housing clients in a nonhospital-based treatment setting for an extended period (averaging about 83 days) with meal support, an interdisciplinary team, and individual and group therapy. *Hospitalization* involves admission to a medical unit at a medical or psychiatric hospital that involves multidisciplinary services comprising psychiatry, psychology, nursing, dietetics, occupational therapy, physical therapy, social services, and general medical services (Foreyt et al., 1998). Inpatient treatment is indicated with the following risk factors (Foreyt et al., 1998; Golden et al., 2003): (1) serious physical complications (malnutrition, dehydration, electrolyte disturbances, cardiac dysrhythmia, arrested growth); (2) extremely low body weight; (3) acute suicide risk; (4) lack of available outpatient treatment; (5) comorbid disorders that interfere with outpatient treatment (i.e., severe depression, obsessive-compulsive disorder [OCD]); and (6) a need to be separated from the current living situation.

There is no evidence suggesting that hospitalization is more effective than outpatient treatment (Crisp et al., 1991; Gowers et al., 2007). Limited research suggests that partial hospitalization/day treatments are effective at reducing eating disorder symptoms at discharge, and when assessed, improvement was sustained at follow-up (Friedman et al., 2016). However, research is biased because of dropout, lack of control groups or no randomized controlled trial of outpatient versus more intensive care, and subjects typically having private insurance and therefore not necessarily being representative (Lock, 2019). Further, publication bias might be an issue because for-profit programs typically would not put forward unsupportive research.

Now that the variety of treatment settings have been covered, both psychotherapy and pharmacologic approaches are discussed separately. There is a paucity of research on eating disorder intervention in adolescents compared with other psychiatric disorders. Additionally, since BED was new to the DSM-5, and because of the limitations in identifying binge eating among children, less treatment research exists but will be provided as available.

Psychotherapy

See Box 12.1 for a list of evidence-based treatment manuals for youths with eating disorders.

ANOREXIA NERVOSA

Much attention in the research literature has centered on the Maudsley model, which was developed by Dare and Eisler at London's Maudsley Hospital in the

Box 12.1

TREATMENT MANUALS FOR EATING DISORDERS

Dalle Grave, R., & Calugi, S. (2020). *Cognitive behavior therapy for adolescents with eating disorders*. New York: Guilford Press.
Le Grange, D., & Lock, J. (2007). *Treatment manual for bulimia nervosa: A family based approach*. New York: Guilford Press.
Lock, J., & Le Grange, D. (2013). *Treatment manual for anorexia nervosa: A family based approach* (2nd ed.). New York: Guilford Press.
Schmidt, U., & Treasure, J. (1997). *Getting better bit(e) by bit(e): A treatment manual for sufferers of bulimia nervosa*. Hove, East Sussex, UK: Psychology Press.
Treasure, J., & Schmidt, U. (1997). *The clinician's guide to getting better bit(e) by bit(e)*. Hove, East Sussex, UK: Psychology Press.

1980s. Called *family-based treatment (FBT)*, the entire family is involved, family is not blamed for the development of the eating disorder, parents are charged with taking control of refeeding the adolescent, and adolescents maintain control of non–weight/eating-related areas of their life (Lock et al., 2001; Lock & Le Grange, 2013). A manualized version of FBT has been published and suggests 10 to 20 family sessions over a period of 6 to 12 months (Lock & Le Grange, 2013). FBT consists of three phases: phase I is focused on weight restoration, with the therapist supporting the parents' effort in refeeding; in phase II, control over food is transitioned back to the adolescent with parent and therapist oversight; and phase III focuses on establishing a healthy identity for the adolescent, including repairing social and family relationships and returning to "normal" adolescent life where the eating disorder symptoms do not need to be central to treatment. Overall, a review of the research indicates that FBT is superior to individual therapy and is the only "well-established" treatment for AN (Lock et al., 2015). FBT is less effective for youths with perseverative thinking or OCD features and those from households without two parents, suggesting that additional work is needed to optimize treatment for some groups (Lock & Le Grange, 2019).

Individual therapy for AN has involved a psychodynamic treatment referred to by different names: "insight-oriented individual psychotherapy," "adolescent focused therapy," or "ego-oriented individual therapy." The aim of this treatment is to identify the central developmental, relational, or emotional challenges that adolescents are avoiding through their eating disorder symptoms and to help them manage these challenges in a more direct and functional way. Treatment spans a 9- to 12-month period and includes several parent sessions. According to a review of this literature, Lock (2019) has categorized this psychodynamic treatment as "the second-best evidence-based approach" for the treatment of AN.

Although currently there is insufficient evidence to be considered an evidence-based treatment for adolescents, cognitive-behavioral therapy—enhanced

(CBT-E; Fairburn, 2008) shows early promise for treating adolescents with AN and is considered an exploratory treatment (Lock et al., 2019). CBT-E is a transdiagnostic treatment for eating disorders, and the detailed manual includes an adaptation for adolescents. Preliminary research has shown that adolescents treated with CBT-E had substantial increases in weight and decreases in eating disorder psychopathology (Dalle Grave et al., 2013, 2019). Additionally, Lock (2019) considers cognitive remediation training an exploratory treatment—although initial evidence suggests this treatment may be best suited as an adjunct to other AN treatments to help improve motivation and reduce attrition (Lock et al., 2013).

Bulimia Nervosa

There is even less research on treatment of BN for adolescents than AN. Therefore, no treatments have been categorized as "well established"; however, FBT adapted for BN (FBT-BN; Le Grange & Lock, 2007) and CBT-guided self-help are considered possibly efficacious (Lock et al., 2015). In FBT-BN, treatment is like that of FBT-AN, except the focus is on disrupting bingeing and purging behavior versus weight restoration. Further, this treatment is more collaborative than FBT-AN, possibly because the BN symptoms tend to be more ego-dystonic than AN (Reinicke, 2017). FBT-BN was shown to have greater abstinence of bingeing and purging than supportive psychotherapy following treatment and at 6-month follow-up (Le Grange et al., 2007). A more recent randomized, controlled trial similarly found FBT-BN to achieve greater abstinence compared with CBT for adolescents (CBT-A) at the end of treatment and 6-month follow-up; however, there was no difference at 12-month follow-up (Le Grange et al., 2015). One randomized, controlled trial examined CBT-guided self-help in which practitioners, over 10 sessions and using motivational interviewing, helped participants progress through the CBT manual (see Box 12.1), which emphasized problem-solving and cognitive restructuring. The guided self-help condition performed as well as family-based therapy (slightly different from FBT-BN in that adolescents could choose any support person) on remission of purging and was more advantageous in terms of rapid reduction of bingeing (although difference disappeared at 6-month follow-up), lower cost, and greater acceptability among clients (Schmidt et al., 2007). The implication of these findings is that guided CBT self-help may represent a first-line intervention. However, guided CBT self-help involves a very structured presentation of CBT, so it resembles CBT interventions more closely than traditional self-help.

A more standard version of CBT was compared, in a German study, to psychodynamic psychotherapy (Stefini et al., 2017). Both conditions achieved the same level of improvement in terms of no longer meeting diagnostic criteria for an eating disorder (33.3% of those receiving CBT vs. 30.2%).

Binge Eating Disorder

As mentioned, because BED is a new diagnosis, there is very little treatment outcome research with adolescents. Further, as previously mentioned, fewer are diagnosed with BED given the criteria may be harder to meet for children.

Interpersonal psychotherapy was discussed in Chapter 10 for depression, and in relation to binge eating, it works to resolve interpersonal problems and the availability of support that are thought to maintain this pattern of eating. Some preliminary evidence has emerged for adolescents with BED (Tanofsky-Kraff et al., 2007, 2010). Dialectical behavior therapy, which involves identifying triggers and teaching coping strategies to manage and tolerate those emotions without engaging in binge eating, is also promising, as is CBT, but these have only been studied in adults (Safer et al., 2010; Wilson et al., 2010). Some adolescents may find online treatments more appealing, so Internet-facilitated CBT self-help may also be a possibility (Bohon, 2019; Jones et al., 2008).

Medication

Compared with the research on psychotherapy for eating disorders, even less information exists to guide medication recommendations. The U.S. Food and Drug Administration (FDA) has not approved any medication for the treatment of AN in adults or adolescents. Medication research in adolescents has methodologic weaknesses, including difficulties with recruitment and dropout; comprises mainly case reports with few randomized controlled trials; and has found little evidence for the efficacy of antidepressants. The overall conclusion is that the selective serotonin reuptake inhibitors (SSRIs) can be used for comorbid disorders, such as depression, anxiety, and OCD, but only after the individual gains sufficient weight; otherwise, low reserves of available serotonin may hinder the potential effectiveness of medication (Lock et al., 2015).

Atypical antipsychotics (usually olanzapine and risperidone) have been studied with adolescents with AN more often than the antidepressants; however, clear evidence of their efficacy is lacking (Couturier et al., 2019; Lock, 2019). Given the lack of evidence, use of antipsychotics is experimental and should only be used for comorbid psychiatric conditions that were clearly present before the AN or to manage behavioral agitation temporarily when nothing else is effective (Lock, 2019).

Fluoxetine (Prozac) is not approved by the FDA in adolescents with BN, but it is approved for adults with BN and for children and adolescents for depression and OCD. The one medication study to date was open-label and involved 10 adolescents who were treated with fluoxetine in combination with supportive psychotherapy (Kotler et al., 2003). Improvements in binge eating and purging were seen, but randomized controlled studies are needed. Lisdexamfetamine dimesylate (Vyvanse) is approved by the FDA for BED in adults but is only approved for use in children and adolescents for attention-deficit/hyperactivity disorder (ADHD). There are no pharmacologic studies published at this time for adolescents with BED.

Despite evidence guidelines cautioning against medication for adolescents with eating disorders, there is a high use of antidepressants in practice. In a case review of more than 500 patients in treatment, 78% of the adolescents were prescribed at least one medication, with no differences for the type of eating disorder (Garner et al., 2016).

Jenny was referred for specialty eating disorder treatment with an outpatient provider experienced in the treatment of adolescent eating disorders while she remained at residential treatment. Her treatment included the following components: efforts to reduce binge eating and purging episodes; psychoeducation; CBT strategies to improve coping, problem-solving, and cognitive restructuring; engagement of her mother in treatment; and efforts to improve interpersonal and social functioning.

Jenny was referred for medical evaluation to ensure she was not experiencing any complications due to her BN; these evaluations did not reveal any remarkable medical issues that prohibited outpatient treatment. Jenny also continued to see the psychiatrist at the residential treatment facility for her depression and was started on an SSRI concurrently with her behavioral therapy. Efforts to reduce Jenny's binge eating and purging were a top priority of treatment. Following a CBT approach, Jenny was tasked with completing self-monitoring of her eating. She had to log what she ate (not counting calories), when she ate, where she ate, and whether she felt she binged or experienced loss of control. Jenny was prescribed to develop a regular pattern of eating with three meals and two to three snacks planned regularly throughout the day. Jenny's treatment team ensured Jenny would be monitored during and after meals closely and regularly made sure food was not in her room. Her meals were planned by staff in collaboration with a nutritionist. Over time, meal monitoring was able to be reduced, and Jenny was given more independence around meals as she demonstrated that she was not bingeing and purging but was maintaining a regular meal pattern. Jenny was weighed weekly as part of treatment.

The clinician also used CBT strategies to help identify triggers for binge eating and purging and provided Jenny strategies to cope more effectively and problem-solve. For example, they worked to identify tools and strategies Jenny could use to distract herself when she had the urge to binge or purge. They also identified alternative behaviors she could do instead and support persons to enlist until the urge passed. The clinician also helped Jenny to identify negative cognitions that were related to her BN, such as, "If I don't throw up, I'll get fat," and how her thoughts, feelings, and behaviors were connected. Jenny was able to identify that she often experiences maladaptive thoughts ("I'm so fat") and feelings (ashamed, sad) before she binges and purges. By challenging and changing those maladaptive thoughts—for example, by catching the thought, "I'm so fat," and changing it to something more helpful, such as, "the way I look doesn't determine my value as a person," Jenny's emotions and behaviors began to improve along with her mood.

Finally, another important component of Jenny's treatment involved enlisting her mother's support by engaging her in treatment, with the aid of an interpreter, and helping Jenny explore strategies for improving her interpersonal relationships. Jenny's treatment team helped her to identify which peers in her social circle were positive influences and worked to increase supportive and positive interactions with those individuals. This was especially important as she transitioned home and to outpatient therapy. They also identified peers with whom continued association would be detrimental for her recovery, such as those she used to use substances with, and problem-solved strategies for Jenny to cease and navigate those relationships and avoid risky situations. Ultimately, Jenny was able to transition home and, with ongoing support in outpatient family therapy, to recover from her eating disorder.

SUMMARY

Although the common belief is that eating disorders are limited to middle-class and upper-class white women, the research indicates that low-SES and minority youths may have comparable rates. Therefore, social workers should screen their adolescent clients in the variety of settings in which they work to appropriately identify such problems. Eating disorders represent a specialty area of practice, so social workers will mainly be involved in referring clients to treatment facilities and providers devoted to such problems. However, these treatment centers typically require private insurance for payment, leaving uninsured clients and those with public insurance without many options.

CASE EXAMPLE 2: INTERPERSONAL THERAPY

By Frances Pollack, Ph.D.

Ana, a 16-year-old Mexican American female, was referred to treatment with a therapist by her pediatrician after she found blood in her vomit. Ana had expressed discontent with her body and reported that she felt "larger" than her friends. Ana saw herself as "fat" although her body mass index was in the healthy weight category (20 kg/m²). She also reported "feeling out of control" when she binged. Ana bought large bags of candy from the local convenience store or took food from her friends' homes when no one was in the kitchen. She hid this food in her bedroom. Ana reported she would go up to her bedroom when she was upset and eat these foods in secret. After her binges, she felt tremendous guilt and feared that she would gain weight. This always resulted in vomiting and sometimes in excessive exercising. After Ana found blood in her vomit, she told her mother, who brought her to the pediatrician for a medical evaluation.

Ana has one older sister and grew up in a low-income household. Her parents had both grown up economically disadvantaged in Mexico and immigrated to the United States hoping for a better life. Her father works long hours as a construction worker, and her mother cleans houses, although she tries to be home for her daughters after school. Most of their extended family members live in Mexico. The family has struggled over the years with financial stability, which has often led to fighting between her parents. The family has had little financial support given the lack of family nearby. Ana attends a public school in a middle-class neighborhood. She does relatively well in school and has always been able to maintain secure friendships. However, as she began to increase the frequency of her bingeing and purging, she began to distance herself from her friendships.

Ana's parents began fighting when she was a young child about financial and relational matters. Ana was aware that her father had at least one affair and suspected there were potentially more. As Ana became a teenager, her mother began to confide in Ana about her relationship with Ana's father, including the affair, the pain the mother experienced, and many other complaints about her husband's character. Ana began to feel both burdened by her mother's stories and more distant from her father.

The pediatrician conducted an initial medical assessment. The pediatrician conducted an electrocardiogram and noted a slightly slow pulse and decreased heart rate. She also noted some minor abrasions around Ana's knuckles due to the vomiting. The pediatrician ordered a complete blood count and a comprehensive metabolic panel including electrolytes, renal function tests, and liver enzymes. Labs confirmed that Ana was medically stable to receive outpatient treatment. Ana saw a nutritionist several times to support a healthy food plan and was medically monitored by her pediatrician. The therapist conducted an initial clinical interview where Ana detailed the history of her eating disorder symptoms and confirmed information provided in the referral from the pediatrician.

Treatment

Interpersonal therapy (IPT) for eating disorders was the primary therapeutic treatment used with Ana. The therapist first explained how IPT worked, including how psychoeducation was an important part of treatment. They began an extensive interpersonal history, involving a comprehensive review of past and present relationships. In IPT, this is called an interpersonal inventory. From this inventory a problem area based on relationships is chosen to work on in therapy.

Ana was asked to keep a journal about the times she binged and purged, logging her food intake, time, and what may have triggered her binge–purge cycle. Ana's journal revealed that the binge–purge cycle typically followed her witnessing her parents fight or conversations when her mother was detailing concerns about her father. IPT for eating disorders posits four interpersonal functioning areas, and one is chosen for the therapeutic work; these include grief, role disputes, role transitions, and interpersonal sensitivities. Accordingly, the therapist selected interpersonal disputes (having extreme tension/distress in one primary relationship) as the focus area for Ana to work on to help with her eating disorder symptoms. The therapist presented the IPT model by describing how problems arising from the relationship with her mother or witnessing her parents fight increase Ana's anxiety and cause stress. Ana then resorts to binge eating and purging to gain a temporary distraction from these intense uncomfortable feelings. IPT works to disrupt the cycle by addressing the interpersonal issues related to causing the increased anxiety and stress or the mood symptoms, which indirectly improves the eating disorder symptoms.

IPT techniques used in Ana's treatment to address role disputes included encouragement of affect, communication analysis, and behavior change techniques. Ana was encouraged and supported to express her feelings to understand them better. The therapist also completed a communication analysis around conversations with her mother when she did not feel heard. The analysis involved a detailed description of the exchanges so that the therapist could help Ana work on communicating with her mother in a more effective way. Communication with Ana's mother seemed to break down when Ana expressed her own feelings or needs and her mother subsequently responded by minimizing or ignoring her. The therapist encouraged Ana to let her mother know that she did not feel heard or understood when this happened. The therapist also supported Ana in leaning more on her friends and maternal aunt for support.

The therapist spoke to Ana about setting boundaries with her mother when it came to speaking about Ana's father. A behavior change technique, in this case a directive technique, was used to help Ana set needed boundaries. Ana feared doing this because she did not want her mother to feel alone. Also, the confidences made Ana feel special. The therapist acknowledged her concerns, while gently pointing out the costs to Ana of being her mother's confidante. The therapist suggested that perhaps there were other ways to connect and feel close and special to her mother, and other people her mother could confide in when distressed. After several sessions on this topic, Ana felt ready to speak with her mother on her own. Ana and the therapist used role playing to practice this interaction. In the following sessions, Ana told the therapist that the conversation with her mother had gone well. After speaking with her daughter, Ana's mother felt badly about inappropriately confiding in her and not listening to her needs.

Progress continued, but, at times, Ana's mother would begin to talk about Ana's father. The therapist taught Ana kind yet firm ways to interrupt her mother in the moment and let her mother know that Ana did not want to speak about her father. Ana and her mother found other things to discuss, and her mother began leaning on her own sister and a good friend to express frustrations about Ana's father. As a result, Ana felt a great sense of relief.

Although Ana and the therapist were working on other coping strategies, such as journal writing, soothing music, and walking, the therapist realized that talking to Ana's parents about the marital conflict and distress was paramount. The therapist brought in the parents, and, in a family session, Ana communicated how hard it was for her and how it often triggered overwhelming feelings that led to binging. The therapist continued a conversation with the parents privately, suggesting they try couple's therapy. According to Ana, the parents did indeed fight less in front of her, and her relationship with her mother improved. Ana's binge–purge cycles significantly decreased. Ana had much more insight into her feelings, how to set healthy boundaries, and how to stop some of the challenging communication problems with her mother.

REFERENCES

American Psychiatric Association. (2022). *Diagnostic and statistical manual of mental disorders* (5th ed., Text Revision). Washington, DC: American Psychiatric Association.

Bahji, A., Mazhar, M. N., Hudson, C. C., Nadkarni, P., MacNeil, B. A., & Hawken, E. (2019). Prevalence of substance use disorder comorbidity among individuals with eating disorders: A systematic review and meta-analysis. *Psychiatry Research, 273,* 58–66. doi:10.1016/j.psychres.2019.01.007

Baker, J. H., Thornton, L. M., Bulik, C. M., Kendler, K. S., & Lichtenstein, P. (2012). Shared genetic effects between age at menarche and disordered eating. *Journal of Adolescent Health, 51*(5), 491–496.

Balakar, J. L., Shank, L. M., Vannucci, A., Radin, R. M., & Tanofsky-Kraff, M. (2015). Recent advances in developmental and risk factor research on eating disorders. *Current Psychiatry Reports, 17*(6), 1–10. https://doi.org/10.1007/s11920-015-0585-x

Bardone-Cone, A. M., Wonderlich, S. A., Frost, R. O., Bulik, C. M., Mitchell, J. E., Uppala, S., & Simonich, H. (2007). Perfectionism and eating disorders: Current status and future directions. *Clinical Psychology Review, 27,* 384–405.

Bohon, A. (2019). Binge eating disorder in children and adolescents. *Child and Adolescent Psychiatric Clinics of North America, 28*(4), 549–555.

Bryant-Waugh, R. (2019). Avoidant/restrictive food intake disorder. *Child and Adolescent Psychiatric Clinics of North America, 28*(4), 557–565.

Bulik, C. M., Blake, L., & Austin, J. (2019). Genetics of eating disorders: What the clinician needs to know. *Psychiatric Clinics of North America, 42*(1), 59–73. https://doi.org/10.1016/j.psc.2018.10.007

Bulik, C. M., Coleman, J. R. I., Hardaway, J. A., Breithaupt, L., Watson, H. J., Bryant, C. D., & Breen, G. (2022). Genetics and neurobiology of eating disorders. *Nature Neuroscience, 25,* 543–554. hhttps://doi.org/10.1038/s41593-022-01071-z

Bulik, C. M., Thornton, L. M., Parker, R., Kennedy, H., Baker, J. H., MacDermod, C., Guintivano, J., Cleland, L., Miller, A. L., Harper, L., Larsen, J. T., Yilmaz, Z, Grove, J., Sullivan, P. F., Petersen, L. V., Jordan, J., Kennedy, M. A., & Martin, N. G. (2021). The Eating Disorders Genetics Initiative (EDGI): Study protocol. *BMC Psychiatry, 21,* 234. https://doi.org/10.1186/s12888-021-03212-3

Caslini, M., Bartoli, F., Crocamo, C., Dakanalis, A., Clerici, M., & Carrà, G. (2016). Disentangling the association between child abuse and eating disorders: A systematic review and meta-analysis. *Psychosomatic Medicine, 78*(1), 79–90. https://doi.org/10.1097/PSY.0000000000000233

Castellini, G., Lo Sauro, C., Mannucci, E., Ravaldi, C., Rotella, C. M., Faravelli, C., & Ricca, V. (2011). Diagnostic crossover and outcome predictors in eating disorders according to DSM-IV and DSM-V proposed criteria: A 6-year follow-up study. *Psychosomatic medicine, 73*(3), 270–279. https://doi.org/10.1097/PSY.0b013e318 20a1838

Crisp, A. H., Norton, K., Gowers, S., Halek, C., Bowyer, C., Yeldham, D., Levett, G., & Bhat, A. (1991). A controlled study of the effect of therapies aimed at adolescent and family psychopathology in anorexia nervosa. *British Journal of Psychiatry: The Journal of Mental Science, 159,* 325–333. https://doi.org/10.1192/bjp.159.3.325

Culbert, K. M., Racine, S. E., & Klump, K. L. (2015). Research review: What we have learned about the causes of eating disorders—A synthesis of sociocultural, psychological, and biological research. *Journal of Child Psychology and Psychiatry, 56,* 1141–1164. doi:10.1111/jcpp.12441

Dalle Grave, R., Calugi, S., Doll, H. A., & Fairburn, C. G. (2013). Enhanced cognitive behaviour therapy for adolescents with anorexia nervosa: An alternative to family therapy? *Behaviour Research and Therapy, 51*(1), R9–R12.

Erkine, H. E., Whiteford, H. A., & Pike, K. M. (2016). The global burden of eating disorders. *Current Opinion in Psychiatry, 29*(6), 346–353. doi:10.1097/YCO.0000000000000276

Fairburn, C. G., Cooper, Z., & Shafran, R. (2003). Cognitive behaviour therapy for eating disorders: A "transdiagnostic" theory and treatment. *Behaviour Research and Therapy, 4*, 509–528.

Fischer, S., Smith, G. T., & Cyders, M. A. (2008). Another look at impulsivity: A meta-analytic review comparing specific dispositions to rash action in their relationship to bulimic symptoms. *Clinical Psychology Review, 28*, 1413–1425.

Foreyt, J., Poston, W., Winebarger, A., & McGavin, J. (1998). Anorexia nervosa and bulimia nervosa. In E. Mash & R. Barkley (Eds.), *Treatment of childhood disorders* (2nd ed., pp. 647–691). New York: Guilford Press.

Friedman, K., Ramirez, A. L., Murray, S. B., Anderson, L. K., Cusack, A., Boutelle, K. N., & Kaye, W. H. (2016). A narrative review of outcome studies for residential and partial hospital-based treatment of eating disorders. *European Eating Disorders Review, 24*(4), 263–276. doi:10.1002/erv.2449

Golden, N., Katzman, D., Kreipe, R., Stevens, S., Sawyer, S., Rees, J., Nicholls, D., & Rome, E.S. (2003). Eating disorders in adolescents: Position paper of the Society for Adolescent Medicine. *Journal of Adolescent Health, 33*, 496–503.

Gowers, S. G., Clark, A., Roberts, C., Griffiths, A., Edwards, V., Bryan, C., Smethurst, N., Byford, S., & Barrett, B. (2007). Clinical effectiveness of treatments for anorexia nervosa in adolescents: Randomised controlled trial. *British Journal of Psychiatry: The Journal of Mental Science, 191*, 427–435. https://doi.org/10.1192/bjp.bp.107.036764

Graves, T. A., Tabri, N., Thompson-Brenner, H., Franko, D. L., Eddy, K. T., Bourion-Bedes, S., Brown, A., Constantino, M. J., Fluckiger, C., Forsberg, S., Isserlin, L., Couturier, J., Karlsson, G. P., Mander, J., Teufel, M., Mitchell, J. E., Crosby, R. D., Prestano, C., . . . Thomas, J. J. (2017). A meta-analysis of the relation between therapeutic alliance and treatment outcome in eating disorders. *International Journal of Eating Disorders, 50*(4), 323–340. doi:10.1002/eat.22672

Grogan, K., MacGarry, D., Bramham, J., Scriven, M., Maher, C., & Fitzgerald, A. (2020). Family-related non-abuse adverse life experiences occurring for adults diagnosed with eating disorders: a systematic review. *Journal of Eating Disorders, 8*, 36. https://doi.org/10.1186/s40337-020-00311-6

Hausenblas, H. A., Campbell, A., Menzel, J. E., Doughty, J., Levine, M., & Thompson, J. K. (2013). Media effects of experimental presentation of the ideal physique on eating disorder symptoms: A meta-analysis of laboratory studies. *Clinical Psychology Review, 33*, 168–181.

Henderson, Z., Fox, J. R. E., Trayner, P., & Wittkowski, A. (2019). Emotional development in eating disorders: A qualitative metasynthesis. *Clinical Psychology and Psychotherapy, 26*, 440–457. https://doi-org.proxy.library.upenn.edu/10.1002/cpp.2365

Hilbert, A., Pike, K. M., Goldschmidt, A. B., Wilfley, D. E., Fairburn, C. G., Dohm, F. A., Walsh, B. T., & Striegel Weissman, R. (2014). Risk factors across the eating disorders. *Psychiatry Research, 220*(1–2), 500–506. https://doi.org/10.1016/j.psychres.2014.05.054

Holland, L. A., Bodell, L. P., & Keel, P. K. (2013). Psychological factors predict eating disorder onset and maintenance at 10-year follow-up. *European Eating Disorders*

Review: The Journal of the Eating Disorders Association, 21(5), 405–410. https://doi. org/10.1002/erv.2241

Hudson, J., Hiripi, E., Pope, H., & Kessler, R. (2007). The prevalence and correlates of eating disorders in the National Comorbidity Survey Replication. *Biological Psychiatry, 61*, 348–358. https://doi.org/10.1016/j.biopsych.2006.03.040

Johnston, O., Fornae, G., Cabrini, S., & Kendrick, T. (2007). Feasibility and acceptability of screening for eating disorders in primary care. *Family Practice, 24*(5), 511–517.

Jones, M., Luce, K. H., Osborne, M. I., Taylor, K., Cunning, D., Doyle, A. C., Wilfley, D. E., & Taylor, C. B. (2008). Randomized, controlled trial of an internet-facilitated intervention for reducing binge eating and overweight in adolescents, *Pediatrics, 121*(3), 453–462.

Kamody, R. C., Grilo, C. M., & Udo, T. (2020). Disparities in DSM-5 defined eating disorders by sexual orientation among U.S. adults. *International Journal of Eating Disorders, 53*(2), 278–287. https://doi.org/10.1002/eat.23193

Keel, P. K., & Forney, K. J. (2013). Psychosocial risk factors for eating disorders. *International Journal of Eating Disorders, 46*(5), 433–439. https://doi.org/10.1002/ eat.22094

Klump, K. L., Culbert, K. M., Slane, J. D., Burt, S. A., Sisk, C. L., & Nigg, J. T. (2012). The effects of puberty on genetic risk for disordered eating: Evidence for a sex differ-ence. *Psychological Medicine, 42*(3), 627–637. https://doi.org/10.1017/S003329171 1001541

Larsen, P. S., Strandberg-Larsen, K., Micali, N., & Anderson, A. M. (2015). Parental and child characteristics related to early-onset disordered eating: A systematic review. *Harvard Review of Psychiatry, 18*(3), 183–202.

Lavender, J. M., Wonderlich, S. A., Engel, S. G., Gordon, K. H., Kaye, W. H., & Mitchell, J. E. (2015). Dimensions of emotion dysregulation in anorexia nervosa and bulimia nervosa: A conceptual review of the empirical literature. *Clinical Psychology Review, 40*, 111–122. https://doi.org/10.1016/j.cpr.2015.05.010

Le Grange, D., Crosby, R. D., Rathouz, P. J., & Leventhal, B. L. (2007). A randomized controlled comparison of family-based treatment and supportive psychotherapy for adolescent bulimia nervosa. *Archives of General Psychiatry, 64*(9), 1049–1056. https://doi.org/10.1001/archpsyc.64.9.1049

Le Grange, D., & Lock, J. (2007). *Treatment manual for bulimia nervosa: A family based approach.* New York: Guilford Press.

Le Grange, D., Lock, J., Agras, W. S., Bryson, S. W., & Jo, B. (2015). Randomized clinical trial of family-based treatment and cognitive-behavioral therapy for adolescent bu-limia nervosa. *Journal of the American Academy of Child and Adolescent Psychiatry, 54*(11), 886–894.e2. https://doi.org/10.1016/j.jaac.2015.08.008

Levinson, C. A., Vanzhula, I. A., Brosof, L. C., & Forbush, K. (2018). Network analysis as an alternative approach to conceptualizing eating disorders: Implications for re-search and treatment. *Current Psychiatry Reports, 20*(9), 67. https://doi.org/10.1007/ s11920-018-0930-y

Lilenfeld, L. R., Wonderlich, S., Riso, L. P., Crosby, R., & Mitchell, J. (2006). Eating disorders and personality: A methodological and empirical review. *Clinical Psychology Review, 26*, 299–320.

Linardon, J., Garcia, X. D., & Brennan, L. (2016). Predictors, moderators, and mediators of treatment outcome following manualised cognitive-behavioural therapy for eating disorders: A systematic review. *European Eating Disorders Review, 25*(1), 3–12. doi:10.1002/erv.2492

Lock, J. (2019). Updates on treatments for adolescent anorexia nervosa. *Child and Adolescent Psychiatric Clinics of North America, 28*, 523–535.

Lock, J., Agras, W. S., Fitzpatrick, K. K., Bryson, S. W., Jo, B., & Tchanturia, K. (2013). Is outpatient cognitive remediation therapy feasible to use in randomized clinical trials for anorexia nervosa?. *International Journal of Eating Disorders, 46*(6), 567–575. https://doi.org/10.1002/eat.22134

Lock, J., LaVia, M. C., & American Academy of Child and Adolescent Psychiatry (AACAP) Committee on Quality Issues (CQI). (2015). Practice parameter for the assessment and treatment of children and adolescents with eating disorders. *Journal of the American Academy of Child & Adolescent Psychiatry, 54*(5), 412–425. doi:10.1016/j.jaac.2015.01.018

Lock, J., & Le Grange, D. (2019). Family-based treatment: Where are we and where should we be going to improve recovery in child and adolescent eating disorders. *International Journal of Eating Disorders, 52*(4), 481–487. https://doi.org/10.1002/eat.22980

Lock, J., Le Grange, D., Agras, W. S., & Dare, C. (2001). *Treatment manual for anorexia nervosa: A family-based approach.* New York: Guilford Press.

Lowe, M. R., & Timko, C. A. (2004). What a difference a diet makes: Towards an understanding of differences between restrained dieters and restrained nondieters. *Eating Behaviors, 5*(3), 199–208.

Mitchison, D., Mond, J., Bussey, K., Griffiths, S., Trompeter, N., Lonergan, A., Pike, K. M., Murray, S. B., & Hay, P. (2020). DSM-5 full syndrome, other specified, and unspecified eating disorders in Australian adolescents: Prevalence and clinical significance. *Psychological Medicine, 50*, 981–990. https:// doi.org/10.1017/S0033291719000898

Mizes, J. S., & Palermo, T. M. (1997). Eating disorders. In R. T. Ammerman & M. Hersen (Eds.), *Handbook of prevention and treatment with children and adolescents: Intervention in the real world context* (pp. 238–258). New York: Wiley.

Molendijk, M. L., Hoek, H. W., Brewerton, T. D., & Elzinga, B. M. (2017).Childhood maltreatment and eating disorder pathology: A systematic review and dose-response meta-analysis. *Psychological Medicine, 47*(8), 1–15. doi:10.1017/S0033291716003561

Morgan, J. F., Reid, F., & Lacey, J. H. (2000). The SCOFF questionnaire: A new screening tool for eating disorders. *Western Journal of Medicine, 172*(3), 164–165. https://doi.org/10.1136/ewjm.172.3.164

Nagata, J. M., Ganson, K. T., & Austin, S. B. (2020). Emerging trends in eating disorders among sexual and gender minorities. *Current Opinion in Psychiatry, 33*(6), 562–567. doi:10.1097/YCO.0000000000000645

Paganini, C., Peterson, G., & Andrews, K. (2021). The mediating role of temperamental traits on the relationship between age of puberty and eating disorders: A mediating analysis through structural equation modelling of Australian eating disorder outpatients. *Journal of Genetic Psychology, 182*(6), 391–405. https://doi.org/10.1080/00221325.2021.1940822

Rasmusson, G., Lydecker, J. A., Coffino, J. A., White, M. A., & Grilo, C. M. (2019). Household food insecurity is associated with binge-eating disorder and obesity. *International Journal of Eating Disorders, 52*, 28–35. https://doi.org/10.1002/eat.22990

Safer, D. L., Robinson, A. H., & Jo, B. (2010). Outcome from a randomized controlled trial of group therapy for binge eating disorder: Comparing dialectical behavior therapy adapted for binge eating to an active comparison group therapy. *Behavior Therapy, 41*(1), 106–120. https://doi.org/10.1016/j.beth.2009.01.006

Saul, J., Rodgers, R. F., & Saul, M. (2022). Adolescent eating disorder risk and the social online world: An update. *Child and Adolescent Psychiatric Clinics of North America, 31*(1), 167–177. doi:10.1016/j.chc.2021.09.004. PMID: 34801153.

Schmidt, U., Lee, S., Beecham, J., Perkins, S., Treasure, J., Yi, I., Winn, S., Robinson, P., Murphy, R., Deville, S., Johnson-Sabine, E., Jenkins, M., Frost, S., Dodge, L., Berelowtiz, M., & Eisler, I. (2007). A randomized controlled trial of family therapy and cognitive behavior therapy guided self-care for adolescents with bulimia nervosa and related disorders. *American Journal of Psychiatry, 164*, 591–598.

Shomaker, L. B., Tanofsky-Kraff, M., Elliott, C., Wolkoff, L. E., Columbo, K. M., Ranzenhofer, L. M., Roza, C. A., Yanovski, S. Z., & Yanovski, J. A. (2010). Salience of loss of control for pediatric binge episodes: does size really matter? *International Journal of Eating Disorders, 43*(8), 707–716. https://doi.org/10.1002/eat.20767

Smith, A. R., Forrest, L. N., Duffy, M. E., Jones, P. J., Joiner, T. E., & Pisetsky, E. M. (2020). Identifying bridge pathways between eating disorder symptoms and suicidal ideation across three samples. *Journal of Abnormal Psychology, 129*(7), 724–736.

Stefini, A., Salzer, S., Reich, G., Horn, H., Winkelmann, K., Bents, H., Rutz, U., Frost, U., von Boetticher, A., Ruhl, U., Specht, N., & Kronmüller, K. T. (2017). Cognitive-behavioral and psychodynamic therapy in female adolescents with bulimia nervosa: A randomized controlled trial. *Journal of the American Academy of Child and Adolescent Psychiatry, 56*(4), 329–335. https://doi.org/10.1016/j.jaac.2017.01.019

Stice, E., Marti, C. N., & Rohde, P. (2013). Prevalence, incidence, impairment, and course of the proposed DSM-5 eating disorder diagnoses in an 8-year prospective community study of young women. *Journal of Abnormal Psychology, 122*(2), 445–457. doi:10.1037/a0030679

Striegel-Moore, R. H., & Cachelin, F. M. (1999). Body image concerns and disordered eating in adolescent girls: Risk and protective factors. In N. G. Johnson, M. C. Roberts, & J. Worell (Eds.), *Beyond appearance: A new look at adolescent girls* (pp. 85–108). Washington, DC: American Psychological Association.

Sundgot-Borgen, J., & Torstveit, M. K. (2004). Prevalence of eating disorders in elite athletes is higher than in the general population. *Clinical Journal of Sport and Medicine, 14*, 25–32.

Swanson, S., Crow, S., Le Grange, D., Swendsen, J., & Merikangas, K. (2011). Prevalence and correlates of eating disorders in adolescents: Results from the national comorbidity survey replication adolescent supplement. *Archives of General Psychiatry, 68*, 714–723. doi:https://doi-org.proxy.library.upenn.edu/10.1001/archgenpsychiatry.2011.22

Tanofsky-Kraff, M., Goossens, L., Eddy, K. T., Ringham, R., Goldschmidt, A., Yanovski, S. Z., Braet, C., Marcus, M. D., Wilfley, D. E., Olsen, C., & Yanovski, J. A. (2007). A multisite investigation of binge eating behaviors in children and adolescents. *Journal of Consulting and Clinical Psychology, 75*(6), 901–913. https://doi.org/10.1037/0022-006X.75.6.901

Tanofsky-Kraff, M., Wilfley, D. E., Young, J. F., Mufson, M., Yanovski, S. Z., Glasofer, D. R., Salaita, C. G., & Schvey, N. A. (2010). A pilot study of interpersonal psychotherapy for preventing excess weight gain in adolescent girls at-risk for obesity. *International Journal of Eating Disorders, 43*(8), 701–706. https://doi.org/10.1002/eat.20773

Thompson, J. K., & Stice, E. (2001). Thin-ideal internalization: Mounting evidence for a new risk factor for body-image disturbance and eating pathology. *Current Directions in Psychological Science, 10*, 181–183.

Treasure, J., Duarte, T. A., & Schmidt, U. (2020). Eating disorders. *Lancet, 395*(10227), 899–911. doi:10.1016/S0140-6736(20)30059-3

Vall, E., & Wade, T. D. (2015). Predictors of treatment outcome in individuals with eating disorders: A systematic review and meta-analysis. *International Journal of Eating Disorders, 48*(7), 946–971. doi:10.1002/eat.22411

van Hoeken, D., & Hoek, H. W. (2020). Review of the burden of eating disorders: Mortality, disability, costs, quality of life, and family burden. *Current Opinion in Psychiatry, 33*(6), 521–527. doi:10.1097/YCO.0000000000000641

Ward, Z. J., Rodriguez, P., Wright, D. R., Austin, S. B., & Long, M. W. (2019). Estimation of eating disorders prevalence by age and associations with mortality in a simulated nationally representative us cohort. *JAMA Network Open, 2*(10). https://doi.org/10.1001/jamanetworkopen.2019.12925

Watson, H. J., Yilmaz, Z., Thornton, L. M., Hübel, C., Coleman, J. R., Gaspar, H. A., Bryois, J., Hinney, A., Leppä, V. M., Mattheisen, M., Medland, S. E., Ripke, S., Yao, S., Giusti-Rodríguez, P., Hanscombe, K. B., Purves, K. L., Adan, R. A., Alfredsson, L., Ando, T., . . . Bulik, C. M. (2019). Genome-wide association study identifies eight risk loci and implicates metabo-psychiatric origins for anorexia nervosa. *Nature Genetics, 51*(8), 1207–1214. https://doi.org/10.1038/s41588-019-0439-2

Whiteside, S. P., & Lynam, D. R. (2001). The Five Factor Model and impulsivity: Using a structural model of personality to understand impulsivity. *Personality and Individual Differences, 30*(4), 669–689. doi:10.1016/S0191-8869(00)00064-7

Wierenga, C. E., Ely, A., Bischoff-Grethe, A., Bailer, U. F., Simmons, A. N., & Kaye, W. H. (2014). Are extremes of consumption in eating disorders related to an altered balance between reward and inhibition? *Frontiers in Behavioral Neuroscience, 8*, 410. https://doi.org/10.3389/fnbeh.2014.00410

Wilson, G. T., Wilfley, D. E., Agras, W. S., & Bryson, S. W. (2010). Psychological treatments of binge eating disorder. *Archives of General Psychiatry, 67*(1), 94–101. https://doi.org/10.1001/archgenpsychiatry.2009.170

Yager, J., Devlin M., J., Halmi, K. A., Herzog, D. B., Mitchell III, J. E., Powers, P., & Zerbe, K. J. (2012). *Practice guideline for the treatment of patients with eating disorders*. Washington, DC: American Psychiatric Association, https://doi.org/10.1176/appi.focus.120404

Yilmaz, Z., Hardaway, J. A., & Bulik, C. M. (2015). Genetics and epigenetics of eating disorders. *Advances in Genomics and Genetics, 5*, 131–150. https://doi.org/10.2147/AGG.S55776

Zucker, N., Merwin, R., Elliott, C., Lacy, J., & Eichen, D. (2009). Assessment of eating disorder symptoms in children and adolescents. In J. L. Matson, F. Andrasik, & M. L. Matson (Eds.), *Assessing childhood psychology and developmental disabilities* (pp. 401–444). New York: Springer.

Trauma- and Stressor-Related Disorders

Ciara Davis is a 10-year-old Black female who presented to treatment at the child and adolescent outpatient clinic of a community mental health center with her mother, Ms. Kimberly Davis, and grandmother, Ms. Gerri Williams. Eight months earlier, Ciara, Ms. Davis, and Ms. Williams (along with several other extended family members and neighbors) had witnessed the shooting of Ciara's adult cousin Jay outside the home where he resided with Ms. Williams. Jay, who was 19 years old, died of his injuries. Jay had been involved with a gang and was known to sell drugs; the shooting was presumed to be related to a dispute with a rival gang, although no arrests had been made. Ms. Williams had allowed Jay to stay with her because he "had nowhere else to go" and expressed guilt that her allowing him to stay in her home had "brought this to my front door." Ciara and her 17-year-old sister Brianna lived with Ms. Davis and their father, Mr. Roy Davis, two blocks away from where the shooting occurred. Ms. Davis worked part-time as a hair stylist and Mr. Davis for the city's sanitation department. Ciara's family was described as close knit and, while her father was typically unable to attend treatment visits because of his work schedule, he was very involved in her life. Ms. Davis reported that she brought Ciara to treatment because, "Ever since she saw Jay get shot, she hasn't been the same little girl, she barely wants to leave the house, has nightmares, and hasn't been doing well in school so far this year. We just don't know how to help her." Neither Ciara nor her family members had received any treatment since Jay's death. Before witnessing her cousin's shooting, Ciara was described as a happy, outgoing girl and a good student.

OVERVIEW

The fifth edition of the *Diagnostic and Statistical Manual of Mental Disorders* (DSM-5) created a new chapter involving the stressor and trauma-related disorders, which include stress and trauma disorders, reactive attachment disorder, disinhibited social engagement disorder, acute stress disorder, and adjustment disorders. This chapter concentrates on *post-traumatic stress disorder*

Child and Adolescent Mental Health in Social Work. Jacqueline Corcoran and Courtney Benjamin Wolk, Oxford University Press.
© Oxford University Press 2023. DOI: 10.1093/oso/9780197653562.003.0013

(PTSD) for the most part, and, at the end of the chapter, we present a case on adjustment disorder.

Following exposure to a traumatic event characterized by threatened death, serious injury, or violence that is beyond the bounds of most human existence, the person with PTSD develops symptoms in four major categories (American Psychiatric Association [APA], 2022; see Table 13.1). *Intrusion* involves the traumatic events being reexperienced through recurrent or intrusive thoughts or images, nightmares, and flashbacks, and psychological and physiologic distress in response to cues of the traumatic event. At least one of six symptoms associated with these experiences is needed to demonstrate intrusion. For *avoidance* the person attempts to protect the self from the negative affect and arousal associated with reexperiencing internal or external cues (or both) of the event. *Alterations in mood* are indicated by at least two of the following symptoms: (1) an inability

Table 13.1 DSM Criteria for Post-traumatic Stress Disorder

Exposure to actual or threatened death, serious injury, or sexual violence and presence of symptoms in three domains:
 I. Intrusion (at least one symptom below)
   1. Recurrent, involuntary, intrusive memories of traumatic event(s)
   2. Recurrent distressing dreams that are related to the traumatic event
   3. Dissociative reactions in which the individual feels/acts as if the traumatic event is recurring
   4. Prolonged psychological distress at exposure to cues related to the traumatic event(s)
   5. Physiologic reactions to internal or external cues to the traumatic event(s)
 II. Avoidance (at least one)
   1. Of distressing memories, thoughts, or feelings
   2. Of external reminders of the event
III. Negative alterations in mood (at least two)
   1. Inability to remember an important part of the event
   2. Persistent and exaggerated negative beliefs or expectations about oneself, others, or the world
   3. Persistent, distorted cognitions about the cause/consequences of the traumatic event(s)
   4. Persistent negative emotional state
   5. Diminished interest/participation in activities
   6. Feelings of detachment or estrangement
   7. Persistent inability to experience positive emotions
IV. Marked alterations in arousal and reactivity (at least two)
   1. Irritability/anger
   2. Reckless/self-destructive behavior
   3. Hypervigilance
   4. Exaggerated startle response
   5. Problems with concentration
   6. Sleep disturbance

to remember aspects of the trauma experience; (2) negative beliefs about oneself, others, and the world; (3) a negative emotional state; (4) diminished interest in activities; (5) disengagement and estrangement from others; and (6) an inability to experience positive emotions. Finally, *increased arousal* is indicated by hypervigilance, insomnia, an inability to concentrate, an elevated startle response, irritability or anger, and self-destructive acts (at least two must be present). Intense anxiety symptoms that are experienced immediately after the traumatic event, but persist for less than 4 weeks, imply a different but related diagnosis: *acute stress disorder* (APA, 2022), which occurs in 21% of the population of youths (Hiller et al., 2016).

Prevalence

For youths, lifetime rates of PTSD range between 1.3% and 6%. Therefore, it is a relatively rare condition, considering that two-thirds of youths experience a traumatic event (Copeland et al., 2007). A meta-analysis on rates of PTSD in trauma-exposed children found the overall rate of PTSD using DSM-IV criteria was 15.9% (Alisic et al., 2014). For preschoolers, rates of PTSD among those who have experienced trauma is 22% (Woolgar et al., 2022). For adolescents specifically, according to the National Comorbidity Survey Replication Adolescent Supplement, a majority of adolescents (62%) have experienced a traumatic event; however, rates of PTSD were 4.7% (McLaughlin et al., 2013). When examining various timepoints after trauma, at 3 months 15% of youths experiencing trauma had PTSD (Hiller et al., 2016), at 6 months 12%, and at 12 months 11%. While relatively rare, PTSD is a serious condition that is associated with deleterious outcomes, including suicidal thoughts and behaviors in adolescents, which surpass those experienced for depression (Panagioti et al., 2015).

RISK AND PROTECTIVE FACTORS

At the heart of the development of PTSD lies a trauma, an environmental event to which the individual has been subjected, even though biological and psychological factors within that individual, and the level of environmental support, may influence whether PTSD develops.

Biological

Biological processes have been associated with the occurrence of PTSD. The extent to which these processes are risk influences for PTSD or result from the person's experiencing certain types of traumatic events is unknown. For PTSD, having a shorter version of the serotonin transporter gene appears to increase one's risk for depression as well as for PTSD after exposure to extremely stressful situations (Bryant et al., 2010; Xie et al., 2009). This same gene variant increases the activation of an emotion control center in the brain known as the amygdala (Bryant et al., 2010). Further, people with PTSD tend to have abnormal levels of some key hormones that are involved in their response to stress (Knapp, 2006). Their cortisol levels are lower than normal, and their norepinephrine and epinephrine levels are higher than average. Scientists have also found that people with PTSD experience alterations in the function of the thyroid gland and in neurotransmitter activity involving serotonin and the opiates (Yehuda, 2006). When people are in danger, they naturally produce high levels of opiates, which temporarily mask emotional pain, but people with PTSD continue to produce those higher levels even after the danger has passed. This may lead to the blunting of emotions often associated with the condition.

Brain-imaging studies show that the hippocampus (a part of the brain critical to emotion-laden memories) appears to be smaller in persons with PTSD (Jatzko et al., 2006). Although most people who experience severe trauma exhibit a normal stress response, the stress response system becomes deregulated and chronically overactive in PTSD, causing compromised immune functioning (Uddin et al., 2010). PTSD has long been linked to an increased risk of numerous physical health problems, including diabetes and cardiovascular disease.

Psychological

Cognitive-behavioral theories attempt to explain the development and maintenance of PTSD, along with learning and emotional processing theory (Gonzalez-Prendes & Resko, 2012). A respondent conditioning theory of PTSD involves conditioned or associative learning (Mowerer, 1960), a process that has been similarly described for other anxiety disorders and obsessive-compulsive disorder (OCD). Cues from the traumatic experience (certain sensory details) may become conditioned to fear based on their association with the trauma. People then avoid these cues, and avoidance of anxiety becomes negatively reinforced when anxiety is reduced as a result. Cognitive theories of PTSD have emerged from Horowitz's (1976) influential information processing model as reviewed by Calhoun and Resick (1993). In the information processing theory of trauma, adjustment to a traumatic event involves incorporation of the experience into cognitive schemas, which are the structures people use to perceive, organize, store, and retrieve experiences and to make meaning of events. In this model, the person may be unable to process exposure to trauma. The trauma remains in active memory, but outside conscious awareness. The defense mechanisms of denial and numbing are activated to prevent the individual from being overwhelmed. The material stays active and is manifested by flashbacks, nightmares, anxiety, and depression. Cycles of denial and numbing alternate with bouts of intrusive thoughts and intense emotion as the individual attempts to integrate the experience into existing cognitive structures.

Social

Two meta-analyses conducted to determine predictors for the onset of PTSD found that social influences, involving trauma severity and lack of social support, posed the largest risks (Brewin et al., 2000; Ozer et al., 2003). In addition to severity, other features of the traumatic experience linked to PTSD involve the degree of exposure to the trauma (intensity, duration, and frequency) and the person's subjective sense of danger (Ford et al., 2006; Memarzia et al., 2021). Certain types of traumatic events may also predispose a person to PTSD, including war-related events (including refugee and immigration status), criminal victimization, exposure to natural disasters (Mineka & Zinbarg, 2006), family violence, maltreatment, and sexual assault. For adolescents, prior trauma exposure is related to the development of PTSD in the face of another event (McLaughlin et al., 2013). For preschoolers, interpersonal trauma was associated with greater risk of developing PTSD (Woolgar et al., 2022).

For youths, living in an adverse family environment, particularly not living with both biological parents (McLaughlin et al., 2013), may predispose those experiencing traumatic events to develop PTSD. Further, children with parents who have PTSD often develop PTSD themselves (Linares & Cloitre, 2004). This may be due to genetic predisposition; exposure to violence that is directed toward a parent, such as community or domestic violence; or the parents' own PTSD, which hampers their parenting abilities. For children of all ages, any threats to a caregiver are risk factors for the development of the disorder (Scheeringa et al., 2006). For adolescents, risk factors at the social level for negative outcomes involved poverty, being born outside the United States, and further trauma exposure (McLaughlin et al., 2013).

ASSESSMENT

Screening for PTSD should take place 3 to 6 months after trauma to detect cases that warrant intervention (Hiller et al., 2018). Recall that *acute stress disorder* should be the diagnosis if the symptoms resolve within 4 weeks. PTSD requires careful differential diagnosis because other disorders may be more appropriate, may share overlapping symptoms, or are comorbid. See Table 13.2 for some diagnostic considerations and Table 13.3 for measurement instruments. Because PTSD often presents with suicidal thoughts and behaviors, assessments for self-harm and suicide risk are important (Panagioti et al., 2015). See Chapter 11.

Readers may also hear the term *complex PTSD* (Guina et al., 2017). The decision was made not to include this term in DSM-5, although it is a diagnosis in the International Classification of Diseases (ICD; World Health Organization, 2018). Generally, it has been referred to in the literature as a complex symptom constellation involving severe emotional dysregulation, in addition to PTSD symptoms, from exposure to sustained, repeated, or multiple traumas. Cloitre et al. (2009)

Table 13.2 CONSIDERATIONS FOR DIFFERENTIAL DIAGNOSIS

Other Diagnosis	Considerations
Attention-deficit/ hyperactivity disorder (ADHD)	In trauma, chronic hyperarousal can resemble hyperactivity and poor impulse control; intrusive thoughts can interfere with attention and concentration
Oppositional defiant disorder (ODD)	Exposure to trauma cues may result in agitation/irritability. Arousal may come off as an angry profile in which irritability, vigilance for threat, and tension are high. Trauma may result in beliefs about the need for control to ward off threat and can lead to conflict/aggression.
Adjustment disorder with anxiety	Number of symptoms or stressful life event is not sufficient for post-traumatic stress disorder (PTSD)
Depression	A traumatic history may result in disorders other than PTSD, and depression in adults is more common than PTSD after trauma. One criterion of the symptom profile involves what look like depression: (1) negative beliefs about oneself, others, and the world; (2) a negative emotional state; (3) diminished interest in activities; (4) disengagement and estrangement from others; and (5) an inability to experience positive emotions.

SOURCE: Information drawn from Cohen et al. (2010); Perrin, Smith, & Yule (2000); and Weinstein, Staffelbach, & Biaggo (2000).

argue that this conceptualization provides coherence to the multiple, diffuse, and sometimes contradictory symptoms apparent in both children and adults. In an Austrian sample of foster children, confirmatory factor analysis provided evidence of construct validity for ICD-11 PTSD and complex PTSD as empirically distinguishable disorders in children (Haselgruber et al., 2020).

During the initial intake appointment, the clinician conducted separate clinical interviews with (1) Ciara and (2) her mother and grandmother. Clinical interviews comprised thorough personal and family histories, review of risk and protective factors, assessment of symptoms of PTSD, and assessment of other disorders important for a careful differential diagnosis, including anxiety, depression, other stress and adjustment disorders, attention-deficit/hyperactivity disorder (ADHD), and psychosis. The clinician also asked Ciara to complete the Child PTSD Symptom Scale (CPSS; Foa et al., 2001) to assess PTSD symptoms and current functioning.

Both Ciara and her caregivers reported that Ciara had experienced a significant traumatic event that is classified in DSM-5 as a PTSD criterion A.2. trauma: witnessing in person a significant traumatic event—the shooting death of her cousin Jay. No other significant traumas in her history were reported. Since that event, Ciara was experiencing the following symptoms: recurrent, intrusive, and upsetting memories and dreams of the event and avoidance of memories of the event. Ciara said, "I don't like to talk about what happened," and Ms. Davis reported that, "Ciara gets upset when we mention Jay. She doesn't like when we try to

Table 13.3 MEASUREMENT INSTRUMENTS FOR POST-TRAUMATIC STRESS DISORDER

Psychometric Support	Measure Name	No. of Items	Completed by[a]	Ages[c]	Link to Measure
Excellent	Child Post-traumatic Cognitions Inventory (CPTCI; Maiser-Stedman et al., 2009)*	25	Y	6–18	http://www.childrenandwar.org/projectsresources/measures/
Good	Children's Revised Impact of Event Scale (CRIES; Perrin et al., 2005)*	8 or 13	Y	8–18	http://www.childrenandwar.org/projectsresources/measures/
Good	Child and Youth Resilience Measure Revised (CYRM; Jefferies et al., 2018)*	17	Y, P	5–23	http://cyrm.resilienceresearch.org/download/
Good	Child and Adolescent Trauma Screen (CATS; Sachser et al., 2017)*	20	Y, P	3–17	https://depts.washington.edu/hcsats/PDF/TF-%20CBT/pages/assessment.html
Good	Child PTSD Symptom Scale (CPSS-5-SR; Foa et al., 2018)*	6 or 24	Y	8–18	http://www.midss.org/content/child-ptsd-symptom-scale-cpss
Adequate	Child Trauma Screen (CTSQ; Kenardy et al., 2006)	10	Y	7–16	https://www.nctsn.org/measures/child-trauma-screening-questionnaire
Adequate	Child Stress Disorders Checklist (CSDC; Saxe 2001 and Saxe et al., 2003)	36	P	2–18	https://www.nctsn.org/measures/child-stress-disorders-checklist

[a] Completed by: Y = youth; P = parent/caregiver; C = clinician; T = teacher.

[b] Intended clinical use: S = screening; D = diagnostic aid or treatment planning; O = outcome monitoring.

[c] Exact age range for specific forms (e.g., self-report, parent report) may vary.

[d] Exact age range not specified.

* Available in multiple languages.

NOTE: Table adapted from Becker-Haimes, E. M., Tabachnick, A. R., Last, B. S., Stewart, R. E., Hasan-Granier, A., & Beidas, R. S. (2020). Evidence base update for brief, free, and accessible youth mental health measures. *Journal of Clinical Child & Adolescent Psychology*, 49(1), 1–17, reprinted by permission of the publisher (Taylor & Francis Ltd, http://www.tandfonline.com).

(continued)

Table 13.3 CONTINUED

References for measures in Table 13.3:

Foa, E. B., Asnaani, A., Zang, Y., Capaldi, S., & Yeh, R. (2018). Psychometrics of the Child PTSD Symptom Scale for DSM-5 for trauma-exposed children and adolescents. *Journal of Clinical Child & Adolescent Psychology, 47*(1), 38–46.

Jefferies, P., McGarrigle, L., & Ungar, M. (2019). The CYRM-R: A Rasch-validated revision of the Child and Youth Resilience Measure. *Journal of Evidence-Based Social Work, 16*(1), 70–92.

Kenardy, J. A., Spence, S. H., & Macleod, A. C. (2006). Screening for posttraumatic stress disorder in children after accidental injury. *Pediatrics, 118*(3), 1002–1009.

Meiser-Stedman, R., Smith, P., Bryant, R., Salmon, K., Yule, W., Dalgleish, T., & Nixon, R. D. (2009). Development and validation of the child post-traumatic cognitions inventory (CPTCI). *Journal of Child Psychology and Psychiatry, 50*(4), 432–440.

Perrin, S., Meiser-Stedman, R., & Smith, P. (2005). The Children's Revised Impact of Event Scale (CRIES): Validity as a screening instrument for PTSD. *Behavioural and Cognitive Psychotherapy, 33*(4), 487–498.

Sachser, C., Berliner, L., Holt, T., Jensen, T. K., Jungbluth, N., Risch, E., Rosner, R., & Goldbeck, L. (2017). International development and psychometric properties of the Child and Adolescent Trauma Screen (CATS). *Journal of Affective Disorders, 210,* 189–195.

Saxe, G., Chawla, N., Stoddard, F., Kassam-Adams, N., Courtney, D., Cunningham, K., Lopez, C., Hall, E., Sheridan, R., King, D., & King, L. (2003). Child Stress Disorders Checklist: A measure of ASD and PTSD in children. *Journal of the American Academy of Child & Adolescent Psychiatry, 42*(8), 972–978.

talk about him or what happened. I don't think it's good that she keeps it all bottled up, but she just doesn't want to talk about it." Ciara also has reportedly refused to go to her grandmother's house or to walk down the block where the shooting occurred since the event. Ms. Williams stated, "The whole family used to come over every Sunday for dinner, and Ciara used to always come visit me after school. Now she won't come by." Since the event, Ciara reported that she often feels "sad" and said, "I just want to stay in my house where it's safe." Additionally, Ciara and her mother reported she has had trouble sleeping well since the event and has an exaggerated startle response. Ms. Davis noted that Ciara has not been doing well in school and that it seems like Ciara has trouble concentrating on her schoolwork. "When she's doing her homework, I find her just staring off in space, or she loses her place. It takes forever, and I have to really keep on her." Previously, Ciara had been a straight-A student, suggesting her academic difficulties were the result of impaired concentration related to PTSD and not a symptom of a learning disorder or ADHD. Loud noises, including fireworks, a car backfiring, or a garbage truck emptying a dumpster cause Ciara to startle considerably. "When that happens, she just practically jumps out of her skin. She starts crying and shaking, and it is so hard to calm her down," said Ms. Davis. The event had occurred 8 months ago, and these symptoms had been present since that time, thus PTSD was the appropriate diagnosis and not acute stress disorder.

Neither Ciara nor her mother and grandmother reported any symptoms of dissociation or symptoms of psychosis. The anxiety she was experiencing (e.g., panic symptoms, avoidance) was related to the traumatic event and thus did not seem better explained by a diagnosis of an anxiety disorder such as generalized anxiety disorder or panic disorder. Given that Ciara reported often feeling "sad" and had difficulties talking about her cousin since his death, the clinician was careful to assess for symptoms of major depressive disorder (MDD) and persistent complex bereavement disorder (listed in DSM-5 as one of the "conditions for further study).

She determined that Ciara's avoidance and intrusive memories were related to the traumatic event and a desire to avoid internal and external trauma reminders as opposed to a focus on thoughts related to her relationship with her cousin Jay, memories of him, and missing him, which would be more characteristic of a bereavement reaction. Thus, persistent complex bereavement disorder was ruled out. In terms of symptoms that might be consistent with MDD, Ciara reported that since the trauma, she has been feeling "sad" most days, and her mother reported that she no longer had much interest in activities she used to enjoy, such as spending time with friends, playing games with her parents, or spending time with her sister doing each other's nails and hair, something she had previously enjoyed very much. She also experienced difficulty concentrating, a third symptom of MDD. Ciara reported that she hadn't been sleeping well since the trauma but said this was because, "when I fall asleep, I have bad dreams about what happened," which is more characteristic of PTSD than insomnia related to MDD. Additionally, Ciara reported that she often thinks about death, stating that she worries "that I could get shot or someone else I love could get shot just walking down the street." Given *the relationship of some of these symptoms to the traumatic event experienced, the clinician determined that a comorbid diagnosis of MDD was not warranted at this time but that careful monitoring of depressive symptoms going forward would be important.*

This was also important because Ms. Davis reported a family history of depression (she herself had experienced a significant depressive episode in her 20s), and an aunt of Ms. Davis's on her father's side of the family had died by suicide. The family history was also positive for substance misuse and legal problems. Ms. Davis's sister, who died from a drug overdose, had two children, Jay and another son Antoine, both of whom used and sold marijuana (and possibly other drugs). Antoine, aged 23, was currently incarcerated for distributing drugs. Both Jay and Antoine had considerable academic difficulties as children but had never received formal evaluations or diagnoses to Ms. Davis's or Ms. Williams's knowledge.

With these exceptions, the family was largely stable; the Davis's nuclear family was close and supportive, and both parents were regularly employed. Ms. Williams, Ciara's grandmother, reported during the intake that she herself had also been having a difficult time dealing with Jay's death, stating, "I understand what she's (Ciara) going through." Ms. Williams reported that she had also been experiencing frequent memories and flashbacks of the event and feeling guilty that her decision to allow Jay to stay with her had resulted in a dangerous situation for her family. At the end of the intake appointment, the clinician suggested to Ms. Williams that she may benefit from treatment herself. Ms. Williams initially stated, "Oh no, I'm just here for Ciara." The clinician explained that "taking care of yourself is a very important part of being able to take care of your family" and that "showing Ciara that you are getting help to deal with this very upsetting event lets her know that it's ok to get help too. I think you'd be setting a great example for her." With support from the clinician and Ms. Davis, Ms. Williams agreed to make an appointment for herself with one of the clinician's colleagues.

INTERVENTION

According to a large population-based study, almost 60% of youths with PTSD in a 1-year period (2012) receive psychotherapy. Almost 10% receive medication (Soria-Saucedo et al., 2018). Over one-third (35%) receive neither, indicating a gap in treatment.

Trauma-Focused Cognitive-Behavioral Therapy

Trauma-focused CBT is an umbrella term for treatments that involve a focus on traumatic memories and their meaning through cognitive restructuring and reframing or exposure (Cary & McMillern, 2012; Morina et al., 2016). This umbrella includes what Curtis and McMillen (2012) have termed the "branded" model developed by Cohen and colleagues (2006). The branded model is manualized in weekly 1½-hour sessions, structured by eight components with the acronym PRACTICE:

P: psychoeducation and parenting skills
R: relaxation
A: affective expression and regulation
C: cognitive coping
T: trauma narrative development and processing
I: in-vivo exposure
C: conjoint parent–child sessions. Note that sometimes parents are in individual meetings (e.g., Cohen et al., 2004; Cohen & Mannarino, 1996, 1998; Deblinger & Heflin, 1996; Kolko, 1996) or conjoint sessions in addition to individual child and individual parent meetings (e.g., Cohen et al., 2004; Deblinger & Heflin, 1996).
E: enhancing safety/future development

The branded version has been widely disseminated through a Web-based training program, funded through the National Child Traumatic Stress Network. For sexual abuse victims, it has been modified in many ways for the needs of community youths (see Table 13.4 and reviews by Cary & McMillen, 2012; Rudd et al., 2019). As is true in other forms of CBT, play can be used within the context of TF-CBT as a way to engage youths in treatment and to teach evidence-based concepts in a developmentally appropriate manner.

At this point, several systematic reviews and meta-analyses have been conducted. We summarize some of the more recent, and others are covered in Table 13.3. Cary and McMillen (2012) found that TF-CBT was more effective than attention control, standard community care, and waitlist control conditions at improving depression and problem behaviors at post-test, although these alternative conditions often caught up at 12-month follow-up. The authors noted, however, that many of the alternative condition interventions had elements of the experimental conditions, such as psychoeducation and exposure. Nonbranded TF-CBT appeared to do as well as the "branded" version.

A review published 4 years later indicated that the overall pooled effect size for TF-CBT was strongest for PTSD (Gutermann et al., 2016). When comparing TF-CBT with treatment-as-usual or active control, CBT showed advantages in small effects for PTSD ($g = .45$) depression ($g = .37$), and anxiety ($g = .42$). The general finding in meta-analysis is that the more well-controlled studies tend to produce smaller effects (Littel et al., 2008). However, in this review, the effect sizes for these three outcomes were higher for the randomized controlled trial studies and reached a medium-effect advantage (Gutermann et al., 2016).

In focusing on the nonoffending parents involved in TF-CBT, a review indicated that parents also benefit from treatment in terms of decreasing caregiver depression, emotional distress, and PTSD (Martin et al., 2019). Further, this review suggests that parent depression, rather than PTSD or distress, influences how well children do in treatment. Similarly, Cary and McMillen (2012) found, in

Table 13.4 ADAPTATIONS OF "BRANDED" TRAUMA-FOCUSED
COGNITIVE-BEHAVIORAL THERAPY

Adaptation	Reference
Language adaptations (German, Chinese)	Cohen et al. (2010)
Ongoing exposure to community violence	Cohen et al. (2011) include addressing safety early in treatment and trauma narrative processing that differentiates between realistic fears and trauma reminders
	Miller-Graff & Campion (2016)
School	Cognitive Behavioral Intervention for Trauma in Schools has the same elements of the branded version of TF-CBT but involves an individual and group format and training is available: http://cbits program.org/course/intro/6148
	A meta-analysis (19 studies; N = 4,655) found that school-based CBT was most successful in reducing trauma symptoms when compared with other types of treatments (d = .68), including play/art therapy, (eye movement desensitization and reprocessing [EMDR]), and mind–body skills (d = .68) (Rolfsnes & Idsoe, 2011)
Ethnic minority	Warfield (2013)
—African American adolescents	Weiner, Schneider, & Lyons (2009)
—Engagement strategies for parents	Staudt (2007)
Natural disasters (Hurricane Katrina)	Jaycox et al. (2010)
Youth in foster care	Dorsey, Kerns, Trupin, Conover, & Berliner (2012)
Engaging foster parents	Dorsey et al. (2014); Weiner et al. (2009)
Youth with incarcerated parents	Morgan-Mullane (2017)
Sexual abuse	CBT was effective for PTSD although not externalizing behaviors (Macdonald et al., 2016).
Adolescents	Amaya-Jackson et al. (2003)
—School version for adolescents experiencing trauma-related symptoms to a wide range of traumas	TARGET model (CBT) (Advanced Trauma Solutions, 2001–2010; Ford et al., 2005)
—Youths in juvenile detention centers	
Child maltreatment	TF-CBT was the best supported treatment following child maltreatment, with evidence that improvements were maintained at longer term follow up (Bennett et al., 2020).

SOURCE: Drawn from reviews in Black, Woodworth, Tremblay, & Carpenter (2012); Cary & McMillen (2012); and Rudd et al. (2019).

their review, that involvement of parents was a positive moderator for child outcome, and Corcoran and Pillai indicated that parent-involved treatment (mostly
TF-CBT) resulted in advantages over child-only treatment on internalizing,
externalizing, sexualized behaviors, and post-traumatic stress symptoms.
However, a review with more recent studies concluded that parents being part of
treatment might not be necessary (Dorsey et al., 2017). This finding is important
for settings like schools where the ability to provide a parent component would be
difficult. For the treatment of trauma in schools, the intervention with the most
empirical support is Cognitive Behavioral Intervention for Trauma in Schools
(CBITS; Stein et al., 2003).

As far as who benefits most from TF-CBT, older children appear to do better
(Cary & McMillan, 2012; Gutermann et al., 2016; Miller-Graff & Campion, 2016;
Newman et al. 2014; Trask et al. 2011). Therefore, treatments for younger children
may need modifications (Cary & McMillen, 2012). A survey of 460 therapists indicated that nondirective play therapy was a popular treatment approach for trauma
in the community (Cohen et al., 2001). A recent systematic review identified
seven studies of child-centered play therapy, although this literature is limited
by a lack of specificity of treatment methods. Generally, results for studies of play
therapy were positive, although there was a great deal of variation in outcomes;
unfortunately, PTSD symptoms generally did not improve (Humble et al., 2019).
In the couple of studies in which it was used as a control condition, nondirective
play therapy was inferior to CBT (e.g., Cohen & Mannarino, 1996, 1998).

Eye Movement Desensitization and Reprocessing

Another treatment used in the community is eye movement desensitization and
reprocessing (EMDR; Curtis & McMillen, 2012). This approach pairs a client's
eye movements with processing of traumatic memories. Shapiro, its creator,
has outlined the method in a book (Shapiro, 2017) and created an international
training program. Recently, a systematic review, comprising eight studies and almost 300 participants, found that EMDR was advantageous to waitlist/placebo
conditions (Moreno-Alcázar et al., 2017). Further, it was similar in effectiveness
to TF-CBT in reducing post-traumatic and anxiety symptoms. EMDR has been
the subject of controversy, with some research suggesting the eye movements are
unnecessary and that the active mechanism of treatment is exposure (Davidson
& Parker, 2001; Herbert et al., 2000). Because of these findings, more research is
needed.

Medication

The U.S. Food and Drug Administration (FDA) has not approved any medications
for PTSD in youths. In a nationally representative study of a private insurer database, 71% of youths who were prescribed medications for PTSD were prescribed

antidepressants, which may reflect the symptom overlap of depression and PTSD, and that antidepressants in general have been widely researched (Soria-Saucedo et al., 2018). Twenty-two percent were prescribed antipsychotics, but these are associated with serious side effects (see Chapter 3), and 7% were prescribed benzodiazepines, which are associated with risk of dependence. Medication use was more common among older youths with medical and mental health comorbidity in the southern United States, which tends to have more areas of rural poverty and a lower number of psychosocial treatment providers.

Ciara's treatment consisted of TF-CBT, which included the following components: familial education, relaxation training, emotion identification and regulation skills, cognitive coping, trauma narration and processing, and in-vivo exposures. Treatment consisted of weekly sessions over the course of 15 weeks that included both individual and family sessions.

The first step of TF-CBT is psychoeducation, which began during the intake and continued throughout treatment as needed. The goal for Ciara and her family was for the clinician to provide education about PTSD, including common trauma reactions for children, and an overview of what to expect in TF-CBT treatment. The therapist explained that Ciara's reaction to witnessing her cousin's shooting was a reaction that many children in the same situation may have, assured her that she was not going crazy, and explained what treatment would entail. Throughout the conversation, she sought to instill hope in Ciara that treatment could help reduce her symptoms. She also explained to Ciara and her family what they could expect from treatment, emphasizing the collaborative nature of CBT, and that they would work together on a weekly basis to face and resolve the traumatic experience.

Additionally, throughout treatment the clinician provided education to Ms. Davis about parenting a child experiencing a trauma reaction. The clinician's goal was to help Ciara's parents learn effective strategies for dealing with challenging behaviors. While Ciara was largely compliant with parental requests, at times her behavior benefited from clinician input. For example, homework completion had become challenging because of poor concentration. The clinician worked with Ms. Davis to help her identify an optimal time and location in the home when homework could best be completed without distraction, instituted frequent breaks and parental checks during homework time, and implemented a reward for completing homework (30 minutes of TV time after dinner). Given Ciara's reported nightmares and sleep difficulties, the clinician also worked with Ms. Davis to ensure that an appropriate nighttime routine and sleep schedule were in place.

Relaxation skills were taught to Ciara and her caregivers as a tool to help her manage intense symptoms of physiologic arousal (e.g., racing heart when reminded of trauma). The clinician began by explaining, "Our bodies have a 'fight or flight' response that kicks in when we are in dangerous situations. Sometimes what happens is that the response kicks in when we are reminded about something scary, even when we aren't in real danger anymore. When that happens, we can experience a racing heart, sweating, difficulty breathing, or other physical symptoms that can be scary or uncomfortable. We can practice ways to help our bodies relax, and these relaxation strategies can help calm our bodies down when we start to have those intense physical feelings." The clinician taught Ciara diaphragmatic breathing ("belly breathing") by explaining the rationale for deep breathing, demonstrating it, and then leading Ciara in practicing it. She helped Ciara demonstrate the technique for her mother and then assigned her to practice it for homework, asking in subsequent sessions whether she was practicing it outside of session, assessing how well it was working for her, and discussing opportunities when it would be useful to employ the skill in her everyday activities. Similarly, the clinician taught Ciara progressive muscle relaxation and discussed other calming activities that may be helpful (e.g., listening to soft music before bed).

Emotion identification and regulation skills and cognitive coping strategies were also an important component of Ciara's treatment. For example, the clinician worked with Ciara to help her label her emotions (e.g., "I'm feeling sad today" or "I don't want to walk that way because going near Grandma's house scares me"), to communicate her emotional experiences to her caregivers effectively, and to understand how those feelings relate to her traumatic experience. They also discussed strategies for increasing experience of positive emotions, such as planning and engaging in pleasant activities (e.g., painting nails with her sister) with family or friends even if she didn't feel like it that day or didn't think it would be fun.

The clinician also provided education about the connection between thoughts, feelings, and behavior (i.e., the CBT triangle) and how a traumatic experience can be associated with certain unhelpful or inaccurate patterns in thinking that can then lead to certain feelings (e.g., sadness, worry) and behaviors (e.g., avoidance). The clinician illustrated this with an example from information Ciara and her family had shared.

> **Clinician:** *You mentioned that when something reminds you about the day Jay was shot you feel scared. What goes through your mind when that happens?*
> **Ciara:** *I think about how I could get shot or my mom or dad or grandma could just get shot walking down the street.*
> **Clinician:** *It sounds like you have thoughts about it being unsafe to be outside. When that happens, you feel scared. What do you usually do when you have those thoughts and feelings?*
> **Ciara:** *I just want to stay home.*
> **Clinician:** *I see. So, when you have the thought that being outside is unsafe and feel scared, you avoid going outside. That makes a lot of sense.*

The clinician, Ms. Davis, and Ciara then discussed the accuracy of this. Ms. Davis explained to Ciara that Jay had "made some poor choices in his life" that resulted in him being in some risky situations and that the path he had taken was very different from the one Ciara was on. Previously, the clinician and Ms. Davis realized, Ciara had not really understood the circumstances of the shooting or Jay's illicit activities. They discussed that, while they could not guarantee that nothing bad would ever happen to her, it was unlikely that Ciara or her parents or grandmother (who were not involved in gangs or illegal activities) would be the target of violence.

Central to Ciara's treatment was the creation of her trauma narrative. Given Ciara's age and cognitive abilities, the clinician and Ciara agreed to write the trauma narrative in the form of a chapter book. Ciara dictated the narrative with support and prompting from the clinician, while the clinician typed it on the computer. They reviewed, edited, and added to the narrative over time. Over the course of four sessions, Ciara's trauma narrative was constructed.

The clinician began the process by explaining that they would work together to write out the story of what had happened the day of the shooting. They would do this gradually, at a pace Ciara was comfortable with and in control of, and that doing so was important for helping Ciara "make sense of what happened that day" and "learn how to handle the thoughts and feelings that come up when you are reminded of that day, so that they aren't so overwhelming and so that you can lead the life you want. Talking through what happened will, over time, help the feelings to not be so strong and intense and help you feel like you are more in control of your mind and body. As you are ready, we will share your story of that day with your mom so that she can help support you in this process."

Ciara's trauma narrative contained chapters describing her life before the shooting and the lead-up to the event (e.g., walking over to and arriving at her grandmother's house), the event itself, and the aftermath (e.g., hearing updates about Jay's condition from family who were at the hospital, hearing that he had died, and the funeral). Throughout, the clinician coached Ciara to share her story while providing support and structure for her. For example, saying, "Today, if you are ready, I'd like for us to write the first chapter of your story, in which we will write about who you were before the shooting occurred. I won't ask anything about the shooting today, we will start to talk about that over the coming weeks though." Then, in subsequent sessions, the clinician and Ciara would review what they had previously written, revise or add to it as needed, and then continue moving the draft forward by writing about what happened next. The clinician was careful to follow Ciara's pace and to try to balance helping her to continue to move the narrative forward without pushing too fast. The clinician helped Ciara to create a complete narrative by asking questions to fill in details, including, "What happened next? What did you see (or smell, hear, feel in your body)?" Ciara was encouraged to experience the feelings associated with the traumatic event and to employ the skills she had learned thus far (e.g., relaxation, cognitive coping) to effectively cope with the feelings. The therapist also helped to correct misinformation. For example, Ciara initially believed the shooting was mostly random and that any of them could have been killed; the therapist and Ms. Davis were able to correct this by providing her with the information that the police believed Jay had been targeted by rival gang members and that random shootings in their area were mostly unheard of. An excerpt from Ciara's trauma narrative is included here to illustrate the level of detail that can be helpful to achieve.

My mom and I walked into Grandma's house. I could smell meatloaf in the oven and heard my cousin Dee and Grandma talking and laughing about something in the other room. It was hot in the living room because Grandma's *house doesn't have air conditioning. We said hi to Grandma and Dee, and then Mom said, "Let's go sit outside while we wait for dinner to be ready." Mom and I went outside and sat on the stoop. It was hot outside and sunny, but we were in the shade on Grandma's stoop. I told my mom a joke about turtles that I'd heard at school that day, and she laughed. Then Jay and Antoine and one of their friends whose name I don't know walked up from around the corner. We said hi to each other. They sat on the neighbor's stoop and were talking to each other mostly and my mom and I kept talking to ourselves. Then Grandma and my cousin Dee came outside, and Grandma said dinner would be ready in 10 minutes. She asked Jay and Antoine's friend if he wanted to stay for dinner, and he said, "Sure." I didn't really notice it, but a car pulled up, a blue car, it wasn't a really busy street but was kind of busy, so I guess I didn't really notice at first, but I looked up and saw a guy in the front of the car holding a black gun. He looked like he was about the age of my cousins, but I didn't see his face very well. It happened really fast—my mom pushed me down on the ground next to the stoop and fell on top of me, and it hurt, and I could hear people screaming and then a few really loud pops and then more screaming and then tires squealing. It was the car driving away really fast I guess that made that noise, but I didn't see because I was on the ground face down with my mom on top of me. Mom started to scream and got up and before I could really figure out what was going on she pulled me up and basically just pushed me into the house and told me to go in the kitchen and stay there. I went into the kitchen, and I could still smell the meatloaf. I could hear everyone out front and everyone was screaming, and my mom was crying really loud and yelling, "Oh my god, oh my god. Call 911." And then I waited for a minute, but then I got worried about my mom. I was so scared hearing everyone screaming, and I didn't know what was happening and didn't want to be by myself, so I went to the living room and looked out the front door, and I saw Mom and Grandma and Aunt Dee and Antoine next door and they were standing over Jay and he was on the ground and there was this huge puddle of blood and I couldn't really see his face because Antoine was over him but he wasn't moving and then I heard sirens and they got louder and louder and two police cars pulled up and the cops jumped out of the car. This big, tall cop saw me and said, "Get inside!" so I ran back in the house, and I was so scared. Then my mom ran in and said, "I told you to stay inside," and I started to cry, and she was crying too, and we sat on the couch together and cried. There were more sirens then and an ambulance came and took Jay to the hospital and Grandma and Antoine went with it and so did Dee, I think. Mom and I sat there crying a few more minutes after that, and Mom called Dad and told him Jay got shot. Dad came over and we locked up Grandma's house and walked home together. They tried to cover my eyes when we walked outside and made me walk the long way around the block so I wouldn't have to walk past all the blood, but I peeked a little and saw it—it was a huge, huge puddle on the neighbor's stoop and sidewalk of bright red blood. It looked like paint and it smelled kind of funny outside, but I don't really know how to describe the smell.*

While Ms. Davis was often involved in portions of Ciara's sessions (e.g., psycho-education, so Ciara could teach her mom the relaxation skills she was learning, to explain the cognitive model), parental involvement was particularly important at the stage that Ciara was ready to share her trauma narrative with her mother. There were several goals to having Ciara share the narrative with her mother. The narrative provided a structure for Ciara and her mother to talk about the trauma and for her mother to gain insight into Ciara's understanding and interpretation of the events and her reactions. The clinician provided structure and support to Ciara as she became increasingly comfortable sharing the narrative and supported Ms. Davis in responding appropriately. Before having Ciara share the narrative with her mother, the clinician met with Ms. Davis individually to prepare her for what she would hear in the narrative and coached her how to stay calm and support Ciara, for example, by role playing giving positive, supportive feedback, such as saying, "Thank you for sharing that chapter with me, it really helps me to understand what that day was like for you." After sharing the narrative with her mother, Ciara decided she would like to share it with her father and Grandmother. The clinician spoke with Mr. Davis by phone to prepare him for that. She also coordinated with Ms. Williams's therapist to determine an appropriate time in Ms. Williams's treatment for that to occur.

In addition to the trauma narrative, the clinician, Ciara, and Ms. Davis arranged for several in-vivo exposures to occur as homework activities that gradually increased in difficulty and occurred after Ciara had completed and shared her trauma narrative with her parents. These included walking to the corner of the block where the shooting had occurred, walking past her grandmother's house, and going to Ms. Williams's house for dinner. Throughout treatment, the clinician infused exposure, when possible, for example, by referring to the event explicitly as "when you saw Jay get shot" versus generically as "the trauma" or "that day."

The final component of Ciara's treatment included providing information about personal safety. This included facilitating discussions with Ciara and her caregivers about staying safe in the community, which included avoiding associations with gangs or persons involved in illicit activity. For example, the clinician worked with the family to develop a plan for if/when Antoine is released from prison to ensure that Ciara and her sister are not around him unless he has demonstrated he is no longer involved in drug activities or associating with dangerous peers.

Ciara responded well to treatment and was discharged after 15 sessions. At that time, she had made significant gains and, in addition to a significant reduction in PTSD symptoms, showed improved mood and academic performance. By the end of treatment, she was able to discuss the events of the shooting with her family calmly without significant distress and to share her sadness and fears with them so that they could help support her in coping with her feelings about the event.

ADJUSTMENT DISORDERS WITH CASE APPLICATION

In DSM-5, adjustment disorders have been placed in the traumatic stress and reactions chapter and involve a reaction within 3 months to a stressful life event that is greater than expected but resolves within 6 months of the resolution of the stressor (APA, 2022). The DSM-5 lists six different types: (1) with depressed mood; (2) with anxiety; (3) with mixed anxiety and depressed mood; (4) with disturbance of conduct; (5) with mixed disturbance of conduct and mood; and (6) unspecified (symptoms vary from the other types). In outpatient settings, adjustment disorders are the most commonly applied diagnosis. They should be considered as an initial option if full criteria for another disorder are not clearly met, considering that adjustment disorder doesn't possess the stigma of other clinical disorders. We include a case here that involves loss.

Violet Smith is a 12-year-old girl who presented to her local community mental health center with her mother, Jennifer Smith, and father, Joshua Smith. Mrs. Smith is a white woman in her 40s who works part time in the office of her local elementary school, and Mr. Smith is a Black Latino male, also in his 40s, who works as an electrician. Violet lives in a low- to middle-income suburban community with her parents, 8-year-old brother, and 5-year-old sister. She is a seventh-grade student at the public middle school in her neighborhood.

Mr. and Mrs. Smith reported that they were seeking mental health services for Violet because they were concerned that she has not been coping well following the death of a classmate. They shared that, 4 months earlier, a classmate of Violet's named Ryan had died of leukemia. Ryan had been ill for more than a year and had been in and out of school during his cancer treatment. Mr. and Mrs. Smith reported that Violet and Ryan had never been particularly close, although they had had classes together for many years. Since Ryan's passing, they reported that Violet is often tearful and fearful that she or others she loves will develop cancer. Violet reported feeling sad and missing Ryan. Before seeking outpatient treatment, Mr. and Mrs. Smith stated that they had consulted with Violet's teacher and school counselor. They reported that these individuals felt that Violet's reaction to Ryan's death was beyond what they would have expected given the closeness of Violet and Ryan's relationship and was more prolonged and severe than her classmates, prompting them to suggest Violet may benefit from working with a therapist.

Violet was generally quiet during the intake appointment but responded appropriately when addressed by the clinician. Her attention was within normal limits for her age, and she demonstrated good insight. Violet presented as a pleasant and likable girl but was noticeably sad when speaking of her classmate's death. Her parents appeared invested in identifying additional support to help Violet manage her distress.

Assessment

The social worker conducted clinical interviews separately, with Violet's parents first, followed by Violet, to understand her current symptoms and relevant historical information.

Violet's parents shared that Violet generally gets along well with her parents and younger siblings, although they noted she has been more withdrawn than usual lately and spending more time in her room. Previously, she would often watch TV or play with her younger siblings in the evening, but since Ryan's death she tends to retreat to her bedroom after dinner. The family history was reported to be remarkable for OCD, anxiety, depression, and PTSD. Mrs. Smith noted that Violet has always had a somewhat anxious temperament, and when nervous about something, such as an upcoming test, she sometimes acts out in anger toward her family; they have not generally seen this behavior when Violet is not anxious and otherwise have never been particularly concerned about anxiety. Violet's mother stated, "Violet has always been a little tightly wound, if you know what I mean, but that's just who she is. I'm kind of like that too. She gets herself a little worked up about big tests, the first day of school, if a friend is mad at her, stuff like that. But I don't think that's really a big deal—it's never been a big issue for her."

In addition to family history, the social worker also inquired about academics. Violet is enrolled in seventh grade and has an Individualized Education Program (IEP) due to "ADHD, reading, and auditory processing issues." Mr. and Mrs. Smith described Violet as a generally good student but noted that she has always struggled in her language arts classes and has benefited from after-school tutoring through a community program. Her parents also reported that Violet becomes easily distracted at school and sometimes has trouble following the rules. Her academic attendance has been consistent.

Socially, Violet reportedly has a similar number of friends as most children her age and several close friends. She is active in several extracurricular activities and enjoys singing, dancing, and basketball. Her parents noted that she has been less interested in socializing with peers since Ryan's death. She continues to see friends outside of school but has been more frequently declining invitations to hang out.

Violet was diagnosed with a reading disability following an evaluation by the district school psychologist at age 8 and with ADHD by her pediatrician at age 10. She reportedly participated in play therapy from fourth to fifth grade. Violet and her family have also tried medication for her ADHD. Her parents reported these interventions have been somewhat helpful, but they discontinued medication because of side effects and have not tried it again because she has been doing well in school with her IEP accommodations. She was born 6 weeks early but discharged home with her mother; her medical and developmental history was otherwise reported to be unremarkable.

Based on parent and child report, Violet was noted to be experiencing excessive sadness and loss of interest across several domains that appeared to be more than a typical bereavement reaction. These symptoms had not been present before her classmate's death and have been persistent since his passing 4 months earlier. These include a loss of interest in social activities with peers and her family, increased tearfulness, and sadness. Violet also has been worried that she or a loved one will die of cancer. Violet stated, "The world is so awful, I don't understand why everyone else seems to be moving on from Ryan dying like that's a normal thing that happens. It's not."

The social worker determined Violet was not showing sufficient symptoms to warrant a diagnosis of MDD or an anxiety disorder and ruled out PTSD, assigning instead a diagnosis of adjustment disorder with mixed anxiety and depressed mood. While a thorough ADHD or psychoeducational evaluation was not conducted, the social worker was able to review documentation from Violet's IEP and records from her pediatrician's office provided by Mr. and Mrs. Smith. These records, along with phone consultations with the school psychologist and pediatrician, substantiated prior diagnoses of ADHD predominantly inattentive type and a specific learning disorder, which the social worker also recorded in Violet's medical record as diagnoses by history. The social worker recommended to the family that Violet begin weekly therapy focused on coping with Ryan's death and increasing Violet's engagement in previously enjoyed activities.

Intervention

In formulating her treatment plan for Violet, the social worker drew from evidence-based CBT strategies for depression and anxiety. The social worker suspected that giving Violet space to talk about and process her reactions to Ryan's death would be important, but that those conversations would be most productive if paired with active intervention strategies.

Treatment began with psychoeducation for both Violet and her parents about typical and prolonged grief reactions and an overview of what to expect from treatment. The clinician validated for Violet that it is normal to have difficulty coping and to experience distress following a loss and that there are a range of different grief reactions that people may have. She explained, "Everyone is different. Some people feel very sad or worried when someone dies or may have trouble adjusting to life without this person being physically present. Others seem to 'get back to normal' quickly, and it can be hard for those who aren't in that place to understand how they are able to do that. Sometimes people feel sad or worried or just don't feel like themselves for a while after losing someone. And if those feelings are sticking around a while or are starting to cause problems with friends, at school, or at home, it can be helpful to get some extra support."

The social worker also explained to Violet's parents that, while there are not necessarily any established evidence-based practices for adjustment disorders specifically, she would utilize elements of evidence-based treatments for depression and anxiety in her work with Violet. The social worker explained that she planned to use CBT approaches to help Violet build coping skills and learn to more effectively manage her thoughts and feelings related to Ryan's death. The social worker explained the CBT model to Violet and her parents. She also explained the particular CBT strategies she planned to employ in their work together. She stated, "There are a few things that I think would be helpful. First, when people are feeling down and have lost interest in doing things they used to enjoy, like hanging out with friends, it can be helpful to start by taking stock of your current activities and behavior and how they affect your mood. Then, we can find ways to increase activities that may help you feel more positive. In addition to doing that, we can talk about how you've been thinking and feeling since Ryan's death and identify some strategies that might help you cope with those thoughts and feelings." Violet's parents were receptive and agreed with the treatment plan the social worker outlined. Violet was initially more skeptical. She asked, "Are we just going to talk about how sad I am that Ryan died? I don't really want to do that."

"That's a great question" the social worker replied, "and thank you for telling me that you'd prefer not to do that. I completely respect that. I'm very happy to talk with you about your reactions to Ryan's death, but we only need to talk about your thoughts and feelings about this in as much detail as you like. There are a lot of things we can try that might be helpful, and they don't require you to share any more than you feel comfortable with. I was thinking we could start by focusing more on actions. For example, since you've shared that you have lost interest in things you used to enjoy, we can start by understanding what you currently are and are not doing in your everyday life, and if there are any small changes we might want to try in terms of your routine or how you spend your free time that might help you to feel a little better." Violet said she felt more comfortable taking an active, behaviorally focused approach, so they agreed to start with behavioral activation strategies before moving into cognitive and affective approaches.

As a first step following psychoeducation, the social worker taught Violet how to complete mood and activity monitoring forms and asked her to closely track her activities and corresponding mood ratings over the course of a week. At the next session, they reviewed the data and identified patterns. For example, they noted that when Violet goes to her room after dinner and stays there alone through the evening her mood is lower than when she is spending time with her family. They proceeded to generate a list of pleasurable activities, and a plan for Violet to engage in more of these by scheduling some over the coming week. For example, they planned for Violet to play a game with her family one evening after dinner, to choose a family movie to watch on the weekend, and to call a friend another evening to say hi. (For a more in-depth review of behavioral activation, see Chapter 10.) Violet responded well to behavioral activation and, with support from her parents, greatly reduced the amount of time she was spending alone. She noticed an improvement in her mood as she made these changes.

While Violet's response to behavioral activation strategies was encouraging, she continued to experience some periods of tearfulness and anxiety about whether she or a loved one might get cancer. While being careful to avoid pressuring Violet to talk about or process Ryan's death, the social worker gently encouraged Violet to begin exploring her thoughts and feelings. The social worker used a thought record to help Violet learn about the connections between her thoughts, feelings, and actions. They started simply with a three-column thought record. The social worker oriented Violet to the thought record in session and asked Violet to complete it over the next week any time she noticed herself experiencing a strong emotion or a shift in how she was feeling. They then reviewed the thought record the following week and identified a few instances in which Violet had experienced distress (see Table 13.5).

One thinking pattern that emerged through Violet's thought records was a tendency for her to feel hopeless because "everyone I love is going to die." A second common theme involved worries that "I (or a loved one) might have/will get cancer."

Table 13.5 Excerpts From Violet's Thought Record

Situation	Thoughts	Feelings/Emotions
Where were you? Who were you with? What were you doing? When was this?	What was going through your mind just then?	Rate from 0–10
Tuesday lying in bed at night, alone, around 10 p.m.	I was thinking, "What's the point in caring about people if they are just going to die?"	Sad, hopeless (8)
Thursday morning around 7:30 a.m. on my walk to school and I had a stomachache	"What if I have cancer? Maybe that's what is wrong with me."	Worried (6)

Violet had the insight to recognize that these concerns had not been present before Ryan's death and responded well to questions from the therapist to help her explore the accuracy and helpfulness of these cognitions.

For example, the clinician asked if Violet had experienced the loss of a friend or loved one before Ryan's death. Violet had lost several family members to chronic health conditions but had never known someone her age who had died. The therapist was careful not to try to assure Violet that she would never lose another friend to disease or that she or a family member would not get cancer, but was able to help her explore whether the possibility of these events occurring was indeed as likely as she might be initially thinking. They also focused on the helpfulness of these thoughts, and with support from the therapist, Violet was able to identify that focusing on the fact that everyone dies eventually and that she or someone she knows may get cancer was detracting from her enjoying time with her loved ones now, which was something she valued. She was also able to conclude that Ryan, based on the person she knew him to be, would likely not want others to stop living their lives in response to his death. Over time, Violet was able to catch herself when she was experiencing one of these "thinking traps" and to implement more helpful coping self-talk in response (Kendall & Hedtke, 2006), such as by telling herself, "Even though I don't know for sure that I won't get cancer, young healthy people like me rarely do" and, "If Ryan were here, he would probably tell me to stop moping around."

As Violet became more comfortable in therapy, she began to talk more about her feelings of sadness and grief and her concerns about illness and death and dying. The social worker was careful not to push Violet to talk about this (which can be iatrogenic) but also tried to provide space and support for Violet to share her reactions to Ryan's death at her own pace. As Violet's mood started to improve following the use of behavioral activation and cognitive restructuring, she gradually started to open up about her reactions to Ryan's death. For example, Violet shared that, "I knew he was sick, but I guess I didn't really get how bad it was. I guess I just didn't really expect him to die because he was young, and he was going to the good hospital in the city." Additionally, she stated, "It makes me wonder what happens when you die and what that's like."

Violet and her parents had shared during intake that the family regularly attended church services. The clinician asked if Violet might find it helpful to talk to her clergy about her questions about death and the afterlife. She agreed to do that, and the social worker helped facilitate this meeting by helping the parents to arrange a time for Violet to meet with her pastor. The social worker also had a brief phone call with the pastor in advance, with the family's permission, to brief him about Violet's questions and concerns. The meeting proved helpful for Violet, and she found comfort in having some of her questions addressed.

Violet met with the social worker for a total of eight individual therapy sessions over the course of 2½ months. The clinician met primarily with Violet for individual sessions and engaged her parents as needed to support their individual work, such as by asking for their input about options for pleasant activities to schedule and engaging them in planning and executing between-sessions homework. Treatment was mutually terminated when Violet's functioning improved such that she was engaging with friends and family in a manner that was in line with her functioning before Ryan's death. At this point she also was no longer tearful, except in rare instances, and she reported that she was generally feeling happier and less worried. Her parents and educators corroborated their perceptions of Violet's improvement.

REFERENCES

Alisic, E., Zalta, A., VanWesel, F., Larsen, S., Hafstad, G., Hassanpour, K., & Smid, G. (2014). Rates of post-traumatic stress disorder in trauma-exposed children and adolescents: Meta-analysis. *British Journal of Psychiatry: The Journal of Mental Science, 204,* 335–340.

American Psychiatric Association. (2022). *Diagnostic and statistical manual of mental disorders* (5th ed., Text Revision). Washington, DC: American Psychiatric Association.

Bennett, R. S., Denne, M., McGuire, R., & Hiller, R. M. (2020). A systematic review of controlled trials for PTSD in maltreated children and adolescents. *Child Maltreatment, 26*(3), 325–343. doi:10.1177/1077559520961176

Black, P. J., Woodworth, M., Tremblay, M., & Carpenter, T. (2012). A review of trauma-informed treatment for adolescents. *Canadian Psychology/Psychologie Canadienne, 53*(3), 192–203. https://doi.org/10.1037/a0028441

Brewin, C. R., Andrews, B., & Valentine, J. D. (2000). Meta-analysis of risk factors for posttraumatic stress disorder in trauma-exposed adults. *Journal of Consulting and Clinical Psychology, 68*(5), 748.

Bryant, R. A., O'Donnell, M. L., Creamer, M., McFarlane, A. C., & Silove, D. (2010). Posttraumatic intrusive symptoms across psychiatric disorders. *Journal of Psychiatric Research, 45*(6), 842–847.

Calhoun, K. S., & Resick, P. A. (1993). Post-traumatic stress disorder. In D. H. Barlow (Ed.), *Clinical handbook of psychological disorders: A step-by-step treatment manual* (pp. 48–98). New York: Guilford Press.

Cary, C., & McMillen, J. C. (2012). The data behind the dissemination: A systematic review of trauma-focused cognitive behavioral therapy for use with children and youth. *Children and Youth Services Review, 34*(4), 748–757.

Cloitre, M., Stolbach, B. C., Herman, J. L., Kolk, B. V. D., Pynoos, R., Wang, J., & Petkova, E. (2009). A developmental approach to complex PTSD: Childhood and adult cumulative trauma as predictors of symptom complexity. *Journal of Traumatic Stress, 22*(5), 399–408.

Cohen, J., Bukstein, O., Walter, H., Benson, R. S., Chrisman, A., Farchione, T., Hamilton, J., Keable, H., Kinlan, J., Schoettle, U., Siegel, M., Stock, S., & Medicus, J. (2010). Practice parameters for the assessment and treatment of children and adolescents with posttraumatic stress disorder. *Journal of the American Academy of Child & Adolescent Psychiatry, 49*(4), 414–430.

Cohen, J., Deblinger, E., Mannarino, A., & Steer, R. (2004). A multisite, randomized controlled trial for children with sexual abuse-related PTSD symptoms. *Journal of the American Academy of Child & Adolescent Psychiatry, 43*(4), 393–402.

Cohen, J. A., Mannarino, A. P., & Murray, L. K. (2011). Trauma-focused CBT for youth who experience ongoing traumas. *Child Abuse & Neglect, 35*(8), 637–646.

Cohen, J., Mannarino, A., & Rogal, S. (2001). Treatment practices for childhood posttraumatic stress disorder. *Child Abuse & Neglect, 25*(1), 123–135.

Cohen, J., Mannarino, A., & Staron, R. (2006). A pilot study of modified cognitive-behavioral therapy for childhood traumatic grief (CBT-CTG). *Journal of the American Academy of Child & Adolescent Psychiatry, 45*(12), 1465–1473.

Copeland, W. E., Keeler, G., Angold, A., & Costello, E. J. (2007). Traumatic events and posttraumatic stress in childhood. *Archives of General Psychiatry, 64*(5), 577–584.

Dorsey, S., Kerns, S. E., Trupin, E. W., Conover, K. L., & Berliner, L. (2012). Child welfare caseworkers as service brokers for youth in foster care: Findings from Project Focus. *Child Maltreatment, 17*(1), 22–31.

Dorsey, S., McLaughlin, K., Kerns, S., Harrison, J., Lambert, H., Briggs, E., Cox, J. R., & Amaya-Jackson, L. (2017). Evidence base update for psychosocial treatments for children and adolescents exposed to traumatic events. *Journal of Clinical Child & Adolescent Psychology, 46*(3), 303–330.

Foa, E. B., Johnson, K. M., Feeny, N. C., & Treadwell, K. R. H. (2001). The Child PTSD Symptom Scale: A preliminary examination of its psychometric properties. *Journal of Clinical Child Psychology, 30*(3), 376–384.

Ford, J. D., Courtois, C. A., Steele, K., van de Hart, & Nijenhuis, E. R. S. (2005). Treatment of complex posttraumatic self-dysregulation. *Journal of Traumatic Stress, 18*, 437–447. doi:10.1002/jts.20051

Gonzalez-Prendes, A. A., & Resko, S. (2012). Cognitive-behavioral theory. In S. Ringel & J. Brandell (Eds.), *Trauma: Contemporary Directions in Theory, Practice, and Research* (pp. 14–40). Thousand Oaks, CA: Sage.

Guina, J., Baker, M., Stinson, K., Maust, J., Coles, J., & Broderick, P. (2017). Should posttraumatic stress be a disorder or a specifier? Towards improved nosology within the DSM categorical classification system. *Current Psychiatry Reports, 19*(10), 66.

Gutermann, J., Schreiber, F., Matulis, S., Schwartzkopff, L., Deppe, J., & Steil, R. (2016). Psychological treatments for symptoms of posttraumatic stress disorder in children, adolescents, and young adults: A meta-analysis. *Clinical Child and Family Psychology Review, 19*(2), 77–93. doi:10.1007/s10567-016-0202-5

Haselgruber, A., Sölva, K., & Lueger-Schuster, B. (2020). Validation of ICD-11 PTSD and complex PTSD in foster children using the international trauma questionnaire. *Acta Psychiatrica Scandinavica, 141*(1), 60–73. doi:10.1111/acps.13100

Hiller, R. M., Meiser-Stedman, R., Fearon, P., Lobo, S., MacKinnon, A., Fraser, A., & Halligan, S. L. (2016). Changes in the prevalence and symptom severity of child PTSD in the year following trauma: A meta-analytic study. *Journal of Child Psychology and Psychiatry, 57*(8), 884–898.

Horowitz, M. (1976). *Stress response syndromes.* New York: Aronson.

Jaycox, L. H., Cohen, J. A., Mannarino, A. P., Walker, D. W., Langley, A. K., Gegenheimer, K. L., Scott, M., & Schonlau, M. (2010). Children's mental health care following Hurricane Katrina: A field trial of trauma-focused psychotherapies. *Journal of Traumatic Stress: Official Publication of the International Society for Traumatic Stress Studies, 23*(2), 223–231.

Macdonald, G., Livingstone, N., Hanratty, J., McCartan, C., Cotmore, R., Cary, M., Glaser, D., Byford, S., Welton, N. J., Bosqui, T., Bowes, L., Audrey, S., Mezey, G., Fisher, H. L., Riches, W., & Churchill, R. (2016). The effectiveness, acceptability and cost-effectiveness of psychosocial interventions for maltreated children and adolescents: an evidence synthesis. *Health Technology and Assessment, 20*(69), 1–508.

Martin, C. G., Everett, Y., Skowron, E. A., & Zalewski, M. (2019). The role of caregiver psychopathology in the treatment of childhood trauma with trauma-focused cognitive behavioral therapy: A systematic review. *Clinical Child and Family Psychology Review, 22,* 273–289. https://doi-org.proxy.library.upenn.edu/10.1007/s10567-019-00290-4

McLaughlin, K. A., Koenen, K. C., Hill, E. D., Petukhova, M., Sampson, N. A., Zaslavsky, A. M., & Kessler, R. C. (2013). Trauma exposure and posttraumatic stress disorder in a national sample of adolescents. *Journal of the American Academy of Child & Adolescent Psychiatry, 52*(8), 815–830.

Miller-Graff, L. E., & Campion, K. (2016). Interventions for posttraumatic stress with children exposed to violence: Factors associated with treatment success. *Journal of Clinical Psychology, 72*(3), 226–248.

Mineka, S., & Zinbarg, R. (2006). A contemporary learning theory perspective on the etiology of anxiety disorders: It's not what you thought it was. *American Psychologist, 61*(1), 10.

Moreno-Alcázar, A., Treen, D., Valiente-Gómez, A., Sio-Eroles, A., Pérez, V., Amann, B. L., & Radua, J. (2017). Efficacy of eye movement desensitization and reprocessing in children and adolescent with post traumatic stress disorder: A meta analysis of randomized controlled trials. *Frontiers in Psychology, 8,* 1750–1750. doi:10.3389/fpsyg.2017.01750

Mowerer, O. (1960). *Learning theory and behavior.* New York: Wiley.

Ozer, E. J., Best, S. R., Lipsey, T. L., & Weiss, D. S. (2003). Predictors of posttraumatic stress disorder and symptoms in adults: A meta-analysis. *Psychological Bulletin, 129*(1), 52.

Panagioti, M., Gooding, P., Triantafyllou, K., & Tarrier, N. (2015). Suicidality and posttraumatic stress disorder (PTSD) in adolescents: A systematic review and meta-analysis. *Social Psychiatry and Psychiatric Epidemiology, 50*(4), 525–537. https://doi.org/10.1007/s00127-014-0978-x

Perrin, S., Smith, P., & Yule, W. (2000). Practitioner review: The assessment and treatment of post-traumatic stress disorder in children and adolescents. *Journal of Child Psychology and Psychiatry, 41*(3), 277–289.

Rolfsnes, E. S., & Idsoe, T. (2011). School-based intervention programs for PTSD symptoms: A review and meta-analysis. *Journal of Traumatic Stress, 24*(2), 155–165.

Rudd, B. N., Last, B. S., Gregor, C., Jackson, K., Berkowitz, S., Zinny, A., Kratz, H. E., Cliggitt, L., Adams, D. R., Walsh, L. M., & Beidas, R. S. (2019). Benchmarking treatment effectiveness of community-delivered trauma-focused cognitive behavioral therapy. *American Journal of Community Psychology, 64*, 438–450. doi:10.1002/ajcp.12370

Scheeringa, M. S., Wright, M. J., Hunt, J. P., & Zeanah, C. H. (2006). Factors affecting the diagnosis and prediction of PTSD symptomatology in children and adolescents. *American Journal of Psychiatry, 163*(4), 644–651.

Shapiro, F. (2017). *Eye movement desensitization and reprocessing (EMDR) therapy* (3rd ed.). New York: Guilford Press.

Soria-Saucedo, R., Chung, J. H., Walter, H., Soley-Bori, M., & Kazis, L. E. (2018). Factors that predict the use of psychotropics among children and adolescents with PTSD: Evidence from private insurance claims. *Psychiatric Services, 69*(9), 1007–1014.

Staudt, M. (2007). Treatment engagement with caregivers of at-risk children: Gaps in research and conceptualization. *Journal of Child and Family Studies, 16*(2), 183–196.

Uddin, M., Aiello, A., Wildman, D., Koenen, K., Pawelec, G., de los Santos, R., Goldman, E., & Galea, S. (2010). Epigenetic and immune function profiles associated with posttraumatic stress disorder. *Proceedings of the National Academy of Sciences of the United States of America, 107*(20), 9470–9475. http://www.jstor.org/stable/25681616

Warfield, J. R. (2013). Supervising culturally informed modified trauma-focused cognitive behavioral therapy. *Journal of Cognitive Psychotherapy, 27*(1), 51–60. doi:10.1891/0889-8391.27.1.51

Weiner, D. A., Schneider, A., & Lyons, J. S. (2009). Evidence-based treatments for trauma among culturally diverse foster care youth: Treatment retention and outcomes. *Children and Youth Services Review, 31*(11), 1199–1205.

World Health Organization. (2018). ICD-11 for mortality and morbidity statistics. Retrieved from: https://www.who.int/classifications/icd/en/

Xie, P., Kranzler, H. R., Poling, J., Stein, M. B., Anton, R. F., Brady, K., Weiss, R. D., Farrer, L., & Gelernter, J. (2009). Interactive effect of stressful life events and the serotonin transporter 5-HTTLPR genotype on posttraumatic stress disorder diagnosis in 2 independent populations. *Archives of General Psychiatry, 66*(11), 1201–1209.

Yehuda, R. (2006). Advances in understanding neuroendocrine alterations in PTSD and their therapeutic implications. *Annals of the New York Academy of Sciences, 1071*(1), 137–166.

For the benefit of digital users, indexed terms that span two pages (e.g., 52–53) may, on occasion, appear on only one of those pages.

Tables, figures, and boxes are indicated by *t*, *f*, and *b* following the page number